# The Future of Health Economics

Edited by
Olivier Ethgen and Ulf Staginnus

Routledge
Taylor & Francis Group

LONDON AND NEW YORK

First published in paperback 2024

First published 2017
by Routledge
4 Park Square, Milton Park, Abingdon, Oxon OX14 4RN

and by Routledge
605 Third Avenue, New York, NY 10158

*Routledge is an imprint of the Taylor & Francis Group, an informa business*

Publisher's Note
The publisher has gone to great lengths to ensure the quality of this reprint but points
out that some imperfections in the original copies may be apparent.

*British Library Cataloguing in Publication Data*
A catalogue record for this book is available from the British Library

*Library of Congress Cataloguing in Publication Data*
Names: Ethgen, Olivier. | Staginnus, Ulf.
Title: The future of health economics / by Olivier Ethgen and Ulf Staginnus.
Description: Farnham, Surrey, UK; Burlington, VT : Gower, [2016] |
Includes bibliographical references and index.
Identifiers: LCCN 2015037279 | ISBN 9781409445432 (hardback)
Subjects: LCSH: Medical economics.
Classification: LCC R728 .E874 2016 | DDC 338.4/73621–dc23
LC record available at http://lccn.loc.gov/2015037279

ISBN: 978-1-409-44543-2 (hbk)
ISBN: 978-1-03-283720-8 (pbk)
ISBN: 978-1-315-55793-9 (ebk)

DOI: 10.4324/9781315557939

Typeset in ITC New Baskerville
Std by Out of House Publishing

# Contents

# List of Figures

# List of Tables

# List of Contributors

**Ulf Staginnus** is a health economist and pharmaceutical executive with 20 years of international experience in the field of market access, pharmacoeconomics, pricing and reimbursement as well as health technology valuations within the biotechnology and pharmaceutical industry. He has a long track record in successfully developing launch pricing and patient access strategies for various innovative drugs across different therapeutic areas such as oncology, cardiology, infectious diseases and orphan drugs within the top ten pharmaceutical companies (Novartis, BMS, Pfizer, GSK Biologics) and biotech start-ups (PTC Therapeutics, Endocyte Inc). The most recent industry positions he has held have included Head of Market Access Europe for PTC Therapeutics and Endocyte Inc, both in Zug, Switzerland; Head of Pricing and Access, Novartis Oncology Europe in Milan, Italy; and Franchise Head, Oncology International Access, Health Economics and Reimbursement with Amgen International in Zug, Switzerland. In 1996, Ulf graduated with an MA in Economics – with a major focus on health economics – from the University of Bayreuth, Germany. During the course of his career he also founded and ran his own consultancy serving biotech and pharma clients in supporting their product pricing, valuations and market access initiatives. He is a regular speaker on access, pricing and health economics-related matters and the author of healtheconomicsblog.com.

**Olivier Ethgen** is an Associate Professor of Health Economics at the Department of Public Health Sciences, School of Medicine, University of Liège in Belgium. He lectures in health economics (theory and applied modeling), decision sciences and pharmacoepidemiology. He is also the Scientific Director of the Economic Evaluation of Medical Innovation Research Unit (EMIR), which is a joint research unit between the Department of Public Health and the School of Business & Management of the University of Liège. Olivier holds a PhD in Public Health Sciences from the University of Liège and an MSc in Mathematical Economics from the University of Paris I – Panthéon Sorbonne. His research interests include financial modeling of patients and market access strategies, multi-criteria decision making and population-based modeling. Olivier has more than ten years of experience as an economic and financial modeler gained in the private sector (IMS Health, Bristol-Myers & Squibb, GlaxoSmithKline Vaccines) and as an independent consultant (SERFAN innovation, a consulting company dedicated to strategic economic research and financial analysis of medical innovation). His experience spans all types of health care technologies, including drugs, biologics, vaccines, devices and diagnostics.

**Lucien Abenhaim:** Lucien is Honorary Professor of Epidemiology at the London School of Hygiene & Tropical Medicine. He was a Professor of Epidemiology and Biostatistics at McGill University in Montreal, Canada, where he was in charge of the pharmacoepidemiology education program (1988–1999). He also spent time at the René Descartes University in Paris (2003–2007). He was an expert at the EMA, the FDA and several European and Canadian agencies. He served as the General Director of Health in France (1999–2003) and as a member of the Executive Council of the WHO (2001–2003). Lucien is Chairman and International Scientific Director for LASER.

**E.I. Hervé Akpo:** Hervé is Manager at the Deloitte Center of Excellence for Market Access Strategy, Health Economics. He worked for five years as a plant molecular biologist at a leading biotechnology firm, with strong expertise in genome-wide genetic and epigenetic markers development associated with key crop traits and their performance in specific environments. This experience gave him proficiency in data analytics. In 2012 he joined Deloitte as a statistician and modeler and has been involved in the development and validation of health economics models, including cost-effectiveness, cost-utility, budget impact and pricing models to secure market access and reimbursement for pharmaceutical and medical devices products. In addition, Hervé has contributed significantly to the implementation and the operationalization of an innovative portfolio management platform that uses real options and Monte Carlo simulations combined with health economics methods to aid investment decision-making processes and licensing in large pharmaceutical companies. Hervé has a PhD in molecular biology and epigenetics.

**Billy Amzal:** Billy graduated from Ecole Polytechnique ("X-Ponts", MSc in maths), from AgroParisTech (MPA and MSc in Statistics) and holds a PhD in Decision Statistics from Paris-Dauphine University, which was awarded by the International Society of Bayesian Analysis and by the International Biometrics Society. Over the past 15 years, Billy has developed quantitative methodologies and hundreds of statistical models to inform and support strategic decision making in health care. He stands as an international statistical expert, especially in the area of clinical trial simulations and modelling, Bayesian modelling and optimal design. Prior to joining LASER, Billy pioneered the model-based drug development initiative at Novartis Pharma. Subsequently, he co-built and led the assessment methodology group at the European Food Safety Authority, establishing the standards, for example, for nutraceuticals evaluations. Billy was also Director of the Data Center at the NIH-funded Program for HIV Prevention and Treatment in Thailand. Billy is now Scientific Vice President at LASER Analytica, teaches pharmacoeconomics in Paris University and acts as a modeling and statistical expert for various national and international public health authorities.

**Eun-Young Bae:** Eun-Young is an Associate Professor at the College of Pharmacy at Gyeongsang National University in South Korea. Before taking up her current position, she was a senior researcher for the Health Insurance Review and Assessment Service (HIRA) from 2003 to 2008, and played a leading role in developing the pharmacoeconomic guidelines in South Korea. Her primary academic interests are in pharmacoeconomics, valuation of health, and reimbursement and pricing policies for pharmaceuticals. She is also interested in eliciting social preference for health care resource allocation. She is currently serving as a member of the Drug Reimbursement Evaluation Committee of HIRA, and is the chair of the Economic Sub-Committee. She has also been a board member of the Korean Association of Health Economics and Policy and the Korean Association of Health Technology Assessment.

**Imene ben Abdallah**: Imene holds a PharmD after defending a thesis in Immunology entitled "Dendritic cells in kidney transplantation: roles and perspectives". She has a specialization in drugs development and in pricing, reimbursement and market access across the different European countries (European University Diploma of Market Access, EMAUD). In Creativ-Ceutical, she has been involved in numerous pricing and market access projects within different disease areas such as schizophrenia, major depression, bipolar disorder, respiratory disease and dermatology. She began her career in medical marketing in the Tunisian pharmaceutical industry, where she worked for two years. Her mother tongue is Arabic and she speaks French and English fluently.

**Stephen Birch**: Stephen is a Professor at the Centre for Health Economics and Policy Analysis at McMaster University in Canada, Chair in Health Economics at the University of Manchester, and Adjunct Professor at the University of Technology Sydney, Australia. He is senior scientist at the WHO Collaborating Centre on Health Workforce Planning at Dalhousie University, Canada and a former member of the UK Department of Health's Centre for Workforce Intelligence. He has served as a consultant on health workforce planning with the WHO and the World Bank as well as many national and provincial health departments. He was a consultant to the Barer-Stoddart report on physician planning in Canada, the Kilshaw report on physician payment reform in Canada and the George Committee on the future of the physician workforce in Ontario. He led research in Canada on the development and application of needs-based models of health care funding and has further developed these models for application to health workforce planning. His main research interests are the economics of health care systems with particular emphasis on equity, resource allocation and alternative delivery models. He has published in more than 200 peer-reviewed journals and was ranked equal first in Canada in the 2012 World Bank publication on the quantity and impact of health economics research. He was Senior Editor for *Social Science and Medicine* from 1997 to 2012 and currently serves on editorial boards of several multidisciplinary scientific journals. He has served on various public boards, including the Local Health Integration Network and the District Health Council in Hamilton, Ontario, the Health Professions Regulatory Council of Ontario and the Community Health Council for York District Health Authority.

**John F.P. Bridges**: John, PhD, is an international leader in the application of stated-preference methods. He is the founding editor of *The Patient: Patient Centered Outcomes Research* and has worked with numerous patient groups, health technology assessment agencies, regulators and international aid agencies to advance and apply these methods to document the preferences of patients and other stake-holders. Within the International Society for Pharmacoeconomics and Outcomes Research (ISPOR) he founded the Conjoint Analysis Working Group (2006–2011), the Conjoint Analysis Task Force (2008–2010) and was the first author on the ISPOR checklist conjoint analysis. In 2006 he received ISPOR's Bernie O'Brien New Investigator Award and in 2011 received an ISPOR Distinguished Service Award for his leadership of conjoint analysis methods. He is the author of more than 100 publications and a frequent speaker on patient engagement, patient preferences and benefit–risk analysis. John is an associate professor in the Department of Health Policy and Management, where he serves as the Director of the Masters of Health Science (MHS) in Health Economics, and has joint appointments in the Department of International Health and Department of Health Behaviour and Society. He is core faculty within the Center for Health Services and Outcomes Research (CHSOR), the Center for Drug Safety & Effectiveness (CDSE), and the Center for Excellence in Regulatory Science and Innovation (CERSI). He is also a Faculty Research Fellow at the National Bureau of Economic Research (NBER) and a Senior Fellow at the Center for Medicine in the Public Interest (CMPI).

**Roman Casciano**: Roman is the General Manager of the LASER Analytica Consulting and Analytics team and is based in New York City. Roman is one of the founders of LA-SER's US- and Germany-based teams (formerly Analytica International Inc.) and has held a variety of roles for the organization since 1997. As an applied health economist and market access strategist, Roman has led hundreds of research engagements in traditional HEOR disciplines such as modeling and database analysis as well as numerous strategic engagements in the pricing and reimbursement context, ranging from traditional pricing research to value message development and communication strategy. Originally taking on the role of Director of Operations for Analytica International, Roman went on to serve as the General Manager for the Germany offices of Analytica from 2004 to 2006 and then subsequently returned to the US and took on the role of President, starting in December 2007. Roman graduated from Cornell University in 1992 with a Master's degree in Engineering and through 1997 worked for HDR Engineering, an environmental services engineering consultancy.

**Joshua Cohen**: Joshua utilizes his background in health economics to examine public policy issues that concern prescription drug reimbursement and patient access to biopharmaceuticals. His areas of research include the impact of comparative effectiveness research on prescribing and reimbursement decisions, patient access to biopharmaceuticals in the US and Europe, ethics regarding the distribution of pharmaceutical care resources, and drug development targeting orphan and neglected diseases.

**Mark Connolly**: Mark is the Managing Director and founder of Global Market Access Solutions, with registered offices in Switzerland and the US. He has formal training in pharmacology and health economics, and received his doctorate from the University of Groningen in health economics. Mark currently holds a guest researcher position with the University of Groningen, Pharmacoeconomics and Pharmacoepidemiology Unit in the Netherlands, working as co-promotor for doctoral researchers.

**Nadia Demarteau**: Nadia has been working in the field of health economics since 1999, first at UCB pharma, then at IMS Health and today in the vaccine division of GSK. She obtained a Bioengineering degree from the Free University of Brussels, followed by a Master's degree in environmental pollution control from Pennsylvania State University where she specialized in environmental economics before moving to the field of health economics when she joined the pharmaceutical industry. She has specialized over time in health economics modeling, investigating new ways to use health economics models to assess the value of vaccines.

**Stephanie R. Earnshaw**: Stephanie is Vice President of Health Economics at RTI Health Solutions. She trained in industrial engineering/operations research and has extensive experience in applying decision-analysis techniques to pharmaceutical/medical diagnostics industry-related issues and health care problems. She has developed decision models to examine the budget impact and cost-effectiveness of pharmaceuticals and diagnostics in cardiovascular disease, gastrointestinal disorders, respiratory disease, transplantation, infectious disease, osteoporosis, men's health and other therapeutic areas. She has used her background to project costs, utilization and clinical outcomes using decision tree, Markov, simulation, mathematical programming and other decision analytic methods. Stephanie also teaches the International Society for Pharmacoeconomics and Outcomes Research (ISPOR) budget impact short courses and the Markov Model Toolkit course offered under the ISPOR distance learning program. She is a member of the ISPOR and the Institute for Operations Research and the Management Sciences (INFORMS). She has presented her research at numerous national and international conferences. She has published in several peer-reviewed journals, including *Annals of Internal Medicine, Archives of Internal Medicine, Journal of General Internal Medicine, Haemophilia, Alimentary Pharmacology & Therapeutics, American Journal of Neuroradiology, Medical Decision Making, Journal of American Society of Nephrology, Stroke, Respiratory Medicine and Value in Health.*

**Dogan Fidan**: Dogan is the Global Head of Early Stage Products in Sanofi's global commercial organization. The remit of this unit is to provide Sanofi R&D and business development with commercial assessment of early-stage projects, as well as to proactively identify patient populations, indications and key product attributes of interest, with a view to building successful health care solution offers to support Sanofi's product portfolio expansion. Dogan has spent the last 12 years in Sanofi (and legacy companies) in health economics, medical affairs and commercial groups, with increasing responsibilities over time. Prior to joining the industry he spent more than three years at NICE, where he acted as a technical lead in health technology appraisals, and four years in clinical medicine and academia in Turkey and the UK. During this period, he held several honorary academic positions at the University of York, London School of Hygiene and Tropical Medicine and Liverpool University, where he worked on projects mainly on middle- and low-income countries sponsored by the WHO and the Wellcome Trust. He also worked as an advisor and trainer on numerous World Bank-sponsored projects for the Turkish Ministry of Health. His research interests include health technology assessment, real-world clinical trials, application of health economics in portfolio management, and patient-centered clinical development. Dogan is a Doctor of Medicine, has a PhD in Public Health, an MSc in Health Economics and an MBA.

**Amiram Gafni**: Amiram is a professor in the Department of Clinical Epidemiology and Biostatistics at McMaster University in Ontario and a member of the Centre for Health Economics and Policy Analysis. He has more than 450 publications in peer-reviewed journals. In the 2011 World Bank rankings of health economics researchers (see *Journal of Health Economics*, 2012, 31:406–39 (Table 5)) he was ranked equal 35th in the world (equal 1st in Canada) based on the volume and impact of his publications. His research interests are in the area of economic evaluation of health care programs (both methods development and empirical applications), modeling of consumers' health-care behavior, models of patient–physician decision making (e.g. shared decision making), policy analysis and risk and decision analysis in health.

**Larry Gorkin**: Trained as a PhD Clinical Psychologist, Larry was drawn to research and began his career as a grant writer to the National Institutes of Health and the pharmaceutical industry. At that time, he was associated with the Brown University School of Medicine, where he received his post-doctorate degree. In 1996, he was employed within health economics at Pfizer world headquarters in New York City. He spent the bulk of the next 13 years as a special advisor to the head of health economics at Pfizer, working on licensing opportunities, critical competitive challenges, etc. After leaving Pfizer in 2009, Larry began a small consulting firm focusing on health economics in drug development, and started writing reports that he placed on the internet gratis on reforming aspects of the industry.

**Lamiae Grimaldi-Bensouda**: Lamiae is one of the founders of the PGRx platform, a widely used pharmacoepidemiological information system. She has more than 12 years' experience in clinical pharmacology (board-certified) and pharmacoepidemiology (PhD), notably in the conduct of real-world studies. Specializing in methodological development as directly applicable to real-world studies, her experience includes the design, conduct and analysis of major, landmark studies. She has the unique experience of both primary data collection from physicians and patients and of the analysis of electronic health care databases. Lamiae has conducted more than 20 major studies involving clinical, patient-reported and functional outcomes assessment internationally and an additional dozen studies using eHCD or EMR, and numerous surveys. She is part of the PROTECT program (Pharmacoepidemiological Research on Outcomes of Therapeutics by a European Consortium) coordinated by the European Medicines Agency (EMA). In 2006, Lamiae established a clinical and academic career as chief resident in clinical pharmacology at a university hospital in France where she ran the regional pharmacovigilance unit. She is now an Associate Professor at the Conservatoire National des Arts & Métiers where she directs a Master Program on Drug Evaluation, Market Access & Public Health and is a Fellow of the Pasteur Institute.

**Eugenia Gruzglin**: Eugenia has more than ten years' experience in the health care industry. She has worked in a variety of therapeutic areas, including oncology, immune-oncology, cardiometabolic disorders and multiple sclerosis, to mention just a few. In addition, she is well familiar with novel technology platforms and a variety of diagnostics. Eugenia received her PhD in molecular oncology from Mount Sinai, NYU, and completed her post-doctoral training at Memorial Sloan-Kettering Cancer Center in New York City. She has coauthored a number of peer-reviewed articles and presented her work at international meetings. Based on her PhD work, she holds a provisional patent in cancer diagnostics and cancer treatment.

**Eddie Hornby**: Eddie is an independent consultant with more than 30 years' experience gained in the pharmaceutical industry internationally in roles including preclinical, biochemistry and pharmacology, clinical trials science and health economics. He has worked in most major disease areas and also in designing cross-functional processes for integrating payer and regulatory insights into early and full clinical plan development and market access planning.

**Claudio Jommi**: Claudio is Associate Professor of Management at the Department of Pharmaceutical Sciences, University of Novara. He is also Director of the Pharmaceutical Observatory at Cergas (Centre for Research on Health and Social Care Management), Bocconi University, and Professor at Bocconi School of Management, Public Management and Policy Department, where he coordinates the specialization in Pharmaceuticals and Medical Technologies, Master in International Health Management Economics and Policy (Mihmep). He is President of the Italian Health Economics Association. He has been visiting professor at Essec Business School, Cergy (Paris), at the Herivan K. Haub School of Business, St Joseph University, Philadelphia (USA), at the Andrija School of Public Health, Zagreb and the University of Claude Bernard Lyon 1 (European Market Access University Diploma). His research activity is focused on pharmaceutical economics, policy and management, health technology assessment and decision making in health care. He has published in many international and national journals, including *Drug Design Development and Therapy, European Journal of Health Economics, Health Policy, International Journal of Health Planning and Management, Journal of Medical Marketing, Pharmacoeconomics, PLOS Neglected Diseases* and *Public Money & Management.*

**Ning Lu**: Ning is a freelance consultant with more than ten years' international consulting and biopharmaceutical experience. Her professional experience spans across pricing and market access, health care systems, hospital management, business analysis and strategy. She has conducted projects in Europe, Asia and the US covering central nervous systems, oncology, gastrointestinal disorders and rare diseases. Most recently she worked as Senior Manager Market Access at Biogen International, focusing on European Market Access. Ning received her MPH from Harvard University and her MBA from the University of Michigan.

**Kevin Marsh**: Kevin is Senior Director of Modeling and Simulation at Evidera. His research interests include the use of economic and decision analysis to inform health decisions, including pipeline optimization, authorization, reimbursement, and prescription decisions. He specializes in decision modeling, MCDA, and a range of economic valuation methods, such as stated preference value approaches. He actively contributes to the methodological development of these techniques. He is currently co-chairing the International Society for Pharmacoeconomics and Outcomes Research Taskforce on the use of MCDA in Health Care Decision-Making. He has applied these and other research techniques for a range of organizations, including both regulatory and industry clients. Kevin completed his PhD at the University of Bath, specializing in economic valuation techniques. After a year at Oxford University, he joined the Matrix Knowledge Group in London, where he built the economics practice. Kevin is an active member of the Campbell and Cochrane Economic Methods Group.

**Thomas Morel**: Thomas is Research Fellow within KU Leuven's Department of Pharmaceutical and Pharmacological Sciences, Belgium. His primary research focus is rare diseases and orphan drug policy. Thomas holds degrees in Economics and Law from the London School of Economics and Political Science and King's College London.

**Cédric Popa**: Cédric is Partner at Deloitte and has led the valuation team in the financial advisory department since 2008. Cédric's experience includes valuations of businesses and intangible assets for commercial and strategic purposes, in litigation contexts for tax purposes and also for financial reporting. Cédric has more than 14 years' experience in various industries, including life sciences, technology, media and communications, manufacturing and food and beverage. In the life sciences sector, his projects have included valuation of the R&D portfolio in a €2 billion-plus pharma acquisition, benchmarking studies on the financial and operating performance of leading pharma companies, co-authoring an article on financial performance of orphan drug companies, market strategy advice to medical device and pharmaceutical companies, and more. He has spoken on valuation issues at several external and in-house seminars and is a member of the UK Society of Share and Business Valuers and of the Royal Institute of Chartered Surveyors. Cédric holds an EMBA from the University of Washington and a BA in Economics and Econometrics from the University of Kent at Canterbury.

**Antonio Ramirez de Arellano**: Antonio is Regional Manager of the Novo Nordisk HEOR European team. He was awarded his BSc degree in Economics from the University of Barcelona, his MSc degree in Health Economics from the University of Barcelona, his MSc degree in Economic and Social Policy Analysis from the Department of Economics, University of York and his PhD degree in Economics from the University of York. The subject of his doctoral thesis was data envelopment analysis (a non-parametric method for estimation of production frontiers). He was a lecturer of Macroeconomics, Microeconomics and Health Economics in the Department of Economic Theory at the University of Barcelona, and he also ran the *Spanish Journal of Health Economics*. From 2000 to 2004 he was the national health system advisor in the cabinet office of the Spanish prime minister. Antonio has worked as a health economist in the pharmaceutical industry (Roche, BMS, Ferrer International and Novo Nordisk).

**R. Ömer Saka**: Ömer leads the Deloitte Center of Excellence for Market Access Strategy, Health Economics. Ömer and his team support medical devices and pharmaceutical companies in three high-level health economics aspects, which include value generation, value illustration and value communication, with related activities spanning from portfolio management to health economics modeling, pricing, writing and adaptation of value dossiers, market access strategy as well as the design and the analysis of observational studies. In the past, Ömer worked for five years at the London School of Economics and Political Science and King's College London. He later joined the National Audit Office of England to lead the health economics and decision modeling practices there. He produced influential work in the area of stroke, which resulted in the implementation of the 2007 UK National Stroke Strategy in a collaborative process with the Department of Health and academic organizations. Ömer has been involved in a number of consultancy projects for governmental organizations in the EU, the UK, Turkey and South Korea. He has published on issues such as the use of health technology assessment methods in orphan drugs policy and has research interests in the use of modeling methods in economic evaluation, comparative health policy analysis and efficient provision of services in hospitals. Ömer is a medical doctor by education.

**Ed Schoonveld**: Ed is a Managing Principal with ZS Associates in New York and is the leader of the firm's market access and pricing practice. He has extensive experience in pharmaceutical marketing and pricing from both the corporate pharma and the consultancy perspective. His team advises drug companies on product pricing and market access strategy, global pricing policy, and internal organizational and process challenges. Most of these projects involve global payer and pricing research through a host of qualitative and quantitative methodologies. Ed's expertise in global pricing and reimbursement is extensive – he has served both on the affiliate level as a general manager of a European affiliate and at corporate headquarters as the responsible leader for global pricing and health economics groups at Wyeth, Eli Lilly and BMS. Ed's considerable experience in the pharmaceutical industry includes various sales, marketing and general management positions with Lederle, Wyeth, Eli Lilly and BMS in the US and Europe. Ed has also led pricing and reimbursement consulting practices for Analytica International, Cambridge Pharma/IMS and his own consultancy firm. Ed is the author of *The Price of Global Health*, a groundbreaking book on global drug pricing. The second edition was published in January 2015.

**Steven Simoens**: Steven is a Professor of Pharmacoeconomics at KU Leuven. He is a health economist and is involved in research and teaching of pharmacoeconomic aspects of medicines, medical devices and related products. He is the current head of the unit Clinical Pharmacology and Pharmacotherapy in the Department of Pharmaceutical and Pharmacological Sciences at KU Leuven. His research interests focus on issues surrounding policy and regulation of the pharmaceutical sector. He has worked extensively in the area of pricing, reimbursement and distribution of orphan medicines and of generic medicines in Europe. Steven also carries out economic evaluations of medicines and medical devices. He has been involved in multiple health technology assessments of antibiotics and of medical devices. He was involved as an expert in drafting the guidelines for pharmacoeconomic evaluations in Belgium. Steven has more than 220 publications in peer-reviewed journals and has given over 240 congress presentations. He is a member of the editorial board of multiple journals. He has lived and worked in England, France, Germany and Scotland.

**Justine Slomian**: Justine trained as a midwife and has professed in this area for three years. In 2013, she also obtained a Master's degree in Public Health Sciences with epidemiology and health economics majors. She is now undertaking a PhD research program at the University of Liège in Belgium. She studies the usefulness and relevance of new information and communication technologies in the management of postnatal stress and depression. She has previously studied the influence of new information and communication technologies in various fields such as osteoporosis, menopausal women or cardiovascular diseases.

**Baudouin Standaert**: Baudouin has a 20-year career in industry (ten years at Amgen and ten at GSK Vaccines). Before that he worked in the public health sector as an epidemiologist on cancer and on infectious diseases as the head of the Provincial Institute of Hygiene in Antwerp, Belgium. He now works on the health economics evaluation of vaccines at a global level worldwide, promoting new ways to assess the total economic value of immunization programs. His main interest is to make complex programs more accessible to decision makers. Baudouin is also linked to the University of Groningen where he was recently promoted with a doctoral thesis on "New ways to explore the economic value of vaccines".

**Mondher Toumi**: Mondher is a medical doctor by training, with an MSc in Biological Sciences and a PhD in Economic Sciences. He is Professor of Public Health at Aix-Marseille University. After working for 12 years as Research Manager in the laboratory of pharmacology at the University of Marseille, he joined the Public Health Department in 1993. He worked from 1995 in the pharmaceutical industry for 13 years. Mondher was appointed Global Vice President at Lundbeck A/S in charge of health economics, outcome research, pricing, market access, epidemiology, risk management, governmental affairs and competitive intelligence. In 2008, he founded Creativ-Ceutical, an international consulting firm dedicated to supporting health industries and authorities in strategic decision making. In February 2009 he was appointed Professor at Lyon I University in the Department of Decision Sciences and Health Policies. The same year, he was appointed Director of the Chair of Public Health and Market Access. He conducted the first European University Diploma of Market Access (EMAUD) in Paris, France. Additionally, he recently created the Market Access Society to promote research and scientific activities around market access, public health and health economics assessment. Since 2009, he has also chaired the Annual Market Access Day, a purely academic event sponsored by EMAUD that has become a reference event in the area. In September 2014 he joined the research unit EA3279 of the Public Health Department, at Aix-Marseille University (France) as Professor. Mondher is also visiting professor at two famous Chinese universities: Shenyang Pharmaceutical University and Beijing University (Third Hospital). In addition to contributing as a reviewer on several journals, he is Chief Editor at the online *Journal of Market Access and Health Policy*. He did two mandates as Co-Chair of the Research Review Committee ISPOR, in 2012 and 2013. He is a recognized expert in drug development and an authority on market access and risk management. He has more than 200 scientific publications and oral communications, and has contributed to several books. He just finished a book on market access, to be published soon.

**Janine van Til**: Janine is a health scientist by training. Janine started her work in preference research with her PhD project called "Integrating preferences into decision making", which was focused on including values in decision making in the treatment of ankle–foot impairments in stroke patients. Janine is currently working as an Assistant Professor in the department of Health Technology and Services Management at the University of Twente in the Netherlands. Her research is focused on using preference methods, mainly discrete choice experiments, best–worst scaling and multi-criteria decision analysis methods to include the stakeholder perspective in health care decisions in the clinical, management and societal context. She has more than ten years' experience in the design and analysis of stated preference surveys, mainly in the field of neurology, oncology and cardiology. Janine is the main supervisor of two PhD students in the field of patient preference research, and is involved in the training of more than five other PhD students. Over the last five years she has successfully written multiple grant proposals, project managed national and international projects, and worked as a consulting researcher on international projects. She is also the main lecturer of the course "Patient Preference Modelling" in the Master Health Sciences at the University of Twente. In her non-research time, Janine likes to read books on the psychology of decision making and fantasy novels, imagine herself doing lots of physical outside activities and taking holidays, and is the proud mother of two very sassy boys.

**Mel Walker**: Mel, BPharm, MRPharmS, PhD, joined Otsuka's European executive team in 2012 with the task of building a cutting-edge patient access function and developing Otsuka's organizational capability to meet the needs of health care systems in Europe. Mel is passionate about the role that a highly ethical and patient-focussed health care company can play in providing better health care for patients. He believes that value can be delivered not only by bringing medicines of real benefit, but also by gaining a better understanding about how medicines should be used within health care systems and using this knowledge to optimize the value delivered to patients at both an individual and a population level. Mel is also passionate about helping health care systems to use data, analytics and change management expertise to improve clinical practice and believes that a holistic approach is essential for a company that wishes to become a trusted and valued health care partner. Mel previously worked for GSK, where he held a variety of senior roles, including leading a team responsible for the delivery of health outcomes plans and reimbursement strategies for the oncology portfolio. He played a crucial role in driving engagement with international value experts involved in the appraisal, reimbursement and access for new medicines as part of the Access to Medicines Leadership, and helped to build broad access capability and drive customer-centric approaches across the CE region as a member of the executive team. Mel has co-authored more than 30 research papers and abstracts, as well as two book chapters, and worked in several therapeutic areas, including oncology, haematology, osteoporosis, rheumatoid arthritis, nephrology, transplantation, obesity, HIV and Alzheimer's disease. He regularly chairs and contributes to international conferences in the areas of market access, the HTA regulatory interface, conditional reimbursement and customer-centric approaches. He is affiliated to the Centre for Socioeconomic Research (University of Wales), sits on the Steering Committee for the Centre for Innovation in Regulatory Science, co-founded the HTAi ISG on HTA Regulatory Interactions and is a member of TOPRA's Advisory Council.

**Michael Wonder:** Michael gained his BSc (Hons) in Biochemistry and Pathology from the University of Melbourne and a B Pharm from the Victorian College of Pharmacy, before working as a hospital pharmacist for five years. He then moved to Novartis Pharmaceuticals Australia as its first Health Economics Manager, working on strategic development and preparation of reimbursement and/or pricing submissions, before being appointed Director of Global Pricing and Market Access Operations for Novartis Pharma AG. Since 2011 Michael has been an independent consultant on biopharmaceutical reimbursement and pricing matters. He has also acted as an expert advisor to the Masters of Science in International Health Technology Assessment, Pricing and Reimbursement at the University of Sheffield and the Distance Learning Certificate Program in Health Economics and Outcomes Research at the University of Washington.

**Julie Zard:** Being an MD, Julie holds a specialized master in "Marketing management for the pharmaceutical industry and biotechnologies" from ESCP – Europe business school in Paris, and has completed the European University Diploma of Market Access from the University of Lyon I. She worked at Takeda France in the public and economic affairs department where she worked on preparation of transparency dossiers for the Transparency Committee and she managed team work with KOLs and consultants. She has worked on several market access topics: HTA overview with an international comparison analysis, products' value stories, core value dossier on products in infectious diseases, payer researches interviewing KOLs, research on risk and market access opportunities in cardiovascular area. She has contributed to a research publication on market access agreements and has strong medical writing skills. Julie has participated in several Global Payer Advisory Boards, producing minutes and slide decks and executive summaries summarizing the meeting outcomes and recommendations. Julie is now pursuing a career as a medical practitioner.

# Introduction

The discipline of health economics has progressed substantially. In the 1960s, it began with cost–benefit analyses of public health programs, such as vaccination, and has evolved into a large discipline of formal health technology assessment (HTA). Cost-effectiveness analysis has become the centrepiece of HTA and is currently performed virtually for each new health care technology. The biopharmaceutical industry and health care payers increasingly rely on cost-effectiveness to assess the value of new technologies and to define their pricing and coverage decision making.

Nonetheless, the affordability criterion of the payers' side is increasing and fuelled by the availability of costly technologies, the growing incidence of chronic diseases and a relatively gloomy economic outlook. In this context, the pricing and market access of medical innovations has without a doubt become a hot topic in recent years. Medical innovation usually occurs in incremental steps and comes at an additional cost to health care systems. Choice and prioritization became unavoidable. The cost debate has now reached a turning point in many health care systems.

The issue of affordability and financial sustainability has triggered the need to think about new concepts going beyond the sole consideration of the "price-per-pill" and the incremental cost-effectiveness ratio. How can health care systems reward innovation and sustain research and development (R&D) investments while also balancing affordability and equitable access to innovation? What assessment criteria should be applied in deciding access and reimbursement? What are the overall value elements that a new treatment brings to patients and society as a whole? What are the perspectives in assessing the cost versus the benefit of innovation? There are many unanswered questions.

The value of treatment continues to be debated intensively at each introduction of innovative products. In recent decades, developments have been made in many areas such as orphan diseases, infectious diseases and cancers. The launch of drugs such as Imatinib in chronic myeloid leukaemia or Sofosbuvir in hepatitis C has brought major advancements for patients. At the same time, these products intensified the debate about the cost of innovative health care technologies.

These debates have not brought forward a single definition of value agreed on by all stakeholders. Therefore, the question arises as to whether all elements that determine the value of a new technology are sufficiently captured in a cost-effectiveness analysis or whether complementary assessment criteria should be considered within a multi-criteria decision analysis framework.

The identification of populations that are expected to benefit the most from a particular treatment, so-called stratified or personalized medicine, is also clearly sought by health care payers. The use of companion diagnostics carries the hope of streamlining clinical decisions and resource allocation with the identification of patient populations most likely to benefit from companion therapies. However, questions remain in the value assessment of these technologies.

Progress in information technology (IT) and the power of the internet have reached the health care industry in a way never observed before. "Big data", "mHealth" or "real-world evidence" are the buzzwords in recent years. It is indeed critical that real-world evidence is collected, processed and analyzed to direct innovation to the populations most likely to benefit and to ensure a wise investment of resources. An increasing number of countries are developing guidance to generate evidence beyond pivotal trials. In many diseases, notably rare diseases, this approach is often the only way to amass significant data for decision making.

There is also the tendency to link real-world outcomes to reimbursement and pricing in pay-for-performance type contracts. We have all witnessed the rise of risk-sharing and other market access agreements between manufacturers and payers. In theory, these agreements can address some of the above issues. They can facilitate faster market access for new medicines while additional real-world evidence is still being generated.

Emerging markets around the world have also been learning from the instituted HTA countries. They have started to introduce guidelines on health economics evaluation and to establish pricing and reimbursement procedures based on economic criteria and relative effectiveness evaluations.

Many books have been written about the theory and methods of health economics. Our aim was not to edit another book further emphasizing the need for cost-effectiveness analysis; instead, we aimed to bring together the most advanced and perhaps unconventional thinkers in the area, from academia to industry, in an attempt to provide forward-thinking ideas on the aforementioned issues.

We have divided the book into three parts:

I. Innovation and market access
II. Technological changes and demographics
III. Decision making and assessment

The first part is devoted to discussions about market access issues of health care innovation.

- Ed Schoonveld starts by insisting on the importance of understanding and defining value in preparing for market access and pricing negotiations. The following questions, among others, are discussed: How do payers perceive value? How can health outcomes and health economics evidence play a role in demonstrating value?
- Then, Larry Gorkin and Eugenia Gruzglin notice that the rapidly improving productivity in drug development will produce a tipping point, in which the unabated approach to ever-increasing drug costs is unsustainable. They

advocate a return to value-based pricing to recalibrate the balance between pricing and value.

- Admittedly, for a new health care technology to fulfil its therapeutic and commercial potential, it is no longer a matter of generating evidence to demonstrate its quality, safety and efficacy to a standard expected by regulators. Michael Wonder and Edward Hornby thus discuss the issues associated with obtaining scientific advice directly from payers. Until relatively recently, this process was considered impossible.
- Market access agreements have been increasingly proposed and implemented during the past few years. Mondher Toumi, Julie Zard, Imene Ben Abdallah, Claudio Jommi and Joshua Cohen provide a thorough description of the emerging market access agreements between the industry and health care payers.
- Among the drugs brought to patients, orphan drugs represent particular challenges. They are produced at a low level but have relatively high prices, in combination with uncertainty over their effectiveness. Thomas Morel and Steven Simoens debate the coverage of orphan drugs, knowing that such drugs are unlikely to be cost-effective.
- Times have changed dramatically for the pharmaceutical industry during the past few years. Market access capabilities, as well as a patient-centred approach to business strategy, have become critical. In this context, Ulf Staginnus suggests how to successfully continue innovating and addressing HTA requirements.

The second part of the book examines a few of the health economics issues that are conveyed by ongoing technical changes and demographics.

- Antonio Ramirez de Arellano provides an overview of experiences in conducting a health economics evaluation of the combination of genetic testing and drugs. The chapter is illustrated with specific examples in which the application of pharmacogenomic testing may be regarded as promising in terms of efficiency.
- Olivier Ethgen, Justine Slomian and Mel Walker introduce a series of health information technology concepts and offer a discussion of the promises of these emerging technologies for health economics in the future.
- Stephen Birch and Amiram Gafni discuss how cost control (and hence the sustainability of healthcare systems) depends on the methods used for planning and evaluating healthcare resource use. They challenge the notion that equitable access to healthcare is unsustainable and show that the continuous increases in healthcare costs are the result of inappropriate assumptions underlying the methods for planning and evaluating healthcare resources. They offer alternative approaches that relate directly to the needs of populations.
- Mark Connolly argues that the typical economic framework for evaluating health conditions ignores the fiscal externalities of health or changes in health status. He then introduces the intergeneration economic framework and shows how the government can expect a return on investment from health.

- To conclude this section, Ning Lu and Eun-Young Bae select two representative Asian countries, China and South Korea, to debate the adoption of health economics. They question whether the need to manage rising health care costs has reached a critical mass and discuss the level of resource infrastructure/capacity development needed for health economics adoption.

The third part of the book comprises a few reflections on how to complement cost-effectiveness to more comprehensively support decision making.

- Janine van Til and John Bridges bring forward the patient perspective. They introduce preference-based methods that enable valuation of healthcare innovation within the context of HTA, assuming that the patient is the best judge of its value trade-offs.
- Olivier Ethgen and Kevin Marsh present the multi-criteria decision analysis framework as an aid to decision making in health care. They describe the necessary steps to implement a multi-criteria decision analysis and provide a few applications to support health care decision making as well as the lessons and challenges identified through these experiences.
- Real-world evidence is increasingly required to defend reimbursement or to keep a product on the market. It is also becoming a critical piece of evidence to anticipate the real-world effectiveness drivers, to predict the potential public health impact and to identify a target population. Billy Amzal, Roman Casciano, Lamiae Grimaldi-Bensouda and Lucien Abenhaim describe the concepts and the practice of relative effectiveness studies.
- Nadia Demarteau, Baudouin Standaert and Stephanie Earnshaw ascertain the limit of cost-effectiveness and introduce the mathematical programming approach to optimize the allocation of health care interventions. The contributors present two applications to cervical cancer prevention and type 2 diabetes.
- Finally, E.I. Hervé Akpo, Cédric Popa, Dogan Fidan and Ömer Saka describe how commercial, research and development (R&D) and health economics models can be interconnected within a framework of product portfolio management under budgetary limitations. They then argue that the use of capital investment appraisal techniques in addition to health economics methods would enhance the efficiency of an investment portfolio decision-making process.

We hope this book contributes new thoughts and perspectives that will advance the field of health economics. The relatively exclusive and narrow microeconomic application of cost-effectiveness analysis that we have observed so far might well be insufficient based on the challenges ahead. New approaches, or at least more comprehensive and complementary approaches, are needed to value innovative technologies. Hopefully, the debates in this book will inspire new ideas and practices among industry practitioners, policy makers, researchers and students.

Olivier Ethgen and Ulf Staginnus

# Part I

# Innovation and Market Access

# Chapter 1

# The Role of Value in Market Access and Pricing Negotiations

*Ed Schoonveld*

## Introduction

Health economists sometimes seem to be their own worst enemy as they tend to insist on presenting evidence of what they think payers should be interested in, rather than focusing on what payers really act on.

How do payers perceive value? How can health outcomes and health economics evidence play a role in demonstrating value? What information can have an impact on market access and pricing decisions? In order to understand this, we must examine the decision-making processes that underlie drug prescribing and funding within each country's health care system. Some global payer systems use cost-effectiveness methodologies for funding decisions, but most don't. Many payers use "benefits"-based drug evaluations that are less directly tied to a cost impact benchmark. Health outcomes data can still have a substantial impact as a means of demonstrating value. It does mean, however, that we need to thoroughly understand the particular way in which we can guide decision making in each specific system. Before we look at the topic in more depth, let us first consider why governments feel the need to interfere in drug pricing and what their mindsets are in doing so.

The drug industry is very different from other industries due to cost structure, intellectual property-related aspects and ethical "right to health care" philosophies. A particularly important aspect is that the drug purchasing decision is not a simple buyer versus seller situation but a more complicated interchange between payer, physician and patient. Whether and how various stakeholders interact and influence drug use is very dependent on the payer system. Understanding this process and its implications goes a long way in the identification of critical success factors for market access and pricing of prescription drugs.

## The Drug Purchasing Process

When you go to a grocery store to buy fruit, you may rest your eyes on a ripe mango and ask the grocer for the price. If acceptable, you may decide to buy the mango. If too expensive, you may decide to buy cheaper oranges instead. Now suppose you tell the grocer that you are still not convinced that the mangos are tastier than the oranges and insist that he lowers the price of the mangos. The angry response from the grocer may be inappropriate for printing, but will give reference to the fact that if I don't like the price of the mangos, I should not buy them. Reading this example

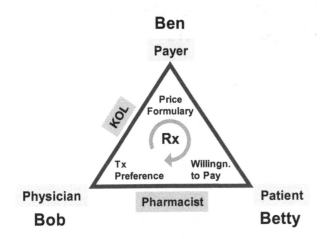

*Figure 1.1* "Dinner for Three"

you may find the suggestion ridiculous; however, this is exactly what is happening for prescription drugs in many countries. Governments in many cases demand that a drug price be lowered rather than deciding not to buy or reimburse it. Why do governments think that it is necessary to insist on a lower price for a product for which they don't appreciate the value that is claimed by the seller?

The situation in the prescription drug purchasing process was once described to me as "Dinner for Three" (see Figure 1.1). Imagine three people, Bob, Ben and Betty, go to a restaurant, where Bob orders a meal, Betty eats and Ben pays the bill. You can imagine the conversation where payer Ben suggests that lobster was perhaps a bit excessive. He would be concerned that absent of an obligation to pay, diner Betty may not be sufficiently cost sensitive and might waste his money. The thought of buying a hot dog on the street corner may very well appeal to Ben. He may even claim that hot dogs are not proven to be less healthy. This example may seem far-fetched, but it illustrates the impact of a situation where a natural balance in decision making is distorted. Many governments have felt compelled to intervene in the pricing and reimbursement process for prescription drugs, particularly as drug cost impacts their budget directly. Unfortunately, as many of these controls are ineffective, they tend to lead to new controls, thus moving further and further away from a balanced system, rather than restoring a form of controlled market. A detailed discussion of these and other factors in the economics of the pharmaceutical industry and global drug pricing can be found in Schoonveld (2015).

## Understanding Payers

Government and private payers, whether central, regional or local, often play a key role in the availability of prescription drugs for physician prescribing. Payers and their systems vary significantly globally. When we try to convince payers of the need to allow broad usage of our product at a reasonable price, we need to try to understand how a payer evaluates our drug and its value proposition within the context of the system, its cost-management practices, and the decision makers' individual priorities.

How can the drug help a payer reach his or her objectives, and what evidence would he or she like to see to buy into any benefit claims that a manufacturer may put forward? As all payers are not the same, we need to consider how different payers might have different reactions to our value proposition. Hospital payers in Germany might have a different view on your drug's value than a US managed care pharmacy director or the national Pharmaceutical Benefits Advisory Committee (PBAC) pricing authorities in Australia. The underlying reason for a different perspective on our value proposition can have various causes:

1.  National vs. regional or local hospital scope of budget responsibilities
2.  Differences in responsibilities with respect to the elements of health care under their remit, such as total medical cost (UK National Health Service or German sick fund) vs. pharmacy cost (for example US Medicare Part D or provincial drug budget holder in Canada)
3.  Political and cultural differences between countries, such as a strong "market" philosophy in the US vs. a social equity-driven mindset in Europe
4.  Legal differences, for example an obligation for health insurance companies to cover anti-cancer drugs in many US states
5.  Differences in the decision-making process and the underlying cost-management principles that payers use in pricing and market access decisions
6.  Specific local preferences and priorities, for example due to a particularly high or low incidence of a condition or cost of an intervention in comparison with other locations

The many differences in situations and perspectives between countries has caused every payer system to be unique, which makes the resulting global drug market access and pricing environment very complex. However, upon closer examination one can see that payers use a limited number of underlying cost-management principles to address their drive to ration healthcare utilization within their budget, as a controlling mechanism of an imperfect market for prescription drugs and to enforce their interests as a buyer.

## Global Payer Archetypes and Segments

Payers around the world have found different ways to address their concerns with respect to pricing and/or reimbursement of prescription drugs, as described in the previous section. In the United States, private payers have instituted formularies, prior authorizations and step edits, together with co-pay and co-insurance rates, to incentivize patients to use generics and preferred brands. In France, the government has instituted a structured evaluation process of the therapeutic benefit of new drugs over existing "comparators" and is controlling price and use of the drugs through price controls and volume agreements. In the United Kingdom, the National Institute for Health and Care Excellence (NICE) reviews the cost-effectiveness of drugs and some other medical treatments, and then provides guidance to the local budget holders with respect to whether they should make the drug available for their patients. In China, the government has a limited number of drugs (usually low-cost options) on national and provincial formularies, whereas many high-cost branded drugs are available to patients on a cash-pay basis only, leaving the funding decision for higher-cost drugs to the individual patient and his/her advising physician. The examples mentioned constitute substantially different systems of market access and pricing control. In examining other countries, we find other variations and methods of control as every country has individual decision-making power. Even within the European Union, although jointly reviewing and approving market authorization through the European Medicines Agency (EMA), individual countries control drug pricing and reimbursement with various control mechanisms. The EMA has no role in these decisions.

What are the commonalities among all the different pricing and reimbursement systems across countries? Despite all being different, there are some fundamental cost-management principles that can serve as descriptive archetypes and which can form a basis for a global segmentation of payer systems. Figure 1.2 shows an approach towards segmenting global payer systems that has proven to be particularly helpful in evaluating payer system reactions to typical outpatient prescription drugs by defining some archetypes. It is not suggested that every country perfectly matches one archetype. As a matter of fact, countries such as Canada exhibit characteristics of more than one archetype. For the purposes of this analysis, countries have been classified by what is generally considered their most restrictive characteristic. Here are the four archetypes, in order of increasing restrictiveness:

1. Emerging cash market
2. Competitive insurance-based market
3. Therapeutic referencing market
4. Health economics-driven market

Now let's have a closer look at each of the archetypes and consider how the global prescription drug market can be segmented on the basis of the predominantly exhibited archetype in each country.

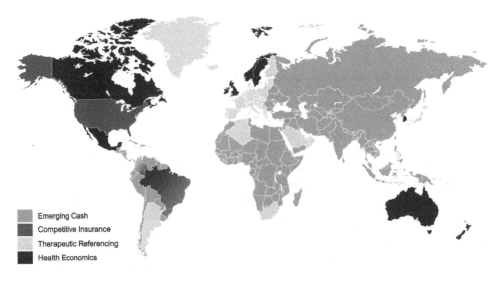

*Figure 1.2* Global payer segments

### Emerging Cash Markets

The emerging cash market is, as the title suggests, representing a large majority of emerging markets, where for many branded drugs there tends to be limited or no health care system coverage. Countries such as China and India fall in this category as the great majority of patients are paying for branded prescription drugs out of pocket without any reimbursement. Since these are prescription drugs, the physician has a strong role in drug choice, but patient affordability and willingness to pay are likely to feature significantly in the physician's decision making. Providing universal health care coverage is on the political wish list of many emerging markets. However, most existing coverage programs do not have sufficient funding to go beyond some form of "essential" drug coverage, usually including generically available drugs only. Selected populations may enjoy broader coverage through employers, but this is typically only a fraction of the population, for example about 5% in India. It is important to have a realistic view on how drug coverage may evolve in the future and to examine this periodically. It is also important to realize that a future introduction or broadening of universal health coverage is likely to lead to more cost controls, whereby a country can look more like one of the other archetypes.

### Competitive Insurance-Based Markets

Competitive insurance-based markets include most of the US market, where health insurance companies are competing to cover patient healthcare needs for a monthly insurance premium. Insurance companies decide on their drug formulary and related co-pays/co-insurance rates, prior authorizations and step edit restrictions on the basis of clinical value and terms offered by competing drug companies. Over the last 10 years, the US market has gradually undergone significant change, as the system has been and continues to be under reform. Insurance plans, in an effort to control their rapidly rising premiums, have continually increased patient co-pay and co-insurance burdens to limit cost and utilization of high-cost biologics and branded drugs with generic "equivalents". Drug companies have utilized various co-pay offset programs to try to mitigate the negative impact of an unfavorable formulary tier placement and associated patient objections. In Medicare Part D, which is managed by private health plans, coupons cannot be used, which is one of the reasons why contracting in this segment has become more aggressive. Since Medicare Part D is a drugs-only coverage plan, insurance companies are incentivized to focus on drug cost only. These patients have their non-drug medical coverage under the traditional Medicare Parts A and B mechanisms. Medicare Part C or Medicare Advantage Plans have drug and other medical care integrated.

The Patient Protection and Affordable Care Act (ACA) or "ObamaCare" has introduced additional insurance plans, targeted at the uninsured population that does not have access to employer-sponsored plans and cannot afford other private options. Federal subsidies have resulted in low monthly premiums for lower-income populations, but the plans, which are offered through a "marketplace" or "exchange", have relatively high deductibles and co-payments (often 50%). The introduction of these plans has further fragmented the US market.

The state-managed Medicaid programs have been much more restrictive in allowing branded drug options on a favorable formulary position. Many state Medicaid programs behave more like a therapeutic referencing market, which is described below.

Over the past few years, Brazil has seen substantial growth in its supplementary private insurance market. United Health Group acquired a 90% stake in Amil, the largest Brazilian private health insurance company. Today, close to 50% of drugs are funded through these private plans, which show similarities to the US managed care model.

### Therapeutic Referencing Markets

Therapeutic referencing markets make their pricing or coverage decisions on the basis of the selection of a "comparator" and a rating of importance of innovativeness or clinical benefits proven over that comparator. Although implemented in slightly different ways, this methodology is used extensively in ex-US countries such as Japan, France, Germany, Italy and Spain. Most payers in these systems use strict criteria for granting favorable benefits or innovativeness ratings, as they are also frequently referred to. Head-to-head superiority data with statistically and clinically significant differences on meaningful outcomes are usually demanded. This is particularly critical when the selected comparator is an inexpensive drug, for example a generic. Many countries in this segment directly control drug price through this methodology. Germany has moved from reimbursement control to price control through introduction of its AMNOG legislation in early 2011. In some countries there is a theoretical possibility to opt out of reimbursement at a higher price; however, in reality this is often not a feasible commercial route.

### Health Economics-Driven Markets

Health economics-driven markets are using cost-effectiveness as the primary metric for pricing or reimbursement decision making. Markets such as the United Kingdom, Australia, Canada, Sweden, South Korea and the public system in Brazil are typical examples of this approach. Payers in these systems tend to use a cost per QALY (quality-adjusted life years) approach. Some markets, such as the Netherlands, and since 2013 France, use cost-effectiveness data in addition to therapeutic referencing, but tend to use less strictly defined cost-effectiveness criteria.

## Payer Perspective on Health Outcomes, Health Economics, Value and Price

Health economics theory provides guidance on how, in a situation with resource constraints, a rational trade-off can be made between value or utility of a drug or treatment and its associated impact on cost. That allows, at least theoretically, for making rational choices between health care spending options. Health economists usually measure the value of changes in patient condition through quality of life (QOL) scales, which allow for weighing the value of life years gained for different situations, such as curing a cancer patient vs. saving the life of a stroke victim. How functional the stroke victim is, for example – fully functional or partly or severely impaired – will have a significant impact on the QOL metric. Academically it makes perfect sense, but not every society and payer within that society is comfortable with handling some of the ethically complex trade-offs that go with such a mechanic decision-making model. In the UK, a lot of debate has emerged over the introduction of value-based assessments, introducing "societal value" as a factor to accept higher or lower cost-effectiveness standards. Not many people will object to spending extra money on saving an infant's life, but translating this to more restrictive coverage for the elderly makes the debate more difficult and may draw comparisons with the US "death panel" fears at the introduction of ObamaCare. These elements are probably the most important reasons why cost-effectiveness is serving as a strict basis for pricing and market access decision making in only about 10% of the global pharmaceutical market (see Figure 1.3).

A particularly difficult challenge is how the relatively academic principles of health economics can be applied in an ethically acceptable way, also considering that at time of launch of a new drug, only data is available on its performance in a controlled clinical setting as defined by Food and Drug Administration (FDA) and EMA type trial requirements. Demanding data on the real-life performance of a drug, before it can be broadly accepted as a viable alternative, can choke off promising new treatment options, much like it is difficult to teach a child to ride a bicycle without at least some risk of falling. Particularly in a field such as oncology, it can be unethical to test a new drug in earlier treatment stages before showing its potential in late-stage disease, where it is much less likely to be cost-effective than in a curative setting. Many drugs that have been initially used for palliative treatment for end-stage cancer patients have over time proven their utility in extending lives in earlier lines of therapy.

In order to truly understand how health outcomes and health economics support pricing and market access decision making, we must first take a closer look at each of these terms and what they entail. We can then evaluate how they can be relevant in each of the global payer archetypes and segments that we identified in the previous section.

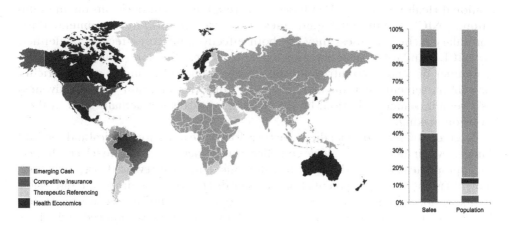

*Figure 1.3* Global payer segments by sales and population

## Health Outcomes

Utilizing health outcomes to more effectively illustrate the impact of a treatment on a patient's well-being can be beneficial in any payer system. The general debilitating nature of an untreated or insufficiently treated condition, or the toxicity and side effects of older treatment options, are frequently underestimated. One reason is that physicians tend to not embellish on issues with current treatments unless there are better options. After all, why raise an issue and upset a patient when there is no alternative solution available?

Showing improved long-term outcomes, such as a reduction in cardiovascular events or improved overall survival, is particularly powerful in payer discussions. In general, long-term outcomes are much more important than shorter-term surrogate endpoints in the impact on overall patient health and associated long-term medical cost. For a lipid-lowering drug, reductions in cardiovascular events will be strongly valued over surrogate low-density lipoprotein (LDL) reduction claims. Similarly, in oncology, overall survival claims are more powerful than tumor response rates. Surrogate endpoints can play an important role in patient management, but are much less meaningful as a measure of value for a drug or treatment unless the relationship with longer-term outcomes can be demonstrated or seems reasonably certain. Payers often simply reject surrogate endpoints on that basis.

Softer health outcomes endpoints, such as non-specific QOL improvement claims, better compliance and fewer side effects, are frequently met with skepticism by payers, unless the claims are clearly linked to long-term outcomes and/or cost savings, and are supported with strong data. In that sense, the term QOL is not of interest to many payers, as it lacks specificity. It is neither emotionally nor economically compelling as it is a very generic term.

## Health Economics

Health economics information that is often considered by private and government payers is cost-effectiveness, usually as a cost per QALY, and/or budget impact. Cost-effectiveness data is required by a minority of healthcare systems. The British National Health Service (NHS) bases many reimbursement decisions on an evaluation by NICE. Within NICE guidelines, drugs are typically not recommended for formulary inclusion unless they are both effective and cost-effective, as defined by NICE standards. Australia, Canadian provinces, Sweden, South Korea and a number of smaller countries use health economics in a similar way in pricing or reimbursement decision making. Some countries mention cost-effectiveness as a reimbursement criterion, but in many cases this is not actually used in their decision making.

Most countries will consider the impact of a drug or treatment on medical and/or drug budget, even if they do not evaluate cost-effectiveness. New drugs that are selectively used for appropriate patients and don't "break the bank" tend to be reviewed in a much more lenient fashion than new potential blockbuster drugs. For these drugs, the discussion frequently focuses on the identification of "appropriate patients" for the new treatment. By selecting only a fraction of the population for which a drug is approved in the FDA or European Medicines Agency (EMA) label, a payer can allow a new treatment, while securing the use of less expensive, perhaps generically available, treatment options first. In reality, this can work well when a payer has the ability to control utilization, for example through the use of step edits, as is done frequently in the United States. In countries where payers have little control over utilization within a relatively broad label, this can become a serious negotiation hurdle.

The drug industry generally experiences health economic requirements as a significant hurdle to patient access. Particularly since it is often practically impossible to have a strong health economic dossier at product launch, health economic requirements at launch indeed have the practical impact of an additional hurdle, in terms of both time and resources required to satisfy rigidly formulated health economic requirements. Moreover, payers tend to mistrust or even reject any health economic data gathered by drug manufacturers.

## Actual Use of Health Outcomes and Economics in Payer Decision Making

### Health Economics-Driven Markets

As suggested by the segment name, health economics-driven markets place the utmost significance on health economic data. In particular cost-effectiveness data, in the form of an incremental cost-effectiveness ratio, is central to coverage decision making. In the UK, the cost per QALY is fairly directly related to the coverage advice of NICE. However, it should be realized that NICE is merely advising on coverage; the actual coverage decisions are made by clinical commissioning groups (CCGs), the local budget holders. CCGs often argue that their financing is inadequate to fund for all NICE-endorsed prescription drugs.

Figure 1.4 illustrates a typical view of cost vs. added outcomes benefit and the related cost-effectiveness plane as used in these markets. It refers to the UK, but will be similar for other health economics-driven markets.

In Canada, the Common Drug Review (CDR) is a joint review from most provinces (excluding Quebec) to evaluate effectiveness and cost-effectiveness of new drugs. A similar review exists for oncology drugs. Provinces tend to use a positive CDR review as a basis for formulary decision making; however, provinces often negotiate with drug companies for confidential provincial agreements after a CDR review is negative. By the CDR's own statistics, roughly half the evaluations end up in a positive advise; however, when considering the large number of partial or conditional coverage approvals, the scorecard looks much more negative. This is not surprising, since Canada has a history of compulsory licensing and subsequent price controls, resulting in average drug price levels that are below those of the United States. Drug companies have been hesitant to allow Canadian prices at much below US levels and have sometimes opted to forego the Canadian market rather than face intense scrutiny over pricing differentials. Provincial listing agreements and more recent pan-Canadian price negotiations have provided opportunities to engage in confidential deals to circumvent the issue.

The Australian PBAC is using cost-effectiveness for national coverage decision making under its Pharmaceutical Benefits Scheme (PBS) drug-listing system. Drug companies need to qualify for formal consideration of cost-effectiveness in the evaluation of the

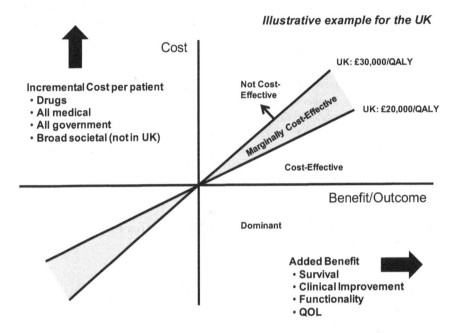

*Figure 1.4* Cost versus added outcomes benefits

reimbursed price. When benefits of a new drug are deemed insignificant, cost-minimization vs. a reference treatment is used as a basis for reimbursement price determination.

Sweden is using cost-effectiveness in a similar way to support coverage decision making by its regional councils, but is taking a broader societal view on cost, allowing for patient economics to be included rather than only department of health expenses. South Korea has adopted cost-effectiveness as a means of controlling drug pricing. It took the South Korean government a long time before its Health Insurance Review and Assessment Service (HIRA) agency developed sufficient expertise to effectively apply the technology. Today, it has been fully adopted; however, it now serves merely as a starting point for price negotiations as the government attempts to further curtail drug spending.

### Therapeutic Referencing Markets

Most therapeutic referencing markets consider health economics data only to inform budget impact of a drug coverage-related decision. Typically, pricing and reimbursement authorities state that the company can submit cost-effectiveness evaluations, but many do not have the internal capability to review the data, and their process often does not offer an opportunity for cost-effectiveness data to impact the pricing or reimbursement decision. Although there is no fixed formula that is valid for all countries, payers in these systems tend to look at budget impact, particularly when this is expected to be high and where there are opportunities to limit use of a certain drug for more "appropriate" populations. Providing information on effectiveness of a drug in sub-populations can strengthen the value proposition for that population, but can also lead to a restriction of use for that specific population. Treatment cost offsets are important to demonstrate, but non-drug medical cost offsets will be convincing only for payers with a broader medical perspective.

The main impact of health outcomes and health economics information on decision making in therapeutic referencing markets is through the assessment of benefits and related "innovativeness" or "value added" rating. This is where patient outcomes data rather than economic data can be leveraged to support value claims. However, it is important that the outcomes data are relevant to the payer and demonstrate, for example, meaningful impact on mortality, avoidance of severe cardiovascular events, reduction in hospitalization days or other clinically and/or economically relevant improvements. Quality of life as a term tends to not impress most payers in the therapeutic referencing market space. The term is too generic for them and without more meaningful specificity it is generally considered irrelevant for coverage decision making.

Figure 1.5 shows a therapeutic referencing market version of the cost-effectiveness plane, discussed earlier in this chapter. As indicated, value is expressed in some form of benefits assessment or innovativeness rating. In this example, the French Amélioration du Service Médical Rendu (ASMR) rating is used, which ranges from I (major benefit) to VI (no benefit, i.e. not reimbursed). The actual reimbursement price premium over the comparator that will be granted or allowed under national law cannot be calculated through a pre-determined formula. However, a small premium is feasible under ASMR IV, whereas a discount is to be expected under ASMR V.

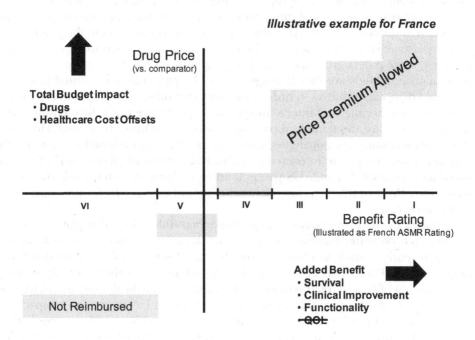

*Figure 1.5* Therapeutic referencing market version of cost versus added outcome benefits

Price premiums for ASMR ratings I–III are much more favorable but more complicated to determine and are influenced by prices in other EU markets. In other therapeutic referencing markets, a similar system of benefits rating exists. In Japan, the relationship is much more defined than in Germany, Italy and Spain. It may be clear from the above that the approach in therapeutic referencing markets is very structured, but the impact on reimbursable price is less mechanistic than the cost-effectiveness assessment under NICE and similar health economics-driven systems. In some markets, such as France since October 2013, cost-effectiveness considerations can play a role in decision making next to the benefits analysis; however, cut-off points in terms of a maximum cost/QALY are usually not defined in these markets.

The use of health economics and health outcomes has some history in the largely private US market. Contrary to the United Kingdom and Canada, the use of strict cost-effectiveness rules and linked-coverage decision making has been met with a lot of resistance among US decision makers and the public, as it was generally felt to be objectionable to determine access to health care through cost cut-offs that are related to an assessment of the value of life. However in, a slightly different way, various health economics and health outcomes aspects influence decision making.

Private payers, such as United Healthcare, Humana or Aetna, review full clinical packages as a primary guide towards an initial decision as to whether, medically speaking, a new treatment should be included in the benefits package. Effectiveness and safety are the primary drivers of this decision. Provided that the medical review has yielded a positive answer, formulary decisions are made on the basis of cost-related issues and concerns. Should utilization be encouraged through a lower patient co-pay? Should prior authorizations and step edits be instituted to avoid overly broad and what the payer would consider "inappropriate" use? Are the restrictions medically justifiable? Do the costs of these programs justify the means? Is managing the drug category important in the context of the per-patient-per-month (pppm) cost to the payer?

The perspective and time horizon of the payer are important considerations in the US. First, some payers are responsible for drug budget only. For example, a private plan, managing Medicare Part D drugs, will not be particularly motivated to accept increased drug expenditures in order to achieve cost offsets through reduced hospitalizations or other medical interventions. These payers are unlikely to bluntly state that they don't care about medical consequences of sub-optimal treatment. However, since their incentives are not aligned with it, we need to ensure broad awareness with employers and the public to overcome payer resistance and "skepticism" of claims and data presented. Second, US payers tend to be fairly short-term oriented. Cost offsets after three or five years are likely to be beyond the time horizon of consideration in most cases.

For most US payer decisions, budget impact considerations can play a substantial role, but cost-effectiveness does not. They have been more sensitive to direct savings incentives, such as offered through shared savings for Accountable Care Organizations. Payers may also choose to take advantage of the gradually starting incorporation of cost in treatment guidelines, issued by medical associations, to support rejection of expensive treatment options. However, lacking a direct impact on their financials, the role of cost-effectiveness in future decision making seems highly uncertain for most health care plans. Few plans, for example Blue Cross Blue Shield, have instituted such reviews for drugs and other treatments.

### Emerging Cash Markets

As described earlier in this chapter, funding decisions in emerging cash markets are subject to dialog between healthcare provider, typically the treating physician and the patient, who will have to pay for the treatment. National health departments tend to have limited interference with drug pricing, as they do not feel a budgetary impact. In some countries, the government does impose pricing restrictions, often based on the prices in a basket of international markets.

Cost-effectiveness evaluations have little merit in communications with physicians and patients, although on a more generic level physicians may claim to look at cost-effectiveness of a treatment. In reality this is seldom the case, or only in very general terms as "cost conscious" rather than driven by detailed cost-effectiveness models. The type of models that are prepared for NICE and SMC in the UK, CDR in Canada and PBAC in Australia have little merit in this setting. By the same token, budget impact assessments are meaningless unless in an exceptional case one would want to educate a patient on long-term personal cost savings for a drug treatment.

## Conclusion

The application of health outcomes and health economics is very different from country to country, as healthcare systems have varying methods of evaluating the value and need for reimbursement coverage of a prescription drug.[1] Cost-effectiveness has only limited application, primarily in health economics-driven systems. However, health outcomes, as a means of demonstrating tangible value, and budget impact analyses have a much broader application globally. To be successful in influencing payers and their decisions, health economists need to always carefully consider the utility of their analyses in the context of the payer system rules and demonstrated past behaviors. Understanding payer systems, rules and the way in which actual decisions are made is the key step in ensuring that health outcomes and economics are adding value in the process. Those who don't understand them are destined to live their lives in oblivion.

## Note

1 More detailed information on global drug pricing and market access issues and the preferences and needs of payers can be found in Schoonveld (2015).

## Reference

Schoonveld, E. (2015). *The Price of Global Health*, 2nd edition. Gower Publishing, London, ISBN 978-1-4724-3880-5.

# Chapter 2

# Productivity, Innovation and Value-Based Pricing

*Larry Gorkin and Eugenia Gruzglin*

## The Recent Rate Reduction in Blockbuster Drug Generation

As we discuss in more detail shortly, only 21 drugs launched in the US from the start of 2005 achieved blockbuster status, which entails $1 billion or more in global annual sales, in 2012. Over that time, then, only about 2.5 drugs per year attained blockbuster status. In contrast, a non-exhaustive search of blockbuster drugs launched in the US between 1998 and 2004 yielded a markedly higher average of seven drugs per year that attained blockbuster status, in at least one of those years.[1] Moreover, given a numerator of 21 blockbuster drugs, and 181 new medical entities approved by the Food and Drug Administration (FDA) during the eight years from 2005 to 2012,[2,3] this implies a blockbuster rate of only 11.8% since 2005.

The rate of blockbuster drug occurrence is important because it is a marker of the growth of sales in the branded pharmaceutical industry in general. Figure 2.1 reveals the growth (annual increase) in prescription expenditures in the US from 1997 to 2012. The growth in US prescription drug sales from 2005 to 2012 ranged between –1% and 9%, mean = 4.25%. In contrast, in the years 1997 to 2004, the growth in US prescription drugs was much greater, ranging between 8% and 18%, mean = 13.5%. These results shadow the earlier finding that the rate of blockbuster generation was nearly three-fold higher in the years 1998–2004 than in the years since 2005.

Figure 2.1 shows that the pharmaceutical industry experienced a decline in growth from 1999, and in 2012 demonstrated negative growth for the first time.

Consistent with this analysis, the Biotechnology Industry Organization (BIO) lobbying group utilized the Bio-MedTracker (BMT) to conduct an outcomes analysis of 4,500 drugs in development from late 2003 to the end of 2010.[5] The overall success rate for drugs from Phase I clinical studies to FDA approval was nearly 9%. These convergent analyses point to the lack of productivity by pharma companies between 2005 and 2012 inclusive. That is, only 9% of drugs that entered human studies were approved, and only 11.8% of those approved drugs became blockbuster agents, then only about 1% of drugs that entered Phase I clinical studies were achieving blockbuster status. It is the blockbuster drugs that provide the bulk of funding for the industry.

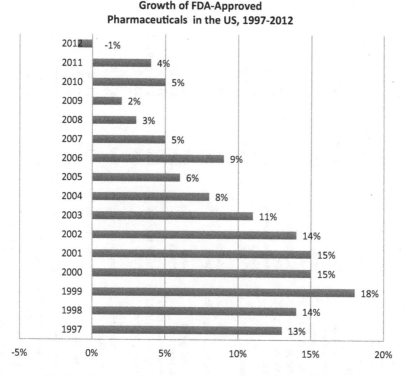

**Growth of FDA-Approved Pharmaceuticals in the US, 1997-2012**

Figure 2.1  Growth in the US market for pharmaceuticals 1997–2012

Adapted/Data from: http://kaiserfamilyfoundation.files.wordpress.com/2013/01/3057-08.pdf.[4]

## End of the "Me-Too" Blockbuster Drug Era

The 21 drugs that attained blockbuster status in 2012 represent a rich source for other information pertinent to the current discussion (see Table 2.1). First, note that in the column devoted to the mechanism of action, there is no mechanism duplicated among the 21 blockbuster drugs listed, though Sutent and Nexavar are assumed to have overlapping kinase targets.[6] Arguably, the lack of a common mechanism is not random, and differs markedly from the prior eight-year period 1997–2004, when it was common for blockbuster drugs to share the same mechanism of action. For example, an analysis of drugs based on US revenue only in 2004, conducted by drugs.com,[7] yielded 33 drugs with sales of more than $1 billion. Of these, nearly two out of three (21/33) shared a mechanism of action with another qualifying drug – for example, four proton pump inhibitors, three statins, three Cox-2 inhibitors, and three atypical antipsychotic agents achieved criterion sales. Back in 2004, very few drugs within a class were tested in appropriately designed, "head-to-head" clinical trials,[8] but nonetheless several members in the drug class succeeded commercially.

Since 2005, such "me-too" drugs, often assumed in the absence of direct head-to-head comparisons data, have been marginalized commercially by key payers in the US

Table 2.1 Blockbusters launched since 2005

| Commercial name | Disease indication | Mechanism of action (generic name) | Company action | US approval | 2012 global revenue |
|---|---|---|---|---|---|
| Baraclude (entecavir) | Hepatitis B | Nucleoside analog | BMS | 3/05 | $1.4 B[9] |
| Xeloda (capecitabine) | Advanced colorectal cancer Metastatic breast cancer | Enzymatic activation oral fluoropyrimidine | Roche | 6/05 | $1.5 B[2A] |
| Orencia (abatacept) | Rheumatoid arthritis | Selective co-stimulation modulator | BMS | 12/05 | $1.2 B[7] |
| Nexavar (sorafenib) | Advanced RCC | Multiple tyrosine kinase inhibitor ras signaling | Bayer/Onyx | 12/05 | >$1.0 B[14] |
| Sutent (sunitinib) | Advanced RCC Gastrointestinal stromal tumors | multiple tyrosine kinase inhibitor VEGF, PDGF | Pfizer | 1/06 | $1.2 B[3] |
| Tysabri (natalizumab) | Multiple sclerosis | α4-integrin blocker MAb | Biogen-IDEC/Elan | 6/06* | $1.1B[5] |
| Prezista (darunavir) | HIV/AIDS | Protease inhibitor | JNJ | 6/06 | $1.4 B[7] |
| Lucentis (ranibizumab) | Age-related macular degeneration | VEGF inhibitor | Roche/Novartis | 6/06 | $1.5 B[2A,2B] |
| Gardasil (HPV) | Cervical cancer prophylaxis | HPV 16, 18 | Merck | 6/06 | $1.6 B[1] |
| Revlimid (lenalidomide) | Multiple myeloma Myelodysplastic syndrome | Anti-angiogenesis | Celgene | 7/06 | $3.2 B[4] |
| Januvia/Janumet (sitagliptin) | Type 2 diabetes | DPP-4 | Merck | 11/06 | $5.7 B[1] |
| Vyvance (lisdexamfetamine dimesylate) | ADHD | Amphetamine-derived prodrug | Shire | 2/07 | $1.0 B[12] |
| Soliris (eculizumab) | Paroxysmal nocturnal hemoglobinuria | Protein C5 binding Mab | Alexion | 3/07 | $1.1 B[13] |
| Isentress (raltegravir) | HIV/AIDS | Integrase inhibitor | Merck | 10/07 | $1.5 B[1] |
| Stelara (ustekinumab) | Psoriasis | IgG1κ Mab interleukin-12/23 | JNJ | 9/09 | $1.0 B[7] |
| Victoza (liraglutide) | Type 2 diabetes | Glucagon-like peptide 1 (GLP-1) | Novo Nordisk | 1/10 | $1.6 B[12] 9.5 B DKK[6] |
| Prevnar 13 (pneumococcal conjugate vaccine) | Prevention: otitis media Streptococcus pneumonia | T-cell dependent immune response | Pfizer | 2/10 | $3.7 B[3] |
| Gilenya (fingolimod) | Multiple sclerosis | Sphingosine-1 phosphate receptor modulator | Novartis | 9/10 | $ 1.2 B[2B] |
| Pradaxa (dabigatran) | Stroke prevention in atrial fibrillation | Direct thrombin | Boehringer-Ingelheim | 10/10 | $1.1B[10] |
| Xgeva/Prolia (denosumab) | Osteoporosis, bone cancer | RANKL-binding IgG2 Mab | Amgen | 11/10 | $1.2 B[11] |
| Incivek (telaprevir) | Hepatitis C | NS3/4A protease | Vertex | 5/11 | $1.16 B[8] |

* The list includes Tysabri, which was launched initially in the US in November 2004 but was removed within a few months (February 2005), due to cases of progressive multifocal leukoencephalopathy.[13] PML is a serious brain disorder, but based on efficacy, Tysabri was returned to the US market in June 2006 and became a blockbuster drug.

Key: B = billion (US$); AIDS = acquired immunodeficiency syndrome; ADHD = attention deficit hyperactivity disorder; BMS = Bristol–Myers Squibb; DPP-4 = dipeptidyl peptidase-4; GSK = GlaxoSmithKline; JNJ = Johnson & Johnson; HIV = human immunodeficiency virus; HPV = human papillomavirus vaccine; MAb = monoclonal antibody; PDGF = platelet-derived growth factor; RCC = renal cell carcinoma; VEGF = vascular endothelial growth factor.

and internationally.[9] Indeed, Light and Lexchin (2012) point out that the number of undifferentiated, "me-too" drugs has decreased dramatically in the past few years.[10]

The industry has responded by warning that payers' systematic refusal to reimburse for "me-too" drugs will hurt innovation in the pharmaceutical industry. According to Stephen Whitehead, chief of the Association of the British Pharmaceutical Industry, an industry trade group,[11] the trend towards value-based pricing, followed by several European governments, including the United Kingdom and Germany, places too much emphasis on "breakthrough treatments", discounting the importance of "incremental advances" in drug development. The incremental approach will, arguably, in the long term produce more clinical advancements than the current paradigm of minimizing "me-too" drugs commercially, and relying on the spontaneous generation of "paradigm-shifting" drugs with markedly improved clinical outcomes.

## Notes to Table 2.1

1. Merck Financial Report 2012. www.mercknewsroom.com/press-release/corporate-news/merck-announces-full-year-and-fourth-quarter-2012-financial-results. 02/01/13.
2a. Roche Financial Report 2012. Fb12e.pdf; www.roche.com/investors/annual_reports.htm. 01/25/13.
2b. Novartis Financial Report 2012. www.novartis.com/downloads/investors/reports/novartis-annual-report-2012-en.pdf. 01/22/13.
3. Pfizer 2012 Annual Report. www.pfizer.com/files/investors/presentations/q4performance_012913.pdf. 01/29/13.
4. Celgene 2012 Proxy Statement. https://materials.proxyvote.com/Approved/151020/20120418/NPS_128362/HTML2/celgene-proxy2012_0021.htm. 01/24/13.
5. Biogen Press Release 2012 Revenues. www.biogenidec.com/press_release_details.aspx?ID=5981&ReqId=1778260. 01/28/13.
6. Novo Nordisk 2012 Annual Report. http://webmedia.novonordisk.com/nncom/images/annual_report/2012/Novo-Nordisk-AR-2012-en.pdf. 02/04/13.
7. Johnson & Johnson 2012 Annual Report. www.2012annualreport.jnj.com/sites/default/files/2012_Johnson_Johnson_Annual_Report_Full%20Report_030613.pdf. 02/22/13.
8. Vertex Reports Full-Year and Fourth Quarter 2012 Financial Results and Provides Updates on Key Development Programs. http://investors.vrtx.com/releasedetail.cfm?ReleaseID=736569. 01/29/13.
9. Bristol Myers Squibb 2012 Annual Report. http://phx.corporate-ir.net/phoenix.zhtml?c=106664&p=irol-reportsannual. 01/24/13.
10. Boehringer Ingelheim Annual Report 2012. www.boehringer-ingelheim.com/content/dam/internet/opu/com_EN/document/01_news/08_APC/APC_2013/BoehringerIngelheim_Summary_Report_2012.pdf. 04/14/13.
11. Amgen Inc. 2012 Annual Report. http://investors.amgen.com/phoenix.zhtml?c=61656&p=irol-reportsannual. 04/04/13.
12. Shire 2012 Annual Report. http://ar2012.shire.com. 03/28/13.

13. Alexion Reports Fourth Quarter and Full Year 2012 Results. http://news. alexionpharma.com/press-release/financial-news/alexion-reports-fourth- quarter-and-full-year-2012-results. 02/14/13.

14. http://seekingalpha.com/article/1214371-onyx-pharmaceuticals-management- discusses-q4-2012-results-earnings-call-transcript?page=3. 02/21/13.

We beg to differ, as Table 2.1 addresses this point, albeit indirectly. More than 30% of the blockbuster drugs listed with approval starting in 2005 were launched after January 1, 2010. Based on the parameter of time to become a blockbuster, drugs launched since 2010 have had significantly less opportunity to achieve this status than drugs launched from 2005 to 2009. Instead of supporting the need for "me-too" drugs, these data demonstrate that the drugs achieving blockbuster status represent innovative products with a novel mechanism of action. Of course, the risk of failure is much greater when developing a potentially innovative product.

## Abandonment of Value-Based Pricing

As long as multiple drugs within a class were able to attain commercial success, with or without demonstrating value-based pricing via cost-effectiveness, the prices of individual drugs were constrained. For example, the most successful class of drugs in 2013, the injected biologics to treat rheumatoid arthritis and other autoimmune conditions, was launched nearly 15 years ago at less than $20,000 annually. This class of drug was expected to generate about $30 billion in 2013, but imagine if the first of this class were launched today: how would this agent be priced? Rather than answer this rhetorical question, we explore the shifting paradigm in pharmaceutical pricing.

Upon realizing that the newly launched "me-too" drugs no longer generate a sufficient return on investment, the pharmaceutical industry has altered the pricing of an innovative drug at launch. Accordingly, companies appear to have abandoned the use of empiric and theoretical pricing models, founded on cost-effectiveness, to determine the value of the new drug. Instead, when the anomalous, innovative drug attains regulatory success, almost all companies seem inclined to simply charge more than the price of the highest branded drug in a particular disease indication and market, in the attempt to pay for the past 30, or the next 30, developmental drug failures.

This pricing effect is evidenced in Table 2.1/Figure 2.2 if one focuses on the 21 drugs launched since 2005, which were blockbusters in 2012, in terms of those that share a common disease indication. There are eight drugs that meet this latter criterion, with two drugs that treat type 2 diabetes, two that treat HIV/AIDS, two that treat multiple sclerosis, and two that treat advanced renal cell carcinoma. These drugs can be utilized to test the hypothesis of increasing price when a new branded drug reaches the market. While the sample size is small, in each of these case studies the launch price of the more recent blockbuster drug was consistently higher than the corresponding market leader or salient comparator drug.

Figure 2.2 demonstrates that almost one quarter of blockbuster drugs have oncology indications, followed by the pharmaceutical compounds indicated for autoimmune diseases (rheumatoid arthritis, MS, and psoriasis), and cardiometabolic disorders.

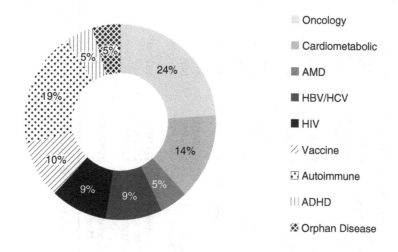

Oncology

Cardiometabolic

AMD

HBV/HCV

HIV

Vaccine

Autoimmune

ADHD

Orphan Disease

*Figure 2.2* Blockbuster drugs launched since 2005 by therapeutic areas

The oral DPP-IV drug, Januvia (100 mg/day), to treat type 2 diabetes, was launched in 4Q06,[14] with the price set at $4.86 per day,[15] or $150 per month. This market leader generated $5.75 billion in 2012.[16] The once-daily, injected GLP-1 agent, Victoza, was approved in the US in 1Q10.[17] The cost of Victoza in the US is about $240/month for the 1.2 mg treatment dose and $360/month for the 1.8 mg dose.[18] The drugs have not been compared in a well-controlled double-blinded study. An open-label study sponsored by Novo Nordisk suggested slightly better efficacy with injected Victoza than oral Januvia,[19] but insufficient to justify the price differential, particularly among most diabetics, who tend to weigh more and require the use of high-dose Victoza. In 1Q13, the FDA approved JNJ's Invokana, an oral drug in a new class known as sodium-glucose co-transporter 2 (SGLT2).[20] Invokana works in the kidneys and allows the body to get rid of excess glucose through the urine. JNJ priced Invokana at $263 per 30 days,[21] markedly higher than oral Januvia, in the absence of head-to-head clinical trials.

Prezista was approved for second-line treatment of HIV/AIDS in 2Q06.[22] At launch, Prezista cost $9,125 annually in the US[23] When launched in 2007, Isentress, in combination with other antiretroviral agents, was also indicated for the treatment of HIV-1 infection in treatment-experienced adult patients.[24] Merck priced Isentress at $9,900 per patient yearly,[25] nearly a 10% increase over Prezista.

In the treatment of multiple sclerosis (MS), when Tysabri was returned to the market in 2Q06, following an 18-month hiatus due to the serious adverse event progressive multifocal leukoencephalopathy (PML), rather than pricing it as "damaged goods", Biogen-IDEC/Elan re-launched the monoclonal antibody at $28,000 annually.[26] At that time, Tysabri was the highest priced branded drug to treat MS on the market.[27] In 4Q10, when Novartis launched Gilenya, this price was

Table 2.2 Oncology drugs launched in the US since 2010 at an annual cost of $90,000+

| Commercial name (generic name) | Disease indication | Mechanism of action | Company United States | Annual cost global revenue | 2012 |
|---|---|---|---|---|---|
| Camprelsa (vandetanib) | Medullary thyroid cancer[33] | Multi-kinase inhibitor (e.g. EGFR, VEGFR, RET) | AstraZeneca | $216,810[34] | $27 M[35] |
| Zaltrap (ziv-aflibercept) | Advanced colorectal cancer[36] | VEGF-trap angio- genesis inhibitor | Sanofi/Regeneron | $132,756[37] | €25 M[38] |
| Pomalyst (pomalidomide) | Third-line multiple myeloma | Thalidomide-like anti-angiogenesis | Celgene | $126,000[39] | N/A |
| Yervoy (ipilimumab) | Advanced melanoma[40] | CTLA4 inhibitor monoclonal antibody | Bristol–Myers | $120,000[41] | $706 M[42] |
| Krypolis (carfilzomib) | Multiple myeloma third-line[43] | Proteasome inhibitor | Onyx | >$120,000[44] | $62 M[45] |
| Cometriq (Cabozantinib) | Medullary thyroid cancer | Tyrosine kinase inhibitor RET, MET and VEGFR2 | Exelixis | $118,900 | N/A |
| Kadcyla (ado-trastuzumab emtansine) | HER2+ metastatic breast cancer | Mab drug conjugate | Roche | $117,600[46] | N/A |
| Xalkori (crizotinib) | ALK-positive NSCLC[47] | Binds competitively to ALK tyrosine kinase | Pfizer | $115,000[48] | $123 M[49] |
| Iclusig (ponatinib) | Chronic myeloid leukemia | Anti-T315I mutation | Ariad | ~$115,000[50] | N/A |
| Zelboraf (vemurafenib) | BRAF v600 advanced melanoma[51] | BRAF v600 inhibitor | Roche | $112,800[52] | $234 M[53] |
| Stivarga (regorafenib) | Second-line, metastatic colorectal cancer[54] | Multiple kinase inhibitor | Bayer/Onyx | $112,200[55] | €32 M[56] |
| Adcetris (brentuximab vedotin) | Hodgkin's lymphoma ALCL[57] | Anti-CD30 monoclonal antibody | Seattle Genetics | $108,000[58] | $138.2 M[59] |
| Inlyta (axitinib) | Renal cell carcinoma[60] | VEGF inhibitor | Pfizer | <$106,800[61] | $100 M[62] |
| Mekinist (trametinib) | Metastatic/unresectable melanoma[63] | MEK inhibitor | GSK | $104,400[64] | N/A |
| Bosulif (bosutinib) | Chronic myelogeneous leukemia, second-line[65] | Kinase inhibitor | Pfizer | <$98,400[66] | Not reported[67] |
| Provenge (sipulecucel-T) | Castration-resistant prostate cancer[68] | Immune response versus PAP | Dendreon | $93,000[69] | $322 M[70] |
| Tafinlar (dabrafenib) | Metastatic/unresectable melanoma[71] | BRAF V600E inhibitor | GSK | $91,200[72] | N/A |
| Erivedge (vismodegib) | Basil cell carcinoma[73] | Hedgehog pathway Roche/Curis inhibitor | $90,000[74] | $29 M[75] | $1.5 M[76] |
| Xtandi (enzalutamide) | Castration-resistant prostate cancer[77] | Androgen receptor inhibitor | Astellas/ Medivation | >$90,000[78] | $71 M[79] |

Key: M = million; Mab = monoclonal antibody; ALCL = analplastic large cell lymphoma; VEGF = vascular endothelial growth factor; PAP = prostatic acid phosphatase; N/A = not applicable; GSK = GlaxoSmithKline.

easily surpassed at $48,000 annually.[28] The latest oral MS drug is Biogen's Tecfidera, approved in the US in 1Q13.[29] Biogen set the price for Tecfidera even higher than Gilenya at launch, at $54,900 annually.[30] It is noted, though, that the 2013 price of Gilenya was higher, at $58,000 annually.

Renal cell carcinoma (RCC) is a difficult-to-treat cancer that accounts for 85% of all renal carcinomas, with an estimated five-year survival rate of less than 10%.[31] The two approved drugs, Pfizer's Sutent and Bayer/Onyx's Nexavar, were priced comparably at approximately $4,600 per month per patient. But when one considers that Sutent includes an anomalous regimen in which usage is for six weeks followed by a two-week hiatus,[32] the price of the more recently launched Sutent is higher than that of Nexavar.

A second approach to confirm that value-based models are being abandoned, and prices are simply being set high, is to present the daunting list of oncology drugs launched since 2010 that have been priced at $90,000 or higher annually (see Table 2.2 and Figure 2.3).

Note that 2013 data include drugs that were launched only before June 4, 2013.

Nineteen oncology drugs that met the criterion of $90,000+ in annual costs are listed. In 2010, only one oncology drug was priced at $90,000+ annual cost. In 2011, another three oncology drugs reached the market ranging from $100,000 to $120,000 annual cost. In 2012, though, a total of 11 oncology drugs that gained FDA approval were priced above $90,000+ annually, including one that was priced above $200,000. By June 2013, already four oncology drugs FDA-approved in this year ranged in price annually from $90,000 to $120,000.

In contrast, only two major oncology drugs since 2010 were launched below this price, Roche's Perjeta (pertuzumab, $71,000) and JNJ's Zytiga (abiraterone, $60,000). The exclusion of Roche's Perjeta is debatable, given FDA labeling for use in combination with Herceptin (trastuzumab) and chemotherapy in HER2-positive metastatic breast cancer patients.[80] The cost of Herceptin plus Perjeta is about $125,000 annually, given that the $71,000 cost of Perjeta is added to the $54,000 cost of Herceptin annually.[81] The idea here is that "two are better than one", but does the efficacy warrant a 230% increase in pricing? Perjeta generated the equivalent of $53.8 million in 1Q13.[82]

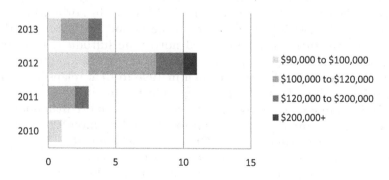

*Figure 2.3* Oncology drugs launched since 2010 at an annual cost of $90,000+

To place this criterion cost of $90,000 in perspective, the median annual wage for a worker in the US in May 2012 was $45,790.[83] Thus, the annual cost of each oncology drug on the list in Table 2.2 is at least twice as great as the median annual income of US wage earners. This trend is not likely to end anytime soon, as 37% of 907 new biotech drugs in development in 1Q13 were cancer treatments.[84]

Of course, oncology therapeutics are not the only drugs that are getting expensive. This trend has been observed in orphan drugs, which treat 200,000 people or fewer in the US[85] These drugs have been priced at beginning "six figures" and much higher, in US dollars. For example, Alexion's Solaris is priced at $440,000 per patient annually[86] and is apparently being prescribed to fewer than 3,000 (if fully compliant) patients worldwide to generate $1.13 billion in 2012 global sales.[87]

It is not only the absolute high-priced drugs but the systemic high pricing of new launches across myriad indications that has occurred. An epidemiologic analysis can be utilized to indicate that a drug to treat a more common disease state, such as type 2 diabetes, can yield comparable results in terms of budgetary impact. For example, high-dose, Nova Nordisk's Victoza, a blockbuster drug launched in 2010, at about $9 per day for most overweight patients, seems to be replacing a drug in the same class that was launched in 2005, Amylin's Byetta,[88] priced at approximately $5 per day, at that time.[89]

Adjusting for disease prevalence and duration of treatment, this is comparable to shifting to a $90,000 drug from a $50,000 oncology product, when one considers the prevalence of type 2 diabetes is more than 100 times that of the key solid tumor, lung cancer, for example, as observed in the following figures:

Lung cancer: 62 cases per 100,000 population[90]
Type 2 diabetes: 83 cases per 1,000 population[91]

When one considers jointly that patients, on average, will be treated for at least 20 times longer for type 2 diabetes than for non-small cell lung cancer (NSCLC), then the ultimate budgetary impact of the two more expensive drugs will be comparable, notwithstanding markedly lower costs per patient for the diabetes compared with the NSCLC drug annually. Thus, innovative products to treat a variety of disease indications are becoming more likely to achieve blockbuster status and seek the same pot of payers' resources.

Another trend relevant to this report is the markedly increasing price of previously launched blockbuster drugs in the US In a 1Q12 report by Forbes, 145% of US sales growth over the last half decade (i.e. in the period highlighted in this report, 2005 to the present) can be attributed not to the introduction of new drugs but to rapidly increasing pricing of launched products, even in the face of decreasing volume.[92] For example, upon launch in 1996 to treat relapsing forms of MS, Biogen sold a four-week supply of Avonex (interferon-ß-1a) to wholesalers for $710, or $9,230 for one year's supply. The price of Avonex more than doubled to approximately $1,500 a month in 2006, and to $2,400 for a month's supply in 2009.[93] A more recent price cited was more than $30,000 annually.[94] The rapid increase in competitors' prices during the period of low productivity is consistent with the thesis of this report. Another implication is that the introduction of a high-priced innovative product can lead companies with drugs already on the market to raise their prices in response to the corresponding competition, as with the launch of oral drugs to treat MS.

## Rebirth of the Blockbuster Drug

In the corresponding time frame, large pharmaceutical companies reduced markedly the size of their sales[95] and marketing[96] forces, and drug company spending on US television advertising decreased a striking 23% from 2007 to 2011.[97] More directly related to this chapter, over the past five years, large pharmaceutical companies have cut thousands of R&D scientists working on drug development in their labs.[98] For example, the largest company, Pfizer, laid off thousands at its central research facilities in Sandwich (UK) and Groton (US), as overall research spending was reduced from $9.4 billion in 2010 (adjusted for the Wyeth acquisition) to $7.8 billion in 2012.[99]

Arguably, all of these actions have occurred because of payers' increasing power to determine criteria for reimbursement. In the US, 84% of branded prescriptions written in 2012 were dispensed as generic drugs.[100] However, the pharmacy benefit managing company, Express Scripts, estimated that $49 billion in brand-name drugs were dispensed in 2011, when a generic equivalent was available.[101] Thus, more work remains to be done, according to managed care.

These findings, however, do not support the "doom and gloom" scenario painted by Stephen Whitehead that "incremental advancement" (via "me-too" drugs) is critical to significant clinical benefits in drug development. Instead, the premise of this chapter is that an increasing number of innovative, actual and potential blockbuster drugs have emerged in recent years. We will review the specific drugs in the next section, but now we want to outline the cultural changes that have allowed an increase in productivity when other operations are being streamlined and de-emphasized.

Improvements in productivity have occurred because of the pursuit of targeted therapeutics that fall into two categories: (1) monoclonal antibodies or other injected, biologic agents designed against cell-surface receptors, or (2) small molecules, administered orally, which can penetrate through cell membranes and reach targets inside the cell. Total sales of recombinant biologic agents nearly doubled from $63.8 billion in 2006 to $124.6 billion in 2012.[102]

A number of factors are contributing to the rebirth of blockbuster drugs. Some of these include the fact that blockbuster status, once achieved, may no longer be assumed until patent loss, creating opportunities for drugs in development or recent launches:

- Greater regulatory focus on safety is one such scenario, with the quintessential example of Avandia (rosiglitazone), the GlaxoSmithKline (GSK) drug to treat type 2 diabetes. In 2006, sales of GSK's Avandia were $3.2 billion.[103] However, in 2007, Dr. Steven Nissen presented a meta-analysis, albeit of mostly short-term studies, that the drug was associated with increased risk of mortality and myocardial infarction.[104] The FDA initiated a Risk Evaluation and Mitigation Strategy (REMS) program that militated against the use of Avandia. By 1Q13, GSK no longer listed Avandia sales separately, but rather included them in a "metabolic" drug category with total sales of only $45 million.[105] Unexpectedly, though, an FDA advisory group recommended that the REMS program be removed or modified to allow more access to Avandia.[106] There is little doubt that Merck's novel blockbuster, dipeptidyl peptidase

IV (DPP-IV) drug, Januvia (sitagliptin), launched in 2006, benefitted from the rapid decline in Avandia prescribing.

- Greater emphasis on clinical efficacy has caused the loss of labeling of approved blockbuster drugs. A complex example is Roche's Avastin, which was approved initially in 2004 on the basis of an overall survival (OS) benefit in the treatment of metastatic colorectal cancer.[107] Since then, many other oncology indications for Avastin have been approved, including the accelerated approval to treat HER2 negative advanced breast cancer, on the basis of improved progression-free survival (PFS). In 4Q11, however, the FDA revoked Avastin's accelerated approval in this indication due to the reliable inability of Roche to demonstrate an OS benefit in metastatic breast cancer.[108] An estimated $1 billion in annual sales was threatened by the revoking of Avastin in advanced breast cancer.[109]

- A clear trend in a number of disease indications is for combination therapy to generate a blockbuster drug, for example a convenient single oral tablet to treat HIV or AIDS. In 3Q12 Gilead's Stribild (elvitegravir, cobicistat, emtricitabine, tenofovir disoproxil fumarate) was approved as a once-a-day combination pill to treat HIV-1 infection among adults naïve to treatment for HIV infection.[110] Gilead's Emtriva (emtricitabine) and Viread (tenofovir disoproxil fumarate) had already been FDA approved for HIV treatment; the new approvals include elvitegravir, an integrase strand transfer inhibitor, that interferes with an enzyme that HIV needs to multiply, and Gilead's cobicistat, which inhibits an enzyme that prolongs elvitegravir's effect. Among 1,408 treatment-naïve adults, double-blinded efficacy for Stribild (88–90%) was statistically comparable to Atripla (efavirenz, emtricitabine and tenofovir, at 84%). Notwithstanding comparable efficacy, Stribild was the highest-priced HIV/AIDS treatment in the US, at $28,500 annually,[111] 35% higher than Atripla ($3.57 billion in global sales in 2012[112]). Stribild generated $92.1 million in 1Q13.[113]

- Consistent with the theme of this chapter, the time between innovative products in a particular disease indication is narrowing. This means that an innovative product may gain and lose blockbuster status much more quickly, yielding a paradigm shift in treatment modalities. For example, as noted in Table 2.1, Vertex's Incivek, to treat the hepatitis C virus (HCV) with injected interferon, attained blockbuster status in 2012, with $1.16 billion in global sales that year. But in 1Q13, worldwide sales contracted by 51% to $222.8 million,[114] as fewer new patients elected to start therapy. The HCV community of patients and physicians has awaited the approval of the filed Gilead drug, sofosbuvir, representing an all-oral regimen for the treatment of HCV.[115]

Some have questioned the improved productivity of industry R&D, citing a KMR Group study released in 3Q12 with regard to success rates of Phase III and Phase II studies. The number of Phase III drugs decreased from 70% to 67% to 65% from 2003 through 2007, from 2005 through 2009, and from 2007 through 2011, respectively.[116] Similarly, the success rates of Phase II drugs fell from 34% to 25% to 22%, respectively, during the same periods.

These findings, though, are not particularly disconcerting to the innovative drug argument because of the marked shift, in the corresponding time frame, from developing "me-too" drugs to developing drugs with a novel mechanism of action. "Me-too" drugs have higher rates of regulatory success, albeit generally in the absence of commercial success. Part of the explanation is that the industry is shifting development to more complex, large rather than simple, small molecular agents, given that the injected biologics advance from pre-clinical to clinical studies at a rate of 12% versus only 2% for the oral agents.[117]

Theoretically, the current pricing strategy, marked by abandoning value-based pricing, is not likely sustainable, if instead of two blockbusters per year, a rapid rise to six, eight or more blockbuster drugs occurs annually. This strategy is bound to stretch payers if the increasing numbers of successful drugs are each priced on the assumption that only two drugs per year will attain blockbuster status, given the empirical finding that generating more blockbuster drugs is accompanied by a multi-fold increase in the annual growth rate for global branded pharmaceutical sales in total.

## Specific Improvements in Drug Productivity Starting in 2010

Starting in 2010, the industry has demonstrated signs of greater productivity, as more recent launches with a novel mechanism of action, albeit with less commercial and sales-force "muscle" behind them, are likely to attain blockbuster status. The thesis is supported by the following review of each drug in the following sections: Class of 2010, Class of 2011, Class of 2012, Class of 2013, and Class of 2014.

This review focuses on innovative drugs that are likely to achieve blockbuster status in the next few years. Accordingly, potential blockbusters that are "me-too" drugs, with small clinical improvements to the standard of care in a disease indication, were not included. For example, the 2Q13 US approval of GSK/Theravance's Breo Ellipta (fluticasone furoate and vilanterol inhalation powder), a once-daily maintenance treatment for chronic obstructive pulmonary disease (COPD),[118] was not included.

Like its predecessor, GSK's Advair (fluticasone and salmeterol), Breo Ellipta is a combination of an inhaled corticosteroid and a long-acting beta2-adrenergic agonist (LABA). The difference is that Breo is administered once daily, whereas Advair is a twice-daily medication. Results of clinical studies did not indicate significantly improved efficacy: safety for Breo versus Advair, notwithstanding the purported convenience and improved adherence of once-daily dosing.[119] Inhaled Advair generated $8.03 billion in 2012[120] and still does not face generic competition in the US, notwithstanding having lost patent protection in 2011. Breo Ellipta will likely attain blockbuster status, even if only one eighth as successful commercially as Advair.

Note that certain developmental drugs that have gained a lot of media attention, such as monoclonal antibodies targeting beta-amyloid to treat Alzheimer's disease (AD), have not been included in this analysis because such projects are considered unlikely to succeed. Indeed, one financial securities analyst equated an investment in Lilly as akin to buying a "lottery ticket", betting on solanezumab approval to treat AD.[121]

Figure 2.4 summarizes the 30 potential blockbuster drugs in terms of type of disease addressed. Among the 30 promising pharmaceutical compounds, half (15 drugs) have an oncology indication, for instance melanoma, prostate cancer, multiple myeloma, among others. In second place are five drugs that have a cardio-metabolic indication that includes three anticoagulation drugs and two compounds for type 2 diabetes.

In this section, the potential renaissance in drug development is evidenced by presenting recent drug launches that contrast with Table 2.1, which listed the relatively

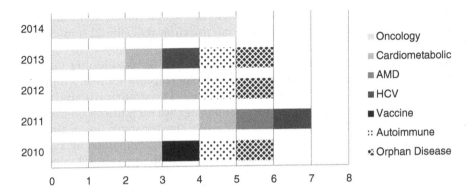

*Figure 2.4* Pharmaceutical compounds with novel mechanism of action, launched since 2010

few drugs launched since 2005 that were blockbuster agents in 2012. The results will support a multi-fold increase in the number of actual and potential blockbuster drugs (Figure 2.3), based on innovation, starting in 2010.

## Class of 2010

Four drugs launched in 2010 had global blockbuster sales in 2012: Pfizer's Prevnar 13 vaccine, Novo Nordisk's Victoza, Boehringer-Ingelheim's Pradaxa and Novartis' Gilenya. In addition, Amgen's Xgeva and Roche's Actemra came close to achieving blockbuster status in the same year. These drugs are listed in Table 2.1 and described below.

**Victoza:** Novo Nordisk's Victoza (liraglutide), to treat type 2 diabetes, was FDA-approved in 1Q10.[122] This long-acting, injectable, GLP-1 peptide analogue was launched as a direct competitor in the class of Amylin's Byetta (exanantide), which received FDA approval in 2Q05.[123] The launch price of the 1.2 mg dose was $8.03 daily.[124] In contrast to blockbuster Victoza, Byetta generated less than $600 million in global sales in 2012.[125] The success of Victoza was due primarily to its demonstrated superiority in the head-to-head trial versus Amylin's Bydureon (a third member of the class, as a once-weekly GLP-1 analogue).[126]

**Pradaxa:** Boehringer-Ingelheim's pradaxa (dabigatran) is a new oral anticoagulant, a direct thrombin inhibitor[127] that was FDA-approved in 2010 to prevent stroke and blood clots among patients with abnormal heart rhythm related to atrial fibrillation (AF).[128] Pradaxa had already attained blockbuster status with $1.43 billion in 2012.[129] Recent data further support substantial benefits for prevention of recurrent deep vein thrombosis (DVT) and/or pulmonary embolism (PE), with low overall bleeding rates, in patients with AF.[130,131] Pradaxa (150 mg BID) costs $250 per 30-day supply[132] and is trying to replace generic warfarin (5 mg daily). Warfarin, in contrast, has a 30-day supply cost of only $4.15 but requires drug safety monitoring, and is not a convenient drug for many patients.

**Gilenya:** Novartis' Gilenya (fingolimid) was the first-to-market, oral treatment of MS, launched in 3Q10,[133] at $48,000 as the annual price.[134] In the Phase III TRANSFORMS study, Gilenya reduced the annualized relapse rate (ARR), relative to interferon-beta-1a (Biogen's Avonex), by 52% at one year, although the absolute rates were quite low (Gilenya 0.5 mg, ARR = 0.16; interferon-beta- 1a IM, ARR = 0.33; p<0.001).[135] Gilenya is the only approved treatment shown to consistently decrease brain volume loss by about one third versus placebo.[136] Brain volume loss is the best magnetic resonance imaging (MRI) correlate of long-term disability. Gilenya generated $1.2 billion in global 2012 sales.[137]

**Prevnar 13:** Pfizer's Prevnar 13 is a vaccine indicated for children aged between 6 weeks and 5 years of age that helps protect against 13 of the most common strains of pneumococcal bacteria that cause invasive pneumococcal disease, including pneumococcal meningitis. In more than 60 countries, Prevnar 13 is offered annually as vaccine coverage against invasive pneumococcal disease for nearly 30 million children.[138] The vaccine was approved subsequently in the US among people 50 years and older to prevent pneumonia and invasive disease caused by the bacterium Streptococcus pneumoniae.[139] The cost of Prevnar 13 in the US is $114 per injection, but it is sold much lower internationally, where charitable organizations, including the Gates Foundation, subsidize the cost.[140] Prevnar 13 generated $3.72 billion in global sales in 2012.[141]

**Xgeva:** Amgen's Xgeva (denosumab), a RANKL-targeted monoclonal antibody, was approved in the US to prevent skeletal-related events (SREs) in patients with cancer that has metastasized and damaged the bone.[142] Xgeva utilized a head-to-head Phase III program against the standard of care, Novartis' Zometa (zoledronic acid), in randomized, double-blinded clinical studies involving patients with breast, prostate and other cancers. For example, an 18% delay in the time to occurrence of the first SREs was observed in breast cancer patients, although no survival difference emerged between the drugs.[143] The modest improvement in efficacy apparently led to a near doubling pricing differential, $1,650 versus $844, respectively, for Xgeva versus Zometa.[144] Xgeva registered revenue that was $64 million short of achieving blockbuster status in 2012.[145]

**Actemra:** The initial interleuken-6 drug, Roche's Actemra (tocilizumab), has been available in Japan since June 2005 to treat a rare disease, called Cattleman's disease.[146] Actemra became a "mainstream" drug, though, with approval in second-line treatment of rheumatoid arthritis in 1Q10,[147] a market that was estimated at $13 billion in 2012.[148] At launch, the US cost of Actemra was estimated to be $1,060 to $2,125 per month, depending on the dose.[149] Accordingly, most doses of Actemra were priced competitively with the market leaders, the tissue necrosis factor-alpha (TNF-alpha) blocking agents ("typically" $15,000 to $20,000 annually).[150] In 2012, Roche increased global sales by 33% to 842 million Swiss francs ($905 million).[151]

With six drugs either having achieved or heading towards blockbuster status, the Class of 2010 is clearly inconsistent with the corresponding mean of approximately two blockbuster drugs per year, on average, from 2005 to 2009. The question is whether the 2010 anomaly is merely an outlier, or a harbinger of a turn-around in R&D innovation. The evidence, we believe, supports the latter conclusion. That is, while remaining an empirical question, an analysis of developmental and approved drugs in 2011 and beyond points to an emergent trend of increased productivity.

## Class of 2011

Seven unique, potential blockbuster drugs, approved in 2011, were identified, including a treatment for advanced prostate cancer, Zytiga, one for hepatitis C, Incivek, two for advanced melanoma, Yervoy and Zelboraf, a treatment for a rare subgroup of non-small cell lung cancer patients, Xalkori, a preventive agent for thrombo-embolism among patients with atrial fibrillation, Xarelto, and an anti-angiogenesis agent to treat age-related macular degeneration (AMD), Eylea.

**Zytiga**: JNJ's Zytiga is an oral medication that targets protein cytochrome P450 17A1[152] and was approved in the US in 2Q11, in combination with the steroid, prednisone, to treat second-line, metastatic castration-resistant, prostate cancer. Zytiga + prednisone prolonged life by 3.9 months versus placebo + prednisone in a clinical trial. In contrast to the tenet of this report, JNJ priced Zytiga in the US at only $5,000 per month, or $40,000 for an expected eight-month course of treatment.[153] Zytiga generated near-blockbuster levels with $961 million in global sales in 2012.[154]

**Yervoy**: Bristol-Myers' Yervoy (ipilimumab) is a CTLA-4 inhibiting, monoclonal antibody, which is a negative regulator of the immune system, and was approved for commercial sale in the US in 1Q11.[155] In a Phase III study, Yervoy established a survival benefit of 3.7 months versus a standard vaccine therapeutic, in the treatment of advanced melanoma.[156] Bristol-Myers priced a four-infusion course of Yervoy at about $120,000.[157] In 1Q13, Yervoy recorded a 49% increase in global revenue to $229 million,[158] as noted in Table 2.2.

**Zelboraf**: Roche's Zelboraf (vemurafenib) was approved in the US simultaneously with a companion diagnostic in 3Q11, for first-line, metastatic or unresectable melanoma, whose tumors express a gene mutation called BRAF V600E.[159] This genotype applies to about 50% of melanoma patients.[160] The risk of death was reduced by 63% for BRAF mutation-positive metastatic melanoma patients who received Zelboraf, versus the standard first-line treatment, dacarbazine.[161] The US cost of Zelboraf is about $56,400 for a six-month course of treatment.[162] Roche registered CHF84 million in global revenue for Zelboraf in 1Q13, up 154% versus 1Q12.[163] This was the equivalent of $90.3 million.[164]

**Xalkori**: Pfizer's Xalkori (crizotinib) is indicated for the treatment of the 3–5% of patients with locally advanced or metastatic NSCLC, which is anaplastic lymphoma kinase (ALK)-positive.[165] Xalkori was approved in the US in 3Q11, with a companion diagnostic assay (Abbott's ALK-FISH test).[166] Pfizer announced pricing of Xalkori at $9,600 per patient per month in the US[167] The actual cost is increased by $1,500 per test, given the approximate 25 ALK screening tests that are performed to find one patient for whom Xalkori is appropriate. Pfizer registered revenue for Xalkori in 1Q13 at $53 million.[168]

**Xarelto**: Bayer/JNJ's Xarelto (rivaroxaban), an oral, once-daily, factor Xa inhibitor, was approved in the US as an anti-clotting agent to reduce the risk of stroke in people who have non-valvular atrial fibrillation.[169] Earlier in 2011, the FDA had approved Xarelto to reduce the acute risk of deep vein thrombosis, and pulmonary embolism following knee or hip replacement surgery. The former indication, stroke prophylaxis in atrial fibrillation opens up a long-term treatment paradigm, as a potential replacement for warfarin. In 4Q11, Xarelto was rejected by US regulators to treat acute coronary syndrome (ACS).[170] Bayer reported that Xarelto generated global sales of €155 in 1Q13,[171] the equivalent of $205 million.

**Eylea:** Regeneron/Bayer's Eylea (aflibercept) to treat patients with wet (neovascular) age-related macular degeneration (AMD) was approved in 4Q11.[172] AMD is the leading cause of blindness in Americans aged 60 years and older. Eylea is a novel fusion recombinant anti-angiographic agent that binds to vascular endothelial growth factor-A (VEGF-A) and placental growth factor (PlGF).[173] The cost of Eylea, per injection, is $1,850, slightly lower than the $1,950 charged by Roche/Novartis for Lucentis.[174] More importantly, Eylea requires fewer injections – once a month for the first three months and then bimonthly – versus monthly for Lucentis. Thus, the annual cost of Eylea is about $8,000 less than for Lucentis. In 2012, Eylea generated $838 million in global revenue.[175]

**Incivek**: The protease inhibitor Vertex's Incivek (telaprevir) was approved in the US in 2Q11, for all treatment lines of hepatitis C in combination with interferon alfa and ribavirin.[176] Incivek improved efficacy about 50% among treatment naïve patients with interferon and ribavirin (standard of care).[177] For 12 weeks of treatment, Incivek costs $49,200, plus $28,800 for the standard of care, totaling nearly $80,000 for a single course of triple therapy.[178] Incivek generated $1.16 billion in 2012,[179] although revenue was decreasing as the market awaited an all-oral treatment regimen for hepatitis C.[180]

## Class of 2012

In 2012, six drugs were already being touted for their blockbuster potential, based on innovation. Some of these had already been approved in the US, or in Europe, whereas others had been filed with regulators during 2012.

**Xtandi**: Medivation/Astellas' Xtandi (enzalutamide) is an oral androgen receptor signaling inhibitor, administered without prednisone, and was approved in the US to treat men with metastatic, castration-resistant prostate cancer in 3Q12.[181] In a study of 1,199 patients who had received prior treatment with docetaxel, the median overall survival with Xtandi was 18.4 months, as compared with 13.6 months for patients randomized to placebo. Xtandi was priced at $7,450 monthly,[182] greater than 50% more than the annual cost of JNJ's Zytiga (see Class of 2011).[183] Net global sales of Xtandi were $71.5 million for the full year 2012.[184]

**Stivarga**: Bayer/Onyx's Stivarga (regorafenib) is an oral multi-kinase inhibitor, targeting vascular endothelial growth factor receptor (VEGFR) 2 and tyrosine kinase with immunoglobulin and EGF homology domain 2 (TIE2) pathways.[185] Stivarga was approved in the US in 3Q12, for the second-line treatment of patients with metastatic colorectal cancer (mCRC).[186] In the Phase III CORRECT study (N = 760), the Stivarga arm resulted in a 23% reduction in overall mortality. According to Bayer, Stivarga was to be priced at $9,350 for a 28-day cycle of treatment.[187] Onyx registered $9.2 million in revenue from Stivarga in 1Q13, and with a 20% royalty agreement, this implied $46 million in global sales.[188]

**Kyprolis**: Onyx's (carfilzomib) is a next-generation, intravenous proteasome inhibitor, approved in the US to treat third-line, multiple myeloma, including the proteasome inhibitor, Velcade (bortezomib), and an immunomodulatory therapeutic.[189] Kyprolis costs $10,000 per 28-day cycle at the recommended dose.[190] Multiple myeloma treatment has been shifting to combination therapy, allowing for more drugs to succeed. Onyx reported global sales of Kyprolis of $58.1 million in 1Q13.[191]

**Eliquis**: Among Factor Xa drugs, Bristol-Myers/Pfizer's Eliquis (apixaban) was approved for commercial sale in the US in 4Q12. It is an oral tablet used to reduce the risk of stroke and systemic embolism in patients with atrial fibrillation that is not caused by a heart valve problem.[192] Eliquis differentiated from JNJ/Bayer's Xarelto by reducing stroke, major bleeding and death versus the "gold standard" warfarin in AF in a Phase III trial.[193] The stroke prophylaxis in AF is considered the largest commercial opportunity for these drugs,[194] given that AF is a primary cause of ischemic stroke among the elderly.[195] Revenue for Eliquis was reported by Bristol-Myers as $22 million in 1Q13.[196] One new oral anticoagulant had already attained blockbuster status, Boehringer-Ingelheim's Pradaxa, with $1.43 billion in 2012.[197]

**Xeljanz**: Pfizer's Xeljanz (tofacitinib) is an oral janus kinase (JAK) inhibitor approved in the US in 4Q12.[198] Efficacy appears nearly comparable to the injected, tumor necrosis factor-alpha (TNF-α) blocking agents combined with methotrexate (e.g. Amgen/Pfizer's Enbrel/etanercept) in the treatment of resistant rheumatoid arthritis (RA),[199] which generate approximately $13 billion in revenue currently in this indication.[200] Accordingly, with the convenience of an oral agent, the opportunity exists for a marked paradigm shift in RA, and possibly other autoimmune diseases, such as ulcerative colitis.[201]

**Kalydeco:** Vertex's Kalydeco (ivacaftor) is an oral drug, approved by the FDA in 1Q12, and indicated for the treatment of 4% of patients with a rare form of cystic fibrosis (CF), who have specific G551D mutation in the CF trans-membrane regulator (CFTR) gene.[202] Kalydeco targets the underlying cause of this disease by reducing the formation of thick mucus build-up in the lungs, digestive tract and other parts of the body, based on the results of two 48-week, placebo control clinical studies.[203] In 2Q13, though, the combination of Kalydeco and VX-661, a CFTR corrector compound, demonstrated significant improvements over placebo in a much wider segment of the CF population, suggesting a viable commercial product heading for blockbuster status. Kalydeco was priced at an annual cost of $294,000.[204]

## Class of 2013

Six innovative, developmental products began to emerge as potential blockbuster drugs in 2013. Five of the six had already been approved in the US, and the other, arguably the most anticipated of all and the first drug listed, was filed with regulators.

**Kadcyla:** Roche's Kadcyla (ado-trastuzumab emtansine) is the first-to-market antibody-drug conjugate (ADC) formulation of Herceptin linked to the chemotherapy drug ImmunoGen's DM1. Kadcyla is indicated to treat HER2-positive metastatic breast cancer patients and was FDA-approved in 1Q13. In the phase III EMILIA trial, T-DM1 generated a statistically significant overall survival benefit in HER2-positive metastatic breast cancer, as compared with GSK's Tykerb (lapatinib) plus Roche's Xeloda (capecitabine). Resubmitted to the FDA in 3Q12,[205] median overall survival was 30.9 months for T-DM1 versus 25.1 months for lapatinib/capecitabine.[206] While one might prefer a Kadcyla head-to-head trial versus Herceptin, Roche reported Kadcyla sales of CHF18 million (approximately $19.5 million) in the truncated 1Q13 for sales.[207] Kadcyla was set at $9,800 per month.[208]

**Xofigo:** Bayer/Algeta's Xofigo (radium-223 dichloride) is injected in patients with castration-resistant prostate cancer (CRPC) that has spread to the bone but not to the other organs. Xofigo is a first-in-class alpha-pharmaceutical targeting bone metastases with high-energy alpha-particles of short range (<100 µm), FDA-approved in 2Q13. In a Phase III, double-blinded randomized study (ALSYMPCA, N = 922), Xofigo significantly improved OS versus placebo (median OS = 14.0 vs 11.2 months, respectively). The median time to skeletal-related events was 13.6 versus 8.4 months, respectively. The cost of Xofigo six-month injection regimen was $69,000.[209]

**Invokana:** JNJ's Invokana (canagliflozin) is the first drug in a new class of type 2 diabetes medication that inhibits sodium-dependent glucose transporter-2 (SGLT-2). Invokana was FDA-approved in 1Q13,[210] as it blocks the reabsorption of glucose by the kidney, and thereby provides improved glycemic control (Invokana 100 mg and 300 mg monotherapy provides significant reduction in A1C by −0.91% and −1.16%, respectively, relative to placebo[211]). Significant improvements were also cited in terms of systolic blood pressure reductions. JNJ priced Invokana at $263 per 30 days.[212]

**Sofosbuvir:** Gilead Sciences' sofosbuvir (formerly PSI-7977), once-daily nucleotide analogue for treatment of chronic hepatitis C virus (HCV) infection, received FDA-expedited review in 2Q13.[213] Gilead acquired Pharmasset in 1Q12 to obtain PSI-7977, an oral nucleotide NS5B polymerase inhibitor to treat hepatitis C, at a cost of $11.2 billion.[214] Sofosbuvir, in combination with Bristol-Myers' daclatasvir, a NS5A replication complex inhibitor, achieved sustained virologic response in 100% of Genotype 1 and 91% of Genotype 2 and 3 treatment-naïve patients, in a Phase II study.[215] This is a desired, all-oral treatment regimen, which avoids the adverse events associated with injected interferon, including serious gastrointestinal, flu-like and central nervous system symptoms.[216] In 2Q13, Gilead filed sofosbuvir and ribavirin (RBV) as an all-oral therapy for patients with Genotype 2 and 3 HCV infection, and for sofosbuvir in combination with RBV and pegylated interferon (peg-IFN) for treatment-naïve patients with Genotype 1, 4, 5 and 6 HCV infection.[217]

**Tecfidera:** In 1Q13, Biogen-Idec's former BG-12, Tecfidera (dimethyl fumarate), was approved in the US, an oral drug candidate to treat remitting-relapsing multiple sclerosis (RRMS).[218] Tecfidera reduced the proportion of patients relapsing by about 50%, relative to placebo, in two studies.[219,220] The annual cost of BG-12 is set at $54,900,[221] and will compete with the new blockbuster oral drug, Novartis' Gilenya.

In its first month of launch, nearly 2,000 patients started Tecfidera, suggesting a strong launch.[222]

**Juxtapid:** Aegerion's Juxtapid (lomitapide), a small molecule microsomal triglyceride transfer protein inhibitor (MTP-I), treats a rare genetic disorder, homozygous familial hypercholesterolemia (HoFH). It was awarded FDA approval in 4Q12.[223] When added to an existing lipid-lowering therapy of HoFH patients Juxtapid reduced mean LDL-C levels by 40%, from a baseline average 336 mg/dL to 190 mg/dL at 26 weeks.[224] While launched at a cost of $235,000 annually, within six months the annual price was raised to $295,000.[225] In 1Q13, Aegerion reported that 75 patients were prescribed Juxtapid, with minimal dropouts from treatment.[226] Approximately 3,500 patients, at the new annualized price, would achieve blockbuster status for Juxtapid.

## Class of 2014

Although early in the process, four drugs have drawn attention for both innovation and the potential for marked commercial success.

**Ibrutinib:** Pharmacyclics' oral inhibitor ibrutinib is for the treatment of chronic lymphocyte leukemia (CLL) patients with deletion in the short arm of chromosome 13. In 2Q13, the FDA granted a "breakthrough therapy designation" for ibrutinib in CLL.[227] The company, along with partner JNJ, recruited 350 patients with relapsed or refractory CLL or small lymphocytic lymphoma (SLL) for a Phase III head-to-head trial that would examine safety and efficacy of ibrutinib monotherapy to Arzerra (fatumumab), a CD-20 inhibitor FDA-approved biologic to treat CLL.[228] The Phase II, RESONATE-17 open-label, single-arm study was to test whether ibrutinib could significantly improve the overall response rate in patients with deletion 17p in patients who did not respond or relapsed at least after one prior CLL treatment.[229]

**GA101:** Roche's GA101 (obinutuzumab) is the first glycol-engineered, type 2 anti-CD20 monoclonal antibody for B-cell malignancy, clinically tested in chronic lymphocytic leukemia (CLL) and non-Hodgkin's lymphoma (NHL) patients.[230] Results from CLL11, Phase III study, investigated efficacy and safety of GA101 or MabThera/Rituxan and chemo compared with chemo alone in 781 previously untreated CLL patients. GA101 plus chemo demonstrated significant 86% (HR=0.14, p<0.0001) reduction in the risk of disease progression, relapse or death. The PFS was more than doubled in the GA101 treated group compared with chemo alone (23 months vs 10.9 months, HR=0.14, 95% CI 0.09–0.21, p<0.0001), while PFS was 10.8 months for chemo compared with 15.7 months for MabThera/Rituxan plus chemo.[231]

**Nivolumab:** BMS' nivolumab is an anti-PD-1 investigational monoclonal antibody that binds to the cell surface of T-cells and allows our own immune system to attack cancer cells that have PD-1 ligand on the cell surface.[232] PD-1 is an inhibitory receptor expressed on activated T cells, which appears to suppress anti-tumor immunity. The long-term, Phase I follow-up study of patients stage IV melanoma demonstrated that 33 out of 107 patients (31%) treated experienced tumor shrinkage of 30% across different doses. The estimated one-year survival rate was 62% and the estimated two-year survival rate was 43%. The median overall across all doses was 16.8 months.[233] A 53% objective response rate was observed among patients receiving the combination of 1 mg/kg of nivolumab plus 3 mg/kg of Yervoy (BMS's CTLA4 monoclonal antibody, Yervoy, approved to treat advanced melanoma), with at least 80% tumor shrinkage within 12 weeks.[234, 235] The estimated one-year survival rate across all cohorts treated with Yervoy/nivolumab was 82%.[236]

**Lambrolizumab:** Merck's lambrolizumab is an anti-PD-1 investigational monoclonal antibody for melanoma treatment. It received a "breakthrough therapy" designation from the FDA in 2Q13.[237] PD-1 is an inhibitory T-cell co-receptor that can lead to suppression of anti-tumor immunity.[238] Results from ongoing a Phase 1b study collected from 85 of 135 patients with advanced melanoma demonstrated that 43 patients (51%) showed an objective anti-tumor response, with 8 patients (9%) showing a complete response at or after 12 weeks.[239] The overall response rate across all doses and schedules was 38%.[240] In general, lambrolizumab is well tolerated. A Phase III study evaluating lambrolizumab in Yervoy-naïve patients with advanced melanoma, and a Phase II/III study in NSCLC, were scheduled to commence in 3Q13.[241]

**Palbociclib:** Pfizer's PD-0332991 is an oral and selective inhibitor of cyclin-dependent kinases (CDK4 and CDK6), which received a "breakthrough therapy" designation by the FDA in 2Q13, for treatment of a subset of post-menopausal, advanced breast cancer.[242] In a Phase II, post-menopausal estrogen-receptor ER+/HER2- advanced breast cancer study, median PFS was 26.1 months with the combination of palbociclib + Novartis' Femara (latrozole), an oral non-steroidal aromatase inhibitor, as compared with 7.5 months with Femara alone, a 63% improvement (p<0.001).[243,244] Pfizer initiated Study-1008 in 3/13, a Phase III trial investigating palbociclib plus latrozole vs latrozole alone, as a first-line treatment for advanced/metastatic, post-menopausal ER+/HER2- breast cancer.[245] If successful, a 2014 launch is possible to treat an estimated 60% ER+/HER2- post-menopausal breast cancer patients.[246]

## Pricing Implications of the Renaissance in Drug Development

Given an average of two-plus new blockbuster drugs emerging annually between 2005 and 2012, particularly when the rate of current blockbuster drugs losing patent protection was multi-fold higher, payers seemed capable of absorbing the successful launch of such blockbuster drugs at this anemic rate. The lack of blockbuster productivity by the industry for the past eight years had led to the bulk of innovative drug launches priced above the cost of the standard of care, within the relevant disease indication, as well as marked price increases in the previously launched blockbuster drugs in the US

Starting in 2010, though, the industry began to enjoy a renaissance in drug development. The number of innovative drugs that were likely to achieve blockbuster status increased reliably from 2010 to 2013, with at least six agents likely to achieve blockbuster status each year. Moreover, the Class of 2014 was beginning to emerge, with five capable entries gathering interest. Thus, results for 2010 should not be seen as an outlier, but as a harbinger of the return to the blockbuster model, which bodes well for increased spending on branded pharmaceuticals generally.

This analysis on the emerging rise in innovative blockbuster drugs does not include touted developmental drugs that are not considered viable or likely blockbuster drugs that are not considered innovative. Of course, if expensive biologics prove sufficiently efficacious to replace oral agents in Alzheimer's disease and other indications, then the described paradigm shift will occur more quickly and have an even greater budgetary impact than suggested in this chapter.

There are already signs of change. Three staff at Memorial Sloan-Kettering Cancer Center in Manhattan wrote an op-ed piece in *The New York Times* in 4Q12 indicating that their facility would not prescribe a recently launched advanced colorectal cancer drug, Sanofi/Regeneron's Zaltrap, to patients.[247] At more than $11,000 per month, Zaltrap was twice the cost of Roche's Avastin for this indication, with comparable efficacy. Quite consistent with the current analysis, these authors noted that the typical new cancer drug launched a decade ago cost about $4,500 per month (in 2012 dollars); since 2010, though, the median price has been around $10,000. In response, Sanofi did not change the official price for injected Zaltrap, which is not purchased directly by patients but sold to clinics and hospitals for administration. Instead, Sanofi said it would offer discounts of 50% to payers,[248] but this was not likely to affect patients' co-payment.

More recently, 120 oncologists wrote more systematically about industry "profiteering" at the expense of blood cancer patients in an article published in *Blood*, the journal of the American Society of Hematology.[249] The authors noted that the cost of medical illness, particularly the cost of the recent drug launches, was the single most frequent cause of personal bankruptcy in the US, according to the specialists, given that patients' co-payments on drug prices average 20% of the total cost of the drug. That means that cancer patients often face having to pay $20,000–30,000 a year, simply to remain alive.

Essentially, the rhetoric of this report is a call for a return to value-based pricing. In this version, a complex approach is assumed in which the onus is on the industry to demonstrate which patients are most likely to benefit both clinically and cost-effectively, either through the use of a validated companion diagnostic or a systematic series of studies differentiating efficacy among salient patient subgroups within the particular disease indication. If these salient subgroups are excluded in the Phase III program, which often occurs in subgroups with significant co-morbidity, then industry can respond with well-designed "real-world" studies that focus on these subgroups. For example, the use of open-label, randomized studies with clinical outcomes, and few inclusionary/exclusionary enrollment criteria, has been advocated. Then the level of "true" innovation relative to the standard of care will direct pricing of the launched product, rather than an *a priori* increase in cost versus the available branded agents.

If there is no return to the value-based pricing model, however, then the 19th-century metaphor of "the tragedy of the commons" seems applicable. This is a dilemma arising from the situation in which multiple individuals, acting independently and rationally consulting their own self-interest, will ultimately deplete a shared limited resource, even when it is clear that nobody's long-term interest is served by this.[250] The *a priori* focus on pricing to pay for past, recent and/or future failures, when productivity is improving markedly, seems to fit the criteria for invoking this metaphor. Obviously, the concern rises exponentially as the number of emergent innovative drugs increases, consistent with the current analysis. Then, truly innovative drugs are likely to be rejected or marginalized by health technology assessors and payers, or even by regulators citing safety concerns. Therefore, the time is now for senior management at large pharma companies to look beyond their short-term self-interest and reutilize health economics models in their pricing decisions. Based on appropriate empiric and theoretical data tied to the competitive landscape and efficacy, safety differentiation provided by their product, the value of the product in the marketplace can be determined, and these analyses should then guide the pricing decision.

## Update on Productivity, Innovation and Value-based Pricing

Larry Gorkin, PhD and Gena Gruzglin, PhD
July 2015

Our premise is that starting in 2005, there was a marked period of poor productivity in which the industry by abandoning value-based pricing derived from well-conducted cost-effectiveness analysis of newly launched agents. Presumably, this approach to pricing compensated for the cost of past and future failed drugs, over 90% of drugs in development. Moreover, formerly successful launches of "me-too" drugs were systematically abandoned by payers, both in the US and in key countries internationally. The payers seemingly accepted this pricing paradigm for anomalous successful drugs, given the overall lack of developmental productivity. From 2010 to 2014, the report highlighted improved productivity in innovative drug development, particularly manifest by an increasing rate of actual or potential blockbuster agents. More specifically, the rate of blockbuster drugs was less than three per year, on average, during the years from 2005 to 2009, whereas the corresponding average rate improved to more than four blockbuster drugs generated annually from 2010, based on global revenue registered in the second quarter of 2014 of at least $250 million (i.e. achieving one quarter of the blockbuster revenue criterion). Many of the drugs launched since 2010, projected as potential blockbuster drugs in the earlier draft, have now fulfilled that promise, a key assumption of this report.

A second assumption is that the trend for improved innovation documented from 2010 through 2014 was likely to extend into 2015 and beyond. Briefly, we list ten new innovative drugs that have good prospects for approval in the next two years and, if approved, likely to achieve blockbuster status: (1) three monoclonal antibodies (Amgen's evolocumab, Sanofi/Regeneron's alirocumab and Pfizer's bococizumab), all PCSK9 (proprotein convertase subtilisin/kexin type 9) inhibitors, have the potential to reshape the dyslipidemia landscape when added to generic, high-potency statin drugs because of marked reductions in low-density lipoprotein cholesterol levels. US advisory committees recommend approval of the drugs, albeit initially in small populations, but blockbuster status would likely follow if the drugs reduce clinical cardiac event rates relative to statin monotherapy; (2) Novartis' Entresto was approved in the US in 2015 to treat heart failure associated with reduced left ventricular ejection fraction levels. As compared to the standard of care, a generic angiotensin-converting enzyme inhibitor, Entresto reduced cardiovascular death and hospitalization by approximately 20% in a Phase III trial; (3) Intercept's obeticholic acid (OCA) has been submitted for the orphan drug indication, primary biliary cirrhosis, in the US and the EU, and will enter a 2,500-patient, placebo-controlled Phase III trial for non-alcoholic steatohepatitis (NASH), a large unmet need. In Phase II,

OCA delivered improvement among 45% of the patients, as compared with only 21% in the placebo arm of the 72-week study; (4) Juno Therapeutics' CAR-T immunotherapies consist of T cells removed from a patient's blood and equipped with targeting mechanisms called chimeric antigen receptors (CARs), which seek out and bind to proteins expressed by cancer cells. The resulting cells are reinjected into the patient to attack malignancies as they would any commonplace infection. In an early-phase study, 20 out of 22 patients with relapsed/refractory B cell acute lymphoblastic leukemia saw remission when treated with Juno's lead agent, JCAR015; (5) in 3Q15, the FDA approved Vertex's cystic-fibrosis drug, Orkambi, which could treat as many as 8,500 patients in the US, with a wholesale cost of $259,000 per patient. Vertex reported that all four combination-treatment arms met their primary endpoint of improvement in homozygous patients' ability to exhale – measured as absolute change from baseline in percent predicted FEV1, as compared with placebo; (6) Opththotech/Novartis' Fovista, an aptamer that inhibits platelet-derived growth factor, subunit B, is being tested in Phase III to treat age-related macular degeneration (AMD). In a Phase IIb study, Fovista in combination with Roche/Novartis' Lucentis, a blockbuster drug in the treatment of AMD, visual acuity was significantly improved when compared with a patient group treated only with Lucentis; (7) Novartis' Cosentyx (secukinumab) is a novel IL-17A inhibitor treatment for plaque psoriasis approved in the US in 1Q15. In a head-to-head double-blinded study of monoclonal antibodies with standard of care, J&J's Stelera (ustekinumab; IL-12/23 inhibitor), Cosentyx achieved significantly better skin clearing; (8) Celgene's GED-0301 is a novel treatment for Crohn's disease that targets Smad7, reducing its protein levels. Researchers found that patients treated with 160 mg of GED-0301 had higher clinical remission rates (62.5–75%) than patients in the placebo group (5–24%); (9) Gilead's Harvoni, an oral combination agent (ledipasvir 90 mg/sofosbuvir 400 mg), eliminates the need for the use of injected interferon, which causes flu-like symptoms. Harvoni replaced Solvadi as a blockbuster HCV drug in 2015, with $3.5 billion in global sales in 1Q15; and (10) in the absence of a head-to-head trial, an all-oral but more complex regimen from Abbott, Viekira Pak (ombitasvir, an NS5A inhibitor, a non-nucleoside polymerase inhibitor, dasabuvir, and ABT-450, a protease inhibitor boosted with Norvir), appears to be more efficacious than Gilead's Harvoni in the treatment of hepatitis C patients with cirrhosis of the liver. Approved in the US in 4Q14, approximately 20% of persons infected with hepatitis C, if not treated, will develop cirrhosis after 20 years of infection.

With these assumptions met, the crux of the argument is that the rapidly improving productivity in development will produce a tipping point, in which the unabated approach to ever-increasing, branded drug costs is unsustainable. Instead, a return to value-based pricing, predicated on established tenets of cost-effectiveness analysis, will be required to recalibrate the balance between pricing and efficacy. It seems that where there has been competition, prices have been moderated. The current "poster-child" for this claim of "too-high" pricing is Gilead's Harvoni (No. 9 in the above list). The cost of the once-daily pill is $94,500 for 12 weeks of treatment, as compared with $84,000 for Solvadi monotherapy.[251] Approved in 4Q14,[252] Harvoni has a large patient pool of 70% of the approximately 3.2 million people in the US who are infected chronically with HCV Genotype 1.[253] Untreated, hepatitis C progresses to advanced fibrosis, cirrhosis, hepatocellular carcinoma (HCC) and premature death. This is not a chronic, lifetime treatment; instead, with 8- or 12-week treatment regimens, Harvoni has demonstrated sustained virologic response (cure) rates of more than 90% in most HCV subgroups treated.[254]

Gilead has faced a backlash from payers over the high cost of its HCV treatments, particularly the US pharmacy benefits manager, Express Scripts.[255] Express Scripts has been able to utilize the competition from Abbott/Abbvie's Viekera Pak to significantly reduce the price of these hepatitis C treatments. By signing an exclusive deal with Abbvie for placement on its formulary plan, this led to a "price war", with Gilead signing an exclusive deal, in response, with CVS. Gilead also surprised relevant parties by noting that the discount for Harvoni in 2015 would be 46%.[256] Clearly, this was not a voluntary acceptance by Gilead that it had overcharged for the drugs in the US, but a powerful display by the pharmacy benefit manager.

The hope was that this reliable increase in productivity and profitability would lead to a return to value-based pricing, reflecting the actual clinical benefits of each innovative therapeutic agent. Unfortunately, this assumption may prove incorrect, as one of the emerging trends seems to be the willingness of pharmaceutical companies and large biotech firms to overpay markedly for small biotechs.

Arguably, this trend has its roots in the Gilead Sciences purchase of Pharmasset to gain the portfolio of hepatitis C drugs. Gilead paid $11 billion for Pharmasset in 4Q11,[257] notwithstanding that the latter had no commercialized product at the time. Reportedly, Pharmasset had planned to sell the cure for hepatitis C for $36,000, but when launched by Gilead, the price of Solvadi had increased to $84,000 for the 12-week course of treatment.[258] More recently, Gilead launched a second-generation, oral cure for hepatitis C, Harvoni, and combined the drugs registered $4.55 billion in 1Q15.[259]

Given this level of success, others have responded by making deals that seemingly imply an inherent commitment to perpetuating ever-increasing prices for newly launched drugs. The leader of this strategy appears to be Celgene, which succeeded unexpectedly in reviving the pariah drug, thalidomide, as a treatment for blood cancers. The next-generation Revlimed costs more than $150,000 annually[260] to treat multiple myeloma, and generated $1.34 billion in global sales for 1Q15. Celgene has made the following three deals recently: (1) in 3Q15, Receptos was purchased for $7.2 billion, to obtain a drug, ozanimod, which is in late-stage clinical trials to treat multiple sclerosis and ulcerative colitis;[261] (2) in 2Q15, an investment of about $1 billion was made in Juno Therapeutics to access the experimental, chimeric antigen receptor T (CAR-T) cells, which involves genetically engineering patients' immune cells which can then recognize and attack tumors;[262] and (3) in 2Q14, the rights to GED-0301 were acquired for between $710 million and $2.6 billion. The deal focused on a late-stage oral antisense drug to treat Crohn's disease.[263]

Other companies are joining this "unbridled exuberance" campaign. One example was Alexion Pharmaceuticals' purchase of Synageva BioPharma for $8.4 billion in 2Q15, which focused on an orphan drug, Kanuma, to treat LAL-Deficiency.[264] The price that Alexion paid was between 10 times and 14 times peak sales of Kanuma, which was more than double the sales multiple typically seen in biotech acquisitions. Presumably, Alexion will be able to price Kanuma consistent with its one drug on the market, Soliris, at about $500,000 annually, to generate $2.2 billion as the latter did in 2014. Another orphan drug deal was BioMarin's purchase of Prosensa for

$840 million in 4Q14, to obtain the rights to a late-stage agent for Duchenne muscular dystrophy.[265] Large pharma Abbott's Abbvie division acquired Pharmacyclics for the US rights to a blood cancer drug, Imbruvica, for $21 billion, which was nearly 30 times sales.[266]

These deals will serve to entrench the commitment to preserving higher and higher pricing of branded drugs at launch. At the same time, payers are organizing a shift from fee-for-service to fee-for-performance, including the government, led by Medicare, and private firms, such as the pharmacy benefit manager, Express Scripts. By providing capitated payments that place clinical practices at risk, the goal is to reduce costs while simultaneously improving health outcomes. Medicare is quickly moving to this risk-sharing model, albeit currently pharmaceutical costs are not the focus of the risk-sharing tests.[267] Clearly, though, pharmaceutical costs will eventually be integrated into these risk-sharing models. Novartis, interestingly, has offered a NICE-type risk-sharing deal for US payers regarding its recently approved treatment for heart failure associated with compromised ventricular functioning, Entresto.[268] The $12.50 daily cost would be reduced, and the company would be repaid upon proof that the drug has kept patients out of the hospital for heart failure. Novartis may even provide remote monitoring of patients to establish early detection of deteriorating status regarding heart failure. Thus, we are heading for the most intense battle over pricing in the US that the industry has ever seen.

## Notes

1  www.drugs.com/stats/top100/sales, accessed 5/20/13.
2  www.drugs.com/newdrugs.html, accessed 9/06/12; www.genengnews.com/insight-and-intelligenceand153/fda-new-drug-approvals-in-2011-outpace-recent-past/77899531/, 1/09/12; www.fda.gov/downloads/AboutFDA/Transparency/.../UCM247465.p..., accessed 9/06/12.
3  www.centerwatch.com/drug-information/fda-approvals/default.aspx?DrugYear=2012, accessed 6/18/13.
4  www.kff.org/rxdrugs/upload/3057-08.pdf, accessed 5/10; www.reuters.com/article/2011/04/19/us-drug-spending-idUSTRE73I4G920110419; www.mmm-online.com/branded-drug-spend-up-but-slower-growth-ahead/article/235233/, accessed 4/05/12; www.nytimes.com/2013/03/19/business/use-of-generics-produces-an-unusual-drop-in-drug-spending.html?pagewanted=all&_r=0
5  www.fiercebiotech.com/press-releases/new-study-shows-rate-drug-approvals-lower-previously-reported-0#ixzz2Pj2Nlk4f
6  Kim *et al.* 2009.
7  www.drugs.com/top200_2004.html, accessed 9/07/12.
8  Hochman and McCormick 2010.
9  Pricing and reimbursement trends in the US: Impact of comparative effectiveness research and cost-effectiveness analysis. FirstWord, Copyright 2011 Doctor's Guide Publishing Limited.
10  Light, D.W. and Lexchin J.R. (2012) Pharmaceutical research and development: what do we get for all that money? *British Medical Journal,* 7 August, 345 doi: http://dx.doi.org/10.1136/bmj.e4348; Pricing and reimbursement trends in the US: Impact of comparative effectiveness research and cost-effectiveness analysis. FirstWord, Copyright 2011 Doctor's Guide Publishing Limited.
11  www.fiercepharma.com/story/uk-pharma-balks-value-based-pricing-ideas/2012-06-06#ixzz25QhbA0we
12  www.bloomberg.com/news/2013-03-14/diabetes-drugs-are-being-evaluated-for-pancreatic-risk.html

13  Wenning *et al.* 2009.
14  www.fda.gov/NewsEvents/Newsroom/PressAnnouncements/2006/ucm108770.htm, accessed 10/17/06.
15  www.usatoday.com/news/health/2006-10-17-diabetes_x.htm
16  www.merck.com/investors/financials/quarterly-financials/home.html, accessed 2/01/13.
17  www.fda.gov/newsevents/newsroom/pressannouncements/ucm198638.htm, accessed 1/25/10.
18  www.thepharmaletter.com/file/40664/denmarks-novo-nordisk-debuts-victoza-in-the-usa-aiming-for-1-billion-global-sales-by-2015.html, accessed 2/17/10.
19  www.medicalnewstoday.com/articles/243855.php, accessed 4/07/12.
20  www.fda.gov/NewsEvents/Newsroom/PressAnnouncements/ucm345848.htm, accessed 3/29/13.
21  www.nytimes.com/2013/03/30/business/invokana-wins-fda-approval-for-diabetes-treatment.html?_r=0
22  www.fda.gov/newsEvents/Newsroom/PressAnnouncements/2006/ucm108676.htm, accessed 6/23/06.
23  www.aidsmap.com/US-activists-applaud-darunavir-iPrezistai-TMC114-pricing/page/1424175/, accessed 6/29/06.
24  www.centerwatch.com/drug-information/fda-approvals/drug-details.aspx?DrugID=966, accessed 9/07/12.
25  www.hivplusmag.com/NewsStory.asp?ID=21001&sd=07/28/2009
26  http://articles.marketwatch.com/2007-07-24/news/30768687_1_tysabri-biogen-idec-avonex-sales
27  www.boston.com/business/globe/articles/2006/06/30/eu_approves_biogens_tysabri_to_be_sold_for_severe_ms_cases/
28  www.bloomberg.com/news/2010-09-30/novartis-gilenya-ms-pill-to-cost-48-000-a-year-update1-.html
29  www.fda.gov/NewsEvents/Newsroom/PressAnnouncements/ucm345528.htm, accessed 3/29/13.
30  www.fiercepharma.com/story/biogen-prices-tecfidera-below-oral-ms-rival-gilenya/2013-03-29
31  http://obroncology.com/documents/OBR_0907_Torisel.pdf
32  www.sutent.com/dosing-of-sutent.aspx, accessed 6/07/13.
33  www.astrazeneca.com/Investors/financial-information/Financial-results, accessed 7/26/12.
34  www.drugs.com/newdrugs/fda-approves-orphan-vandetanib-advanced-medullary-thyroid-cancer-2598.html, accessed 4/06/11.
35  www.zacks.com/ZER/rd_get_pdf.php?r=AZN
36  www.fda.gov/NewsEvents/Newsroom/PressAnnouncements/ucm314372.htm, accessed 8/03/12.
37  www.washingtonpost.com/blogs/ezra-klein/wp/2012/10/15/a-cancer-center-says-no-to-an-11000-treatment-will-others-follow/
38  http://en.sanofi.com/Images/31972_20-F_2012.pdf
39  www.biopharmatoday.com/2013/02/latest-news-from-the-pink-sheet-daily-celgenes-pomalyst-clears-fda-for-multiple-myeloma.html
40  www.fda.gov/newsevents/newsroom/pressannouncements/ucm1193237.htm, accessed 3/25/11.
41  www.fiercepharma.com/story/120k-price-tag-yervoy-hailed-potential-blockbuster/2011-03-28#ixzz25wAwXOYt
42  Bristol Myers Squibb 2012 Annual Report. http://phx.corporate-ir.net/phoenix.zhtml?c=106664&p=irol-reportsannual, accessed 4/11/13.
43  www.fda.gov/Drugs/InformationOnDrugs/ApprovedDrugs/ucm312945.htm, accessed 7/20/12.
44  www.myelomabeacon.com/news/2012/07/20/fda-approves-kyprolis-carfilzomib-for-relapsed-and-refractory-multiple-myeloma/
45  www.onyx.com/view.cfm/651/onyx-pharmaceuticals-announces-2013-updates-and-reviews-2012-achievements-at-jp-morgan-healthcare-conference, accessed 5/9/13.

46 www.pharmatimes.com/article/13-02-25/FDA_OK_for_Roche_s_Herceptin_successor_Kadcyla.aspx

47 www.fda.gov/NewsEvents/Newsroom/PressAnnouncements/ucm269856.htm, accessed 8/26/11.

48 www.forbes.com/sites/matthewherper/2011/08/26/pfizer-wins-approval-for-xalkori-lung-cancer-drug-that-heralds-age-of-expensive-personalized-medicines/

49 www.pfizer.com/files/annualreport/2012/financial/financial2012.pdf

50 www.nytimes.com/2012/12/15/business/fda-gives-early-approval-to-leukemia-drugiclusig.html?_r=0

51 www.fda.gov/NewsEvents/Newsroom/PressAnnouncements/ucm268241.htm, accessed 8/17/11.

52 www.reuters.com/article/2011/08/17/roche-zelboraf-idUSN1E77G0BW20110817

53 Roche Financial Report 2012. Fb12e.pdf; www.roche.com/investors/annual_reports.htm, accessed 4/9/13.

54 www.fda.gov/NewsEvents/Newsroom/PressAnnouncements/ucm321271.htm, accessed 9/27/12.

55 www.fiercebiotech.com/story/breaking-bayer-onyx-nab-speedy-fda-approval-blockbuster-cancer-drug-regoraf/2012-09-27

56 www.annualreport2012.bayer.com/en/healthcare.aspx, accessed 5/9/13.

57 www.fda.gov/NewsEvents/Newsroom/PressAnnouncements/ucm268781.htm, accessed 8/19/11.

58 www.fiercepharma.com/story/seattle-genetics-prices-adcetris-above-100k/2011-08-22#ixzz25w8TF9VO

59 http://investor.seattlegenetics.com/phoenix.zhtml?c=124860&p=irol-newsArticle&ID=1784376&highlight=Adcetris, accessed 5/9/13. www.fda.gov/NewsEvents/Newsroom/PressAnnouncements/ucm268781.htm, accessed 8/19/11.

60 www.fda.gov/Newsevents/Newsroom/PressAnnouncements/ucm289423.htm, accessed 1/27/12.

61 www.inpharm.com/news/171119/fda-approves-pfizer-cancer-drug-inlyta, accessed 1/30/12.

62 www.pfizer.com/files/annualreport/2012/financial/financial2012.pdf, accessed 5/29/13.

63 www.fda.gov/NewsEvents/Newsroom/PressAnnouncements/ucm354199.htm, accessed 5/29/13.

64 www.biocentury.com/DailyNews/topstory/2013-05-29/fda-approves-gsk-melanoma-drugs, accessed 5/29/13.

65 www.fda.gov/NewsEvents/Newsroom/PressAnnouncements/ucm318160.htm, accessed 9/04/12.

66 www.fiercebiotech.com/story/pfizer-wins-fda-approval-orphan-chronic-myelogenous-leukemia-drug/2012-09-04

67 www.pfizer.com/files/annualreport/2012/financial/financial2012.pdf, accessed 5/29/13.

68 www.fda.gov/BiologicsBloodVaccines/CellularGeneTherapyProducts/ApprovedProducts/ucm210012.htm, accessed 4/29/10.

69 www.fiercebiotech.com/story/dendreon-provenge-cost-93k-full-course-treatment/2010-04-29

70 http://investor.dendreon.com/releasedetail.cfm?ReleaseID=742694, accessed 2/25/13.

71 www.fda.gov/NewsEvents/Newsroom/PressAnnouncements/ucm354199.htm, accessed 5/29/13.

72 www.biocentury.com/DailyNews/topstory/2013-05-29/fda-approves-gsk-melanoma-drugs, accessed 5/29/13.

73 www.cancer.gov/cancertopics/druginfo/fda-vismodegib, accessed 1/30/12.

74 http://prescriptions.blogs.nytimes.com/2012/01/30/f-d-a-approves-drug-for-an-advanced-skin-cancer/

75 www.roche.com/med-cor-2013-01-30-e.rtf;

76 http://investors.curis.com/releasedetail.cfm?releaseid=741656, accessed 2/20/13.

77 www.fda.gov/NewsEvents/Newsroom/PressAnnouncements/ucm317838.htm, accessed 8/31/12.

78 www.nytimes.com/2012/09/01/business/fda-approves-prostate-cancer-drug.html

79   www.astellas.com/en/ir/library/pdf/3q2013_pre_en.pdf, accessed 2/01/13.
80   www.fda.gov/NewsEvents/Newsroom/.../ucm307549.htm, accessed 6/08/12.
81   http://seekingalpha.com/article/679041-breast-cancer-seeking-the-next-blockbuster, accessed 6/22/12.
82   www.roche.com/investors/ir_update/inv-update-2013-04-11.htm
83   www.bls.gov/oes/current/oes_nat.htm#00-0000, accessed 3/29/13.
84   www.nasprx.org/news/119072/PhRMA-Reports-907-New-Biotech-Drugs-in-Development.htm, updated 3/11/13.
85   www.fda.gov/ForIndustry/DevelopingProductsforRareDiseasesConditions/default.htm, updated 9/25/12.
86   www.forbes.com/sites/matthewherper/2012/09/05/how-a-440000-drug-is-turning-alexion-into-biotechs-new-innovation-powerhouse/
87   www.hartfordbusiness.com/article/20130214/NEWS01/130219899/ct-alexions-4q-net-zooms-68%89-on-hot-soliris-sales
88   www.fda.gov/Drugs/InformationOnDrugs/ucm091496.htm, accessed 4/28/05.
89   Bond 2006.
90   http://seer.cancer.gov/statfacts/html/lungb.html, updated 10/10/11.
91   www.diabetes.org/diabetes-basics/diabetes-statistics/, released 1/26/11.
92   www.forbes.com/sites/matthewherper/2012/03/21/will-the-drug-industrys-shocking-reliance-on-price-increases-come-to-an-end/
93   www.oocities.org/thjuland/inter-fer.html, updated 4/16/2013.
94   http://prescriptions.blogs.nytimes.com/2011/07/20/study-examines-high-drug-costs-vs-benefits-for-m-s-patients/
95   www.fiercepharma.com/story/nine-10-big-pharmas-cut-sales-reps-2010/2011-07-08
96   www.fiercepharma.com/story/analysts-more-pharma-cuts-especially-marketing/2010-11-29
97   http://prescriptions.blogs.nytimes.com/2012/02/02/drug-makers-dial-down-tv-advertising/
98   http://sciencecareers.sciencemag.org/career_magazine/previous_issues/articles/2011_12_09/caredit.a1100136
99   www.fiercebiotech.com/story/pfizer-shuttering-covx-research-unit-san-diego/2013-02-16#ixzz2TqKXLRXO
100  www.nytimes.com/2013/03/19/business/use-of-generics-produces-an-unusual-drop-in-drug-spending.html?pagewanted=all
101  http://aishealth.com/archive/ndbn012513-02, accessed 2/04/13.
102  http://pipelinereview.com/index.php/2013050950921/Press-Room/Blockbuster-Biologics-2012-sales-are-double-that-of-2006-driven-by-strong-growth-of-recombinant-antibodies.html
103  www.bizjournals.com/triangle/stories/2010/07/26/story11.html?page=all
104  Nissen S.E. and Wolski, K. (2007) Effect of rosiglitazone in the risk of MI and death from CV causes. *The New England Journal of Medicine*, 356, 2457–71. www.ncbi.nlm.nih.gov/pubmed/17517853.
105  www.gsk.com/content/dam/gsk/globals/documents/pdf/Investors/quarterly-results/2013/Q1-2013-US-dollar-translation.pdf, accessed 4/24/13.
106  www.gsk.com/media/press-releases/2013/gsk-statement-in-response-to-fda-advisory-committees-vote-on-ava.html, accessed 6/06/13.
107  Hurwitz *et al.* 2004.
108  www.fda.gov/NewsEvents/Newsroom/ucm279485.htm, accessed 11/18/11.
109  www.nytimes.com/2011/11/19/business/fda-revokes-approval-of-avastin-as-breast-cancer-drug.html?_r=0
110  www.fda.gov/NewsEvents/Newsroom/PressAnnouncements/ucm317004.htm, accessed 8/27/12.
111  http://finance.yahoo.com/news/ahf-gilead-stribild-not-covered-123000993.html, accessed 9/24/12.
112  http://investors.gilead.com/phoenix.zhtml?c=69964&p=irol-newsarticle&ID=1781144, accessed 2/04/13.

113  http://investors.gilead.com/phoenix.zhtml?c=69964&p=irol-newsarticle&ID=1719172, accessed 7/2612.

114  www.fiercepharma.com/story/vertex-sales-lag-hep-c-patients-pass-incivek/2013-01-30#ixzz2TFFpOpEi

115  www.pharmatimes.com/Article/13-04-10/Gilead_files_hepatitis_C_drug_sofosbuvir_in_the_US.aspx

116  www.pharmalot.com/2012/09/are-drug-pipelines-really-getting-better/

117  www.genengnews.com/insight-and-intelligenceand153/studies-suggest-that-when-it-comes-to-drug-development-success-size-matters/77899586/, accessed 4/09/12.

118  www.fda.gov/NewsEvents/Newsroom/PressAnnouncements/ucm351664.htm, accessed 5/10/13.

119  www.chimeraresearchgroup.com/2013/03/a-look-into-relovairs-upcoming-fda-advisory-committee/

120  www.gsk.com/content/dam/gsk/globals/documents/pdf/Investors/quarterly-results/2012/Q4-2012-US-dollar-translation.pdf, accessed 2/06/13.

121  http://investorplace.com/2011/12/eli-lilly-lly-stock-solanezumab-alzheimers-drug/

122  www.fda.gov/newsevents/newsroom/pressannouncements/ucm198638.htm, accessed 1/25/10.

123  www.centerwatch.com/drug-information/fda-approvals/drug-details.aspx?DrugID=879, accessed 5/20/13.

124  http://diabetes.webmd.com/news/20100126/new-diabetes-drug-victoza-approved, accessed 1/26/10.

125  www.evaluategroup.com/Universal/View.aspx?type=Entity&entityType=Product&id=20500&lType=modData&componentID=1002, accessed 5/20/13.

126  Buse et al. 2013.

127  http://prescribersletter.therapeuticresearch.com/pl/ArticleDD.aspx?nidchk=1&cs=&s=PRL&pt=5&fpt=2&dd=271220&pb=PRL#PLVOICES385

128  www.fda.gov/NewsEvents/Newsroom/PressAnnouncements/ucm230241.htm, accessed 10/19/10.

129  www.aboutlawsuits.com/pradaxa-blockbuster-despite-bleeding-problems-45767/, accessed 4/26/13.

130  www.boehringer-ingelheim.com/news/news_releases/press_releases/2013/21_february_2013dabigatranetexilate.html

131  www.boehringer-ingelheim.com/news/news_releases/press_releases/2013/21_february_2013dabigatranetexilate.html

132  http://prescribersletter.therapeuticresearch.com/pl/ArticleDD.aspx?nidchk=1&cs=&s=PRL&pt=5&fpt=2&dd=271220&pb=PRL#PLVOICES3853

133  www.fda.gov/NewsEvents/Newsroom/PressAnnouncements/ucm226755.htm, accessed 9/22/13.

134  www.bloomberg.com/news/2010-09-30/novartis-gilenya-ms-pill-to-cost-48-000-a-year-update1-.html

135  Cohen et al. 2010.

136  Kappos et al. 2010; Cohen et al. 2010.

137  www.novartis.com/investors/financial-results/annual-results-2012.shtml

138  http://seekingalpha.com/article/1320731-pfizer-s-prevnar-13-the-world-s-leading-vaccine-and-its-competitors, accessed 4/13/13.

139  www.fda.gov/NewsEvents/Newsroom/PressAnnouncements/ucm285431.htm, accessed 12/30/11.

140  http://seekingalpha.com/article/1320731-pfizer-s-prevnar-13-the-world-s-leading-vaccine-and-its-competitors, accessed 4/04/13.

141  http://pfizer.newshq.businesswire.com/press-release/pfizer-reports-fourth-quarter-and-full-year-2012-results-provides-2013-financial-guida, accessed 1/29/13.

142  www.fda.gov/NewsEvents/Newsroom/PressAnnouncements/ucm234346.htm, accessed 11/19/10.

143  Stopeck et al. 2010.

144  http://online.wsj.com/article/SB10001424052748704410404575623530026654838.html, accessed 10/18/10.

145 www.amgen.com/media/media_pr_detail.jsp?year=2013&releaseID=1777310, accessed 1/23/13.
146 www.roche.com/media/med-cor-2010-01-11.htm
147 www.fda.gov/NewsEvents/Newsroom/.../ucm197108.htm, accessed 1/10/10.
148 www.pharmalot.com/2012/03/pfizers-rheumatoid-arthritis-pill-not-a-slam-dunk/#comments, accessed 3/20/12.
149 www.rheumatology.org/publications/hotline/2010_02_03_tocilizumab.asp
150 www.biomedreports.com/2011030164443/achieving-long-term-treatment-for-severe-autoimmune-diseases-with-neovacs-kinoid-polyclonal-antibody-active-immunotherapy.html
151 www.thepharmaletter.com/file/120336/fda-accepts-file-for-new-actemra-formulation-in-rheumatoid-arthritis.html, accessed 2/28/13.
152 www.fda.gov/NewsEvents/Newsroom/PressAnnouncements/ucm253055.htm, accessed 4/28/11.
153 www.fiercepharma.com/story/jjs-prostate-drug-zytiga-gets-final-nod-europe/2011-09-07
154 http://files.shareholder.com/downloads/JNJ/2456791146x0x627475/56b0526b-477f-4bb9-8ada-9d7cc646bdd4/JNJ_Q4_2012_Sales_of_Key_Products_Franchises.pdf
155 www.fda.gov/newsevents/newsroom/pressannouncements/ucm1193237.htm, accessed 3/25/11.
156 Hodi *et al.* 2010.
157 www.fiercepharma.com/story/120k-price-tag-yervoy-hailed-potential-blockbuster/2011-03-28#ixzz25wAwXOYt
158 http://news.bms.com/press-release/financial-news/bristol-myers-squibb-reports-first-quarter-2013-financial-results, accessed 4/25/13.
159 www.fda.gov/NewsEvents/Newsroom/PressAnnouncements/ucm268241.htm, accessed 8/17/11.
160 Sosman, *et al.* 2012
161 www.roche.com/media/media_releases/med-cor-2012-02-20.htm
162 www.reuters.com/article/2011/08/17/roche-zelboraf-idUSN1E77G0BW20110817
163 www.roche.com/investors/ir_update/inv-update-2013-04-11.htm
164 www.x-rates.com/average/?from=CHF&to=USD&amount=1&year=2013, accessed 5/12/13.
165 Garber 2010.
166 www.fda.gov/NewsEvents/Newsroom/.../ucm269856.htm, accessed 8/26/11.
167 www.forbes.com/sites/matthewherper/2011/08/29/gene-test-for-pfizer-cancer-drug-to-cost-1500-per-patient/
168 http://pfizer.newshq.businesswire.com/press-release/pfizer-reports-first-quarter-2013-results, accessed 4/30/13.
169 www.fda.gov/NewsEvents/Newsroom/PressAnnouncements/ucm278646.htm, accessed 11/04/11.
170 www.forbes.com/sites/larryhusten/2012/06/21/fda-rejects-acs-indication-for-rivaroxaban-xarelto/
171 www.investor.bayer.com/berichte/quartalsberichte/, accessed 4/25/13.
172 www.fda.gov/NewsEvents/Newsroom/.../ucm280601.htm, accessed 11/18/11.
173 Ohr and Kaiser 2012.
174 www.pharmatimes.com/article/12-10-22/Eylea_and_Lucentis_matched_in_new_study.aspx
175 http://investor.regeneron.com/releasedetail.cfm?ReleaseID=740288, accessed 2/14/13.
176 www.fda.gov/NewsEvents/Newsroom/PressAnnouncements/ucm256299.htm, accessed 5/23/11.
177 Jacobson *et al.* 2011.
178 Wu, W. (2011). New agents for Hepatitis C: Triple therapy/twice as good/one big bill. www.eugenegi.com/pdf/EGI_newsletter_Oct11.pdf, accessed 10/11.
179 http://investors.vrtx.com/releasedetail.cfm?ReleaseID=736569, accessed 1/29/13.
180 http://seekingalpha.com/article/763801-vertex-pharmaceuticals-ceo-discusses-q2-2012-results-earnings-call-transcript?page=3, accessed 7/31/12.
181 www.fda.gov/NewsEvents/Newsroom/PressAnnouncements/ucm317838.htm, accessed 8/31/12.

182 www.bizjournals.com/sanfrancisco/blog/biotech/2012/09/medivation-xtandi-zytiga-prostate-cancer.html?page=all

183 www.bloomberg.com/news/2012-05-16/j-j-s-zytiga-helps-eliminate-early-stage-prostate-cancer.html

184 http://investors.medivation.com/releasedetail.cfm?ReleaseID=744267, accessed 2/28/13.

185 Wilhelm, S., Adnane, J., Lynch, M., et al. (2009). Regorafenib: A new oral multikinase inhibitor of angiogenic, stromal and oncogenic (receptor tyrosine) kinases with potent preclinical antitumor activity. Molecular Cancer Therapeutics, 8(Suppl 1): doi: 10.1158/1535–7163. TARG-09-B4. Abstract presented at the American Association for Cancer Research, Boston, MA.

186 www.fda.gov/NewsEvents/Newsroom/PressAnnouncements/ucm321271.htm, accessed 9/27/12.

187 http://articles.chicagotribune.com/2012-09-27/lifestyle/sns-rt-us-bayer-cancerbre88q138-20120927_1_colon-cancer-bayer-drug-cancer-drug

188 www.onyx.com/view.cfm/667/onyx-pharmaceuticals-reports-first-quarter-2013-financial-results

189 www.fda.gov/NewsEvents/Newsroom/PressAnnouncements/ucm312920.htm, accessed 7/20/12.

190 www.myelomabeacon.com/news/2012/07/25/questions-and-answers-about-the-fdas-approval-of-kyprolis-carfilzomib/

191 www.onyx.com/view.cfm/667/onyx-pharmaceuticals-reports-first-quarter-2013-financial-results, accessed 5/07/13.

192 www.fda.gov/NewsEvents/Newsroom/PressAnnouncements/ucm333634.htm, accessed 12/28/12.

193 Granger, C.B., et al. (2011).

194 www.forbes.com/sites/matthewherper/2011/08/29/analyst-says-xarelto-niche-still-secure/

195 Ogilvie et al. 2010.

196 http://news.bms.com/press-release/financial-news/bristol-myers-squibb-reports-first-quarter-2013-financial-results, accessed 4/25/13.

197 www.aboutlawsuits.com/pradaxa-blockbuster-despite-bleeding-problems-45767/, accessed 4/26/13.

198 www.fda.gov/NewsEvents/Newsroom/PressAnnouncements/ucm327152.htm, accessed 11/06/12.

199 www.accessdata.fda.gov/drugsatfda_docs/.../103772s5145LBL.pdf, accessed 10/11/06.

200 www.pharmalot.com/2012/03/pfizers-rheumatoid-arthritis-pill-not-a-slam-dunk/#comments, accessed 3/20/12.

201 Sandborn et al. 2012.

202 www.fda.gov/NewsEvents/Newsroom/PressAnnouncements/ucm289633.htm, accessed 1/31/12.

203 www.centerwatch.com/drug-information/fda-approvals/drug-details.aspx?DrugID=1184, accessed 5/20/13.

204 http://blogs.wsj.com/health/2012/01/31/fda-approves-vertexs-kalydeco-but-it-wont-come-cheap/

205 http://oncologystat.com/news/Genentech_Resubmits_TDM1_to_FDA_with_Overall_Survival_Benefit_US.html, accessed 8/28/12.

206 www.onclive.com/conference-coverage/esmo-2012/Updated-Data-Show-T-DM1-Improves-Overall-Survival-in-HER2-Positive-Breast-Cancer, accessed 10/01/12.

207 http://investor.immunogen.com/releasedetail.cfm?ReleaseID=75962, accessed 4/26/13.

208 www.firstwordpharma.com/node/1060822

209 www.dailyrx.com/xofigo-approved-fda-treat-advanced-prostate-cancer-bone-metastasis,

210 www.fda.gov/NewsEvents/Newsroom/PressAnnouncements/ucm345848.htm, accessed 3/29/13.

211 www.invokanahcp.com/clinical-research-results/monotherapy-vs-placebo/a1c-reductions, accessed 5/20/13.

212 www.nytimes.com/2013/03/30/business/invokana-wins-fda-approval-for-diabetes-treatment.html?_r=0
213 www.bloomberg.com/news/2013-06-07/gilead-s-hepatitis-c-drug-to-get-priority-review-by-fda.html
214 www.reuters.com/article/2012/01/17/idUS215805+17-Jan-2012+BW20120117
215 www.businesswire.com/news/home/20120419005320/en/All-Oral-Combination-Investigational-Hepatitis-HCV-Compounds-Daclatasvir
216 Fried *et al.* 2002.
217 www.gilead.com/news/press-releases/2013/4/gilead-submits-new-drug-application-to-us-fda-for-sofosbuvir-for-the-treatment-of-hepatitis-c
218 www.drugs.com/newdrugs/fda-approves-tecfidera-new-multiple-sclerosis-3731.html, accessed 3/27/13.
219 Fox *et al.* 2012.
220 Gold *et al.* 2012.
221 www.fiercepharma.com/story/biogen-prices-tecfidera-below-oral-ms-rival-gilenya/2013-03-29
222 http://pull.db-gmresearch.com/cgi-bin/pull/DocPull/576-EBDF/11366304/0900b8c086c40667.pdf, accessed 5/06/13.
223 www.fda.gov/NewsEvents/Newsroom/PressAnnouncements/ucm333285.htm, accessed 12/26/12.
224 www.centerwatch.com/drug-information/fda-approvals/drug-details.aspx?DrugID=1242, accessed 5/20/13.
225 www.bizjournals.com/boston/blog/bioflash/2013/05/aegerion-stock-soars-on-price-boost.html
226 http://ir.aegerion.com/releasedetail.cfm?ReleaseID=760329, accessed 4/30/13.
227 http://finance.yahoo.com/news/pharmacyclics-says-fda-grants-breakthrough-103538512.html, accessed 4/08/13.
228 www.news-medical.net/news/20130423/Enrollment-for-Pharmacyclics-Phase-III-study-using-ibrutinib-in-CLL-patients-completed.aspx
229 http://ir.pharmacyclics.com/releasedetail.cfm?releaseid=754820, accessed 4/08/13.
230 www.gene.com/media/press-releases/14327/2013-01-30/obinutuzumab-ga101-significantly-improve
231 www.roche.com/media/media_releases/med-cor-2013-05-16.htm
232 Krempski, *et al.* 2011.
233 www.ascopost.com/ViewNews.aspx?nid=4189, accessed 6/04/13.
234 http://news.bms.com/press-release/rd-news/bristol-myers-squibb-announces-phase-1-results-first-trial-combining-immune-ch&t=635063503845866356, accessed 6/02/13.
235 www.onclive.com/conference-coverage/asco-2013/Combining-Ipilimumab-and-Nivolumab-Shows-Promise-in-Advanced-Melanoma, accessed 5/15/13.
236 http://online.wsj.com/article/BT-CO-20130606-706213.html
237 www.onclive.com/web-exclusives/PD-1-Targeted-Antibody-Lambrolizumab-Receives-FDA-Breakthrough-Designation, accessed 4/24/13.
238 www.chemotherapyadvisor.com/lambrolizumab-mk-3475-safe-exhibits-early-evidence-of-anti-melanoma-activity/article/295884/#, accessed 6/02/13.
239 www.onclive.com/web-exclusives/PD-1-Targeted-Antibody-Lambrolizumab-Receives-FDA-Breakthrough-Designation, accessed 4/24/13.
240 www.chemotherapyadvisor.com/lambrolizumab-mk-3475-safe-exhibits-early-evidence-of-anti-melanoma-activity/article/295884/#, accessed 6/02/13.
241 www.dailyfinance.com/2013/06/02/merck-announces-presentation-of-interim-data-from-/
242 http://finance.yahoo.com/news/pfizer-palbociclib-pd-0332991-receives-120000060.html
243 http://press.pfizer.com/press-release/pfizers-palbociclib-pd-0332991-receives-food-and-drug-administration-breakthrough-therapy, accessed 4/10/13.
244 Finn, R.S., *et al.* (2012).

245  http://clinicaltrials.gov/ct2/show/NCT01740427?term=0332991+and+pfizer&rank=2, updated 5/13.
246  Decision Resources. Event Driven Pharmacor Report. 2012.
247  Bach, P.B., *et al.* (2012).
248  www.nytimes.com/2012/11/09/business/sanofi-halves-price-of-drug-after-sloan-ketteri ng-balks-at-paying-it.html
249  Experts in chronic myeloid leukemia. Price of drugs for chronic myeloid leukemia (CML), reflection of the unsustainable cancer drug prices: Perspective of CML experts. *Blood*, 2013; doi:10.1182/blood-2013-03-490003, 4/25/13.
250  Hardin 1968.
251  www.nytimes.com/2014/10/11/business/harvoni-a-hepatitis-c-drug-from-gilead-wins-f da-approval.html?_r=0
252  www.fda.gov/NewsEvents/Newsroom/PressAnnouncements/ucm418365.htm, accessed 10/10/14.
253  Manos, M.M., *et al.* (2012).
254  www.gilead.com/~/media/Files/pdfs/medicines/liver-disease/harvoni/harvoni_pi.pdf, accessed 10/10/14.
255  www.fiercepharma.com/story/express-scripts-assembling-anti-sovaldi-coalition-shut-o ut-gilead-hep-c-dru/2014-04-08
256  www.cnbc.com/2015/02/04/pricing-wars-heat-up-over-hepatitis-c-drugs.html
257  www.bloomberg.com/news/articles/2011-11-21/gilead-to-acquire-pharmasset-for-11-billion-to-add-hepatitis-c-medicines
258  www.fiercepharma.com/story/riled-84000-sovaldi-senate-panel-digs-gileads-pharmasset-buy/2014-07-14
259  http://investors.gilead.com/phoenix.zhtml?c=69964&p=irol-earnings, accessed 4/30/15.
260  http://seekingalpha.com/article/1309651-celgenes-star-drug-revlimid-and-its-competitors, accessed 3/30/13.
261  www.nytimes.com/2015/07/15/business/dealbook/celgene-agrees-to-7-2-billion-deal-for-receptos.html
262  www.nytimes.com/2015/06/30/business/celgene-to-pay-1-billion-for-biotech-coll aboration-with-juno.html
263  www.genengnews.com/gen-news-highlights/celgene-to-develop-nogra-crohn-s-drug-for-up-to-2-6b/81249784/, accessed 4/24/14.
264  www.thestreet.com/story/13140427/1/alexion-pays-hefty-84b-to-acquire-synagev a-expand-rare-disease-drug-business.html, accessed 5/06/15.
265  www.fiercebiotech.com/story/biomarin-buys-prosensa-840m-shoots-early-ok-duchenne-drug/2014-11-24#>
266  www.chicagotribune.com/business/breaking/ct-abbvie-pharmacyclics-0 527-biz-20150526-story.html
267  www.hhs.gov/news/press/2015pres/01/20150126a.html
268  www.wsj.com/articles/novartis-looking-at-ways-to-win-over-cost-concerned-health-insurers-1436522314, accessed 7/10/15.

## References

Bond, A. (2006). Exenatide (Byetta) as a novel treatment option for type 2 diabetes mellitus. *Proceedings Baylor University Medical Center*, 19, 281–4.

Buse, J.B., Nauck, M., Forst, T., *et al.* (2013). Exenatide once weekly versus liraglutide once daily in patients with type 2 diabetes (DURATION-6): A randomised, open-label study. *Lancet*, 381, 117–24.

Cheetham, P.J. and Petrylak, D.P. (2012). Alpha particles as radiopharmaceuticals in the treatment of bone metastases: Mechanism of action of radium-223 chloride (Alpharadin) and radiation. *Oncology*, 26, 330–7.

Cohen, J.A., Barkhof, F., Comi, G., *et al.* (2010). Oral fingolimod vs. intramuscular interferon in relapsing multiple sclerosis. *New England Journal of Medicine*, 362, 402–15.

DiMasi, J.A., Feldman, L., Seckler, A. and Wilson, A. (2010). Trends in risks associated with new drug development: Success rates for investigational drugs. *Clinical Pharmacology & Therapeutics*, 87, 272–7.

Fang, J., Mensah, G.A., Croft, J.B. and Keenan, N.L. (2008). Heart failure-related hospitalization in the U.S., 1979 to 2004. *Journal of the American College of Cardiology*, 52, 428–34.

Fox, R.J., Miller, D.H., Phillips, J.T., *et al.* (2012). Placebo-controlled Phase 3 study of oral BG-12 or glatiramer in multiple sclerosis. *New England Journal of Medicine*, 367, 1087–97.

Fried, M.W., Shiffman, M.L., Reddy, R., *et al.* (2002). Peginterferon alfa-2a plus ribavirin for chronic hepatitis C virus infection. *New England Journal of Medicine*, 347, 975–82.

Garber, K. (2010). ALK, lung cancer, and personalized therapy: portent of the future? *Journal of the National Cancer Institute*, 102, 672–5.

Gold, R., Kappos, L., Arnold, D.L., *et al.* (2012). Placebo-controlled Phase 3 study of oral BG-12 for relapsing multiple sclerosis. *New England Journal of Medicine*, 367, 1098–107.

Hardin, G. (1968). The tragedy of the commons. *Science*, 162, 1243–8.

Hochman, M. and McCormick, D. (2010). Characteristics of published comparative effectiveness studies of medications. *Journal of the American Medical Association*, 303, 951–8.

Hodi, F.S., O'Day, S.J., McDermott, D.F., *et al.* (2010). Improved survival with ipilimumab in patients with metastatic melanoma. *New England Journal of Medicine*, 363, 711–23.

Hurwitz, H., Fehrenbacher, L., Novotny, W., *et al.* (2004). Bevacizumab plus irinotecan, fluorouracil, and leucovorin for metastatic colorectal cancer. *New England Journal of Medicine*, 350, 2335–42.

Jacobson, I.M., McHutchison, J.G., Dusheiko, G., *et al.* (2011). Telaprevir for previously untreated chronic hepatitis C virus infection. *New England Journal of Medicine*, 364, 2405–16.

Kappos, L., Radue, E.-W., O'Connor, P., *et al.* (2010). Placebo-controlled study of oral fingolimod in relapsing multiple sclerosis. *New England Journal of Medicine*, 362, 387–401.

Kim, A., Balis, F.M. and Widemann, B.C. (2009). Sorafenib and sunitinib. *The Oncologist*, 14, 800–5.

Krempski, J., Karyampudi, L., Behrens, M.D., *et al.* (2011). Tumor-infiltrating programmed death receptor-1+ dendritic cells mediate immune suppression in ovarian cancer. *Journal of Immunology*, 186, 6905–13.

McHutchinson, J.G., Manns, M.P., Muir, A.J., *et al.* (2010). Telaprevir for previously treated chronic HCV infection. *New England Journal of Medicine*, 362, 1292–303.

Ogilvie, I.M., Newton, N., Weiner, S.A., *et al.* (2010). Underuse of oral anticoagulants in atrial fibrillation: a systematic review. *American Journal of Medicine*, 123, 638–45.

Ohr, M. and Kaiser, P.K. (2012). Aflibercept in wet age-related macular degeneration: a perspective review. *Therapeutic Advances in Chronic Disease*, 3, 153–61.

Poordad, F., McCone, J., Bacon, B.R., *et al.* (2011). Boceprevir for untreated chronic HCV Genotype 1 infection. *New England Journal of Medicine*, 364, 1195–206.

Ricotta, D. and Frishman, W. (2012). Mipomersen: A safe and effective antisense therapy adjunct to statins in patients with hypercholesterolemia. *Cardiology in Review*, 20, 90–5.

Sandborn, W.J., Ghosh, J., Panes, J., *et al.* (2012). Tofacitinib, an oral janus kinase inhibitor, in active ulcerative colitis. *New England Journal of Medicine*, 367, 616–24.

Sosman, J.A., Kim, K.B., Schuchter, L., *et al.* (2012). Survival in BRAF V600-mutant advanced melanoma treated with vemurafenib. *New England Journal of Medicine*, 366, 707–14.

Stopeck, A.T., Lipton, A., Body, J.J., *et al.* (2010). Denosumab compared with zoledronic acid for the treatment of bone metastases in patients with advanced breast cancer: A randomized, double-blind study. *Journal of Clinical Oncology*, 28, 5132–9.

Sullivan, R., Peppercorn, J., Sikora, K., *et al.* (2011). Delivering affordable cancer care in high-income countries. *Lancet Oncology*, 12, 933–80.

Wenning, W., Haghkia, A., Laubenberger, J., *et al.* (2009). Treatment of progressive multifocal leukoencephalopathy associated with natalizumab. *New England Journal of Medicine*, 361, 1075–80.

Yakisich, J.S. (2012). An algorithm for the preclinical screening of anticancer drugs effective against brain tumors. *ISRN Pharmacology*, 513580, doi:10.5402/2012/513580.

# Chapter 3

# Early Optimization of Draft Evidence Plans for Market Access

*Michael Wonder and Edward Hornby*

## Introduction

The global pharmaceutical industry continues to evolve. Developments in genomics, proteomics, immunology and cellular biology are set to promise a plethora of new targets for pharmacotherapy. The hope is that the targeted use of new medicines by specific patients (i.e. personalized medicine) based on the molecular characteristics of their disease and/or genetic polymorphisms relevant to the medicine's metabolism and toxicity will lead to improved clinical outcomes (Day *et al.* 2011). Nonetheless, the industry is also facing a myriad daunting challenges – numerous patent expirations, longer product development times, continued low output, increased stakeholder demands and increasing costs – so the "business as usual" operating model is no longer an option (Kaitlin 2010).

For a new medicine to fulfill its therapeutic and commercial potential (i.e. successful market access), it is now simply no longer a matter of generating evidence to demonstrate its quality, safety and efficacy to a standard expected by those responsible for making a decision on its marketing authorization ("regulators"). Nowadays, successful market access for a new medicine not only requires market authorization with an acceptable (i.e. competitive) label, but also that those who are responsible for making a decision on whether or not it is worth paying for ("payers") have the necessary clinical and other evidence they need to make a timely and favourable pricing and reimbursement (P&R) determination at the proposed price. Typically this means that the clinical evidence available at the end of a new medicine's phase III clinical trial programme to demonstrate its therapeutic value is both strong and relevant to the decisions payers are called upon to make. This poses strategic and operational challenges for the global pharmaceutical industry because payers' clinical evidence needs often differ both qualitatively and quantitatively from regulators' clinical evidence needs. Necessarily, forward planning of phase III programmes must change to ensure that phase III clinical trials are intentionally designed and conducted to provide evidence for payers as well as for regulators. Market access success in the major markets is increasingly unlikely if payers' evidence needs are not explicitly factored into the design and conduct of phase III programmes from the beginning.

The means by which a pharmaceutical company seeks to ensure that the trial programme for a compound in clinical development will meet the evidence needs of the regulators is to obtain scientific advice from both local and international key clinical opinion leaders and the regulators at or before the compound's major development milestones, such as before the commencement of phase III. Scientific advice from the former is usually obtained via the convening of local and/or international advisory boards; for the latter it is obtained by direct engagement with the regulators (e.g. at the end of phase II meetings). There is a transparent, long-established process whereby a pharmaceutical company can obtain scientific advice from regulators (e.g. the FDA and the EMA) on a compound's proposed phase III clinical trial programme (FDA 2015; EMA 2015a; MHRA 2015).

## Objectives and Chapter Outline

The objective of this chapter is to introduce and discuss the issues associated with obtaining scientific advice on new health care technologies directly from payers. Until relatively recent times, it has not been considered possible to do this.

In the first section, we outline the concept of early engagement and its potential scope. In the second section, we describe the various models of engagement and discuss their pros and cons. In the third section we report on recent engagement activities. This is followed by a discussion on the issues associated with successful implementation and a future outlook. The chapter ends with a provocative conclusion.

For the purpose of this chapter we have defined payers as those who are charged with the responsibility of making assessments, recommendations or decisions on the reimbursement and pricing of new health care technologies.

- Strictly speaking they are not always payers as some may not always finance or reimburse the cost of health care but instead advise those who are.
- While the ultimate decision maker is usually an elected official, such decisions are complex and invariably require expert technical advice.
- Expert technical advice is usually provided by an organization (e.g. National Institute for Health and Care Excellence (NICE) in the United Kingdom) or an independent expert committee (e.g. Pharmaceutical Benefits Advisory Committee (PBAC) in Australia).
- Different organizations/expert committees may exist for different health care technologies.
- Each organization/expert committee is comprised of individuals with a variety of training, expertise and values.

## Early Engagement

Early engagement is a process whereby a developer of a new health care technology seeks to conduct dialogue with one or more pricing and reimbursement agencies (payers) in the early stages of its development (i.e. before the key evidence plan is generated and before starting phase III clinical trials) about their likely evidence requirements when called upon later to make a pricing and reimbursement (coverage) decision about the technology when the evidence is realized. While there has been greater focus and attention on new medicines, there is no reason why seeking early scientific advice cannot be extended to include other technology types.

Early engagement has both short- and broader long-term benefits. In the short term, the advice will help to inform the expensive phase III investment decisions of the developers of new health care technologies, which will hopefully lead to improved development programmes, more effective or useful medicines and yield more relevant evidence for payer (and regulator) decision making. In the long term, early engagement should result in improved patient access to new health care technologies and gains in population health.

## Early Engagement Models

Scientific advice can be obtained using a number of payer engagement models, which have been used in practice and which are described briefly below.

### Indirect Model

Involves an expert advisory board comprised of "payer experts" from a given jurisdiction or set of jurisdictions who offer scientific, strategic and operational advice as if they were the actual payers in those jurisdictions. They may be proxies for payers at the national, regional or even local (institutional) level. The "payer experts" are either former payers or have acted in the past as expert advisors to payers.

### Direct Bipartite Model

Engagement with a single payer may be with a single payer organization, which will provide scientific advice from the perspective of the jurisdiction's P&R system for medicines. The jurisdiction may be at the national, regional or even local (institutional) level. The payer organization could be public or private. In some jurisdictions, it might not be possible, for legal and other reasons, to engage with the actual decision makers (e.g. the PBAC). In such instances, however, it should be possible to engage with their departmental advisors and administrators (e.g. the PBAC Secretariat).

### Direct Tripartite Model

This involves engagement with both a payer and a regulator for a given jurisdiction who provide "joint" or "parallel" scientific advice from the perspective of the systems they represent and that relates to the evidence issues of overlapping or common interest. Insofar as the medicine regulators operate only at the national level, tripartite engagements are more likely to take place at the national level for payers. While there is nothing to preclude the involvement of private payers, tripartite engagements are probably more likely to be with public payers given all medicine regulators serve public interests.

In direct engagement models, analogous with taking early scientific advice from regulators, the advice received is deemed not to be binding on any party to the exercise.

The various models of engagement are summarized in Table 3.1.

*Table 3.1* Models of engagement

| Attribute | Indirect | Direct bipartite | Direct tripartite |
|---|---|---|---|
| Participants | Ex-payers, payer advisors (i.e. academics and practicing health care professionals) | Payers | Payer, regulators |
| Location | Company's office or independent site | Payer's office | Payer's or regulator's office |
| Payment/fee for advice | Advisor paid as consultants | Free or fee for service | Free or fee for service |
| Level | National, regional, local | National, regional, local | National or regional/ national |
| Public/private | Either | Either | Either/public |
| Advantages | Advice from more than one jurisdiction at the same time, multiple compounds per meeting | Direct advice | Efficient. Direct advice. Regulator and payer able to hear each other's advice and adjust accordingly (when possible) |
| Disadvantages | Advice might not be contemporary | Costly, not possible in all jurisdictions, only 1–2 compounds/meeting | Costly, not possible in all jurisdictions, long lead time, only 1–2 compounds/meeting |

There are variations to these models:

- Multi local bipartite – multiple payers from the same or different levels from the same jurisdiction (e.g. payers from a hospital network).
- Multi national bipartite – multiple payers from the same level from different jurisdictions (e.g. payer networks such as the European network for Health Technology Assessment, EUnetHTA 2015).
- Multi national tripartite – multiple payers and regulators from the same level from different jurisdictions (e.g. a joint meeting between the International Conference on Harmonisation of Technical Requirements for Registration of Pharmaceuticals for Human Use (ICH), member representatives from the EUnetHTA and a technology developer).

The key points to note are as follows:

- The models of engagement are not mutually exclusive.
- All models need not be considered/adopted for a given project.
- Different models could be applied at different major development milestones for a given project.

This chapter focuses on the direct bipartite and direct tripartite models.

### Scope of Advice

Scientific advice can relate to any issue that is pertinent to the development of evidence for payers. The following points illustrate the potentially broad scope of discussion. The topics listed are not exhaustive, nor are they necessarily in a logical or priority order.

- Interpretation of P&R submission guidelines, methods guidance, previous HTAs, etc. and their relevance for the evidence plans for the compound under discussion.
- Health system priorities for the disease area and the evidence of unmet needs.
- Payer-relevant treatment pathway positioning options for a new medicine (related to unmet needs) and the outline evidence plans relevant to them.
- Trial design considerations/preferences to support each proposed position, e.g. trial population, duration, comparators, outcome(s), etc.
- Economic evaluation design considerations/preferences, e.g. form of evaluation and approaches to benefit measurement, modeling vs. trials, relevant trial(s) for economic evaluation, approaches to the generation of QALYs.
- Potential for demonstrating cost-effectiveness (and hence P&R potential) based on insights from models that payers have developed or accepted, e.g. acceptable range of the cost-effectiveness ratio, expected value of perfect information calculations to highlight greatest areas of uncertainty and assist with trial design and formulating P&R expectations, Bayesian simulations.
- Budget impact/affordability considerations.
- Practical considerations, e.g. difficulty of blinding in a trial against the preferred comparator, ethical issues.
- Methodological issues, e.g. selection of instruments/research to derive QALYs, extrapolation of long-term outcomes, planning for indirect comparisons.
- Balancing the evidence requirements of a regulator and a payer.

## Engagement Activities

We are aware of several recent pilot direct bipartite and direct tripartite engagement projects. They are described below and summarized in Table 3.2.

### EU Headquartered Multinational Pharmaceutical Company

We reported the results of a pilot project conducted in 2007–2008 to engage directly with eight payers in seven countries for a new oral treatment for patients with chronic plaque psoriasis prior to the commencement of the phase III clinical trials.

The agencies were asked questions about the likely evidence requirements for a development compound that might be the subject of a P&R submission sometime in the future. A briefing book was produced, giving some background on the compound, its proposed positioning in current and anticipated future treatment pathways, and outlined several key questions. The questions related to various aspects of the proposed phase III clinical trials, such as:

- What is the most relevant target population for the compound?
- With which alternative therapies should the compound be compared?
- What outcomes (e.g. clinical, health-related quality of life) should be measured?

- Over what time period should measurement be made (i.e. length of patient follow-up)?
- Should the issue of non-responders be examined and how should "non-response" or "treatment failure" be defined?
- Are there relevant subgroups of the target patient population that should be considered?

The pilot project demonstrated that a feasible process of early dialogue could be established. Although there was some variation in the advice obtained from the agencies, the similarities far outweighed the differences. Several important conclusions were reached about the viability of the company's aspirations for product positioning, the desirability of particular comparisons, the outcomes to be used in trials and the length of trial follow-up (Backhouse *et al.* 2011).

### NICE (England)

Since 2008 and following the pilot mentioned above, NICE has provided a scientific advice consultancy service to companies about a technology they have in development that, if and when licensed, may be referred to the Institute for assessment and appraisal. NICE was the first payer to offer such scientific advice as a regular service.

Each individual scientific advice project consists of the following stages:

- Telephone or email NICE to discuss your request and the availability of slots.
- Submit a request for an advice appointment.
- Agree terms and sign contracts (one month before briefing book submission).
- Initial payment.
- Submission of a briefing book by the company.
- NICE confirms project size.
- NICE clarifies any issues relating to the briefing book in writing and the company responds in writing.
- Face-to-face meeting attended by company representatives, NICE staff and experts.
- Written advice report from NICE.
- Follow-up and clarification by the company if required.
- Final payment.

The advice given by NICE is in response to the written questions asked and the documentation submitted. The advice cannot account for future changes and developments in scientific knowledge or appraisal requirements and hence is non-binding.

NICE also welcomes requests from companies to provide scientific advice in conjunction with other agencies (NICE 2015).

The Institute recently reported on trends in its early engagement service; over the last few years, requests for scientific advice have diversified into personalized medicine, regenerative medicines and products for rare and very rare diseases (Maignen *et al.* 2014).

### CVZ (The Netherlands)

The tasks of the Dutch Health Care Insurance Board (College voor zorgverzekeringen, CVZ) include providing advice and implementing the Dutch statutory health

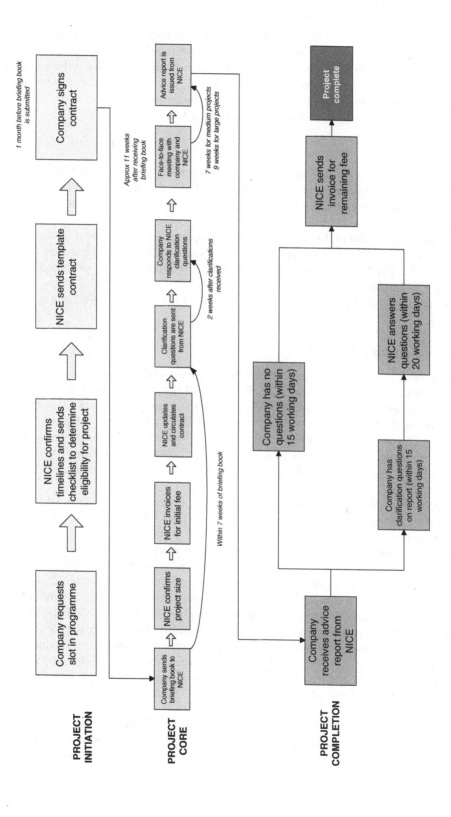

*Figure 3.1* NICE scientific advice process map

insurance. The CVZ has frequently provided pre-submission advice to pharmaceutical companies on the optimal presentation of realized data pre-submission.

Six members of the CVZ participated in a pilot relating to supplying the pharmaceutical industry with pre-phase III scientific advice. The CVZ found that it was time consuming and decided that it would be feasible to do this only on a broader scale. The CVZ has since participated in other pan-European activities (CVZ 2012).

### TLV (Sweden)

In Sweden, pilot tripartite scientific advice meetings were held in 2009–2010 between the Dental and Pharmaceutical Benefits Agency (TLV), the Medical Products Agency (MPA) and pharmaceutical companies. Meetings were typically held at the end of phase II.

The outcome of the evaluation of the pilot project was positive; the TLV and MPA have continued to offer joint scientific advice to the pharmaceutical industry from 1 January 2011. The advice given is not binding for the MPA, the TLV or the company (TLV 2015a, 2015b).

Like the CVZ, the TLV has since participated in other pan-European engagement activities.

### Tapestry Networks (Europe)

In 2010, pilot projects were conducted linking payers and regulators from five EU Member States (the UK, France, Italy, Sweden and the Netherlands) with pharmaceutical companies and other stakeholders under the Tapestry Networks banner. The pilots provided a forum for developers of new medicines to receive integrated feedback on a pipeline medicine's expected value and how best to demonstrate its value.

The pilots were the first to include patients in early engagement with payers to inform a pharmaceutical company's investment decisions for a medicine in development.

Participating stakeholders and Tapestry jointly designed the process, with guidance from existing early scientific advice processes and input from key European health care leaders.

The launch meeting resulted in an agreement on a multi-stakeholder consultation process that included input and participation by regulators, payers, patient advocates and clinical experts (see Figure 3.2). All participating institutions considered issues of therapeutic value, and a narrower group of payers considered and advised on questions of economic value that flow from a compound's therapeutic benefits. While the launch meeting participants expressed an interest in the possibility of being able to reach a common perspective across institutions regarding the compound's therapeutic value, they recognized that economic value determinations are solely the remit of Member States.

Participants at the launch meeting agreed the following six principles to guide the design and conduct of the pilots:

- Agree to non-binding outcomes to increase willingness to experiment, but with an expectation of "engagement and commitment" from the parties befitting the importance of this initiative. Additionally, advice should not displace or supersede existing channels for regulatory and reimbursement approval.

*Figure 3.2* Tapestry Networks scientific advice process map

- Focus on the methodology of value assessment (as opposed to an early read on the potential for reimbursement or pricing).
- Foster open dialogue and equal standing for all parties in the discussion.
- Create an environment that supports mutual learning.
- Encourage transparency by publishing findings and keeping the process and participation in the pilots as transparent as possible, while making sure advice specific to a company's medicine remains confidential (as is customary).
- Ensure that multiple Member States participate.

In 2009, Tapestry launched disease-specific working groups for two diseases, type 2 diabetes and breast cancer, which were chosen for their high unmet need and their impact on health care systems. The same three multinational pharmaceutical companies took part in separate pilots for the two diseases: Johnson & Johnson, AstraZeneca and GlaxoSmithKline. Additional pilots have been conducted for compounds in other therapeutic areas: Alzheimer's disease (AD), melanoma, non-small cell lung cancer and bacterial infection.

Thus the advice sought and received appears to have been at the level of approaches to the treatment for a given disease with any intervention, rather than advice focused on a planned development programme for a specific compound.

The pilots resulted in substantial insights for the participating companies. The pilots also enabled participants to gain a better understanding of other stakeholders' perspectives on the specific compound as well as the key challenges of developing medicines in the particular therapeutic areas. The consultations demonstrated the need to balance depth and breadth of discussion, as well as the challenge of seeking clarity among stakeholders despite the substantial uncertainties that drug developers face. Participants also identified the alignment and mutual education among participating stakeholders as an important measure of success (Tapestry Networks 2015).

### Green Park Collaborative

The Green Park Collaborative – International (GPC-I), chaired jointly by Health Technology Assessment International (HTAi) and the Center for Medical Technology Policy in the US, was an international initiative to explore the feasibility of developing guidance for health technology developers on the design of clinical trials to yield evidence that meets the needs of payers (Green Park Collaborative 2015). The aim was to produce prototype "evidence guidance documents" to provide therapeutic area-specific trial design recommendations as well as general methodological advice. The prototype guidance documents developed by the GPC-I were not intended to represent consensus statements on the part of all participating stakeholders but rather to demonstrate the feasibility of and inform the subsequent development of authoritative written scientific guidance beyond the prototype phase.

The GPC-I developed a pilot evidence guidance document that offered recommendations on the design of clinical trials of new medicines for patients with Alzheimer's disease from a payer perspective. The GPC-I also conducted a pilot project to develop general (i.e. non-disease-specific) methodological guidance on issues of trial design and evidence generation.

The development of the evidence guidance document was led by a technical working group of international AD experts that included researchers, patient representatives, payers and regulators. A life sciences advisory group outlined the questions that an evidence guidance document on treatments for AD should answer, and provided technical, methodological and logistical input to ensure applicability of the guidance on drug development. The GPC-I steering group included payers and regulators from around the world.

The GPC-I pilot project on AD was completed in early 2013 and continues with a focus solely on the American market (GPC-USA); it therefore has limited relevance to informing global payer decision making. The GPC-USA focuses on developing methodological standards to support cancer and diabetes research. Working groups are developing effectiveness guidance documents on:

- patient-centered outcomes (diabetes);
- treatment sequencing and prioritization (cancer);
- next-generation sequencing tests for diagnosis and treatment (cancer).

## CIRS (Europe)

The Centre for Innovation in Regulatory Science (CIRS) is an organization that facilitates the meeting of the international pharmaceutical industry, regulatory authorities and academia to debate and develop regulatory policy. The CIRS has developed a programme to address the increasing impact of HTA and payer activities on medicine development, regulation and patient access to innovative medicines, and has conducted a number of workshops and industry and agency meetings to discuss related issues and challenges. It has not sponsored or facilitated any specific direct engagement activities (CIRS 2015).

## EUnetHTA (Europe)

Common interests and policies in relation to HTA have been explored and developed at the strategic level in the European Union for ten years. EUnetHTA has been

Table 3.2 Summary of recent direct bipartite and tripartite engagement projects

| Model | Period | Project initiator/sponsor | Jurisdiction/s | Stakeholders | Funding | Form of advice | Binding advice |
|---|---|---|---|---|---|---|---|
| Direct bipartite | 2007–2008 | Novartis | UK, Australia, Canada, the Netherlands, US (public and private) | Single pharmaceutical company, payers | Self-funded | Verbal | Non-binding |
| Direct bipartite | 2008– | NICE | UK | Individual pharmaceutical companies, payer | Fee-paying service | Verbal followed by written advice | Non-binding |
| Direct bipartite | | CVZ | The Netherlands | Individual pharmaceutical companies, payer | Self-funded | Unknown | Unknown |
| Direct tripartite | 2009–2010 | MPA/TLV | Sweden | Individual pharmaceutical companies, payer, regulator | Fee-paying service (MPA) | Verbal | Non-binding |
| Direct tripartite | 2010–2012 | AstraZeneca, GlaxoSmithKline and Johnson & Johnson | EU (US FDA was an observer) | Three pharmaceutical companies, payers, regulators, clinical experts, patient group representatives | Self-funded | Verbal with participants received a set of informal minutes after each consultation | Non-binding |
| Direct tripartite | 2011–2012 (AD pilot) | CMTP (US) | US, UK, Canada, France, Italy, Australia, Norway, Denmark, the Netherlands | Three pharmaceutical companies, payers, regulators, consultants, academics | California HealthCare Foundation, Kaiser Foundation Community Benefit Program, the United Healthcare Foundation, the National Pharmaceutical Council, and Pfizer | Written guidance in the form of prototype evidence guidance documents | Non-binding |

NICE = National Institute for Health and Clinical Excellence; UK = United Kingdom; US = United States; CVZ = College voor zorgverzekeringen; MPA = Medical Products Agency; TLV = Tandvårds-och läkemedelsförmånsverket; EU = European Union; FDA = Food and Drug Administration; AD = Alzheimer's disease; CMTP = Center for Medical Technology Policy.

a platform for supporting this process since its inception in 2006. EUnetHTA continues collaborative production of HTA information between partner organizations that include the major EU HTA agencies.

Since 2011, EUnetHTA has collaborated with the EMA on the process for production of European Public Assessment Reports (EPARs), which are published by the EMA for every medicine authorized through the centralized procedure in the EU. The EPARs reflect the scientific conclusions reached by the Agency's Committee for Medicinal Products for Human Use (CHMP) at the end of the evaluation process, after the deletion of commercially confidential information.

The EMA and EUnetHTA have considered how the information on the assessment of the risks and the benefits of a medicine contained in an EPAR can best be used in the assessment of the relative effectiveness of new medicines carried out by HTA agencies in the Member States.

The EMA and the EUnetHTA group have also agreed to explore other areas of possible collaboration or exchange of information in future that will include parallel scientific advice on clinical development programmes. This was part of the EMA work plan for 2012 (EUnetHTA 2015). The EMA and the EUnetHTA recently published a report on their 2012–2015 joint work plan (EMA 2016).

### EMA (Europe)

The EMA offers scientific advice and protocol assistance to developers of new medicines in parallel with HTA bodies.

A pilot for parallel scientific advice was launched in July 2010. Around 25 procedures had been finalized or were ongoing as of November 2013, covering diseases such as diabetes, heart failure, lung cancer, breast cancer, pancreatic cancer, melanoma, mesothelioma, asthma, rheumatoid arthritis, multi-resistant infection, food allergies, diabetic gastroparesis, Alzheimer's disease, depression, osteoporosis and three rare conditions.

The following health care guidance and HTA agencies took part in different procedures in the pilot in various ways (EMA 2015b):

- Agenzia Italiana del Farmaco (Italy);
- College voor Zorgverzekeringen (Netherlands);
- Gemeinsamer Bundesausschuss (Germany);
- Haute Autorité de Santé (France);
- L'Agència d'Avaluació i Qualitat Sanitàries de Catalunya (Spain);
- National Institute for Health and Care Excellence (England);
- Tandvårds-och Läkemedelsförmånsverket (Sweden);
- Vertragspartner Medikamente (Austria).

A joint EMA–HTA workshop on parallel scientific advice was held on 26 November 2013. Following the workshop, and based on the experience gained by all stakeholders, draft best-practice guidance for EMA–HTA parallel scientific advice was developed and published for public consultation in May 2014. The guidance details the timelines and actions whereby applicants can seek simultaneous feedback on their development plans from regulatory and HTA agencies. The final guidance will take into account feedback from all stakeholders.

## Issues

Taking early scientific advice from payers is now an established reality; making it work with the aim of developing more clinically useful and valuable medicines requires more than simply seeking advice. Planning to take full advantage of the advice process and planning how to implement the advice received both matter.

### Attendance and Conduct

Those representing the developer should be experienced in their respective disciplines and be fully briefed on the health care system and the payer. Ideally they should be members of the compound's project team who play an active decision-making role in its clinical development.

### Timing of Advice

The appropriate time in which to obtain scientific advice is a challenging issue. While a strong argument could be made that such activities should occur much earlier ("it's never too early until it's too late"), the advice offered will probably be of a more general nature as the phase III clinical trials are yet to be designed. Nonetheless, some useful advice may be given on issues with long lead times (e.g. the validation of surrogate outcomes and the development of instruments to measure health-related quality of life).

### Briefing Materials

A key element of early engagement is the production and timely supply of briefing materials. It is beyond the scope of this chapter to provide detailed guidance on their preparation. Nonetheless, below are some salient points for potential applicants to consider:

- Keep the materials as short as you can (i.e. no more than 50 pages).
- Be sure the briefing materials make reference to local treatment guidelines and local competitors (comparators).
- Be sure to have studied any recent relevant health technology assessments and appraisals/decisions.

The objective should be to obtain scientific advice rather than strategic advice; nonetheless, high-value strategic advice will no doubt be provided with well-thought-out scientific questioning and the ensuing dialogue.

### Transparency

To date, all of the compound-specific scientific advice meetings have been held in private and none of the advice has been made public. While some might argue that engagements should be transparent and the scientific advice made public, it is likely that payers and technology developers will want all activities to remain confidential for the foreseeable future. The case for transparency will build if and when payers are prepared to provide written advice. Technology developers might be more prepared to release details of such activities if and when the technology concerned gains market access.

### Written Advice

Technology developers will want to receive written advice to support and clarify the verbal advice, but some payers might be hesitant to do so (at least in the short term), either because of resource constraints or because of legal issues (written advice could be seen as binding). This concern may be unfounded as technology developers might not be seeking this since they would want the same conditions for themselves (i.e. they would want to reserve the right to change their phase III clinical evidence plans in the light of further scientific advice and/or changed market conditions).

### Integration with Other Scientific Advice

Insofar as a technology developer may well seek scientific advice from multiple regulators and payers in different jurisdictions, there is a reasonable chance that the advice might not be entirely consistent on all aspects. It is conceivable that some advice will be declined, as it will not be possible for the phase III clinical trials to address all issues. Technology developers will need to give careful thought about where they should seek scientific advice and the order in which such advice should be obtained. Those providing advice late in the sequence should be informed in the briefing materials of the advice given earlier by other regulators and payers.

### Impact on Development

It is unclear as to what impact the scientific advice will have on an actual development compound's phase III clinical trial programme, costs and timelines. Stakeholder advice to companies in the Tapestry Network pilots ranged from confirming the value of pursuing a programme, to recommending that a study be redesigned and advising that a study not be pursued (Tapestry Networks 2015).

## Future Outlook

### Tripartite Engagements

A logical extension of bipartite early scientific advice engagements (meetings involving only regulators and developers or only payers and developers) was to conduct tripartite interactions involving each of the three stakeholders. This area is likely to develop further, as illustrated by the ongoing EMA/EUnetHTA collaboration. There are clear potential benefits to all parties from tripartite dialogue. For example, an early and more comprehensive mutual understanding of the expected phase III evidence needs of both regulators and payers might lead to developers producing a single concise clinical evidence file (one dossier) that simultaneously meets the needs of both decision makers and that is sufficient to ensure quicker patient access (EUnetHTA 2015).

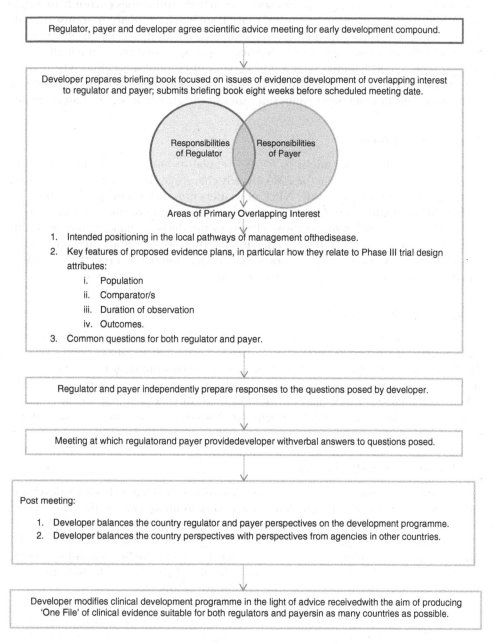

*Figure 3.3* Indicative schematic representation of the tripartite scientific advice process

### Payer Guidance Notes

An alternative model is for payers and regulators to collaborate in the production of separate or joint disease-specific evidence development guidance notes based on a synopsis of the key evidence issues and recurrent weaknesses arising from their assessments/appraisals. The purpose would be to enhance the efficiency and focus of the scientific advisory meetings. Notably some regulatory authorities currently maintain published advice to sponsors of clinical trials. If such written advice to sponsors could be prepared in future with the involvement of payers and a focus on effectiveness (beyond efficacy), considerable efficiencies might be gained from which all parties and patients would benefit. Such guidance should be published alongside any current HTA guidance. This has the advantage that technology developers would be much less likely to avoid payer issues since they would also then be "regulatory" issues.

### Fee for Service Models

Another operating model might be for the regulators and payers to apply a fee for scientific advice. We note that the EMA already charges for providing scientific advice (EMA 2015c). On the payer side, NICE now offers bipartite scientific advice for a fee (NICE 2015). While this might address cost issues, it might not solve the competency issue. The best model is to get those closest to the decision makers to provide the scientific advice. Under a fee for service model, those who provide advice might do this full time and thus have less exposure to the decision makers (i.e. they do not sit in on actual decision-making meetings/sessions).

### Feedback Loops/Networks

An enhanced operating model would be one where the developer provides feedback to the regulator and payer on whether the advice they gave had an influence on the phase III clinical trials and if not, why not. A developer reserves the right to not accept such advice if the weight of advice from other regulators/payers suggests another course be taken. Such trade-offs are inevitable in multinational evidence planning. Ideally, feedback would be given face to face, but that might not always be feasible. A more viable option is to provide written feedback in the local registration and reimbursement dossiers.

### Payer Collaboration/Networks

While early engagement seems a worthwhile endeavor from a technology developer perspective, it will present a challenge for payers to implement as they are already overworked and no doubt underfunded. The major agencies could never cope with the demand if all technology developers were to seek scientific advice even only once for each new technology currently in development. The burden will fall on the health care system's officials rather than on the actual payers (i.e. decision makers). Possible solutions to this resource conundrum are as follows:

- Create a fee for service model as per the current NICE approach. This will be somewhat costly for some. Agencies offering advice will need to ensure that those providing the advice are sufficiently knowledgeable and experienced. In other words, they need to be close to the decision makers.

- Payers develop a collaborative network with other payers (in other jurisdictions) to enable a payer in one jurisdiction to give advice that will serve as a proxy for a payer in another jurisdiction.
- Payers develop collaborative networks with the major regulatory agencies. This is important, as the regulatory world is not static; ongoing developments in clinical trial design will have an impact on the type of phase III evidence that will be generated in the future.
- Development of internationally accepted published advice to sponsors and a library of regulator- and payer-endorsed protocol guidance in all major disease areas.

### Other Ongoing Developments

Early engagement needs to be considered in the light of other important ongoing developments in the regulatory and reimbursement domains, such as:

- the emerging comparative effectiveness research movement in the US (and elsewhere) (Neumann *et al.* 2011);
- the ongoing debate in certain jurisdictions about whether regulators or payers should be responsible for making decisions on the comparative (relative) efficacy and comparative (relative) effectiveness of new medicines (Eichler *et al.* 2010);
- calls for regulators to raise the approval bar for market authorization of new medicines (Naci *et al.* 2012);
- the introduction of process by the US FDA (e.g. fast track designation, breakthrough therapy designation) that will result in new technologies coming to market with less mature clinical data;
- the Canadian Agency for Drugs and Technologies in Health  (CADTH) now offers a scientific advice service.

Early engagement would only support and perhaps enhance all of these (proposed) initiatives. Insofar as the case of a new medicine's value-based price will be supported by the strength and relevance of the underlying clinical and economic evidence base, one could present a sound argument that early engagement is an important clinical development and commercial activity.

## Conclusion

Insofar as early engagement with payers is still in its infancy, it would be improper to draw any firm conclusions. It is too early to determine whether early engagement will become a significant success to drive real change and improve the quality of evidence for payers and patient access to new medicines, or whether it will end up being just another nice talkfest. Nonetheless, the early signs from the pilot projects look promising. Momentum for early engagement is building, with opportunities to engage directly with payers (and regulators) in a given jurisdiction and in other jurisdictions increasing all the time. We note that NICE has expanded its scientific advice service to offer advice with the EMA and the Medicines and Healthcare Products Regulatory Agency (MHRA) (NICE 2015).

All parties appear to agree that the advantages of early engagement outweigh its disadvantages. Nonetheless, non-trivial resource challenges remain. We are yet to see its full benefits. Likewise, we are yet to see whether the scientific advice has made a material change to a compound's development plan.

There has been no experience to date with other technology types or technology mixtures (i.e. co-dependent technologies). We note that NICE has recently commenced a scientific advice service for developers of devices and diagnostics (NICE 2015). There is also limited experience to date in some large and important countries such as the US and the Far East. There are additional challenges in the US given there are multiple payers and they are private (most payers in the pilots to date are public payers). We foresee a role for some pilot projects in these areas.

We think that early engagement has the potential to cause a paradigm change to the industry's current clinical development-operating model. By gaining a greater understanding, appreciation and respect for each other's roles and the immense challenges in medicine development, we feel it could lead to a positive change in relationships, with less of an adversarial undertone. We are hopeful that early engagement will lead to stakeholders being seen as "partners in evidence development". We also expect that the early scientific advice currently offered by NICE and that may also be offered by the EUnetHTA/EMA in future could become an obligatory step in obtaining P&R if not marketing authorization.

Like the participants of the Tapestry Network's pilot projects, we think that multi-country, multi-stakeholder consultation is probably the most appropriate operating model to:

- evaluate novel and strategic development questions in early-stage assets;
- clarify how current methods of value assessment differ in their approach to a new medicine;
- address requirements for post-launch data to evaluate effectiveness.

While the participants in the Tapestry Network's pilot projects identified several critical success factors for their engagement pilot projects, we feel there are some additional success factors for long-term success whereby early engagement is a routine service offered by all the major payers. We have outlined above some of the significant obstacles to its long-term success along with some potential solutions to the current barriers.

We are of the view that the best operating model will be one implemented through (more formal) collaborative payer/regulatory networks. We foresee limited success for engagement initiatives coordinated by independent not-for-profit organizations that are not technology developers, payers or regulators. We feel that efforts to develop payer evidence guidance notes should start with thematic issues (e.g. validation of surrogate outcomes) rather than focus on a given disease/condition such as AD, as they will have more widespread usefulness. This is a more efficient and equitable approach.

As we noted earlier, planning by technology developers to take full advantage of the available advice process and how to implement the advice received both matter.

Within pharmaceutical companies, the nature of advice received may highlight that a development, previously addressing the needs of regulators only, now has added complication that affects timelines, costs and overall feasibility. Careers may be on the line, so the advice received may be challenged by members of project teams whose incentives may not be aligned well with the overall goal of optimal market access. Invariably, the price and sales volumes of new medicines are forecast much in advance of the availability of the evidence to support them. The expected size and costs of phase III development programmes are still predominantly forecast based on regulatory planning only, though this is slowly changing. Thus, when the nature of the expected evidence is properly revealed in early payer engagement, forecasts and forecasters in clinical and marketing divisions may be called to task by their management. Their incentive remains to avoid such a personally uncomfortable situation, which includes avoiding taking or considering advice from payers. Prior awareness of this common structural (perverse) disincentive to taking and implementing scientific advice from payers is important. Development of processes to ensure early scientific advice received is made available highly visibly throughout a development organization matters. Dissemination should include management layers above project teams. Management often provide incentives to their subordinates for successful regulatory agency outcomes rather than successful market access outcomes. This should be changed and subordinates have also to work for ensuring successful outcomes with payers. Shareholders in pharmaceutical companies as well as other stakeholders, including regulators, payers and patients, should expect no less.

## Disclaimer

Any views/opinions expressed in this chapter are based on our own thoughts and experiences and do not necessarily represent the views of any former employers.

## References

Backhouse, M., Wonder, M., Hornby, E., *et al.* (2011). Early dialogue between the developers of new technologies and pricing and reimbursement agencies. A pilot study. *Value Health*, 14, 608–15.

CIRS, Center for Innovation in Regulatory Science (2015). *Past Workshops and Publications 2012–2010.* CIRS, London (available online at: http://cirsci.org/content/past-workshops-publications-2011-2010).

CVZ (2012). International cooperation: organisations and activities (viewed 2 October 2012 at: www.cvz.nl/binaries/live/cvzinternet/hst_content/en/documents/international-cooperation-organisations-and-activities.pdf).

Day, R., Lipworth, W. and Kerridge, I. (2011). Death of the 'blockbuster' and 'pivotal' clinical trial; rethinking the drug development process. *Journal of Pharmacy Practice & Research*, 41, 94–6.

Eichler, H.G., Bloechl-Daum, B., Abadie, E., *et al.* (2010). Relative efficacy of drugs: an emerging issue between regulatory agencies and third-party payers. *Nature Reviews Drug Discovery*, 9, 277–91.

EMA, European Medicines Agency (2015a). Scientific advice (available online at: www.ema.europa.eu/ema/index.jsp?curl=pages/regulation/general/general_content_000050.jsp&jsenabled=true).

EMA, European Medicines Agency (2015b). Partners & Networks, Health-technology-assessment bodies (available online at: www.ema.europa.eu/ema/index.jsp?curl=pages/partners_and_networks/general/general_content_000476.jsp&).

EMA, European Medicines Agency (2015c). Scientific advice (available online at: www.ema. europa.eu/ema/index.jsp?curl=pages/regulation/general/general_content_000050. jsp&jsenabled=true).

EMA, European Medicines Agency (2015d). General principles: EMA–FDA parallel scientific advice (available online at: www.emea.europa.eu/ema/index.jsp?curl=pages/regulation/general/general_content_000062.jsp).

EMA, European Medicine Agency (2016). Cooperation between regulators and HTA bodies creates synergies (available online at: www.ema.europa.eu/ema/index.jsp?curl=pages/news_and_events/news/2016/04/news_detail_002510.jsp&mid=WC0b01ac058004d5c1).

EUnetHTA, European network for Health Technology Agencies (2015). Joint Action 2, 2012–15 (available online at: www.eunethta.eu/activities/EUnetHTA Joint Action 2%282012–15%29/eunethta-joint-action-2-2012-2015).

FDA, U.S. Food and Drug Administration (2015). Scheduling and conduct of regulatory review meetings with sponsors and applicants (available online at: www.fda.gov/BiologicsBloodVaccines/GuidanceComplianceRegulatoryInformation/ProceduresSOPPs/ucm079448.htm).

Green Park Collaborative (2015). (Available online at: www.greenparkcollaborative.org).

Kaitlin, K.I. (2010). Deconstructing the drug development process; the new face of innovation. *Clinical Pharmacology & Therapeutics*, 87, 356–61.

Maignen, F.M., Ospienko, L., Gajraj, E. and Chivers, R. (2014). Trends in early engagement between industry and HTA; analysis of scientific advice provided by NICE since 2009. *Value Health*, 17, A441.

MHRA, Medicines and Healthcare products Regulatory Agency (2015). Scientific advice for license applicants (available online at: www.gov.uk/medicines-get-scientific-advice-from-mhra).

Naci, H., Cylus, J., Vandoros, S., *et al.* (2012). Raising the bar for market authorisation of new drugs. *British Medical Journal*, 345, e4261.

Neumann, P.J., Lin, P.J. and Hughes, T.E. (2011). U.S. FDA Modernization Act, Section 114: uses, opportunities and implications for comparative effectiveness research. *Pharmacoeconomics*, 28, 687–92.

NICE, National Institute for Health and Care Excellence (2015). About NICE, Scientific advice consultancy service (available online at: www.nice.org.uk/aboutnice/scientificadvice/AboutScientificAdvice.jsp).

Tapestry Networks (2015). (Available online at: www.tapestrynetworks.com/).

TLV (2015a). Joint scientific advice meetings between the Dental and Pharmaceutical Benefits Agency (TLV) and the Medical Products Agency (MPA) (available online at: www.lakemedelsverket.se/english/product/Medicinal-products/Scientific-advice/Pilot-project-of-joint-scientific-advice-meetings-arranged-by-the-TLV-and-the-MPA/).

TLV (2015b). Pilot project of joint scientific advice meetings will be evaluated (available online at: www.lakemedelsverket.se/english/All-news/NYHETER-2010/Pilot-project-of-joint-scientific-advice-meetings-Medical-Product-Agency-MPA-and-the-Dental-and-Pharmaceutical-Benefits-Agency-TLV/).

# Chapter 4

# An Overview of Market Access Agreements

*Mondher Toumi, Julie Zard, Imene Ben Abdallah, Claudio Jommi and Joshua Cohen*

## Introduction

Market access was originally defined by the World Trade Organization (WTO). According to the WTO, market access for general goods refers to the conditions, tariff and non-tariff measures, agreed upon by members for the entry of specific goods into their markets.

Likewise, market access for drugs can be defined as referring to the rules and conditions put in place to allow a pharmaceutical company to enter a specific market with its product. Those rules could be classified as generic rules; arrangements that apply for all products, and specific rules; i.e. arrangements aimed at optimizing a patient's access to a specific drug. In this chapter, they are referred to as market access agreements (MAAs).

MAAs have been widely and increasingly implemented over the past few years. Ando *et al.* (2011) found that between 2010 and 2011, there was nearly double the total number of MAAs as there were in 2009. Furthermore, it is a growing phenomenon across various countries, such as Italy and Australia, while a significant number of new countries, such as New Zealand, Belgium, Poland and Hungary, are beginning to witness MAAs. Carlson *et al.* identified 148 arrangements in their study spanning 20 years between 1993 and 2013 (Carlson *et al.* 2014). Also, the initial confusions about the definition, taxonomy and best practices of these schemes are gradually giving way to clearer taxonomies as reported by the International Society for Pharmacoeconomics and Outcomes Research (ISPOR) good practices task force on performance-based risk-sharing arrangements (PBRSA) (Garrison *et al.* 2013).

Historically, there have been non-written agreements between manufacturers and payers on the drug development and commercialization risk share. In these agreements, manufacturers bear the risks in development and charge for the cost of its failure. Once the product reaches the market and a price is set between payers and manufacturers, the payers endorse the post-approval risk. Now however, the risk has shifted towards the industry and MAAs have changed this landscape according to a number of parameters, which aim at minimizing the post-approval uncertainty for the payer and shifting it towards the manufacturer. This has mainly been driven by an increased price of pharmaceutical overtime, and payers getting worried about uncertainties associated with very highly priced products.

In this chapter, we will shed more light on these agreements, their different types, why and how they are put in place in different countries, their outcomes, and finally the possible perspectives for MAAs.

## Rationale Behind Market Access Agreements

It has been budget constraints, as well as experiences from past launch stories, that have pushed payers to become more and more critical when assessing the value of a drug coming on the market. Many times, the expected benefits of innovative drugs failed to be realized once the drug was on the market, thus emphasizing the important gap between the price of the drug and its true benefit. This gap between "expected benefit" and "actual medical benefit" was difficult to manage for payers, which led them to become more demanding about the requirements for proof of the evidence of a new drug's value.

Clinical development plans of new molecules aim to demonstrate the safety and clinical benefit of the product. However, they rarely allow for anticipating the added value from a payer's perspective. Most often, even if this added value is likely, it is not always evidenced before the launch, and uncertainty on the added benefit remains.

It was in this context, and to reduce the uncertainty related to a drug's value, that numerous agreements between payers and manufacturers were made. It is interesting to note that most of these market access agreements are in fact disguised price discounts on which both the payer and the manufacturer agree. As such, it appears legitimate that as long as the uncertainty over the drug's value exists, the price should account for this uncertainty or be conditional until the benefit is proven.

Based on these, we can already consider two types of agreements – the first where the price includes the cost of uncertainty, and the second where the price is conditional until the benefit is evidenced – or even a mix of the two.

## Different Definitions and Taxonomies of Market Access Agreements

### Different Definitions

There was some initial confusion surrounding the exact definition of MAA, due in part to a lack of a single common definition. In fact, a number of different definitions, as well as taxonomies, can be found in literature. Taxonomies however, are becoming more consolidated, as demonstrated by examples such as the Morel *et al.* (2013) taxonomy, shown in Figure 4.1, and the guidelines by ISPOR (Garrison *et al.* 2013).

MAAs are often called risk sharing agreements. But while risk sharing implies both a risk and a share, in a payment for performance (P4P), for example, the risk is only on the manufacturer as it would receive payment only if the drug performs. Also, in a cost-sharing agreement there is no risk sharing. Therefore risk sharing is not an appropriate name for these agreements. Consultants call them innovative contracting, while in the UK the Department of Health (DoH) adopted a new terminology, the patient access scheme (PAS).

Risk sharing, cost sharing and payment for performance are often put in the same basket and called risk-sharing agreements, whereas in reality there are some structural differences. Some often quoted definitions are presented below:

- Risk-sharing agreements:
    "A contract between two parties, who agree to engage in a transaction in which there are uncertainties, regardless of its final value. Nevertheless, one party, the company, has sufficient confidence in its claims of either effectiveness or

efficiency that it is ready to accept a reward or a penalty depending on the observed performance of its product" (de Pouvourville 2006).

- Cost-sharing agreement:
  "Type of a commercial agreement between health care payer and the drug manufacturer implemented to reduce pharmaceutical expenditure. The cost of the drug (according to its list price) is "shared" between the two parties either for all patients on treatment, or for patients who did not respond to the treatment. In the latter case, it is a part of a payment by performance agreement" (Jarolawski and Toumi 2011).
- Payment for performance:
  "A performance-based agreement can be defined as one between a payer and a pharmaceutical, device or diagnostic manufacturer, where the price level and/or revenue received is related to the future performance of the product in either a research or a real-world environment" (Towse and Garrison 2010).

In practice, many MAAs are a mix of a financially based agreement and payment by performance. An example of these mixed types of agreements for Italy is given in Table 4.1.

Chronologically, de Pouvourville was the first to define risk sharing in literature as "a contract between two parties, who agree to engage in a transaction in which there are uncertainties regardless of its final value. Nevertheless, one party, the company, has sufficient confidence in its claims of either effectiveness or efficiency

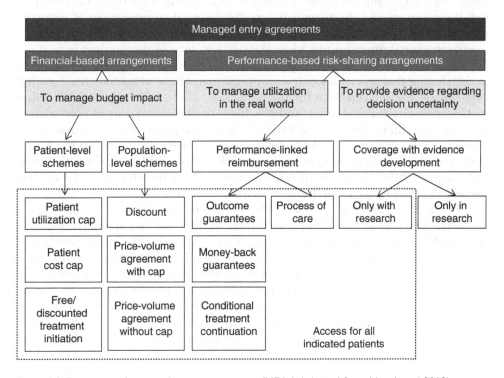

*Figure 4.1* Taxonomy of managed entry agreements (MEAs) (adapted from Morel *et al.* 2013)

*Table 4.1* Mix of market access agreements (MAAs) in Italy for oncological drugs

| Cost sharing | Sunitinib (SUTENT®), erlotinib (TARCEVA®) | |
|---|---|---|
| Discount of 50% on the drug price for the first cycles of therapy | Description of the scheme | 50% discount on sunitinib or erlotinib for NHS, for the first three months (two cycles) of treatment |
| **Risk sharing** | **Cetuximab (ERBITUX®) (metastastic colo-rectal cancer)** | |
| A patient is treated at full cost until follow-up; if the patient shows disease progression, then the manufacturer has to pay back 50% of the treatment cost | Description of the scheme | 50% payback for patients with disease progression after two months of treatment |
| **Payment by performance** | **Everolimus (AFINITOR®) (pNET and breast cancer HER2 negative)** | |
| A patient is treated at full cost until follow-up; if the patient shows disease progression, then the manufacturer has to pay back the full cost | Description of the scheme | Full price for the six months of treatment, then 100% payback for non-responding patients |

that it is ready to accept a reward or a penalty depending on the observed performance of its product" (de Pouvourville 2006). For example, the reward could be a higher price, or an extension of a license, and a penalty could be a lower price, with or without the reimbursement of excess profit in case the claims are not justified. Under such an arrangement one can talk of risk sharing since the concerned parties, the company and the payer, support the financial consequences of reducing uncertainty. Such an arrangement necessarily includes the design and the cost of the observational procedure to assess the performance of the product in real life (de Pouvourville 2006). Interestingly, the author restricts the scope of his definition to risk sharing that represents only a very small proportion of agreements, focusing explicitly on risk management for the payer side. Towse and Garrison also define such agreements as risk sharing, and also focus on the uncertainty of product performance – defining them as "agreements between a payer and a pharmaceutical company where the price level and/or revenue received are related to the future performance of the product in either a research or real-world environment" (Towse and Garrison 2010). They clearly differentiate between the efficacy and the effectiveness by referring to research and real-world evidences.

Adamski *et al.* (2010) proposed a wider perspective in calling those agreements risk-sharing arrangements. They defined them as "agreements concluded by payers and pharmaceutical companies to diminish the impact on the payer's budget of new and existing medicines brought about by either the uncertainty of the value of the medicine and/or the need to work within finite budgets". In practice, the agreement lies in setting the scope and realizing the mutual obligations among both payers and pharmaceutical companies, depending on the occurrence of an agreed condition, the "risk". This "risk" varies, and can include pharmaceutical expenditure higher than agreed thresholds, or the health gain from a new product being lower in practice, thus reducing its value. Adamski *et al.* explicitly focused on the cost-containment role of such agreements and the fact that the risk lies more on the budget-impact side than the intervention-performance side. It is noticeable that Adamski and his co-authors are payers and thus focus on budget impact, while the authors, who focus on uncertainty of the performance, are academics.

So, we can see that there is no consensus regarding the definition of these agreements. They may be defined as the outcome of a compromise between health care payers and the industry on the drug's price and reimbursement status, health technology assessment (HTA) recommendation and/or formulary listing, or as an alternative to simply bringing the drug's list price closer to the level of a currently used treatment option. This solution is deemed unacceptable by the industry, particularly when many generic therapeutic options are available in a disease area. In de Pouvourville's definition, agreements whose sole aim is to implement cost-containment measures are not included. In such agreements, there is no uncertainty about health outcomes. These financial agreements are also often called risk-sharing agreements, although most do not involve sharing risk. In fact, in most of the identified agreements, the risk is shifted solely on to the manufacturer, rather than being shared between both parties. Patient access schemes is another description that was proposed by the Department of Health in the UK. However, some schemes have led to restricted access rather than optimized patients' access.

### A Possible Definition

In this book, we have decided to use the terminology of market access agreement (MAA), as it is thought to cover all types of agreements under a general term. An MAA is defined as "an agreement between two or more parties, who agree on the terms and conditions under which a product will get access to the market". MAAs can be grouped into two types of agreements: financial agreements and outcome-based agreements. The latter include both P4P and coverage with evidence development (CED) types of agreements, which are presented below.

### Different Taxonomies

In addition to the various terminologies describing these schemes, experts have proposed a number of classifications.

Morel *et al.* (2013) classify agreements into two main types – those that measure health outcomes in characterizing performance (i.e. performance-based risk-sharing schemes) and those that do not consider outcomes but focus on keeping expenditure within agreed limits (i.e. financial-based arrangements).

Adamski *et al.* (2010) similarly suggest that agreements may be classified into two categories: financial- and performance-based/outcome-based models. Other classifications distinguish between population-versus patient-level schemes, the latter characterizing a situation where value for money is guaranteed without the need for subsequent review of the reimbursement decision (Adamski *et al.* 2010).

Towse and Garrison also made the distinction between outcome-based and non-outcome-based in their taxonomy, and also between agreements that specified how evidence would be translated into revisions of price, revenues, and/or use, and agreements that instead specify an evidence review point where renegotiation would occur (Towse and Garrison 2010).

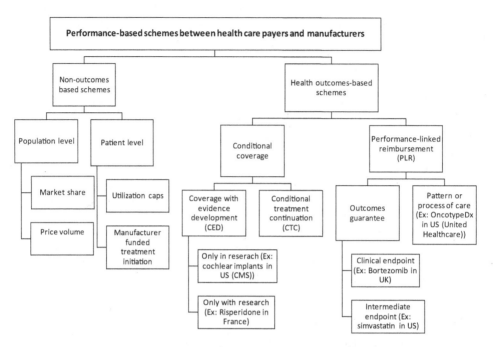

*Figure 4.2* Taxonomy of performance-based health outcomes reimbursement schemes (adapted from Carlson *et al.* 2010)

Carlson *et al.* (2010, 2014) based their taxonomy on an inventory of published schemes categorized in terms of timing, execution, and health outcomes. They made a clear distinction between schemes that are health outcomes-based and those that are not, setting aside the research component (Carlson *et al.* 2010, 2014). This taxonomy (Figure 4.2) allows identification of the various sub-types of agreements. It is useful for reviewing all potential agreements that might apply for a given intervention in order to prepare for negotiation with payers. However, it remains complex for daily practice and classification of agreements. Table 4.2 offers an overview of the various agreements and their characteristics.

### Simplified Taxonomy

MAAs can thus be grouped into two types:

- "Financial agreements are commercial agreements between two or more parties entering into a deal for goods acquisition. For example, a price volume agreement, discount or rebate, price cap, or cost sharing" (Toumi and Michel 2011).
- "Outcome-based agreements are part of an insurance or warranty facility: the payer agrees to a price under the insurance that the product will deliver a

*Table 4.2* Characteristics of market access agreements (MAAs)

| MAA category | Commercial agreement | Payment for performance agreement | Coverage with evidence development |
|---|---|---|---|
| **Contract type** | • Traditional commercial contract | • Long-term risk-shifting agreement (outcomes guarantee) applied on per-patient basis | • Provisional agreement (risk sharing or shifting) until new evidence develops from a cohort of patients |
| **Underlying concept (payer perspective)** | • Reducing pharmaceutical expenditure | • Avoiding inefficient expenditure on treating patients who do not respond to a drug and who cannot be identified ex ante (by linking the payment to drug's performance) | • Avoiding inefficient expenditure until uncertainty about drug's effectiveness is reduced, by linking final reimbursement (and/or pricing) decision to drug's performance |
| **Types** | • Price–volume agreement <br> • Market cap <br> • Flat price (per patient, regardless of number of doses administered) <br> • Cost sharing <br> • Rebate <br> • Discount | • Payment for performance <br> • Pay-back for non-performance <br> • Payment for management of events which the drug failed to prevent <br> • Payment for management of side effects | • Temporary coverage on a condition that new evidence reduces uncertainty <br> • Real-life effectiveness <br> • Higher effectiveness in a subpopulation of patients <br> • Actual daily dose as a daily price may be based on an expected daily dose while in real life daily dose may be higher <br> • Long-term effect <br> • Improved patient's adherence <br> • Reduction of use of health care resources <br> • Reduction of use of other medication having serious side effects |
| **Examples** | • PAS on ranibizumab in England/Wales (flat price) <br> • Price–volume agreements in France and Italy <br> • Market cap on drugs in Italy and UK | • PAS on Velcade in England/Wales <br> • P4P schemes on oncology drugs in Italy | • CED on Duodopa® in Sweden <br> • CED on multiple sclerosis drugs in England/Wales <br> • CEDs on rosiglitazone, risperidone and omalizumab in France |

predefined outcome. This regroups into two kinds of MAA: payment for performance (P4P) and conditional coverage agreements" (Toumi and Michel 2011).

These two types of market access agreements are further subdivided into two categories: MAA at population level and MAA at individual levels (Table 4.3).

*Table 4.3* Taxonomy of market access agreements (MAAs)

|  | Population level | Patient level |
| --- | --- | --- |
| Financial based | Discounts/Rebates<br>Price/volume agreement | • Capping<br><br>• Manufacturer-funded<br>treatment initiation |
| Outcome based | Coverage with evidence<br>development (CED) | • Payment for performance<br>reimbursement (P4P) |

### Financial Agreement

Financial agreements are commercial agreements between two or more parties entering into a deal for goods acquisition. The aim of these agreements is cost containment and they do not involve any risk sharing.

In order to maintain high list prices (which are used internationally by payers as a reference when setting a price for a new drug), pharmaceutical companies have been entering into more and more complex agreements with payers, that conceal the actual price at which the drug is purchased. This can be achieved by implementing price–volume mechanisms, market caps, etc. Most of these agreements are more or less complex price discounts.

### Payment for Performance (P4P)

When reimbursement depends on real-life outcome assessed for individual patients, it is an outcome-based agreement. In a P4P agreement, payment is decided for individual cases, which will allow for minimizing the possibility of paying for non-responders and maximizing the likelihood that the manufacturer receives a price reflecting the drug's true value. The analysis is done on an individual basis and is potentially infinite in duration. P4P does not seek to gather new or comparative evidence but rather to justify reimbursement of a drug.

• Conditional treatment continuation

Among payment for performance agreements, we can also distinguish a type of payment for performance where continuation of coverage for individual patients is conditional upon meeting short-term treatment goals (e.g. tumor response or lower cholesterol). This form of P4P was termed conditional treatment continuation (CTC) by Carlson *et al.* (2010).

• Prospective P4P

Another type of agreement is the prospective P4P agreement, which has recently been implemented in oncology in two countries for two different products (according to the authors' confidential insight). The specific conditions of the schemes cannot be revealed as they are protected by confidentiality agreements; however, a description of the rationale and the pros and cons of such an agreement can be given.

In this model, the insurance would pay on a periodic basis (quarterly, for example) for as long as the patient benefits. It could be overall progression-free survival in oncology or until next flare or relapse in ulcerative colitis, etc.

- The advantages of this type of agreement would be:
  - the reduction of decision uncertainty inherent in purchasing new technologies by replacing a single upfront payment with a payment stream with an equivalent expected value conditional upon delivery of promised health gain;
  - the reduction of the initial and expected total budget impact of the technology through the progressive reimbursement process;
  - the prompt and easier implementation for innovative technologies into a health care system.
- The limits of such schemes are as follows:
  - The uncertainty risk is shifted on to the payer, who covers a drug that has yet to prove its efficacy. Today payers pay for proven efficacy and eventually cover with evidence development. Here the payer will discover over time the drug's added benefit and pay for it despite the absence of specific evidence at time of launch.
  - This is different from usual P4P as the payer has not just some understanding of the benefit but also some doubt about transferability in real life. In which case the question is how long life expectancy is increased, and there is no strong evidence about it. So the payer pays as long as the patient survives up to a cap, but with no idea how long the patient may survive and which proportion may reach the capped survival.
  - The lack of comparative studies makes it difficult to assess whether the given product is doing better than a reference product in real life or not. Patients' eligibility criteria should be very strict and documented or some patients might wrongly be assigned to that new treatment and the added benefit will not be real.
  - Such schemes do not generate evidence over a limited period of time and will likely last as long as the drug is patented.
  - The potentially substantial administrative costs associated with monitoring patients' response to treatment.
- The conditions for eligibility of prospective P4P:
  - A new treatment for diseases with no major benefit over the next best alternative or population poorly serviced by existing alternatives, which demonstrated a good benefit with a high unproven potential.
  - Ideally, the treatment duration should be short, coupled with a long-lasting health benefit after the end of the treatment.
- There should be a general consensus on performance indicators to be used.
- The drug must belong to a range of high–priced drugs to compensate for the substantial administrative costs associated with monitoring over time.
- It is likely that payment caps will need to be implemented, to avoid paying with no limits.

### Coverage with Evidence Development

CED is a conditional outcome-based agreement. It allows conditional funding for new, promising drugs while more conclusive evidence is being gathered to address uncertainty regarding clinical or cost-effectiveness at population level (NHS Quality Improvement Scotland 2008). CED agreements suggest the demonstration of benefit in a study over which both parties will have agreed on the trial's design and implementation processes. In some cases, the threshold for the evidence of a particular benefit may, or may not be predefined. In other cases, different commercialization prices are predefined, based on the level of the benefit.

Finally, the sums that are paid to the manufacturer during the period awaiting the final results of the agreed upon study could be claimed as payback in case the performance of the drug does not meet the predefined expectations. Anglo-Saxon legal experts call this type of scheme an "escrow agreement". In an escrow agreement, the amount due by the payer to the manufacturer is put aside in a frozen bank account or placed with a lawyer (CARPA account). If, by the end of the study, the results confirm the drug's performance according to the scheme, then the frozen amount is given to the manufacturer. Otherwise, it is delivered to the health insurance.

The scheme transparency also varies from one CED to another. Even though they have a limited duration, it is not always clear at implementation how much the price revision will be, because the minimum threshold for improving the endpoint, and the relation ship between magnitude of improvement and price, are not defined. As relevant data from ongoing or prospective studies are made available, this will lead to price negotiations between payers and manufacturers.

The aim of CED agreements is to minimize the possibility of financing non-cost-effective drugs and maximizing the likelihood that the manufacturer receives a price reflecting the drug's true value.

CED agreements are temporary arrangements that are terminated when evidence from a cohort of patients is produced. Their temporary nature allows for developing new evidence on real-life health outcomes and identifying elements such as the duration of treatment, the appropriate dose, the target population, etc.

CED aims to reduce two types of uncertainties:

- how efficacy results in clinical trials translate in to real-life benefit;
- the study design, which might not produce conclusive evidence about the real intrinsic value of the product, for example by using the wrong comparator.

## Payer's and Manufacturer's Motivations to Implement MAAs

MAAs have emerged as the subsequent answer to two issues: restricted budgets and uncertainties surrounding the real benefits of new products. In reality, some represent real tools of management for budget-constraints management, and others for payers' uncertainty.

CED is a specific tool for managing uncertainty, whereas commercial agreements and payment for performance agreements are used to control the budget and health expenditures. In theory, both are expected to manage uncertainty. However, payers often expect a discount and find that the P4P is a good way to achieve that discount, which appears to actually make a lot of sense. In reality however, when a clear uncertainty pops up as a concern for payers, there develops an opportunity to run a study to address this specific concern. In that case the CED is explicitly a tool to address the uncertainty that raises the payer's concern.

### The Increasingly Cost-Sensitive Environment

The growing cost pressures on health care budgets, leading to authorities' cost-containment measures, are driving these agreements. In fact, the increasing number of launches of new, expensive technologies that are supported by public budgets has put considerable strain on European health care systems, with most of them in deficit.

### The Uncertainty Related to Drugs' Performance

In most developed countries, public authorities and payers are placing increased emphasis on the post-marketing monitoring of drugs. Pressures on health care budgets certainly drive this change, but this emphasis extends farther than merely budget impact and pricing issues.

In contrast to the initial paradigm that prevailed in the 1990s, public authorities and payers are now questioning the effectiveness of new products: the clinical efficacy demonstrated through pre-marketing studies is considered a necessary but not sufficient condition to verify the value of a new product.

In fact, trials do not ensure effectiveness due to a number of biases (e.g. experimental setting, selection of patients, choice of the comparator, use of intermediate endpoints, trial duration) of which payers and health authorities are becoming less tolerant.

### The "Trust Crisis"

In the current pharmaceutical industry crisis, there is a need to restore trust, as the uncertainty related to a drug's performance has become a critical issue for payers. Even though the risk often appears to be linked to pharmacovigilance, the uncertainty related to the risk of having a lower-than-expected performance in real life is frequent. In that case, MAAs can allow the net price paid by the payers to be linked to the actual added value of the drug. It can also allow payers to reverse decisions more easily.

In practice, payers' main goal is to control expenditure, while manufacturers aim to keep high listed prices for drugs in order to optimize international reference pricing and avoid cross-reference pricing and parallel trade.

There are, however, a number of other reasons to implement MAAs on both sides, which are presented in Table 4.4, where the main motivations are highlighted.

Some other benefits that could motivate payers to implement MAAs are to collect valuable post-marketing data on the drug and its benefits over time with possible increased coincidental information, which could be useful for another product (de Pouvourville 2006).

Some risks may arise when applying MAAs (de Pouvourville 2006). For example, manufacturers may produce data that are useful to competitors (i.e. second movers on the market of the drug).

*Table 4.4* Payers' and manufacturers' motivations for implementing MAAs

| Payers' motivations | Manufacturers' motivations |
|---|---|
| • To provide patients with access while staying within budget | • To optimize international reference pricing |
| • To control expenditure | • To capture product's value (ensure profitability) |
| • To improve ICER of expensive products (and stay within a fixed threshold) | • To reduce the cost of an additional clinical trial |
| • To prioritize certain interventions to patients who most need it | • To achieve access for patients and further explore drug's potential |
| • To align with a national/regional policy that prioritizes certain health outcomes | • To achieve competitive advantage (over cheaper or equally priced comparator drugs) |
| • To avoid pressure from patient associations, government or media | • To capture value of non-clinical or real-life benefits of the drug |
| • To prevent media coverage of negative reimbursement decisions | • To obtain comparative real-life effectiveness data versus a comparator |
| • To expand the list of innovative accessible interventions in the country (favourable publicity) | • To mitigate a failure to achieve reimbursement or HTA recommendation and achieve global coverage (for policy reasons) |
| • To reduce uncertainty about effectiveness or non-clinical drug benefits (e.g. compliance) | • To improve company's image |
| | • To create opportunity to develop partnerships with payers |

Any plans to establish an MAA should be preceded by a comprehensive and transparent analysis of stakeholders' motivations.

## International Comparison of MAA Health Policies

### Market Access Agreements Across Countries

Across countries and the different policies, MAAs are not the same, and implementations differ. For example, most CEDs and P4Ps were implemented outside of the US between 1998 and 2009 (Carlson *et al.* 2010). In Europe, where MAAs are also very common, there is a big variability in schemes' implementation. These differences are presented in Table 4.5.

- The price–volume schemes are extensively implemented due to the fact that relatively high volumes of sales can be achieved. They are used either as a leverage to control drug use in target populations, or as a tool to control the budget impact.
- In practice, a mix of commercial agreements and P4Ps is agreed upon and implemented.
- Commercial agreements are most common in France, Spain and Italy. Price volume agreements in France do not apply on the first box that is sold, but in an incremental way, with prices varying when reaching over a certain volume plateau. In most countries, these agreements are implemented from the first box that is sold, meaning that the sales volume reached will condition the unit price and apply to the total sales.

Table 4.5 Differences in MAA schemes across some European countries

| Market access agreements | FR | UK | DE | IT | ES | NL |
|---|---|---|---|---|---|---|
| **Commercial agreements** | | | | | | |
| Market cap | √ | √ | | √√ | √ | |
| Price–volume | √√ | | √ | √ | | √ |
| Flat price | √ | √ | √ | √ | √ | √ |
| Discount | √ | √ | √ | √ | √ | √ |
| Rebate | √ | √ | √ | √ | √ | √ |
| Cost-sharing | | √ | √ | √ | | |
| **Payment for performance** | | | | | | |
| Pay back for non-performance | | √ | √ | √ | √ | |
| Payment for performance | | √ | √ | √ | √ | |
| Payment for non-prevention management | | | √ | | | |
| Payment for side effects management | | | √ | | | |
| **Coverage with evidence development** | | | | | | |
| Real-life effectiveness | √ | √ | √ | | | √ |
| Subpopulation efficacy/effectiveness | √ | √ | √ | | | √ |
| Long-term effectiveness | √ | √ | √ | | | √ |
| Actual daily dose | √ | | √ | | | √ |
| Improved adherence | √ | | √ | | | |
| Resource use reduction | √ | | √ | | | |
| Comparative clinical trials | √ | √ | | | | |

- In Italy, the use of MAAs has increased. They are mainly negotiated and decided at national level with the Agenzia Italiana del Farmaco (AIFA), and primarily managed at local level. Besides commercial agreements, including cost-sharing agreements, for oncology drugs there has been a tremendous increase in P4P contracts. These contracts may rely on oncology registries and provide for a full (or partial) payback in the case of patients who do not respond to treatment (Figure 4.3).
- CEDs are usually implemented in Belgium, the Netherlands, Sweden or Portugal for expensive drugs. Sweden is the most active country in implementing CEDs, but they are increasingly being used in France after a long period of reluctance. Initial reimbursement or pricing decision is reviewed after 1.5–3 years.
- Swedish TLV, operating under the cost-effectiveness paradigm, does not reimburse drugs with uncertain or high incremental cost-effectiveness ratio (ICER). For instance, Duodopa®, which is indicated for advanced-stage Parkinson's disease, went through a five-year CED scheme aimed at reducing uncertainty of its ICER. The product, at launch, was given a price and reimbursement rate that was conditional on carrying out a study. The post-marketing study was conducted without the TLV's approval of the design due to shortages in the methodology. For that reason, at the beginning, Duodopa® was not granted reimbursement at the agreed conditional price. This led to non-reimbursement. Afterwards, a second study was conducted with the TLV that allowed the evidencing of the added value of Duodopa® and to confirm reimbursement at the initial conditional price.

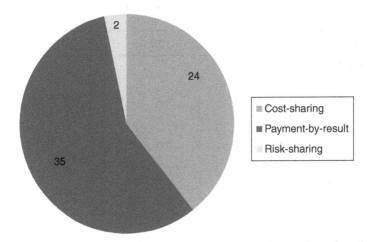

*Figure 4.3* Typology of MAA in Italy for oncology drugs (61 evaluated agreements)*
* Last update: June 2015.

- MAAs in Germany are not very diffused and were primarily introduced at *Lander* (regional) level, contracting with the Krankenkasse (German health insurance). A mix of methods (price-volume, outcome-based, etc.) is used and they have been increasingly used also by private insurers.
- MAAs in the UK have been introduced, together with the Cancer Drugs Fund and higher thresholds for end-of life treatments, to cover drugs that otherwise would have not been recommended because of an incremental cost-effectiveness ratio (ICER) over the threshold.

### Comparative Resistance Among Some Countries

Resistance varies across countries. For instance:

- In Denmark:
  - there is resistance to the administrative burden of access schemes.
- In France, there is:
  - reliance on payback agreements as this is quite certain based on pre-specified criteria that usually allow budget constraints to be addressed;
  - resistance to the concept of risk sharing as there is uncertainty and such agreement would be acceptable only in exceptional cases;
  - little interest in outcome-based agreements as the payers' ability to cross check those outcomes is complex and burdensome;
  - lack of transparency because those agreements are not publicly available and are kept confidential between manufacturer and pricing committee;
  - CEDs with real-life studies are increasingly implemented to address actual payers' concerns about transferability of clinical trials in real life.

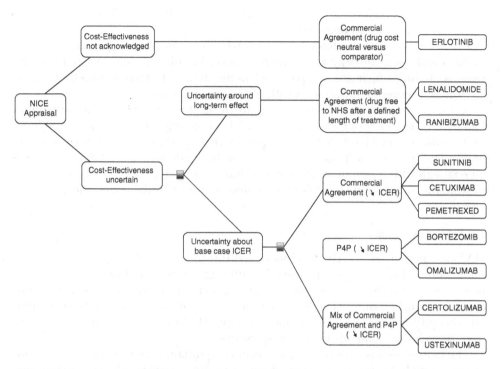

*Figure 4.4* Classification of patient access schemes (PAS) according to UK NICE's consideration of the cost-effectiveness evidence and the design of the PAS

- In Spain:
  - price–volume agreements, discounts and rebates are already being used;
  - risk-sharing agreements at a regional level have been piloted in some hospitals, with details still being kept confidential;
  - the regional authority of Catalonia initiated the first official risk-sharing agreement in oncology and formalized the first guidelines for MAAs at regional level (Mora-Ripoll *et al.* 2014).

### Regional MAA Growth in Europe

Types of MAA and implementations vary across not just countries, but also across regions within the same country. The increasing budget pressures at regional levels have contributed to create a new major hurdle for pharmaceuticals' market access.

The lack of market access culture in the field forces, and the large number of regions, has led to a poorly managed process for gaining regional market access. There is a trend to structure the regional management of MAAs that goes from the pragmatic prioritization and segmentation, as in Italy (Compagni *et al.* 2008), to a sophisticated segmentation process, as in the UK (Toumi *et al.* 2011).

In practice, the balance of power and level of autonomy are very different from one country to another. Generally, the federal/central government sets a vision, while the local/regional authorities will decide on implementation. Payers at a national level decide on price, reimbursement and national MAA recommendations, while payers at a regional level manage entry date, possible local MAA, prescription restrictions and local recommendations.

Until now, the industry has not yet succeeded in addressing regional hurdles in a rational and systematic way as is done for national bodies. This is due to numerous reasons, among which are complex and quite atomized markets, non-transparent rules, and divergent requirements within the same country.

At the national level, decision makers focus on the scientific evaluation, and on budget impact to a lesser extent, as the bill is ultimately paid at the regional level; while at the regional level, decision makers are mainly concerned with the budgetary impact, but of course will also look at the scientific evidence. This explains why commercial agreements are more frequent in Italy and Spain, for instance, in order to provide the opportunity for regions to achieve a more affordable net price.

### The Italian Case Study

MAAs are negotiated by AIFA and managed through the onco-registry by hospitals (clinicians and hospital pharmacists). Even though regions do not negotiate MAAs, most regions govern market access through regional formularies, tenders and actions on prescribing behaviour (Fattore and Jommi 2008; Jommi *et al.* 2013). Some regions are also putting pressure on hospitals to apply MAAs and ask for reimbursement from the relevant company for non-responders.

The reason for this regional pressure over cost containment is that in Italy, regions are responsible for any deficit they incur on health care expenditure. They decide the overall structure of their (regional) health care system (quasi-market mechanisms, accreditation of providers, cost-containment actions including pharmaceuticals), provided that they give the "essential level of health care" determined by the central government (Tediosi *et al.* 2009). Regions are also accountable for 50% of the possible deficit on hospital drugs budgets (3.4% of health care budget) (Jommi *et al.* 2013; Jommi and Minghetti 2015).

A 2010 study in Italy highlighted the variability of patients' access to oncology products among Italian regions (IRs) (Russo *et al.* 2010). The percentage of patient access by IRs, among the 14 oncology products investigated, ranged from 50% to 85.7% (Table 4.6). Regional formularies have gained a more important role and this represents a further barrier to patients' access to drugs in Italy. Results from this study show that regions with binding formularies show a less rapid access of oncology drugs to market than regions without a regional formulary. The study also shows that a much faster patient access for oncology drugs was achieved with products receiving a market authorization combined with a risk-sharing agreement.

### The Swedish Example

In Sweden, funding is local (county council), and MAAs are negotiated locally. Thus, they are less visible internationally, less transparent, and an increase in MAAs implies more requirements to negotiate and administer.

One example is Roche's bevacizumab, in which case Stockholm County Council agreed in April 2008 that if patients with advanced cancer exceeded an accumulated dose of 10,000 mg of bevacizumab, the additional costs would be covered by the

Table 4.6 Percentage of patient access by Italian region to oncology drugs (2010 onwards)

| Italian regions | No. of available products | % of patient access[a] | % of a stable patient access[b] |
|---|---|---|---|
| Campania | 12 | 85.7 | 85.7 |
| Friuli Venezia Giulia | 12 | 85.7 | 85.7 |
| Lombardia | 12 | 85.7 | 78.6 |
| Marche | 12 | 85.7 | 78.6 |
| Piemonte | 12 | 85.7 | 85.7 |
| Toscana | 12 | 85.7 | 71.4 |
| Veneto | 12 | 85.7 | 71.4 |
| Abruzzo | 11 | 78.6 | 71.4 |
| Lazio | 11 | 78.6 | 78.6 |
| Liguria | 11 | 78.6 | 71.4 |
| Puglia | 11 | 78.6 | 78.6 |
| Calabria | 10 | 71.4 | 57.1 |
| Emilia Romagna | 10 | 71.4 | 71.4 |
| Sicilia | 10 | 71.4 | 71.4 |
| Umbria | 10 | 71.4 | 64.3 |
| Basilicata | 9 | 64.3 | 57.1 |
| Prov. Aut. di Bolzano | 9 | 64.3 | 42.9 |
| Prov. Aut. di Trento | 8 | 57.1 | 42.9 |
| Sardegna | 8 | 57.1 | 50.0 |
| Molise | 7 | 50.0 | 35.7 |
| Valle d'Aosta | 7 | 50.0 | 21.4 |

(a) Computed with respect to the 14 oncology products with market access in Italy.
(b) The purchase date has been defined according to the handling month in which the volume corresponded to at least the 20th percentile of the overall volume of the given product.

company. The scheme has since been extended and other regions in Sweden have been offered similar schemes.

There are examples of local MAAs growing in other countries as well, such as the Spanish regions and the UK through general practitioners.

## MAA Best Practice

All MAAs do not follow the same processes and are applied differently according to various parameters (underlying rationales for manufacturer and payer, the type of drug, the country, etc.). Even though each agreement is unique, it is possible to define a general implementation guide for MAAs that consists of identifying the rationale behind MAA typology, the implementation process, and the evaluation of these agreements.

### Factors Underlining MAA Typology

#### When Should MAAs Be Considered?

Table 4.7 lists the factors that indicate that an MAA (P4P or CED) should be considered within a market access strategy for a drug. The right-hand column contains the payer's point of view and therefore defines what evidence should be provided.

*Table 4.7* Rationale behind MAAs: factors to consider

| Factors favouring risk-sharing | Assessment/rationale points to consider |
|---|---|
| 1. Disease with high unmet needs | • Outcomes, side effects, administration |
| 2. Disease is severe or life-threatening | • Mortality rates, burden of disease |
| 3. Uncertainty related to patient population | • Identification of patients, similar indications, degree of off-label use in therapy area |
| 4. An objective and measurable outcome, ideally with biomarkers | • Primary versus proxy outcome |
| 5. An innovative treatment with uncertainty over expected risks and benefits | • New drug class, new treatment approach, new endpoint |
| 6. High cost per treatment | • Total potential population (on/off-label) |
| 7. Large budget impact | • High-cost therapy |
| 8. Strong political support and/or patient demand for drug access | • Political priority<br>• Well-organized patient groups |

### The Implementation Process

*Requirements for Implementing MAAs*

In order to conclude an MAA, a number of elements must be in place. The PBRSA identified a number of requirements for implementation (Garrison *et al.* 2013):

- Measuring appropriate outcomes that should be clinically robust, plausible, appropriate and monitorable.
- Acceptable costs: costs of the schemes to the health care system should be proportionate to the potential gains.
- Realistic time horizon: it should have a clear target date. According to Hutton *et al.* (2007), an MAA longer than three years will be irrelevant in the face of changing clinical practice and technological advancement.
- It is important that all relevant new data can be acquired within a realistic period before entering a scheme.
- Funding arrangements must be clear, whether it is the manufacturer's or the payer's responsibility.
- Define how responsibility for data collection and analysis is allocated.
- Define the process for analyzing and reviewing the evidence in order to make a revised decision on price, revenue or coverage.
- Define whether any rebates or discounts will be paid during the course of the scheme, based on provisional results, for instance.

In general, schemes must not involve appreciable administrative burden, and future schemes must take into consideration possible changes that may impact the agreement, such as changes in therapeutic guidelines. Also, exit strategies must be considered in case the new drug turns out to be worse in reality, which would lead to withdrawal during the lifetime of the scheme (Adamski *et al.* 2010).

*Challenges in MAA Implementation*

Apart from the fact that both parties must agree on the design for the control scheme, there are some practical difficulties in MAA implementation. Firstly, collection of cost data requires good information systems and careful sampling to avoid biases. This could force companies to invest more time and money in initial studies. Then there is also a question concerning the transferability of the results of a given agreement as cost data or quality of life data may be more country dependent than clinical results. And finally, analytical expertise and a good information system need to be available for the payer in order to design the protocol and monitor it over time.

## Evaluation

In theory, evaluation of MAAs should include the overall costs involved in implementing and conducting the schemes as well as the outcomes.

The Task Force report on PBRSA indicates that evaluation should rely on process indicators for the scheme's success (Garrison *et al.* 2013). "It will be an important part of the design of any PBRSA (utilization or CED) scheme to define the metrics by which the success of that scheme can be assessed".

The Task Force identified the following questions as process indicators of success:

- Were the intended outcome measures collected?
- Was uncertainty in associated parameter estimation reduced for the outcomes that were the focus of the scheme?
- Did the scheme keep within budget?
- Was the integrity of the design/estimation maintained?
- Did the governance arrangements work?
- Did the process to underpin a decision with further evidence work?

According to the Task Force, "The appropriate decision making will require the ability to show that the agreed outcome adjustments were made to guarantee the cost-effectiveness of the intervention" (Garrison *et al.* 2013).

Until now, little was published on MAAs' evaluations and results. A systematic literature review conducted by Barros (2011) found that the studies referring to the UK multiple sclerosis (MS) risk-sharing scheme (40% of all studies) reported a few costs, whereas other studies included qualitative discussions of costs and benefits without evaluating the overall economic impact of the scheme. Other articles (Boggild *et al.* 2009; Pickin *et al.* 2009) were published regarding early results in monitoring MS study. They reported that "baseline characteristics and a small but statistically significant progression of disease were similar to those reported in previous pivotal studies". However, a conclusion of both articles is that it is too early to determine the cost-effectiveness of the disease-modifying drugs.

It is important to note that not all proposed schemes will be accepted, even though the majority are. It will depend on "the payer's needs in terms of clinical effectiveness, cost-effectiveness, and/or budget impact and the needs of the manufacturer in terms of pricing, access and revenues" (Carlson *et al.* 2010). Among the schemes that had sufficient details available for evaluation (46 out of 53), 72% gained unlimited access to the market and 28% gained limited access to the market (research participation, cost-effective subgroups, and prior authorizations). Hopefully, more publications on evaluation of MAA schemes will be found as these agreements become more transparent.

## Impact of MAAs on Product Uptake

The main rationale for manufacturers to enter into MAAs is to ensure profitability and optimize sale volumes and market share of a specific drug while avoiding negative impacts of international reference pricing. Patients on the other hand, expect that those agreements will allow them to obtain access to expensive innovative products.

The adoption of such schemes and contracts is not without impact on the market uptake, which may be either positive or negative depending on the clinical or the financial outcomes. The direct and indirect impacts on sales and implications of MAAs will be presented in this section based on actual cases.

### An Example of Multiple Sclerosis (MS) Biologic Drugs MAAs in the UK

This is an example of how sales are impacted by MAAs, showing how the "Patient Access Scheme" led to UK sales being the lowest in the EU5 (the UK, Germany, France, Spain and Italy). In 2004, uptake was very slow; 20% of eligible patients were still waiting to see a specialist doctor and only 8% of MS patients received disease-modifying treatment (Figure 4.5). By 2007, there were 11.5% of MS patients receiving treatment in the UK vs. 35% in Western Europe and 50% in the US, implying that the market access agreement for MS biologic drugs did not help British patients' access (Figure 4.6).

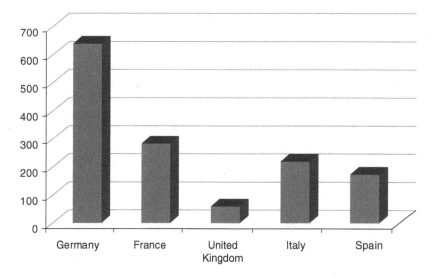

*Figure 4.5* Sales of disease-modifying drugs affected by PAS in the UK (computed by the authors from IMS data sources)

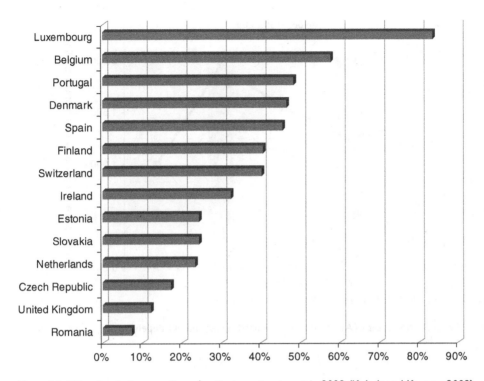

*Figure 4.6* MS estimated proportion of patients on treatment in 2008 (Kobelt and Kasteng 2009)

### Example of Bevacizumab's Uptake in Metastatic Colorectal Cancer (mCRC) Across the EU

Utilization rates of Avastin in mCRC varied across the EU, depending on HTA and funding schemes. Funding based on disease-related group (DRG) and lower price in France resulted in a higher utilization rate, while the same type of funding at a higher price in Germany resulted in relatively low usage of Avastin. MAA based on payment by performance in Italy allowed faster penetration and higher price, while the lack of NICE's recommendation in the UK caused virtually no use. While this is based on common sense, the example is well illustrated in Figure 4.7.

Another example (Figure 4.8) shows that bevacizumab uptake in Italy would have been much slower without a risk-sharing scheme for the drug.

Also in France, early uptake (prior to EMA license) was made possible due to ATU (pre-registration usage authorization) and unrestricted funding based on DRGs.

### Enbrel (Etanercept)

Other collaborative agreements to improve compliance may enhance patients' access. An example is the MAA that was adopted in Germany for Etanercept (Enbrel®) for rheumatoid arthritis between Wyeth pharmaceuticals and the third largest statutory health insurance (SHI) fund in Germany (Taunus BKK) in 2008. Wyeth would agree

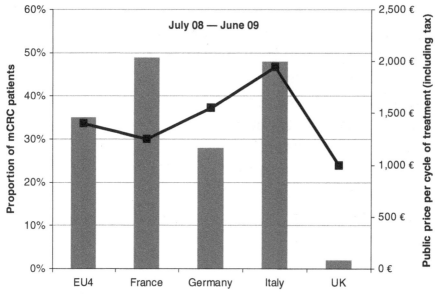

Toumi M., et al Atlanta 2009 mCRC-metastatic colorectal cancer

*Figure 4.7* Utilization rates of Avastin in mCRC varied across the EU, depending on HTA and funding schemes

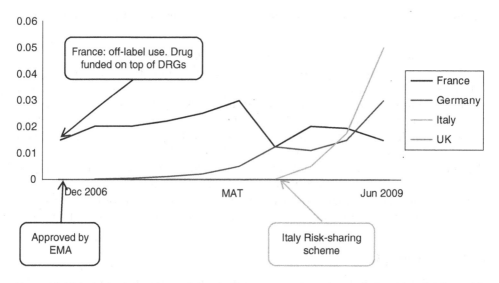

*Figure 4.8* Risk-sharing schemes can dramatically impact uptake and use in Italy, analysis performed by the authors from Synovate database

to fund and provide compliance support to patients taking Enbrel, which in turn would significantly improve the treatment's effectiveness. Being an injectable drug, Enbrel's effectiveness would greatly depend on patients' compliance. In fact, one third of patients will discontinue the treatment within the first three months due partly to lack of compliance.

The company offered a telephone support service, homecare visits by qualified nurses, and the promotion of regular patient communications about treatment, as well as tips on how to self-inject and the importance of maintaining therapy.

This scheme allowed patients to become more compliant with the treatment and to remain on treatment for a longer time, thus experiencing a more effective treatment. "Since the scheme, Enbrel has shown a more positive sales trend than its competitors and Wyeth has expanded the deal to over 100 other German sick funds, with some even eliminating co-payments on the drug to improve uptake" (Pugatch *et al.* 2010).

## Some Specific Case Studies

### Example of Performance-based Model in the UK: Use of β Interferons and Glatiramer for the Treatment of MS

A most prominent example of a risk-sharing concept based on the conditional demonstration of a drug's effectiveness and efficiency in real life (CED) is this agreement between the payers and the pharmaceutical industry, which was asked to demonstrate its claims in terms of the impact of the treatment on quality of life and its efficiency, measured by an incremental cost-effectiveness ratio per QALY (quality-adjusted life year).

In its initial appraisal, NICE refused to fund the β interferons in the treatment of MS on clinical and cost-effectiveness grounds (the calculated cost/QALY was £42,000 to £98,000 over 20 years and would rise to a maximum of £780,000/QALY over 5 years).

Under external pressure, in 2002 the government established a scheme with the four manufacturers where a cohort of approximately 10,000 patients would be followed for over 10 years with the cost of drugs reduced or refunds given if the cost/QALY over an envisaged 20-year horizon was more than £35,000/QALY, i.e. fund a maximum value of £35,000/QALY or less (Adamski *et al.* 2010). Patients would be followed using the Kurtzke Expanded Disability Status Scale (EDSS), which was the same outcome measure used in the trials.

The initial assessment, published in 2002, highlighted important issues concerning the study's methodology, insisting on the need to have longer-term follow-ups before securing meaningful results (NICE 2002). The patients included in this study had initiated treatment from May 2002 to April 2005.

In this case, the agreement restricted access and led to much lower usage rates than the drugs would have achieved otherwise with positive recommendation from NICE. In fact, the UK ranked 13 out of 14 developed countries for use of new disease-modifying drugs in 2010 despite the agreement being in place since 2002 (Toumi and Michel 2011).

This experimental CED for MS drugs in UK was inconclusive at seven years from its launch, and the scheme was heavily criticized for a number of reasons, which payers need to consider for future scheme evaluations. These include (Adamski *et al.* 2010) the following:

- The model:
  - Flaws in the actual model (difficulties in fully mapping out the quality of life and natural history of MS to the trial outcomes, which were based on changes in EDSS scores).
  - Concerns that the model was heavily influenced by assumptions about future discounting and did not account, for example, for the cost of azathioprine.
  - The model did not appear to fully account for patients discontinuing treatment early because of side effects.
- The length of follow-up:
  - Concerns that within ten years the β interferons and glatiramer acetate might have been replaced by newer drugs, counteracting the whole rationale behind the scheme.
- Funding and administration support:
  - Primary care trusts generally did not receive any additional funding to cover the cost of these drugs.
  - Hospitals also did not receive additional funding for more extensive follow-up consultations and for completing the necessary forms, reducing their involvement in practice.
  - Concerns generally with the necessary infrastructure required, including specialist nurses, as well as concerns over where the funding of the additional administrative burden would come from.

### Three Examples of CEDs in France

Three requests of the French Haute Autorité de Santé (HAS) for real-life comparative studies were identified. These were expected to reduce uncertainty about drugs' real-life performance and enable final pricing.

In 2005, the French pricing committee CEPS (Comité économique des produits de santé) asked the manufacturer of the injectable antipsychotic risperidone (RisperdalConsta LP) to perform a one-year study that should demonstrate evidence of reduction in the rate of hospitalizations for patients treated with this drug as compared with other antipsychotics (to be designed under the supervision of the Ministry of Health) (HAS 2010a; Renaudin 2010). This escrow MAA assumed that while the drug would be granted a premium list price (approximately 15-fold premium versus generic injectable LP antipsychotics, and almost 60% versus oral risperidone from Janssen Cilag), the company would be paid based on the price of the cheapest comparator. Then, the difference would be deposited as public funds with the Caisse des Dépôts et Consignations until results from the study were available. Should the results show evidence of reduction in hospitalization rate, money would be transferred to the company. Otherwise, social security services would receive the funds.

Another MAA requested by CEPS and the Transparency Commission in 2004 was a real-life use study for glitazones (pioglitazone and rosiglitazone) in type 2 diabetes.

This two-year observational study intended to develop evidence that would support or invalidate the manufacturer's claim of a superior real-life efficacy (time to introduction of an add-on therapy) as compared with what was previously observed in clinical trials.

In 2006, Xolair's launch in France was conditional upon conducting a study that would demonstrate a positive impact in real life. The prospective study was conducted on a cohort of 1,000 patients who were followed for two years (HAS 2012). The main criterion was the onset of a severe asthma exacerbation defined by at least one of the following events: hospitalization, ER visit, oral corticoid prescription, and increase in oral corticoid dose by at least 20 mg equivalent prednisone.

Five years after the initial HAS ruling of minor improvement of clinical benefit (Amélioration du Service Médical Rendu (ASMR) IV) for Risperdal Consta LP, the requested study provided evidence that in a cohort of more than 1,600 patients followed for 1 year, patients treated with the drug had a lower relative risk of hospitalization as compared with other antipsychotics (HAS 2010a). Thus, the premium list price was maintained.

Similarly, results of Xolair's study showed real-life benefit with a better control of persistent severe asthma in terms of prescriptions and hospitalizations and/or ER visits (44% decrease) (HAS 2012).

On the contrary, the observational study for rosiglitazone (AVANCE) did not support the manufacturer's claims of a superior real-life efficacy, as the study largely repeated the efficacy data, which had been shown in clinical trials (Renaudin 2010; HAS 2010b). Consequently, the pricing committee CEPS cut the drug's price by 30% and requested rebates for the drugs that had already been purchased. The reimbursement level also dropped from 65% to 35%. The actual amounts of the rebates were not published by the HAS, however.

### Two Examples of CEDs in Sweden

The Swedish TLV uses cost-effectiveness analysis to inform its decision making, thus it will not recommend reimbursement of drugs that show uncertain or high ICER value (depending on a specific disease threshold).

Two CEDs implemented in Sweden are worth mentioning:

1. Levodopa/carbidopa's (Duodopa®) went through a temporary (five-year) MAA aimed at generating real-life evidence that would allow a reduction of the value of ICER and uncertainty around it, and help achieve the final pricing path and reimbursement in Sweden (Persson 2010; TLV 2008). Briefly, at the time of initial manufacturer submission, while the product was granted provisional reimbursement at a premium price, the follow-up studies and additional cost-effectiveness analyses allowed TLV to give a positive final reimbursement decision and premium price.
2. Rimonabant, a drug used in the treatment of obesity, was granted provisional reimbursement status for two years. At the end, TLV's final decision was conditional on providing additional data that would evidence cost-effectiveness of the drug as well as long-term effects in real practice (TLV 2006 and 2008; Persson *et al.* 2010).

These two CEDs enabled the payer to collect evidence that led to re-evaluation of the real-life cost-effectiveness of concerned drugs, and final reimbursement and pricing decisions were delivered. Following these decisions, the drugs were financed without employing any further MAA.

### Example of MAAs in Italy

Sixty-one various MAAs on oncology drugs were identified in Italy until May 2015, but there were no detailed technology appraisals available on AIFA's website (AIFA 2010). The MAAs involved "cost sharing" and/or pay-backs for non-responding patients (100% or 50% of the drug's cost, all on a per-patient basis).

While the drugs' safety and efficacy were monitored in patient registries, it is note-worthy that those MAAs did not seek to address uncertainty about a clearly specified health outcome, and data collection in the registries seemed not systematic with a high potential for various biases (Gallo and Deambrosis 2008).

In contrast, the CRONOS project launched by AIFA to evaluate real-life effec-tiveness of Alzheimer's disease drugs (donepezil, rivastigmine and galantamine) col-lected and analyzed well-defined health outcomes from a cohort of patients. It was carried out in a nationally representative sample of patients with Alzheimer's disease over a period of two years. The state reimbursed medicines only in patients who responded at four months of treatment (while the cost for non-responders was cov-ered by manufacturers) (AIFA 2000; Adamski et al. 2010).

AIFA announced that following an analysis of patients' registries, which were a part of P4P and commercial agreements for expensive cancer drugs, it would reduce their list price by 30–40% in 2011 (Jack 2010). While scheduled price revision was assumed at the launch of these P4P schemes, they had not been designed to address uncertainty about (cost-effectiveness of) the drugs and it is unlikely that the registry data had the sufficient quality to provide more robust estimates than those available at the drugs' launch.

The Italian CED for Alzheimer's disease drugs (CRONOS) provided new real-life effectiveness data and allowed AIFA to reimburse these medicines, with some restric-tions with respect to diagnosis and continuation of treatment and prescription lim-ited to specialist physicians (AIFA 2004).

In conclusion of the above case studies, the payers had a diversity of approaches towards how to sponsor provision of the drug for patients during its CED testing period. In France, drugs in one CED were financed by the payer at a premium price, but in case of unfavourable results, the difference between the cost of a cheaper com-parator and the premium price was returned to the payer. In Sweden, the drugs were financed at a premium price, and in Italy at a premium price with payment limited to patients who responded to treatment (for the CRONOS MAA). In the UK, the MS disease-modifying drugs were financed at a premium price, but the scheme assumed sliding reduction of the price as soon as unfavourable interim evidence from the CED became available.

## Overview of MAA Trends in Other Countries

MAAs hold a certain amount of confidentiality, and it is difficult to determine the exact number and details of the agreements in place in various countries. Most of the information presented below for each country was extracted from the

Espín *et al.* (2011) report prepared on MAAs in different European countries based on results from a survey, literature review, conferences and other grey literature for the European Commission. In other countries such as Latin American countries and Australia, information was extracted from published literature.

## MAA is a Growing Phenomenon in Various Countries

As mentioned previously, risk-sharing agreements have been increasing in recent years, with 148 risk-sharing agreements between 1993 and 2013. The country with the greatest number of new agreements was the UK (40%), with Italy and Australia among other important markets. A significant number of other countries are also beginning to see MAAs, such as New Zealand, Belgium, Poland and Hungary (Carlson *et al.* 2014).

## MAAs in Australia

Australia is one of the countries in which MAAs have been expanding rapidly (Wonder 2013). Indeed, as at "30 June 2012, there were 76 deeds of agreement in place or in development" (DHA 2012; Wonder 2013).

In 2012, 15 new drugs were listed, of which 8 received a recommendation for an MAA by the Pharmaceutical Benefits Advisory Committee (PBAC). It was noted that seven of the eight were recommended fully or in part on an incremental cost-effectiveness analysis basis, suggesting that "it is highly likely that a new medicine recommended by the PBAC on an incremental cost-effectiveness analysis basis will be associated with a RSA". Among the eight drugs, three of them were indicated in oncology, two were for Hepatitis C and one was recommended for an orphan indication (Wonder 2013).

No detailed information was given on the type of MAA recommended, except for sapropterin hydrochloride (an orphan drug in phenylketonuria), where it was specified that the PBAC recommended an agreement with a 100% rebate in case the number of patients with BH4 deficiency should exceed 20. There were only 12 patients treated with sapropterin in Australia in 2011–2012 (Wonder 2013).

## MAAs in Latin America

Health technology assessment has started developing recently in Latin American countries, especially with the creation of a new HTA network in the Americas (Red de Evaluación de Tecnologís Sanitarias) by the Organizacion Panamericana del Salud (Pan-American Health Organization), basically to address the fragmentation of the health care systems in the region and the lack of resources and expertise for some countries. This has boosted the development of HTA in Latin America.

Cuba, Brazil, and Mexico have recently developed and published methodological guidelines in economic evaluation, indicating that there is a growing interest in evaluating health-related products, drugs, and technologies used by the population (Banda 2009; ISPOR 2012). However, until now in these countries, decisions regarding drug approval have been made on the basis of efficacy and safety, and not on cost.

So far, these countries have no experience in P4P contracts or conditional reimbursement. Only in Brazil have discussions regarding these programs started. However, according to current Brazilian regulations, risk-sharing negotiations are not allowed, though this might potentially change in the next few years. It is expected that the P4P will develop fast in Latin America as increasing forums and discussions at authorities' levels are ongoing.

### MAAs in India: Different Market Access Pathway

A study explored the opportunity of implementing MAAs in India using desk and primary research interview of key stakeholders (Kirpekar 2012). The author concluded that it was difficult to implement such agreements in India.

Results from the desk and primary research showed the following:

- Recent developments in India, including the introduction of compulsory licensing for sorefanib, may generate greater pressure on the pharmaceutical industry to reduce price.
- Physicians consider most of the current patient access schemes, with a few exceptions, as marketing schemes rather than genuine patient assistance programs. Only those schemes implemented closely with locally based foundations/cancer institutes are considered by physicians to be true assistance programs.
- Existing hurdles for patient access schemes that were identified by the majority of respondents are:
  - bureaucracy and the informal economy (which creates difficulties with means-testing) – these are the two most important reasons for the schemes not "taking off";
  - general ignorance about the potential of such schemes and cynicism surrounding them;
  - unethical medical practice, knowledge gap and a lack of streamlined infrastructure for scheme delivery.

"Establishing cost-sharing schemes in India remains a challenge because of the fractured infrastructure, porous supply-chain and unethical medical practice" (Kirpekar 2012).

### MAAs in South Korea

Market access for oncology drugs in South Korea was compared with that of Australia and the UK through a review of HTAs (Espín *et al.* 2011). These showed that the South Korean HTA process was new and not well defined, and that the pharmaco-economic assessment was still evolving.

While cost-effectiveness is the main driver for a positive recommendation, South Korea's approach appears to be less rigorous and mainly aimed at financial agreements such as price discounts and price–volume agreements, which play a major role in determining reimbursement (Saraf and Akpinar 2012).

### Other Asian Countries

In Asian countries such as Indonesia, Malaysia, China, etc., access to medication is predominantly from out-of-pocket funding, and despite this, "patient-pay access schemes" are being increasingly used through some specific private or institutional insurers.

## Perspectives

### MAAs are a Growing Trend and are Shifting towards Conditional Access

Since 2003, there has been a steady growth in MAAs, with approximately 148 separate agreements in 2013 (Carlson *et al.* 2014). However, there are probably even more MAAs put in place every year as most are private agreements and are not publicly disclosed. It is not known whether these agreements correspond to one or ten new molecules every year, as very little information regarding these schemes is made publicly available.

While commercial agreements and P4Ps have the potential to incur savings for individual national payers, care should be taken so that the real cost of purchasing drugs in MAAs, rather than their list price, is what should be increasingly used for international reference pricing in Europe (Jaroslawski and Toumi 2011).

Individual patient P4P has proven difficult to implement and manage because it incurs an administrative burden on hospitals, which already suffer from lack of resources. Ideally, such agreements should be for a limited time until there is sufficient real-life evidence to confirm the value of the products or to address the uncertainty. However, in most cases these agreements last throughout the product's life cycle, and the rationale for maintaining them is unclear. CED meanwhile, which has grown the in Nordic countries, the Netherlands, and France, seems to represent a powerful tool for reducing the uncertainty about a drug's real-life performance. Every question or issue raised could lead to a specific study. This procedure allows rapid market access for new molecules or interventions, without having to wait for the company to generate evidences, thus giving patients a chance to access innovative treatments earlier. Moreover, it does not hypothecate the payer's budget thanks to the escrow agreement. Consequently, CED is bound to develop in most countries as a reference tool for managing payers' uncertainty.

On the other side, P4P seems to be gradually reaching its limits, whereas commercial agreements are becoming adjustment variables for list prices in order to define the price that will satisfy all parties without affecting international reference pricing. At this stage this is pure speculation from the authors based on their personal experiences and interactions with payers. Different geographical areas may have different appreciations, as such, it may be very true for France and less so for Italy.

Today in the UK, all PASs are just financial discounts that are aimed at bringing down the net price to a level that makes the drug cost-effective for the NHS. These PASs are now confidential, making it impossible for third parties to know the actual net price. This prevents external reference pricing using the net price, restricted instead to using the listed price.

A shift is foreseen, moving from where regulatory approvals and market access are achieved through a decision point, towards a decision window through conditional approvals and conditional access. CED comes at a cost, which is mostly covered by the industry, whereas in P4P agreements most of the (hidden) cost is covered by the payer, such as the NHS. Parallel advice and regulatory adaptive pathway may become a new way to address uncertainty associated with market access for highly innovative products with a large benefit-effect size.

### Future of MAAs

Some authors foresee the use of MAAs only in specific situations. For instance, de Pouvourville (2006) considers that MAAs will be useful only in a specific setting, i.e. for innovative drugs where there is little competition, and which target very specific populations for which it is more obtainable to demonstrate a benefit claim. Likewise, Adamski *et al.* (2010) believe there are only a limited number of situations in which risk-sharing schemes should be considered in the future, and describe the key issues that payers need to take into consideration.

Situations where MAAs would work are:

- a novel treatment in a high-priority disease area with an expected net health gain;
- new drugs that are effective in priority disease, but with potential concerns about long-term safety;
- new drugs that could have a substantial beneficial impact on service delivery and patient safety; however, this has been difficult to prove in phase III trials;
- likely health gain that can be determined within a limited time frame;
- proposed PAS in priority disease areas would substantially lower health service costs to enhance reimbursement, having factored in all administrative costs (Adamski *et al.* 2010).

## Conclusion: Are MAAs a Temporary Solution?

There are numerous challenges in the current health care environment: the economic crisis has been only partially resolved, HTA processes are becoming more complex, criteria for benefit recognition are changing, and the regions' hurdles are increasing as budget holders are held responsible for the deficit. All these issues necessitate a number of changes.

### Paradigm Shift in the Pharmaceutical Industry

Originally, risk-sharing agreements were non-written: and in the pre-marketing period, the company would endorse the development risk while in the post-marketing phase it was the payer who would endorse the post-marketing risk. In the new risk-sharing agreements however, it is the company that endorses both pre- and post-marketing risk through P4P, CED, etc. It is therefore a shift towards an insurance business model.

### From Decision Point to Decision Window

In more and more countries, pricing and reimbursement decisions are no longer made at a fixed time point but over a period of time during which pharmaceutical companies are expected to provide additional information to reduce any uncertainty around the value of a new product.

It is a general fact that risk-averse attitudes have increased in the majority of countries where approvals have become conditional. Recently, regulators have been dealing with three main facts: conditional approvals, the lack of efficacy now considered as an adverse event (and as such, to be reported by prescribers), and risk management plans that have been instituted to track the lack of efficacy as one of the potential adverse events. The first two are relatively more recent in the EU compared to the US, and effectiveness has become a potential outcome of a risk management plan.

Therefore, there has been a move from a decision point for regulatory approval, pricing and market access decisions towards a time frame that has turned into a decision window, which is well illustrated by CED. This allows regulators and payers to minimize the risk associated with the introduction of a new product, while also contributing to the increased dialogue between regulators and payers. More and more, risk management plans will bolster payers' insight and CED will bolster regulators' insight.

### Which MAA in the Future?

Of the three main types of MAA described above;

- CED will probably continue to expand and multiply. It is the most promising agreement as it diminishes uncertainty, while moving towards a value-based pricing, and constitutes an incentive for the pharmaceutical companies for R&D.
- Commercial agreements will remain attractive as long as there will be international reference pricing, in order to maintain a good listed price.
- P4Ps will probably gradually decrease, because it does not support a robust concept that brings an added value (e.g. effectiveness). It is also difficult to monitor and incurs a high administrative burden. Some companies may be tempted to offer a P4P to obtain a discount without actually using the term discount.

The potential impact of MAAs is that they will allow for managing some of the uncertainties and fine tune commercial agreements. However, MAAs do not address the issue of affordability, and public health priorities. Moreover, there are a number of challenges with MAAs which are difficult to implement as they may increase burden and costs.

Some changes have been witnessed with regard to the tools that support decision making, such as managing the risk on an ongoing basis, anticipating at all levels of go/no-go decision the room for access, and developing real-world data-analysis capability.

Another interesting aspect is the question of how MAAs will integrate with adaptive pathways. On the one hand, adaptive pathways would anticipate marketing authorization for a limited population sub-group, provided that real-world data are collected (i.e. implicitly implying something similar to MAA), and on the other hand, once a product has gained full approval, real-world data have been collected already and only commercial agreements may be justified.

Hence, it is not precluded that MAAs might experience further evolution in the coming years, with the increasing pressures for better health and right prices, and the growing dynamics of interrelated drug markets (reference pricing, etc.).

## References

Adamski, J., Godman, B., Ofierska-Sujkowska, G., *et al.* (2010). Risk sharing arrangements for pharmaceuticals: Potential considerations and recommendations for European payers. *BMC Health Service Research*, 10, 153.

AIFA, Agenzia Italiana del Farmaco (2000). Protocollo di monitoraggio dei piani di trattamento farmacologico per la malattia di Alzheimer (available online at: www.agenziafarmaco.gov.it/wscs_render_attachment_by_id/111.72724.11504520512382ba1.pdf ?id=111.72754.1150452053514).

AIFA, Agenzia Italiana del Farmaco (2004). Progetto Cronos: i risultati dello studio osservazionale (available online at: www.agenziafarmaco.gov.it/it/content/progetto-cronos-i-risultati-dello-studio-osservazionale).

AIFA, Agenzia Italiana del Farmaco (2010). Oncology registries.

Ando, G., Reinaud, F. and Bharath, A. (2011). Global pharmaceutical risk-sharing agreement trends in 2010 and 2011. *Value in Health*, 14, PHP148.

Banda, D. (2009). Health technology assessment in Latin America and the Caribbean. *International Journal of Technology Assessment in Health Care*, 25, 253–4.

Barros, P.P. (2011). The simple economics of risk-sharing agreements between the NHS and the pharmaceutical industry. *Health Economics*, 20, 461–70.

Boggild, M., Palace, J., Barton, P., *et al.* (2009). Multiple sclerosis risk sharing scheme: Two year results of clinical cohort study with historical comparator. *British Medical Journal (Clinical Research Edition)*, 339, b4677.

Carlson, J.J., Gries, K.S., Yeung, K., *et al.* (2014). Current status and trends in performance-based risk-sharing arrangements between healthcare payers and medical product manufacturers. *Applied Health Economics and Health Policy*, 12, 231–8.

Carlson, J.J., Sullivan, S.D., Garrison, L.P., *et al.* (2010). Linking payment to health outcomes: A taxonomy and examination of performance-based reimbursement schemes between healthcare payers and manufacturers. *Health Policy*, 96, 179–90.

Compagni, A., Cavalli, L. and Jommi, C. (2008). Pharmaceutical companies and Italian Regional Governments: Managing relationships in an increasing institutional complexity. *Health Policy*, 87, 333–41.

de Pouvourville, G. (2006). Risk-sharing agreements for innovative drugs: A new solution to old problems? *European Journal of Health Economics*, 7, 155–7.

DHA, Department of Health and Ageing (2012). Annual Report 2011–2012 (available online at www.health.gov.au/internet/main/publishing.nsf/Content/annual-report2011-12).

Espín, J., Rovira, J. and García, L. (2011). Experiences and impact of European risk-sharing schemes focusing on oncology medicines. EMINET (available online at: http://whocc.goeg.at/Literaturliste/Dokumente/FurtherReading/Experiences%20and%20impact%20of%20European%20risk-sharing%20schemes.pdf).

Fattore, G. and Jommi, C. (2008). The last decade of Italian Pharmaceutical Policy: Instability or consolidation? *Pharmacoeconomics*, 26, 5–15.

Gallo, P.F. and Deambrosis, P. (2008). Pharmaceutical risk-sharing and conditional reimbursement in Italy. In Central and Eastern European Society of Technology Assessment in Health Care, CEESTAHC (available online at: www.ceestahc.org/pliki/symp2008/gallo.pdf).

Garrison, L.P., Towse, A., Briggs, A., *et al.* (2013). Performance-based risk-sharing arrangements – good practices for design, implementation and evaluation: Report of the ISPOR

Good Practices for Performance-Based Risk-Sharing Arrangements Task Force. *Value in Health*, 16, 703–19.

HAS, Haute Autorité de Santé (2010a). Avis de la Commission de la transparence – RISPERDALCONSTA L.P. (available online at: www.has-sante.fr/portail/upload/docs/application/pdf/2010-06/risperdalconsta_-_ct-7257.pdf).

HAS, Haute Autorité de Santé (2010b). Avis de la Commission de la transparence – AVANDIA (available online at: www.has-sante.fr/portail/upload/docs/application/pdf/2010–11/avandia_avandamet_-_ct-9105.pdf).

HAS, Haute Autorité de Santé (2012). Avis de la commission de transparence – XOLAIR (available online at: www.has-sante.fr/portail/upload/docs/application/pdf/2012-07/xolair_06062012_avis_ct10947_130712.pdf).

Hutton, J., Trueman, P. and Henshall, C. (2007). Coverage with evidence development: An examination of conceptual and policy issues. *International Journal of Technology Assessment in Health Care*, 23, 425–32.

ISPOR, International Society for Pharmacoeconomics and Outcomes Research (2012). Pharmacoeconomic guidelines around the world (available online at: www.ispor.org/peguidelines/index.asp).

Jack, A. (2010). Italy to cut cost of cancer drugs. *Financial Times*, London.

Jaroslawski, S. and Toumi, M. (2011). Market access agreements for pharmaceuticals in Europe: Diversity of approaches and underlying concepts. *BMC Health Service Research*, 11, 259.

Jommi, C. and Minghetti, P. (2015). Pharmaceutical pricing policies in Italy. In Babar, Zaheer-Ud-Din, (ed.). *Pharmaceutical Prices in the 21st Century*. Springer, London, pp. 131–50.

Jommi, C., Costa, E., Michelon, A., *et al.* (2013). Multi-tier drugs assessment in a decentralised health care system. The Italian case-study. *Health Policy*, 112, 241–7.

Kirpekar, S. (2012). Failure for cost-sharing schemes to take off in India: What can be the access solution? *Value in Health*, 15, A628.

Kobelt, G. and Kasteng, F. (2009). Access to innovative treatments in multiple sclerosis in Europe. A report prepared for the European Federation of Pharmaceutical Industry Associations – EFPIA (available online at: www.comparatorreports.se/Access%20to%20MS%20treatments%20-%20October%202009.pdf).

Mora-Ripoll, R., Gilabert-Perramon, A., Espinosa-Tome, C., *et al.* (2014). Guidance for risk sharing agreements/pay per results schemes for pharmaceuticals in Catalonia (Spain). *Value in Health*, 17, A447.

Morel, T., Arickx, F., Befrits, G., *et al.* (2013). Reconciling uncertainty of costs and outcomes with the need for access to orphan medicinal products: A comparative study of managed entry agreements across seven European countries. *Orphanet Journal of Rare Diseases*, 8, 198.

NHS Quality Improvement Scotland (2008). Coverage with evidence development in NHS Scotland – Discussion paper November 2008 (available online at: www.healthcareimprovementscotland.org/previous_resources/hta_report/evidence_development_in_nhssco.aspx).

NICE, National Institute for Health and Care Excellence (2002). NICE Technology Appraisal Guidance TA32 – beta interferon and glatiramer acetate for the treatment of multiple sclerosis (available online at: www.nice.org.uk/Guidance/TA32).

Persson, U. (2010). European Market Access University Diploma. Paris, 2010. European Market Access Environment. The Swedish Experience.

Persson, U., Willis, M. and Odegaard, K. (2010). A case study of ex-ante, value-based price and reimbursement decision-making: TLV and rimonabant in Sweden. *European Journal of Health Economics*, 11, 195–203.

Pickin, M., Cooper, C.L., Chater, T., *et al.* (2009). The Multiple Sclerosis Risk Sharing Scheme Monitoring Study – early results and lessons for the future. *BMC Neurology*, 9, 1.

Pugatch, M., Healy, P. and Chu, R. (2010). *Sharing the Burden: Could risk-sharing change the way we pay for healthcare?* The Stockholm Network, London.

Renaudin, M.N. (2010). Risk sharing for reimbursement and pricing of drugs: The French practical example. *ISPOR Connections*, 16, September/October.

Russo, P., Mennini, F.S., Siviero, P.D. and Rasi, G. (2010). Time to market and patient access to new oncology products in Italy: A multistep pathway from European context to regional health care providers. *Annals of Oncology*, 21, 2081–7.

Saraf, S. and Akpinar, P. (2012). Similar HTA, different access outcome? Comparison of orphan oncology drug assessment in South Korea, Australia and the UK. *ISPOR 5th Asia-Pacific Conference*, September 2012, Taipei, Taiwan, PHP78.

Tediosi, F., Gabriele, S. and Longo, F. (2009). Governing decentralization in health care under tough budget constraint: What can we learn from the Italian experience? *Health Policy*, 90, 303–12.

TLV, Tandvårds- och läkemedelsförmånsverket (2006). Lakemedelsformansnamnden (LFN) Beslut (Decision) 1023/2006. Stockholm, 2006.

TLV, Tandvårds- och läkemedelsförmånsverket (2008). Lakemedelsformansnamnden (LFN) Beslut (Decision) 0625/2006. Stockholm, 2008.

Toumi, M. and Michel, M. (2011). Define access agreements. Published on Pharmaceutical Market Europe (available online at: www.pmlive.com/Europe).

Toumi, M., Flostrand, S. and Millier, A. (2011). Segmentation of regional payers. *Journal of Medical Marketing: Device, Diagnostic and Pharmaceutical Marketing*, 11, 244–53.

Towse, A. and Garrison, L.P. (2010). Can't get no satisfaction? Will pay for performance help? Toward an economic framework for understanding performance-based risk-sharing agreements for innovative medical products. *Pharmacoeconomics*, 28, 93–102.

Wonder, M. (2013). PBAC recommendations and risk sharing arrangements – when does an optional extra become a standard accessory? (Available online at: http://pbacandrsas.blogspot.fr/#!).

# Chapter 5

# Coverage of Orphan Drugs

*Thomas Morel and Steven Simoens*

## Introduction

According to European Union legislation, an orphan drug is a medicinal product intended for a rare disease or a medicinal product that would not be developed without incentives because its sales are unlikely to generate sufficient return on investment. An additional requirement to qualify as an orphan drug is that no satisfactory method exists to diagnose, prevent or treat the disease, or if such a method exists, that the medicinal product will be of significant benefit to those affected by that disease (European Commission 2000). Orphan drugs are used to manage rare diseases, which are life-threatening or chronically debilitating diseases with a prevalence of 5 out of 10,000 individuals or less.

In an increasing number of European countries, economic evaluation is used to inform pharmaceutical coverage decisions, within health technology assessment. How can this be carried out? First, the results of an economic evaluation are expressed in the form of an incremental cost-effectiveness ratio. This ratio relates the difference in costs between the drug and the comparator to the difference in effectiveness. The effectiveness can be expressed, for example, by quality-adjusted life years, a measure that accounts for both quantity of life and quality of life. The incremental cost-effectiveness ratio is then compared with a threshold incremental cost-effectiveness ratio. The threshold ratio corresponds with the maximum cost per unit of health that a health care payer is willing to pay for a drug. Thus, a health care payer is likely to accept a drug that exhibits an incremental cost-effectiveness ratio below the threshold value and is likely to refuse a drug that has a ratio exceeding the threshold value (Simoens 2010a). Also, drugs that are more cost-effective are rewarded by means of a more favour able coverage.

## Health Technology Assessment of Orphan Drugs

Health technology assessment is an important requirement that exists in several European countries and is now also increasingly applied elsewhere. Health technology assessment can be defined as a "multidisciplinary process that summarises information about the medical, social, economic and ethical issues related to the use of a health technology in a systematic, transparent, unbiased, robust manner. Its aim is to inform the formulation of safe, effective, health policies that are patient focused and seek to achieve best value" (EUnetHTA 2012). The end product of the health technology assessment process is the coverage decision.

In the case of orphan drugs, economic evaluation within the health technology assessment framework may (e.g. in England and Wales, Scotland, the Netherlands or Sweden) or may not (e.g. in France or Belgium) be applied (Denis *et al.* 2009; Denis *et al.* 2010). Ideally, the health technology assessment process to guide the coverage decision of an orphan drug should consider multiple criteria that reflect the specific characteristics of orphan drugs (see below). Such decision-making criteria may include the rarity and the severity of the disease (i.e. the unmet need), the availability of alternative health technologies, the impact of the orphan drug on the disease (i.e. whether the drug's objective is symptomatic, palliative, or to modify the disease), the use of an orphan drug in a single or in multiple indications, the level, quality and uncertainty of clinical evidence and research undertaken, and the manufacturing complexity involved in producing the orphan drug (Hughes-Wilson *et al.* 2012).

Multi-criteria decision analysis allows decision makers to consider multiple dimensions in the coverage decision (Hughes-Wilson *et al.* 2012). Under this approach, an expert panel identifies and quantifies the relative importance of the relevant decision-making criteria. The degree to which an orphan drug attains each criterion is then assessed. The scores of an orphan drug on the different criteria are aggregated with a view to calculating the overall performance of the orphan drug. Decision makers then allocate resources based on the ranking of drugs according to their performance scores until the budget is exhausted (Baltussen and Niessen 2006; Simoens 2010b).

The nature of health technology assessment varies between European countries both in terms of the assessment of the evidence and the appraisal focus of the evidence, as well as in the role of health technology assessment within each health care system. For example, if we consider a sample of orphan drugs approved by the European Medicines Agency and then evaluated by a few European health technology assessment bodies and/or payers to decide on their coverage, it is striking to realize to what extent access decisions for the very same orphan drug may differ from one country to another (Table 5.1).

For instance, dasatinib (Sprycel®) was designated as an orphan medicinal product in 2005 and was granted the European marketing authorization the following year for the treatment of "adult patients with newly diagnosed Philadelphia-chromosome-positive chronic myelogenous leukaemia in the chronic phase" and "adult patients with chronic, accelerated or blast phase myelogenous leukaemia with resistance or intolerance to prior therapy including imatinib mesylate". Four health technology assessment bodies (namely the Scottish Medicines Consortium, the French Haute Autorité de Santé, the Dutch College voor Zorgverzekeringen, and the National Institute for Health and Clinical Excellence for England and Wales) then reviewed the value of dasatinib in the second therapeutic indication mentioned above and appraised it quite differently. While the review outcomes from the French and Dutch health technology assessment bodies were positive, the Scottish institution recommended its restricted use to a sub-population and finally the English institution ruled out its use entirely.

This brief analysis on diverging health technology assessment decision outcomes may reflect different societal and health care system priorities, but ultimately creates a

Table 5.1 Examples of diverging health technology assessment decision outcomes in a sample of orphan drugs

| Compound (brand name, manufacturer) | Indication | Scotland (SMC) appraisal | | France (HAS) appraisal | | Netherlands (CVZ) appraisal | | England & Wales (NICE) appraisal | |
|---|---|---|---|---|---|---|---|---|---|
| | | Year | Outcome | Year | Outcome | Year | Outcome | Year | Outcome |
| Alglucosidase alfa (**Myozyme®, Genzyme**) | Pompe disease | 2007 | Not recommended | 2006 | ASMR II | 2006 | Recommended | | n.a. |
| Anagrelide (**Xagrid®, Shire**) | Reduction of elevated platelet counts in "at risk" patients with essential thrombocythaemia | 2005 | Recommended | 2005 | ASMR IV | 2005 | Restricted | | n.a. |
| Dasatinib (**Sprycel®, BMS**) | Chronic, accelerated or blast phase CML with resistance or intolerance to prior therapy including imatinib mesilate | 2007 | Restricted | 2007 | ASMR II | 2007 | Recommended | 2012 | Not recommended |
| Imatinib (**Glivec®, Novartis**) | Chronic myeloid leukaemia | 2003 | Restricted | 2002 | ASMR I | 2001 | Recommended | 2003 | Recommended |
| Lenalidomide (**Revlimid®, Celgene**) | Multiple myeloma | 2008 | Not recommended | 2007 | ASMR III | 2007 | Restricted | 2009 | Recommended |
| Sorafenib (**Nexavar®, Bayer**) | Renal cell carcinoma | 2006 | Not recommended | 2006 | ASMR II | 2006 | Restricted | 2009 | Not recommended |
| Trabectedin (**Yondelis®, PharmaMar**) | Advanced soft tissue sarcoma | 2008 | Not recommended | 2008 | ASMR V | 2008 | Not recommended | 2010 | Recommended |

n.a.: not assessed (NB: unlike the SMC, the HAS and the CVZ, NICE does not appraise every new health technology, but appraises those agreed with the UK Department of Health) potential for inequitable access to orphan needs across European countries, for patients with the same condition. The current standard health technology assessment process may be ill-suited for some orphan drugs, as it tends to magnify the uncertainty in efficacy which is often more common in orphan drugs due to accelerated regulatory requirements allowing for early filing.

## Economic Evaluation of Orphan Drugs

In the jurisdictions where pharmaco-economic evaluation is a key element of the health technology assessment process, orphan drugs are unlikely to be cost-effective when their incremental cost-effectiveness ratio is compared with a threshold value (e.g. the threshold of £20,000–30,000 per quality-adjusted life year used by NICE (Drummond et al. 2007; Rawlins and Cuyler 2004). This is because orphan drugs tend to have low volume with high prices in combination with uncertainty over their effectiveness. This implies that coverage of an orphan drug may improve the clinical outcomes of patients suffering from the rare disease, but coverage would generate a decrease in population health that is larger than the improvement in the outcomes of patients using the orphan drug (Simoens et al. 2012). In turn, this raises the question of whether society needs to provide incentives to the pharmaceutical industry to develop orphan drugs when the costs surpass the value that society attaches to the health benefits produced by orphan drugs (opportunity cost) (McCabe et al. 2005).

In order to answer this question, some other characteristics of orphan drugs need to be noted (Simoens 2011). First, orphan drug coverage is based on the principle of social solidarity in which vulnerable groups receive support. For instance, European Union legislation states that "patients suffering from rare conditions should be entitled to the same quality of treatment as other patients" (European Comission 2000). Second, orphan drugs tend to target life-threatening diseases for which an alternative therapy is unlikely to be available. For instance, treatment is estimated to be available for only 10% of rare diseases (Tambuyzer 2010). Of note, the absence or the unclear definition of a relevant comparator (because of the usually poor understanding of the natural history of the disease) or standard of care makes any economic modelling challenging. Furthermore, there is some evidence suggesting that individuals are willing to give up cost-effective treatments for common diseases in return for the provision of treatment to patients with a disease for which no alternative health technology exists (Nord 1993; Ubel and Loewenstein 1996). Third, in light of the often high prices, patients are unlikely to be able to afford orphan drug therapy if such drugs are not covered (Orofino et al. 2010). For instance, a study of the cost of muscular dystrophy in Australia showed that while some coverage of the standard of care was available from the Australian government, individuals with muscular dystrophy still had to bear one third of the financial costs, and their relatives a further 21% (Access Economics 2007). In general, the budget impact of orphan drugs is substantial: a study showed that the orphan drugs budget was expected to increase to 4.6% of total pharmaceutical expenditure in Europe by 2016 (Shey et al. 2011).

As a result, innovative schemes have been developed that take account of the specific characteristics of orphan drugs and that can inform the coverage decision more adequately by tackling the clinical and economic uncertainty of orphan drugs (Figure 5.1).

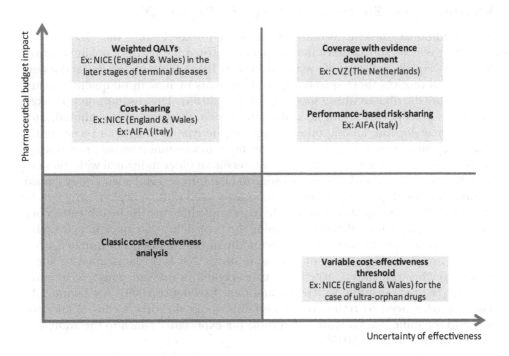

*Figure 5.1* Mechanisms for the management of the clinical and economic uncertainty of orphan drugs

## Variable Cost-Effectiveness Threshold for Orphan Drugs

One approach consists of selecting a higher value for the threshold incremental cost-effectiveness ratio for drugs to which society attaches a high social value (Drummond *et al.* 2007). As illustrated in Figure 5.1, it has been suggested that NICE establish an ultra-orphan drugs evaluation process and committee, which would be modelled on the existing conventional process but be tailored for ultra-orphan drugs. The reference incremental cost-effectiveness ratio would be developed from currently marketed ultra-orphan drugs that are in the range of £200,000–300,000 per quality-adjusted life year (i.e. a ten-fold increase on the decision rules currently applied in conventional appraisals) (National Institute for Health and Care Excellence 2006). In light of their specific characteristics, orphan drugs may attract a high social value, although future research needs to elicit social values ascribed to different drugs and other health technologies (Simoens 2010b), particularly to trade off "rarity" versus "non-rarity" for diseases with similar severity. This approach would increase the probability of an orphan drug being cost-effective and, therefore, the probability of receiving coverage. For instance, a review of Belgian coverage dossiers of orphan drugs suggested that a number of elements were considered by the Drug Reimbursement Committee, including price, employment opportunities, (restrictions on) the size of the patient population, the funding of diagnostic tests by the company, and (a reduction of) the dosage (Denis *et al.* 2011).

## Weighted Cost-Effectiveness Ratio for Orphan Drugs

The traditional health economics approach based on the incremental cost-effectiveness ratio assumes that "a quality-adjusted life year is a quality-adjusted life year is a quality-adjusted life year" (Weinstein 1988). This implies that it does not matter who receives those quality-adjusted life years or how those quality-adjusted life years are distributed within society (Simoens 2010b). This assumption is unlikely to hold in practice. According to a literature review, the value of a quality-adjusted life year may depend, among other things, on the type of individual receiving the quality-adjusted life year (e.g. patients suffering from a common versus a rare disease, or a young infant affected by a rare disease versus an older individual with the same rare disease) (Dolan *et al.* 2005). In order to take into account such equity considerations, weighted quality-adjusted life years associated with an orphan drug may be calculated. Weighted quality-adjusted life years would increase the health gain generated by an orphan drug, thereby increasing the probability that an orphan drug has an incremental cost-effectiveness ratio below the threshold value. For instance, when assessing the cost-effectiveness of end-of-life drugs, NICE recommended to attach greater weights to quality-adjusted life years accrued in the later stages of terminal diseases (National Institute for Health and Care Excellence 2009) (see Figure 5.1). These weights need to reflect the uncertainty about the drug's clinical effectiveness and the value that patients with a short life expectancy attach to the additional months of life (Simoens 2010b).

## Coverage with Evidence Development

Coverage with evidence development purports to tackle more directly the uncertainty around the clinical evidence supporting an orphan drug. The clinical evidence on orphan drugs tends to be limited relative to drugs aimed at common diseases (Dubois 2010; Dupont and Van Wilder 2011; Kesselheim 2010; Wild *et al.* 2011; Joppi *et al.* 2012) and is associated with uncertainty at product launch due to the fact that it is difficult to recruit a sufficient number of patients and medical centres in clinical trials and that many of the approved orphan drugs are based on surrogate endpoints only (e.g. time to progression, response rate, or progression-free survival) (Joppi *et al.* 2009). Also, orphan drug trials are sometimes halted early when an interim analysis demonstrates clinical superiority of the orphan medicine over the comparator in terms of an intermediate outcome measure (Simoens 2011).

In response to this, the US Centers for Medicare and Medicaid Services have issued guidance about so-called "coverage with evidence development", offering the option for drug coverage subject to the condition that further evidence about comparative effectiveness is gathered (Tunis and Pearson 2006). This, in essence, implies that initial coverage is granted based on surrogate outcome measures for a limited period of time subject to the commitment to further clinical investigation, which will inform the final coverage decision (Clarke 2006).

Coverage with evidence development schemes usually draws on patient registries of rare diseases in order to achieve a sufficient sample size and to collect the necessary data on the longer-term effectiveness and cost-effectiveness of orphan drugs (Owen *et al.* 2008). Setting up patient and disease registries is recommended by European

Union policy as they allow evidence to be gathered on the effectiveness of the treatment and are an action line in rare disease plans that many countries have in place (Doulet 2011; EUCERD 2012).

For example, in 2006 the Netherlands introduced a coverage with evidence development scheme in university hospitals, whereby access to a number of expensive orphan drugs (for inpatient use) is granted, while additional real-life effectiveness outcomes and health economics (e.g. resource use) data are generated to reduce the level of uncertainty around the drug. A budget impact greater than €0.6 million per annum was the main criterion to justify the inclusion of a new orphan drug into the scheme. In 2012, 11 orphan drugs (mostly enzyme-replacement products) were included in the Dutch scheme. The costs of the drugs in university hospitals are totally refunded for a maximum of four years. After this time frame, a re-evaluation takes place and the product may be listed permanently on the Dutch drug formulary. Recent developments illustrated the opposite situation where the Dutch Healthcare Board issued advice, on the basis of the outcome of a four-year coverage with evidence development programme, not to reimburse two orphan drugs that target lysosomal storage disorders, subsequently leading to public outcry (Simoens et al. 2013).

Because widespread approval of an orphan drug is not withheld until research findings are available, the Dutch scheme appears to be a balanced compromise, as patients get access to the new drug while the uncertainty around the clinical and economic dimensions is addressed by generating long-term effectiveness data. Other positive features of this scheme include the fact that is institutionalized by law and that it sets clear criteria for its implementation (i.e. uncertainty in effectiveness with a budget impact >0.6 million p.a.) and therefore applies only to "some" orphan drugs. Limitations of this national scheme, however, relate to the fact that it is country-specific. In a population of the size of one country such as the Netherlands, it is difficult to recruit a sufficient number of patients and to generate robust and unequivocal analyses on the effectiveness of a new health technology. The risk for patients to be denied the right to continue or initiate a therapy on the basis of insufficient data may be unethical and not acceptable for patients and society. As a result, coverage with evidence development schemes may be best suited in a cross-border (European) context, where more patients and more data can be pooled together to reach indisputable significance.

## Risk-Sharing Schemes Linked to Outcomes Guarantees

In a risk-sharing scheme, the manufacturer shares the risk with the health care payer that the orphan drug may not be effective for a specific patient. If the orphan drug does not have the expected improvement in health outcomes, the manufacturer loses some (or all) product revenue or needs to provide an alternative therapy (Cook et al. 2008). For risk-sharing schemes to work, it needs to be possible to assess the effectiveness of the orphan drug in a "real-life" (as opposed to experimental) environment on scientifically validated clinical endpoints and patient-reported outcomes (Dubois 2010). Such schemes also require physicians to be trained in the appropriate use of the orphan drug, and necessitate the implementation of a tracking system to follow up its use (Simoens 2011).

In general, risk-sharing schemes have been referred to by different names, including performance-based agreements or outcomes guarantees, and can take the form of simple "no cure, no pay" and "money-back guarantee" schemes or the form of more sophisticated schemes where, for example, the price of the drug is adjusted to ensure an agreed threshold value for the cost-effectiveness ratio (Sudlow and Counsell 2003). For payers, risk-sharing schemes offer the potential for efficiency gains by directing scarce resources toward the patients likely to receive the most benefit (i.e. who would respond to therapy) and reduce the risk of paying for expensive drug with uncertain added value (Carlson *et al.* 2010; Stafinski *et al.* 2010; Towse and Garrison 2010). For drug manufacturers, risk-sharing schemes secure both the coverage of the drug and predictable revenues. Besides, they usually allow the negotiation of discounts to payers while avoiding any negative impact on the international reference drug pricing lists (Annemans *et al.* 2011).

Italy is one of the few European countries where risk-sharing schemes have been implemented regularly. No specific law regulates them; rather, they are part of the coverage negotiation and are decided on an ad-hoc basis once a newly launched drug presents some uncertainty over its value. In October 2010, 18 contracts covering 17 drugs were in force (Garattini and Casadei 2011). Over one third of these contracts dealt with orphan drugs in the field of oncology – five of them being "payment-by-results", and the other two "cost-sharing" schemes (Table 5.2). While "cost-sharing" schemes do not include any clinical evaluation and merely consist of a discount on the initial treatment costs for all eligible patients, "payment-by-results" contracts link coverage level to previously agreed clinical and health outcomes. The manufacturer is expected to pay back half (i.e. risk-sharing) or the full price (payment-by-results) for each non-responder or patient having discontinued treatment. To manage these various schemes, the Italian authorities have set up a web-based nationwide registry to document all data from monitored patients who are receiving one of the targeted drugs.

*Table 5.2* Italian risk-sharing schemes at the end of 2010

| Compound (brand name, manufacturer) | Indication(s) | Type of scheme (start date) |
| --- | --- | --- |
| **Dasatinib (Sprycel®, Bristol Myers Squibb)** | Chronic myeloid leukaemia | Payment by results (2007) |
| **Lenalidomide (Revlimid®, Celgene)** | Multiple myeloma | Cost sharing (2008) |
| **Nilotinib (Tasigna®, Novartis)** | Chronic myeloid leukaemia | Payment by results (2008) |
| **Sorafenib (Nexavar®, Bayer)** | Renal cell carcinoma | Cost sharing (2006) |
| | Hepato-carcinoma | Payment by results (2008) |
| **Temsirolimus (Torisel®, Wyeth-Pfizer)** | Renal cell carcinoma | Payment by results (2008) |
| **Trabectedin (Yondelis®, PharmaMar)** | Advanced soft tissue sarcoma | Payment by results (2009) |

Adapted from Garattini and Casadei (2011)

In Italy, risk-sharing schemes mainly attempt to reduce the cost for new orphan drugs to the national health system. The objective is to limit pharmaceutical spending to the most effective drugs, or even to the individual patients who respond best to treatment. Another interesting, while more complex, example of a risk-sharing scheme linked to outcomes guarantee applied to an orphan drug which has been well reported in the literature is Australia's Bosentan Patient Registry (see Box 5.1).

Overall, risk-sharing schemes are not without controversy and some have argued that the money should be better allocated to funding a properly designed clinical trial of the drug (Raftery 2010). Furthermore, risk-sharing schemes rely on complex data collection, analysis procedures, and information systems and databases, which entail an extra administrative burden and additional costs for the manufacturer, health care payer and administrators. Also, besides the fact that drug manufacturers need to have sufficient confidence in their claims of product effectiveness to accept the future rewards or penalties based on observed performance, both payers and manufacturers also need to agree on the set of objective outcomes or health measures that will determine treatment effectiveness (Annemans *et al.* 2011).

## Box 5.1  The Australian Bosentan (Tracleer®) Patient Registry

Bosentan (Tracleer®), a dual endothelin receptor antagonist, was the first oral agent approved in Australia for the treatment of idiopathic pulmonary arterial hypertension. This is a progressive disease of the small pulmonary arteries that is characterized by vascular proliferation and re-modelling. It results in a progressive increase in pulmonary arterial resistance and, ultimately, right ventricular failure and death. A rare disease with poor prognosis, idiopathic pulmonary arterial hypertension has an estimated incidence of 1–2 cases per 1 million each year and a prevalence of 15 cases per 1 million (NORD 2012; Orphanet 2012).

At the time of the Pharmaceutical Benefits Advisory Committee recommendation, only two short-term randomized controlled trials were available to provide evidence that bosentan administration was associated with improved cardiopulmonary haemodynamics, improved exercise capacity (as measured by the six-minute-walk distance test) and increased delay to clinical worsening. As is often the case in rare diseases research, links between intermediate outcomes and long-term survival were not well established.

Therefore, a health economics model based on long-term follow-up of these trials (up to 2.2 years) was developed to predict the cost, hospitalization and mortality rates of a population of idiopathic pulmonary arterial hypertension patients treated with bosentan therapy plus conventional therapy ("bosentan therapy") versus conventional therapy alone ("conventional therapy") over a 15-year period (Wlodarczyk *et al.* 2011). The model assumed that bosentan would reduce mortality from 26.6% to 5.2% per annum, thereby increasing life expectancy from 2.8 years to 6.7 years.

The model predicted that after 5, 10 and 15 years, the difference in average cumulative costs between bosentan therapy and conventional therapy would be $AU116,929, $AU181,808 and $AU216,331 for each patient, respectively. It adds that there would be an associated increase in average life expectancy of 1.39, 2.93 and 3.87 years at 5, 10 and 15 years, with an incremental cost-effectiveness ratio at 15 years of $AU55,927 per life-year saved. Removing the continuation criteria from the model increased the incremental cost-effectiveness ratio to $AU62,267.

In Australia, a cost-effectiveness ratio of < $AU60,000 for each life-year saved is usually considered acceptable (George *et al.* 2001). In this instance, the incremental cost-effectiveness ratio was considered high but acceptable in the presence of a risk-sharing scheme. Therefore, a three-year risk-sharing scheme was established between the Australian government and the drug manufacturer (Actelion), whereby the price of bosentan would be directly linked to the observed survival of idiopathic pulmonary arterial hypertension patients treated with bosentan under the Australian Pharmaceutical Benefits Scheme.

To facilitate monitoring of bosentan-treated patients and to collect survival data to assess the accuracy of modeled data afterwards, a register managed independently by the Centre of Clinical Research Excellence in Therapeutics at Monash University and overseen by an advisory board was established: the Bosentan Patient Register. The drug manufacturer was to bear the cost of the establishment and operations of the register.

The driving idea of this scheme was that the price of bosentan would be altered in the event that the observed survival in Pharmaceutical Benefits Scheme-treated patients would differ from that predicted by the economic model. In concrete terms, mortality rates from the registry were to be plugged into the original model and the price of bosentan adjusted to maintain the original incremental cost-effectiveness ratio.

The Bosentan Patient Register was initiated in 15 specialized pulmonary arterial hypertension centres. Between 2004 and 2007, a total of 528 patients (mean age: 59 years) were enrolled. The observed mortality rate in idiopathic pulmonary arterial hypertension was 11.8% per annum (95% CI, 8.8–14.8) compared with the 5.2% predicted by the economic model (Keogh *et al.* 2011). However, the Bosentan Patient Register population was generally older, with more advanced functional deficit, than patients enrolled in the randomized controlled trials on which the risk-sharing scheme was based. Thus, an age- and severity-adjusted mortality rate was calculated and resulted in a revised estimate of 8.8%.

The input of the observed raw mortality rate of 11.8% p.a. into the original health economics model would have resulted in an incremental cost-effectiveness ratio of $AU80,735 per life-year gained and a 23.7% price reduction would have been required to maintain the original incremental cost-effectiveness ratio of $AU62,267. By using the adjusted mortality rate of 8.8%, the incremental cost-effectiveness ratio was reduced to $AU69,811 and a 13.5% reduction in bosentan price would have been necessary (Wlodarczyk *et al.* 2011). In 2008, however, sitaxentan, a new oral idiopathic pulmonary arterial hypertension treatment, was listed on the Pharmaceutical Benefits Scheme at a 15% discount to bosentan. On the basis of cost minimization, bosentan was forced to reduce its price to that of sitaxentan. After this price reduction the incremental cost-effectiveness ratio for bosentan was similar to that originally proposed and hence no additional price reduction was sought by the Pharmaceutical Benefits Advisory Committee.

## Conclusions

Given that in some instances there is uncertainty surrounding the value of orphan drugs, innovative schemes are being implemented in European countries to facilitate coverage of orphan drugs. In this respect, it should first be noted that there is a lack of alignment between the centralized regulatory system and the non-centralized market access process. In particular, whereas the European Medicines Agency allows for a degree of uncertainty surrounding an orphan drug in the marketing authorization procedure, this same uncertainty is sometimes held against an orphan drug in national coverage procedures.

Coverage with evidence development schemes appear to be appropriate coverage instruments to the extent that they are limited to the few drugs where uncertainty and/or budget impact is (are) high and that a sufficient number of patients can be enrolled to allow for meaningful conclusions on treatment effectiveness. Coverage with evidence development schemes are tools to collect additional evidence; they are ill-suited to address cost-effectiveness or affordability concerns and cannot be applied across the board because of the logistic implications. Risk-sharing schemes may also gain traction as payers and manufacturers get experience with them, although further research is needed to check whether risk-sharing is aligned with societal preferences. In the future, payers may implement a combination of these instruments, as illustrated by the bosentan case. Finally, there is a need for further research to systematically review all access schemes applied to orphan drugs. Today, there is no comprehensive overview and understanding available of the use of access schemes for orphan drugs. Research to map and analyze such schemes across key European markets may offer valuable insights to identify or suggest a standard template for setting up effective access schemes that best address uncertainty.

## References

Access Economics (2007). *The cost of muscular dystrophy*. Muscular Dystrophy Australia, Melbourne (available online at: www.mda.org.au/media/accesslaunch/ExecutiveSummary5.pdf).

Annemans, L., Cleemput, I., Hulstaert, F. and Simoens, S. (2011). Valorising and creating access to innovative medicines in the European Union. *Frontiers in Pharmacology*, 2, 1–6.

Baltussen, R. and Niessen, L. (2006). Priority setting of health interventions: the need for multi-criteria decision analysis. *Cost Effectiveness and Resource Allocation*, 4, 14.

Carlson, J.J., Sullivan, S.D., Garrison, L.P., *et al.* (2010). Linking payment to health outcomes: a taxonomy and examination of performance-based reimbursement schemes between health-care payers and manufacturers. *Health Policy*, 96, 179–90.

Clarke, J.T. (2006). Is the current approach to reviewing new drugs condemning the victims of rare diseases to death? A call for a national orphan drug review policy. *Canadian Medical Association Journal*, 174, 189–90.

Cook, J.P., Vernon, J.A. and Manning, R. (2008). Pharmaceutical risk-sharing agreements. *Pharmacoeconomics*, 26, 551–6.

Denis, A., Simoens, S., Fostier, C., *et al.* (2009). *Policies for orphan diseases and orphan drugs*. Belgian Health Care Knowledge Centre (KCE), Brussels.

Denis, A., Mergaert, L., Fostier, C., *et al.* (2010). A comparative study of European rare disease and orphan drug markets. *Health Policy*, 97, 173–9.

Denis, A., Mergaert, L., Fostier, C., *et al.* (2011). Critical assessment of Belgian reimbursement dossiers of orphan drugs. *Pharmacoeconomics*, 29, 883–93.

Dolan, P., Shaw, R., Tsuchiya, A. and Williams, A. (2005). QALY maximisation and people's preferences: a methodological review of the literature. *Health Economics*, 14, 197–208.

Doulet, N. (2011). *Disease registries in Europe*. Orphanet Report Series, Rare Diseases Collection, Paris (available online at: www.orpha.net/orphacom/cahiers/docs/GB/Registries.pdf).

Drummond, M.F., Wilson, D.A., Kanavos, P., *et al.* (2007). Assessing the economic challenges posed by orphan drugs. *International Journal of Technology Assessment in Health Care*, 23, 36–42.

Dubois, D. (2010). Grand challenges in pharmacoeconomics and health outcomes. *Frontiers in Pharmacology*, 1, 7.

Dupont, A.G. and Van Wilder, P.B. (2011). Access to orphan drugs despite poor quality of clinical evidence. *British Journal of Clinical Pharmacology*, 71, 488–96.

EUnetHTA (2012). *The EUnetHTA Project.* European Commission, Brussels (available online at: http://eunetha.eu/).

European Commission (2000). Regulation (EC) No 141/2000 of the European Parliament and the Council of 16 December 1999 on orphan medicinal products. *Official Journal of the European Communities*, L 18/1.

European Union Committee of Experts on Rare Diseases (2012). *EUCERD Report on the State of the Art of Rare Disease Activities in Europe – Part V: Activities in EU Member States & Other European Countries in the Field of Rare Diseases.* EUCERD, Paris (available online at: www.eucerd.eu/?post_type=document&p=1390).

Garattini, L. and Casadei, G. (2011). Risk sharing agreements: what lessons from Italy? *International Journal of Technology Assessment in Health Care*, 27, 169–72.

George, B., Harris, A. and Mitchell, A. (2001). Cost-effectiveness analysis and the consistency of decision making: evidence from pharmaceutical reimbursement in Australia (1991 to 1996). *Pharmacoeconomics*, 19, 1103–9.

Hughes-Wilson, W., Palma, A., Schuurman, A. and Simoens, S. (2012). Paying for the Orphan Drug System: break or bend? Is it time for a new evaluation system for payers in Europe to take account of new rare disease treatments? *Orphanet Journal of Rare Diseases*, 7, 74.

Joppi, R., Bertele, V. and Garattini, S. (2009). Orphan drug development is not taking off. *British Journal of Clinical Pharmacology*, 67, 494–502.

Joppi, R., Bertele, V. and Garattini, S. (2012). Orphan drugs, orphan diseases. The first decade of orphan drug legislation in the EU. *European Journal of Clinical Pharmacology*, 69, 1009–24.

Keogh, A., Strange, G., McNeil, K., *et al.* (2011). The Bosentan Patient Registry: long-term survival in pulmonary arterial hypertension. *International Medicine Journal*, 41, 227–34.

Kesselheim, A.S. (2010). Using market-exclusivity incentives to promote pharmaceutical innovation. *New England Journal of Medicine*, 363, 1855–62.

McCabe, C., Claxton, K. and Tsuchiya, A. (2005). Orphan drugs and the NHS: should we value rarity? *British Medical Journal*, 331, 1016–9.

National Institute for Health and Care Excellence (2006). *Appraising orphan drugs.* National Institute for Health and Clinical Excellence, London (available online at: www.nice.org.uk/niceMedia/pdf/smt/120705item4.pdf).

National Institute for Health and Care Excellence (2009). *Appraising life-extending, end of life treatments.* National Institute for Health and Clinical Excellence, London (available online at: www.nice.org.uk/guidance/gid-tag387/resources/appraising-life-extending-end-of-life-treatments-paper2).

National Organization for Rare Disorders (2012). *Report on pulmonary arterial hypertension.* National Organization for Rare Disorders, Washington (available online at: www.rarediseases.org/rare-disease-information/rare-diseases/byID/706/viewAbstract).

Nord, E. (1993). The trade-off between severity of illness and treatment effect in cost-value analysis of health care. *Health Policy*, 24, 227–38.

Orofino, J., Soto, J., Casado, M.A. and Oyaguez, I. (2010). Global spending on orphan drugs in France, Germany, the UK, Italy and Spain during 2007. *Applied Health Economics Health Policy*, 28, 301–15.

Orphanet (2012). *The portal for rare diseases and orphan drugs.* Orphanet, Paris (available online at: www.orpha.net/consor/cgi-bin/index.php).

Owen, A., Sprinks, J., Meehan, A., *et al.* (2008). A new model to evaluate the long-term cost effectiveness of orphan and highly specialised drugs following listing on the Australian

Pharmaceutical Benefits Scheme: the Bosentan Patient Registry. *Journal of Medical Economics*, 11, 235–43.

Raftery, J. (2010). Multiple sclerosis risk sharing scheme: a costly failure. *British Medical Journal*, 340, c1672.

Rawlins, M.D. and Culyer, A.J. (2004). National Institute for Clinical Excellence and its value judgments. *British Medical Journal*, 329, 224–7.

Schey, C., Milanova, T. and Hutchings, A. (2011). Estimating the budget impact of orphan medicines in Europe: 2010–2020. *Orphanet Journal of Rare Diseases*, 6, 62.

Simoens, S. (2010a). Health economic assessment: cost-effectiveness thresholds and other decision criteria. *International Journal of Environmental Research and Public Health*, 7, 1835–40.

Simoens, S. (2010b). How to assess the value of medicines? *Frontiers in Pharmacology*, 1, 115.

Simoens, S. (2011). Pricing and reimbursement of orphan drugs: the need for more transparency. *Orphanet Journal of Rare Diseases*, 6, 42.

Simoens, S., Cassiman, D., Dooms, M. and Picavet, E. (2012). Orphan drugs for rare diseases: is it time to revisit their special market access status? *Drugs*, 72, 1437–43.

Simoens, S., Picavet, E., Dooms, M., *et al.* (2013). Cost-effectiveness assessment of orphan drugs: a scientific and political conundrum, *Applied Health Economics and Health Policy*, 11, 1–3.

Stafinski, T., McCabe, C.J. and Menon, D. (2010). Funding the unfundable: mechanisms for managing uncertainty in decisions on the introduction of new and innovative technologies into healthcare systems. *Pharmacoeconomics*, 28, 113–42.

Sudlow, C. and Counsell, C. (2003). Problems with the UK Government's risk sharing scheme for assessing drugs for multiple sclerosis. *British Medical Journal*, 326, 383–92.

Tambuyzer, E. (2010). Rare diseases, orphan drugs and their regulation: questions and misconceptions. *Nature Reviews Drug Discovery*, 9, 921–9.

Towse, A. and Garrison, L.P. (2010). Can't get no satisfaction? Will pay for performance help?: toward an economic framework for understanding performance-based risk-sharing agreements for innovative medical products. *Pharmacoeconomics*, 28, 93–102.

Tunis, S.R. and Pearson, S.D. Coverage options for promising technologies: Medicare's 'coverage with evidence development'. *Health Affairs*, 25, 1218–30.

Ubel, P.A. and Loewenstein, G. (1996). Distributing scarce livers: the moral reasoning of the general public. *Social Science and Medicine*, 42, 1049–55.

Weinstein, M.C. (1988). A QALY is a QALY – or is it? *Journal of Health Economics*, 7, 289–90.

Wild, C., Hintringer, K. and Nachtnebel, A. (2011). Orphan drugs in oncology. *Pharmaceutical Policy and Law*, 13, 223–32.

Wlodarczyk, J., Reid, C.M. and Pater, G. (2011). Funding linked to ongoing research: impact of the Bosentan Patient Registry on pricing in Australia. *Value in Health*, 14, 961–3.

Chapter 6

# Innovating in the Changing Market Access Environment

*Ulf Staginnus*

## Introduction

The pharmaceutical industry has changed dramatically over the past few years after decades of steady growth. The economic crisis hit government finances and health care budgets hard and brought medical expenditures, especially those of pharmaceutical companies, and measures to save money under the spotlight. Budgetary deficits have caused health care payers around the world to introduce new cost-containment measures and changes in how drugs are being assessed in order to be reimbursed (the most significant being the change in Germany brought by AMNOG and the benefit assessments by IQWIG linked to pharmaceutical pricing). A strong push towards generics and the introduction of biosimilars are also high on the current health policy agenda. High unmet need areas such as cancer experience numerous drug entrants (e.g. for melanoma) that compete for funding and reimbursement, and HTA agencies are becoming much stricter on the type of data (overall survival, head-to-head studies) required for reimbursement. At the same time the gradual shift to "outcomes-based" and/or "risk-sharing" agreements (e.g. Italy, the UK, regions in Spain, Germany) is further complicating the cost–benefit relation of R&D investments. As this trend will increase, pharmaceutical company risk will increase as it will make it much more difficult to exactly forecast the expected revenues generated from the drug portfolio under development and will create significant transactional cost via administration onto the manufacturer and health authorities, yet at the same time presenting an opportunity to overcome access (cost) related hurdles.

## Market Access

Considering the above developments, "market access" capabilities as well as a more patient-centered approach to business strategy (e.g. targeted therapies) and conduct are of paramount importance to the future of the research-based industry. In the end, whatever one wants to call that new kid on the block, the matter comes down to the right evidence development and creation of convincing data to payers, which will have a remarkable impact on how successful business is done in future years and who will gain a competitive advantage. As a result, skills and experiences that are related to understanding this new environment are now even more in high demand. In particular, those individuals who comprehend not only payer business models but also how the decisions of these organizations are affected by outside influencers will be invaluable in determining the future pricing models and positioning of drugs. This shift from the "physician-prescriber" to a "stakeholder-payer" model will make the ability to influence payers of utmost importance to drug manufacturers. Consequently, the companies will need fewer people whose primary added value is being able to access physicians. Instead, they will seek individuals who are sophisticated in working with payers to position and price their products. The industry is in for a big change and that may open up great opportunities for those companies that manage to concentrate their development on high unmet needs areas coupled with a different approach to product commercialization.

## Organization and Capabilities

These days almost every pharmaceutical, biotech and medical device company is (re) organizing the area that deals with payer requirements, dossier submissions and market access. Over the course of the past 20 years the industry has seen many changes, and different models to organize functions related to market access have been tried and altered again over time.

In the late 1990s health economics was a new and coming discipline with mostly only a single or a handful of individuals per company and most often still considered a marketing "gimmick" and "nice to have" rather than a strategic function. That often resulted in health economists being placed in departments such as "marketing services" or similar ancillary functions.

With the introduction of some sophisticated HTA agencies, such as NICE, and their formal processes of product evaluation, a fundamental change went through the industry and larger health outcomes units were formed and typically placed into the R&D organization and/or clinical development units. That was also the dawn of a time that I like to call the phase of "statistical overkill". Economic models became almost overly complex and sophisticated, attempts were made to calculate confidence intervals around CE ratios, and all sorts of analytical refinement was added, which gave the user an illusion of a precision that cannot exist however. Nonetheless, the fundamental problem of how to best allocate scarce resources and reduce time for patients to access innovative medicines has probably not been greatly improved (TUFTS 2012; Wilking and Joensson 2005).

It is almost certainly fair to say that some irritation over this issue has been building up among health economists, policy makers and budget holders. Others would even go so far as to say the concept of cost-effectiveness, at least as it has been applied in some jurisdictions, is a too narrow way forward (Bridges 2006). It is also not an uncommon viewpoint among the health economics community, especially among the liberal economists, that this technocratic and static "point in time snapshot" cannot be an appropriate methodology for such a complex matter as health care.

Over the last years analyses became, on the technical front, somewhat more "pragmatic" again and in many countries relative effectiveness and budget impact evaluations are playing a much more important role than cost-effectiveness (notably, Germany opted for a system that is not applying a cost per QALY metrics determining reimbursement).

Non-satisfaction with the access issues related to cost per QALY assessments, together with public pressure, initiated the risk-sharing/patient access scheme stage that we then entered. Patient groups articulated strongly the perceived discrimination by HTA assessment bodies, especially related to cancer drug funding in the UK, and risk-sharing approaches took up quite significantly as a way to bridge either budgetary considerations and/or evidence matters at launch coupled with meeting the needs of patients to have access to novel and innovative medicines (Ethgen and Staginnus 2011). Companies are addressing this environmental shift by adding capabilities and have increased sophistication and analytical skills in dealing with such access-related matters. While in the past those issues were managed by professionals falling into "categories" such as health economics, pricing and government affairs, we are experiencing an era that is characterized by the emergence of the broad term "market access".

This evidently is nothing really new, nor is market access a specific capability, as the disciplines summarized under this umbrella phrase are still the same as before, but depending on who is in "charge" the matter either swings from extremely policy focused to a very technical approach and/or variations thereof. For that reason we have to be careful that it does not become a buzzword but rather that we clearly define roles and responsibilities within an organization to address the ultimate objective, which is rather patients' access to medicines.

In order to get structure in the maze let's focus on the key elements of market access from a payer/decision-maker perspective. To me, two major points that come to mind are:

- clinical (relative efficacy/effectiveness), so in simple words the proof that B (new treatment) is really better than A (current treatment);
- pricing (overall net cost).

There are, of course, many other elements in a holistic approach to patient access and these two elements are cutting things far too short, yet in essence decision making mostly comes down to these two items. These are our key variables in successfully introducing a new medicine to the market and to get it reimbursed.

Therefore, we have to address within the company the organizational set-up and skills to most effectively deliver the access strategy in order to be able to address the above points. That requires the clarification of one major organizational principle first, namely: what is the role of "Global", versus the role of the "Region" (e.g. Europe, emerging markets, etc.) versus the role of the "Country affiliate" in relation to market access? Not surprisingly, in that regard different models can be applied.

Based on numerous discussions with industry "veterans", and the personal experiences I made in several companies, what seemed to work most smoothly in organizations was the application of the catholic principle of subsidiarity (Lagler and Messner 1952), effectively practiced by the Roman Empire for almost 2,000 years. Subsidiarity is an organizational standard that states that matters ought to be handled by the smallest, lowest or least centralized competent authority. Decisions should therefore be taken at a local level if possible, rather than by a central authority. Central authority should have a subsidiary function, performing only those tasks that cannot be performed successfully at a more immediate or local level.

Applying this principle to a pharmaceutical company, and more specifically to market access, would mean to sufficiently empower the countries. Is it not very apparent anyhow that someone else other than the countries would know better what "works and doesn't work" locally? Not only the regulatory side of things but rather the soft facts, the relationships and proximity to the various stakeholders, the same language, the culture of communication and local negotiation styles determine what makes the unique difference and puts the affiliate market access organization in the most favorable spot when appropriately supported, rather than being too closely "gated" (sometimes patronized) by Global or the Region. Especially when looking at the increasing regionalization of decision making in many markets (e.g. Italy, Spain, Sweden) it appears that such a model is most likely to be poised for success in the long run.

An overall market access organization should be lean, agile and direct without too many "intermediaries"; in other words, having someone in Global sending an email to ask a question to someone else in the Region who in turn sends an email to an affiliate, etc. and all the way back. That is inefficient and burdensome. To look at this more specifically, what should be the tasks of the various levels of a successful and nimble organization?

Let's start with "Global":

The global organization and its personnel are close to the R&D strategy and developments as well as to the overall commercial vision and objectives. It is therefore ideally placed to set the framework (e.g. overall pricing principles) and general health economics/access strategy and philosophies (e.g. are certain strategies and other novel access approaches being used proactively or only reactively?), inform and influence pipeline developments, access intelligence regarding competitors, provide core datasets on clinical studies, and perform the main technical analysis to support the reimbursement dossier, such as indirect comparisons, extrapolations and creation of other essential evidence elements. More importantly, the Global market access organization should inform via consultation with the Country/Region the clinical trial design regarding the inclusion of payer relevant endpoints.

The "Region", meanwhile, usually overseeing a varying number of affiliates, is ideally placed to be the "voice", "coach" and "advocate" of these countries. An instrumental role, to start with, is the role of the Region in pricing, which includes the management of day-to-day pricing challenges but also the key input and reality check into strategic pricing of development compounds at Global level as well as the implementation of the global pricing strategy with the countries via launch sequencing and price management. International price referencing and other cost-containment measures as well as the developments on patient access and risk-sharing schemes require a strong knowledge and execution of tactical pricing, price optimization and coaching at the Regional level. In addition to that, the Region, due to its proximity and multi-issue experience, is best suited to coach and train the countries in dealing with payer objections and handling of questions via best practice sharing, etc. The Region should also support local health economics and outcomes research activities as well as modelling exercises. A healthy combination of health economics and pricing skills also makes the Region ideally suited to deal with overall market access challenges in a broad fashion and to educate and share experiences with the affiliates about what has worked well in other markets, and to help in the hands-on execution locally of the broader market access strategy. Negotiation support and trainings round up the regional responsibilities.

On the country level resides the accountability to implement strategies and the pricing and reimbursement dossiers/submissions (strongly supported by the Region) as well as the actual price negotiations and dealing with local market access challenges, supported by the Region or Global if needed. The countries will also monitor and influence health policy developments and will feed important needs for pipeline products to the global organization (e.g. trial designs and comparators, data creation needs, modelling, etc.). It is important that the various levels of the organization allow for an open culture of communication and information sharing without relating to a "post office" model (the aforementioned chain of email questions floating vertically back and fourth through the organization).

That leads us to discuss the topic of governance. Governance processes and tools are an important element of ensuring consistency and compliance. At the same time, however, governance should not suffocate innovation, bureaucracy, delays and internal frustrations. To follow the principle of subsidiarity, and with sufficient empowerment, more than a few "signatures" in a fairly lean and efficient process should ideally not be required. In case of ambiguity the final decision-making authority (within the global guidance, of course) should lay with the country, provided the right people with experience and seniority are in place; again, they usually know best.

One additional topic we still need to deal with is how to manage the various functions involved in the market access process (in the end, market access is of course an orchestrated approach of the various roles). We are having health economics and outcomes research, patient advocacy, communication, government relations, and pricing. These are the typical roles that are usually being hosted under the roof of market access.

An important aspect of a synchronized performance of the various functions is the understanding of the importance of multidisciplinary thinking and action. What is meant by that is the matter of pricing and reimbursement submissions is becoming increasingly complex and requires broad skills that range from understanding the various payer archetypes across the globe as much as the evidence requirements, modelling aspects and the microeconomics and international implications of pharmaceutical pricing and health policy regulations. When slicing responsibilities too thin there are too many "chefs" in the kitchen, which results in them stepping on each other's toes and thus creates undesired silos. In addition, there is the risk of forming narrowly focused experts that act like "scalpels" when what you actually need is more of a "Swiss knife". That is of paramount importance for the Region – a place that should be lean and be able to deal with multiple access challenges requiring a broader combination of skills coupled with commercial experiences and abilities to present, convey messages and provide overall direction.

In an overly divided organization, countries' general managers might get confused about who is doing what and actually prefer to deal with one person on the next corporate level (e.g. Region) related to access rather than with another "guy" each time there is a slightly different problem.

Of course there is no recipe that fits all; depending on business and company size, geographical expansion and portfolio, organizational modifications are required. However, and to give a specific example, various organizations decided to have a pricing, health economics/access role under one leadership, or at least "roof", rather than having three different headcounts or functions. Health economics analyses, apart from the dossier requirements, are performed in order to support a certain price target (at least that is the theory; often it works the other way around unfortunately). Separation of health economics and pricing (talking here about strategic pricing, not the day-to-day pricing analytics) often leads to inefficiencies and frictions. For example, the separation of these two functions in some companies caused confusion about who "owns" the payer insights and who is responsible for identifying the specific payer needs, interpreting them and developing strategies to address these. Health economics by itself may not always have the leverage to influence clinical development. A survey showed that only 15% of the top 20 pharma companies regularly involve health economics experts in clinical trial designs (Mansell 2012). There is a need to have alignment with commercial teams who are typically more receptive to pricing arguments. That leads to the often posed question: where should health economics and strategic pricing reside? There is no clear answer to this question as it depends on the size and nature of the organization, but a "central" and strategic location, e.g. part of "access", within the organization chart is probably more suitable rather than being tossed in within other functions, such as medical or marketing.

To summarize, in my experience across the industry the following points have proven to work better than others when designing a market access organization:

- Management of the function needs knowledge of the discipline, to ensure credibility, knowledge of the payer and environment, and an ability to lead and rally people to a common cause with no formal authority while maintaining efficacy and harmony of the function.
- Subsidiarity – empower the countries and let them decide within the framework of the overall strategy how to write their P&R dossier, how to engage, what tactics to pursue, etc.
- A lean but well-functioning Region with not too thinly sliced roles and responsibilities that can coach, share experiences, fire fight and bring specific expertise and serves as the voice of the countries.
- A Global department with the right technical as well as practical expertise (ideally people who have had prior country experience) and focus: Global and the Region need to see themselves and work together as one team without duplicating efforts.
- A culture of innovative approaches to market access and pricing.
- People with broad hands-on experiences, commercial savvy and able to present to and communicate well with non-experts.
- Lean processes and governance, flexibility and empowerment, a culture of trial and error rather than a culture of excessive control and risk aversion.

Now let's also look a little at the capabilities. Most health economists up until the late 1990s were first of all economists before they became health economists. Today I feel that component is missing in some institutions – training is too limited and wholly focused on technical, microeconomic/econometric analysis and doesn't teach the big picture as well as broad economic theory and thinking. Forgetting the roots leads to the stoic application of cost-utility analysis without seeing the health care system as a whole, and without understanding of its nuances and incentive structures it is difficult to find broader solutions on a macro level. It is of course imperative to have the technical skills, but the challenges of the times to come need leaders with vision and courage to try new things, leaders who have learned to think broadly and understand the different schools of thought in (political) economics. It is easier to comprehend the details of analyzing the specific technology and health issue than to learn to think conceptually – my plea would be for more economics mainstream skills added to the capabilities of employees on all levels.

## R&D Productivity and Innovation

Most recently, a lot has been spoken about the declining R&D productivity and the lack of breakthrough medicines. Many companies have moved away from the blockbuster model to more specific disease areas with high unmet need. Human biology is complex and innovation is often achieved only in incremental steps. Oncology is a perfect example. Look, for instance, at the area of metastatic colorectal cancer, where the successive introduction of new chemotherapies improved overall survival from about five months with best supportive care in 1993 to almost two years with targeted therapies in 2011 (Lucas *et al.* 2011). Yet payers are less and less willing to pay for incremental innovation. As already stated, to overcome the increasing budgetary constraints, new models for market access emerged. Options applied are various, such as the evolving trend of risk-sharing agreements, pay-for-performance contracts, alternative pricing models or reimbursement with evidence developments (some authors like to refer to them as "market access agreements"). All those schemes are designed to allow patients access to the medicines while at the same time maintaining affordability criteria and/or allowing for additional evidence being generated until a final reimbursement and pricing decision is made by the authorities. While these measures allow for incremental innovation to be rewarded, they obviously do not address the more fundamental issue of how to broadly improve R&D productivity. So apart from the scientific challenges and other incentives, is there perhaps also a factor related to the environment for innovation?

Culture may play an important role in that; scientists, like all creative people, need an environment that encourages collaboration, allows for trial and error, lets you be different if you want to be, have the freedom to investigate, have the possibility of fast and flexible joint ventures with whoever is needed. Maybe we need looser and faster partnerships, a closer link to universities, labs, start-ups, etc. But this all requires a lean, innovative, can-do culture with an entrepreneurial spirit. However, what we often find is that scientists, as well as those in other departments, are bugged down by inefficiency, over-complication, too much paper stuff to be done, inappropriate leadership that micromanages and delegates too little and therefore will not allow things to flourish. Or as Steve Jobs put it once, "Innovation has nothing to do with how many R&D dollars you have. When Apple came up with the Mac, IBM was spending at least 100 times more on R&D. It's not about money. It's about the people you have, how you're led, and how much you get it" (Fortune 1998).

We might also want to stop seeing our competitors only as that but rather form intelligent partnerships across companies when deemed appropriate (we already see many more of these), develop projects together when indicated, and jointly understand which drug combinations do benefit patients.

New breakthrough medicines are the challenge of the future and in order to discover and develop such you need science and economics savvy, yet pragmatic leaders, those who can understand the opportunities and limitations of the science in the same way as the requirements on the payers' side in order to lead development and hence a solid market access strategy. However, once you have a loser in your portfolio it will stay a loser whatever resources you throw at it – that is the big change that has come around. Yet many people seem to have not yet fully understood that and carry forward products with a too weak value proposition instead of assuming the sunk cost and quickly shifting the remaining development budget into more promising candidates. In that regard, targeted therapies based on biomarkers have brought forward some interesting developments lately.

Discovery in human biology and drug development needs a flexible and open-minded environment, so why not work on that end first, talk to each other earlier, try to build frameworks of collaborations and organizations that foster scientific progress and find truly promising drug candidates (and be ready to kill those early that are not delivering) rather than wasting time on some of these surface-based market access discussions that often jump the horse from the wrong end by trying to "fix" things when it is already too late. Let's rather talk about how to become an agile, innovative and forward-looking industry that will be admired for its breakthrough products. A business that fosters a culture of true innovation, evolution, entrepreneurship and with a focus on distinctive, head-to-head evidence generation – that is where the "market access" movement should be starting to put the focus to begin with. The early and consistent involvement of health economists in the development decision making and pricing, so often spoken about but not systematically done, would be a great start.

## New Ways of Pricing Pharmaceuticals

Pricing has undoubtedly become a big challenge for the industry. Over the last six years, especially in Europe, strong cost-containment measures on pricing have been implemented, which caused the "perfect pricing storm". Most regulations on price were either mandatory and/or arbitrary price cuts, changes related to international price referencing (new rules, frequency of revisions, country basket, exchange rate discussions, etc.) and other health policy changes related to pricing. The most significant news in Europe came from Germany with the implementation of the IQWIG assessment and the entire AMNOG process marking the end of free pricing, at least in the long run, in Germany. In the UK, everyone anxiously observed the neverending debate over the creation of a value-based pricing system that finally failed to deliver. Pricing considerations are also currently happening in other markets where the pendulum might swing towards even more reference pricing in a worse case. In Italy, high-cost oncology drugs must undergo a mandatory risk-sharing/pay-for-performance contract, in that regard actually the most advanced system in Europe so far. The list of new regulations and cost-containment policies continues to grow across the globe.

The issue that has come to the forefront, considering the current financial situation of many health care systems, is that of affordability. In many areas, especially oncology, infectious diseases (most recently the HCV drug-pricing discussions) or rare diseases, it is questionable whether the price-per-pill concept is sustainable everywhere considering the pricing of "me too" products (as outlined in Chapter 2) and the issue of combination of drugs. If we look at the latest launches in the area of melanoma, for example, with Ipilimumab and Zelboraf, both drugs if used for the same patient exceed easily €100,000 annual treatment cost. If we now add even more drugs working on other targets (e.g. PD1 inhibitors), the overall treatment cost for one melanoma patient becomes prohibitive. Other issues might arise with orphan and ultra-orphan drugs such as Glybera, a recently launched gene therapy for treatment of lipoprotein lipase deficiency (LPLD), which causes life-threatening pancreatic attacks, with a cost of more than €1 million. According to the CEO of the manufacturer, most likely a novel financing mechanism will be developed with annual payments spread over several years given that the administration is required only once (Moran 2012).

These examples make it clear that the present approach of price per unit (pill/vial) only might not be sustainable in certain disease areas in the long run. The current surge in risk-sharing agreements points towards new and somewhat promising solutions but might be only an intermediate step and perhaps a little too short-sighted for the future. The pharmaceutical industry may have to learn from other industries and work on different models (for instance, drugs with varying dosages per patient and uncertain frequency and length of treatment, or chronic diseases requiring regular infusions – see Figure 6.1), payments based on outcomes (results), coverage with evidence development or certain fidelity models, etc.

The sky is the limit in terms of theoretical opportunities to develop different approaches to pricing than the price-per-unit model, with the advantage of balancing return of investment for the manufacturer, budget predictability and affordability from a payer's perspective, but practically speaking this would require major political willingness on the part of governments and payers to change current policies and to engage, so unfortunately we see little of it thus far. In addition, many operational hurdles would have to be overcome to make these alternative models work. Several opponents correctly say, why go through the trouble with novel pricing schemes and the currently offered market access agreements? A simple discount

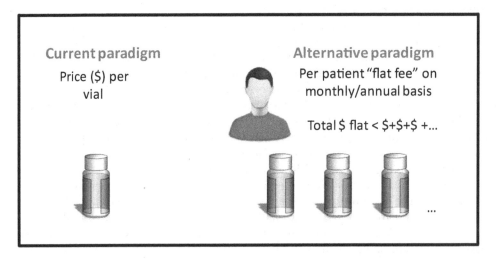

*Figure 6.1* Example of an alternative pricing model (per patient flat fee independent of number of vials used)

would be much easier for all involved but that is unfortunately only possible as long as these discounts are guaranteed to be confidential. Otherwise it would trigger the spillover effects (in economists' terms: "negative externalities") of international price referencing. Apart from the fact that they don't solve the inherent short-comings of price-per-pill concepts in certain diseases (e.g. think of drugs based on weight), confidential discounts would only adjust the magnitude of the "problem".

In fact, various manufacturers have already embarked on negotiations with governments in order to implement innovative pricing models to foster fast patient access to novel medicines (Espín *et al.* 2011; BBC 2014). It remains to be seen whether more authorities will come to recognize the potential for win–win solutions and be able to move away from sole external reference pricing.

## Health Economics Evidence Generation: Real-Life Data

The shortcomings of data available at launch have led to various constructs of conditional reimbursement or coverage with evidence development/outcomes research requirements to prove the value of a medicine to reimbursement authorities and payers over time. In numerous geographies this is not an easy undertaking, often ending up in the set-up of prospective chart reviews (usually to understand patient management), collection of observational data from cohort studies (that is what most people would see as real-life data) or registry creation coupled with the well-known issues of timing as well as administrative, technical and legal hurdles involved. However, everyone talks about real-life evidence now. On many occasions payers or other institutions/stakeholders also do not have the data (especially in Europe) to conduct such analyses on a wide-scale basis. Novel technologies, such as social media or web-based registries, should offer options for additional and faster data collection in the near future. In that regard many researchers argue the need to really beef up IT capabilities in data tracking and mining on the various levels in the health care system. Weeding through patients' charts somewhere in the hospital basement should be a thing of the past very soon.

## Summary

Launching innovative pharmaceuticals has become more and more difficult over recent years and market access is the main hurdle to overcome. The industry is responding with increasing the personnel dealing with access-related matters, and refocusing business and geographical expansion into emerging markets and into specialty areas with high unmet medical need. The financial crisis put additional and immense strain on budgets and created many extra hurdles. New capacities and organizational models are being brought forward to prepare for this changing environment. While improving skills, knowledge and processes in these access-related areas is essential, the changes have to start earlier and the basic problem that needs to be addressed is increasing R&D output and more diligent assessment of pipeline assets and combining these with a sound data-creation strategy that meets payer-relevant endpoints. Additionally, health policy discussions must address the issues created through external price referencing and political willingness is needed to look beyond the usual dealings to open up opportunities for novel commercial strategies and better remuneration for innovation in relation to the value those new medicines ought to deliver. In sync with this, real-life data-creation strategies will become more important in the future and increasing IT capacities and creation of electronic databases, social media and other data-collection forums should facilitate opportunities to better analyze the impact of treatments in real life. Therefore health economics will maintain a very central role in strategizing and creating the required evidence for HTA/pricing and reimbursement submissions and the influence of health economics on R&D and business development decision making and trial designs must further increase in the future. Following that line of thought, the future of health economics as a discipline might lie in its ability to develop beyond its microeconomic application in cost-utility analysis and look at the allocation of health care resources in its complexity from a more holistic perspective, coupled with novel pricing and data-creation strategies that allow for better value generation, capturing and demonstration.

## References

BBC (2014). *Unique 'pay if you clear' proposal for new hepatitis drug* (available online at: www.bbc. com/news/uk-scotland-29569242).

Bridges, J.F. (2006). What can economics add to health technology assessment? Please not just another cost-effectiveness analysis! *Expert Review in Pharmacoeconomics and Outcomes Research*, 6, 19–24.

Espín, J., Rovira, J. and García, L. (2011). Experiences and impact of European risk-sharing schemes focusing on oncology medicines. EMINET (available online at: http://ec.europa. eu/enterprise/sectors/healthcare/files/docs/risksharing_oncology_012011_en.pdf).

Ethgen, O. and Staginnus, U. (2011). Risk-sharing: The need to think differently. *ISPOR Connections*, 17, May–June.

Fortune (1998). November 9.

Lagler, E. and Messner, J. (1952). Das Subsidiaritätsprinzip als wirtschaftliches Ordnungsprinzip [German]. In *Wirtschaftliche Entwicklung und soziale Ordnung*. Degenfeld-Festschrift, Vienna, pp. 81–92.

Lucas, A.S., O'Neil, B.H. and Goldberg, R.M. (2011) A decade of advances in cytotoxic chemotherapy for metastatic colorectal cancer. *Clinical Colorectal Cancer*, 10, 238–44.

Mansell, P. (2012). Health economics increasingly factored into clinical trial design. Pharmatimes (available online at www.pharmatimes.com/Article/12-09-04/Health_economics_increasingly_factored_into_clinical_trial_design.aspx).

Moran, L. (2012). First gene therapy nears landmark European market authorization. *Nature Biotechnology*, 30, 807–9.

TUFTS (2012). U.S. offers patients faster, greater access to cancer drugs than Europe. *Impact Report*, 14, July–August.

Wilking, N. and Joensson, B. (2005). *A pan-European comparison regarding patient access to cancer drugs*. Karolinska Institute, Stockholm.

# Part II

# Technological Changes and Demographics

# Chapter 7

# The Increasing Economic Expectations of Stratified and Personalized Medicine

*Antonio Ramirez de Arellano Serna*

## Introduction

The introduction of pharmacogenomics in clinical practice can provide physicians with tools to assess risks and benefits associated with using available medicines for particular patients, and to select therapies tailored to each patient or subgroup of patients. The use of pharmacogenomic testing in clinical practice is limited thus far. Nevertheless, current and emerging advances suggest that better targeted and more effective pharmacogenomic-based treatments have the potential to yield significant gains in personal health, population health and cost-effective resource allocation. Current "trial and error" approaches to pharmaceutical therapy contributes to nearly 3 million incorrect or ineffective drug prescriptions annually in the US (SACGHS 2007). In contrast to that approach, pharmacogenomics has great potential to increase the safety and effectiveness of drugs by identifying those at risk of adverse events, and by helping physicians to prescribe drugs and dosages in ways that are more likely to fit individual patient responses. A potential barrier to the widespread implementation of pharmacogenomic-based diagnostic screening could be the lack of evidence on whether testing provides good value for money. In general terms, testing before treating is economically viable if the savings gained by avoiding ineffective treatment and adverse events are greater than the cost of testing. The goal of this chapter is twofold: first, to provide an overview of experiences so far in conducting economic evaluation studies focused on the combination of genetic testing and drug. Second, to analyze specific examples where the application of pharmacogenomic testing may be regarded as promising in terms of efficiency.

## Stratified Medicine: A Potential Area for Applying Pharmacoeconomics

The decoding of the human genome, at the beginning of the last decade, has led to scientific breakthroughs which permit a better understanding of the disease mechanisms. Likewise, the identification of pharmacological responses creates opportunities for a better correspondence among patients and therapies. In the extreme, when such a correspondence is very accentuated we refer to individualized or personalized medicine. The anticancer vaccine Oncophage® (vitespen) accounts for an example of personalized medicine. In order to produce this vaccine, cancer cells from a patient are extracted and through a specific laboratory procedure, the vaccine is administered after the patient recovers from surgery. The cancer vaccine, suitable for this patient only, stimulates a series of immunological responses against cancer cells that remain in the body. On the other hand, we refer to stratified or segmented medicine in the case of those therapies linked to a biological biomarker or genetic profile which is able to predict disease progression and/or pharmacological response. In this sense, pharmacogenomics is linked to the concept of stratified medicine and refers to the science and technologies associated with dividing patients or populations into groups on the basis of their biological response to drug treatment using a prognostic test (Hopkins *et al.* 2006).

Figure 7.1 illustrates the two categories of stratified medicine: stratification of patients and stratification of diseases. In the first category, the relevant aspect lies in the patient's response in terms of safety. The possibility to use diagnostic tests to determine the speed for the metabolism of drugs (e.g. identification of the type of the polymorphic enzyme CYP) might allow us to identify the appropriate dose for obtaining the expected therapeutic benefit for the patient. About 30 different enzymes, each made by a different gene or set of genes, control how humans metabolize drugs. A variation in, or the presence or absence of, any of these genes can affect both the minimum dosage that will be effective and the maximum dosage that an individual can tolerate without suffering any adverse reaction.

An illustrative example of this kind would be the oral anticoagulant treatment with Sintrom® (acenocoumarol) for patients affected by atrial fibrillation. Serious bleeding events and strokes can be caused by under- and overdosing of Sintrom®, with a direct impact on mortality and reductions in quality of life. According to the genetic profile of each patient (i.e. identification of polymorphisms CYP2C9/VKORC1), a

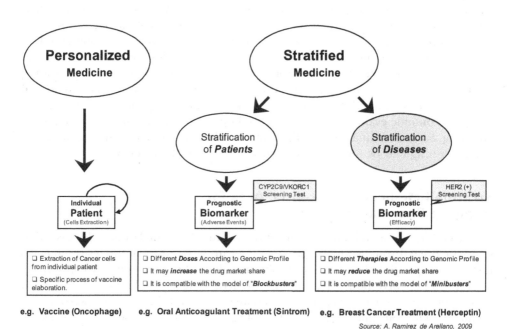

*Figure 7.1* Stratification of patients versus stratification of diseases

specific and different dose can be prescribed for each patient, resulting in a reduction of severe side effects. The estimated cost savings in the US of preventing adverse events associated to the oral anticoagulant Sintrom® with the use of genetic testing are $940 million per year. In this regard, the estimated cost of genetic screening test for CYP2C9/VKORC1 is only $160 million per year (Aspinall and Hamermesh 2007).

The second category of stratification, the most common form when we refer to pharmacogenomics, implies the segmentation of diseases. In this case, patients with similar clinical symptoms and diagnostic are prescribed different therapies on the basis of their molecular profile. For instance, breast cancer patients can be divided into two groups according to the results of the diagnostic testing: group of HER2 positive (with overexpression of HER2 protein) and group of HER2 negative (without overexpression). In the first group, patients would be eligible for the treatment with Herceptin® (trastuzumab), a monoclonal antibody therapy which reduces the likelihood of cancer metastasizing to other parts of the body by a remarkable 53% compared with conventional therapy alone. On the contrary, HER negative patients would receive conventional chemotherapy, since their genetic profile suggests that Herceptin® will not be an effective option. It is clear that identifying which patients should and which patients should not be treated with Herceptin® can save tens of thousands of euros.

The potential net cost saving in the US of not using Erbitux® (cetuximab) for metastatic colorectal cancer patients, with mutated KRAS gene, would be $740 million per year, being the cost of testing if KRAS gene has been mutated of only $13 million (Shankaran *et al.* 2009).

The incorporation of pharmacogenomics into clinical practice has the potential to improve efficacy and reduce toxicity, by allowing the choice of the right drug for the right patient in the right disease at the right dose (Pirmohamed and Lewis 2004). In the same line, payers are beginning to recognize the real and increasing cost of administering ineffective drugs and treating side effects. In this context, pharmacogenomics drugs must be subject to economic evaluation studies, given their substantial development costs and complexity (i.e. simultaneous combination of biomarker and drug) and their potential efficacy for only small subsets of a patient population.

## Economic Evaluation of Pharmacogenomics: A Review of the Current Evidence

### Validity of Pharmacogenomic Tests

The validity and usefulness of a diagnostic test can be evaluated on the basis of the ACCE criteria (analytic validity, clinical validity, clinical utility and ethical implications) (CDCP 2010). The key attributes of a genetic testing are the following:

- **Analytic validity**: it refers to how accurately and reliably the test detects the presence or absence of a particular gene or genetic change. In other words, can the test accurately detect whether a specific genetic variant is present or absent? A genetic test can be applied to expected clinical use if it exhibits acceptable accuracy, precision, specificity and sensitivity.
- **Clinical validity**: it refers to how well the genetic variant being analyzed is related to the presence, absence or risk of a specific intermediate or final health outcome

(e.g. disorder or disease). The genetic variant must identify patients with a higher likelihood of benefit–risk or those at higher risk of an adverse event, or potentially both. The performance attributes of a test are penetrance, clinical sensitivity and specificity, positive and negative predictive values, and attributable risk.

• **Clinical utility**: it refers to whether the test can provide information about diagnosis, treatment, management or prevention of a health outcome (e.g. disorder or disease) that will be helpful to a patient. In other words, the clinical utility of the test accounts for the strength of the association between the tests results and a particular treatment response, whether beneficial or toxic, and the size of the difference between treatment response between tested and untested groups. A clinical study validation for a drug used in conjunction with a predictive biomarker should be performed for the assessment of a drug's safety and efficacy, as well as for verification of the clinical utility of the biomarker in guiding the drug's use.

The estimated clinical validity and utility of a series of genetic tests and biomarkers in the study of Wong and colleagues (2010) are listed in Table 7.1. A majority of biomarkers (63%) were estimated to exhibit clinical validity, only one biomarker (Alpha-adducin Gly460Trp) did not show clinical validity, and the remainder were unclear. However, the clinical utility of most of the biomarkers was unclear, with only two having utility (human leukocyte antigen B*5701 and HER2 overexpression), two likely to have utility (Oncotype-DX® and TPMT variants) and one not having any clinical utility (Alpha-adducin Gly460Trp). The conclusion that may be obtained from this analysis is that the use of pharmacogenomic testing so far is affected by a certain lack of evidence regarding the clinical utility; that is to say, the ability of those genetic tests to influence drug response.

### Assessment of Cost-Effectiveness Results: Combining Biomarker and Drug

The use of pharmacogenomics tests to predict health status and drug response promises safer and more effective drug treatments. The economic viability of pharmacogenomics-based diagnostic screening will depend on specific circumstances of its use. If the potential savings gained by avoiding ineffective treatment and adverse events are greater than the cost of testing, there is scope for demonstrating value for money. Economic attractiveness will depend on the nature of the indication (monogenic or complex, common or rare), the test cost, treatment cost, treatment benefits with and without the test, and the prevalence of the pharmacogenomics variant (Stallings *et al.* 2006).

The first experiences of treatments based on pharmacogenomics include Herceptin® (trastuzumab), a monoclonal antibody that targets the protein product of the HER2 oncogen expressed in a subpopulation of breast cancer patients; Gleevec® (imatinib), a drug designed to treat patients with chronic myeloid leukemia resulting from the so-called "Philadelphia chromosome" translocation; and a test linking hypersensitivity reactions to the HIV/AIDS drug Ziagen® (abacavir) to the HLA-B*5701 haplotype (Shah 2003). The number of cost-effectiveness studies dealing with pharmacogenomic-based test/treatment combinations has increased in recent years. As a consequence, the National Institute for Clinical Excellence (NICE) in England and Wales has published, in the last few years, two Final Appraisal

*Table 7.1* Estimates of clinical validity and utility of genetic tests/biomarkers

| Genetic variants | Diseases/Disorders | Clinical validity | Clinical utility |
|---|---|---|---|
| Thiopurine Methyltransferase TPMT 2/3A/3C | IBD, cancer – ALL, Crohn's, rheumatoid arthritis | Yes | Likely |
| CYP2C9/VKORC1 | Atrial fibrilation, venous thromboembolism | Yes | Unclear |
| Angiotensin converting enzyme I/D polymorphism | Nephropathy, hypercholesteraemia | Unclear | Unclear |
| Uridine Diphosphate Glucuronosyltransferase 1A1 | Colon cancer | Yes | Unclear |
| Dopamine D$_2$ receptor | Nicotine addiction | Unclear | Unclear |
| Factor V Leiden | Oral contraceptive associated VTE | Yes | Unclear |
| Oncotype-DX® gene expression profile | Breast cancer | Yes | Likely |
| Human leukocyte antigen B*5701 | HIV | Yes | Yes |
| HER2 Overexpression | Breast cancer | Yes | Yes |
| Alpha-adducin Gly460Trp | Hypertension | No | No |
| Mitochondrial mutation A1555G | Infection | Yes | Unlikely |
| Methylenetetrahydrofolate Reductase C6771 | Rheumatoid arthritis | Unclear | Unclear |
| CYP2C19*2/3 | Helicobacter pylori-associated duodenal ulcer | Yes | Unclear |
| EGFR Overexpression | Non-small-cell lung cancer | Yes | Unclear |
| Serotonin receptor 2A rs 7997012 | Depression | Unclear | Unclear |
| Six polymorphisms in neurotransmitter-receptor-related | Schizophrenia | Unclear | Unclear |

Determinations (FADs) in relation to the combined use of biomarker and drug. In December 2010, NICE recommended that Herceptin® (trastuzumab) be available for women with HER2-positive advanced breast cancer, indicating that HER2 levels of 3+ should be measured using validated techniques and in accordance with published guidelines. In June 2009, NICE recommended the use of the drug Erbitux® (cetuximab) in combination with chemotherapy as a first-line treatment for patients with metastatic colorectal cancer (mCRC) who have "wild-type" KRAS tumours. Despite these breakthroughs, it could be said that the use of economic evaluation in combining a therapy and a diagnostic is still emerging.

Figure 7.2 exemplifies the current evidence in terms of cost-effectiveness results from and analysis carried out by Wong *et al.* (2010). In this analysis, the selection of original publications of economic evaluation in pharmacogenomics was made on the basis of two criteria:

- The pharmacogenomics testing must indicate variable response to a specific drug therapy in terms of either treatment benefit or risk. Therefore, biomarkers that provided information only on a patient's disease risk or disease-related sequelae, irrespective of therapy, were excluded.

- The instrument to select the economic evaluation studies was the Quality of Health Economic Studies (QHES) rating scale developed by Chiou and colleagues (2003).

The analysis identified 34 cost-effectiveness analysis (CEA) studies of pharmacogenomics applications that met the inclusion criteria: 21 studies exhibited alternative result indicators (i.e. cost per life years gained and cost per event avoided), 10 studies exhibited the relevant indicator used by most economic evaluation agencies (i.e. cost per quality-adjusted life years (QALYs)).

The results in terms of cost per QALY, using as a threshold for willingness to pay of £30,000, indicate that "Oncotype-DX" and "Test for HLA-B*5701 and treat with non-abacavir regimen in HIV patients" would strictly be the only ones eligible for a positive recommendation (and consequently, a positive reimbursement decision) by an evaluation agency (e.g. NICE). Close to the border of a hypothetical positive recommendation there may be the "genetic testing of six polymorphism guiding clozapine treatment in schizophrenia patients" and the "test for CYP2C9/VKORC1 variants for warfarin dosing in AF" with an ICER of £30,855 and £39,287, respectively. In the latter case, an alternative analysis focused on the testing of the same variants for warfarin dosing in non-valvular atrial fibrillation patients shows a very negative outcome (£109,986/QALY).

It is worth noting that this update on the status of economic evaluation shows that in the topic of cancer, in which pharmacogenomics research is most active and possibly promising, the results do not appear favourable in terms of cost-effectiveness. More precisely, in the case of the "six strategies testing for HER2 and trastuzumab", the HercepTest with FISH confirmation of 2+ and 3+ results exhibit an ICER which

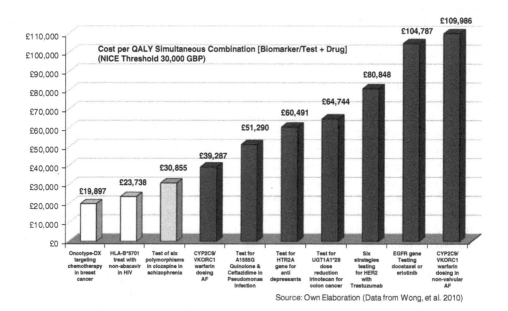

Source: Own Elaboration (Data from Wong, et al. 2010)

*Figure 7.2* Cost-effectiveness analysis results of combining therapy and biomarkers

ranges from £59,835 to £117,780 (Elkin *et al.* 2004). The assessment of differences in the cost of treating typical patients with different genotypes provides a simple answer to the question: "What is the cost of genomic variation?" If that cost is greater than the cost associated with pharmacogenomic testing, it makes economic sense to consider applying the genomic testing to therapeutics. However, the current economic evidence does not seem to offer an optimistic view.

### Key Factors Affecting the Cost-Effectiveness Results of Pharmacogenomics

A clinical biomarker or genetic test is not defined by its technology or biological basis but rather by its reliable, predictive correlation to differential patient responses. However, population variability in efficacy or safety is not by itself sufficient for a stratified medicine to emerge. The clinical variability must be sufficiently large to provide the incentive for the search for an optimal drug. Specially, a viable pharmacogenomics testing must possess a suitable, meaningful therapeutic benefit that exceeds the costs of identifying the appropriate patients (Trusheim *et al.* 2007).

The key factors that are likely to determine the cost-effectiveness of pharmacogenomic testing are:

- prevalence of genetic mutation;
- prevalence of the disease or health outcome (e.g. adverse event) in the population;
- strength of the association between the genetic mutation and clinical outcomes (penetrance);
- availability of alternative interventions that can be implemented on the basis of genetic information;
- level of effectiveness of the genetic test to identify the mutation carrier;
- relative effectiveness of alternative interventions;
- cost of alternative interventions;
- cost of standard of care;
- cost of avoided adverse events;
- cost of the pharmacogenomic test;
- quality of life values associated to the disease or health outcome.

The former key variables can affect, to a greater or lesser extent, the results of an economic evaluation study. When the "prevalence of genetic mutation" is low, few patients in the population would have their responder status affected by the outcome of a diagnostic test. The screening of a whole patient population in order to identify a small subset of patients with the genetic mutation might not be regarded as an efficient intervention, since non-responder costs are less significant to overall costs. In the case that the "prevalence of the disease or health outcome" is low, the economic burden for the health system might not be relevant. Hence, it might not be worth the extra cost of the screening. The necessary conditions for a test being informative, such as clinical validity, clinical utility and analytic validity, are closely related to the "penetrance", "availability of alternative interventions" and "effectiveness of the genetic test", respectively. If those conditions are not fully met, cost-effectiveness results will be negatively affected.

The "relative effectiveness of alternative options" (or in other words, clinical variability in efficacy) must be sufficiently large. This is in line with the intrinsic definition of an informative biomarker which associates a treatment to a patient population showing a differential and substantial clinical response. The "cost of alternative interventions" becomes a crucial variable in pursuing favorable cost-effectiveness results. In short, if such a cost is relatively low in relation to the cost of standard of care, the comparison between genotyping versus not genotyping becomes irrelevant. However, if this cost is substantially high, the use of testing may not guarantee reasonable cost-effectiveness results, since pharmocogenomic testing is not a panacea. In the case that the use of a biomarker is aiming to rule out standard treatments or avoid adverse events in a subgroup of the patient population, those costs must be sufficiently high. Again, the extra cost of the screening must be offset by potential cost savings of avoiding sufficiently expensive treatments or expected side effects. The "cost of the test" is probably the most crucial factor. In short, one major challenge of pharmacogenomics testing is that current biomarkers/genetic tests are not sufficiently mature and there is still significant scope for price reduction. For a cost-effectiveness analysis of pharmacogenomics, the "cost of the test" might include the price of the test as well as cost of genetic counseling (direct costs) and patient time costs to attend testing, counseling and follow-up (indirect costs) (Philips *et al.* 2003). Finally, "quality of life" is a factor to be taken into account mainly in those disease areas (e.g. cancer) where current treatments induce side effects associated to a negative impact on quality of life. The use of genetic platforms to discriminate subgroups of patients between low and high risk of metastasis can help in the clinical decision-making process to rule out adjuvant chemotherapy for those patients who will not get any therapeutic benefit. It is entirely possible that QALYs will be the same or even greater for those patients not taking the chemotherapy drug. In conclusion, the expanded use of pharmacogenomics testing offers many potential clinical benefits but also many economic challenges. As an illustrative example, Table 7.2 shows the parameters as well as their ranges for sensitivity analysis of a cost-effectiveness model of a screening test to identify genetic polymorphism in genes CYP2C9 and VOKRC1 in patients treated with acenocoumarol, compared with non-application of the test. The polymorphisms in the CYP2C9 and VOKRC1 genes are associated with an increased incidence of episodes of major bleeding in patients under oral anticoagulant treatment.

The analysis carried out by Lindner and colleagues (2009) in the Spanish NHS yields an incremental cost per major bleeding avoided of €1,355 in the base case scenario. When we take into consideration that the cost of dealing with a major bleeding accounts for €5,451, we can reach the conclusion that the treatment with acenocoumarol guided by a genetic screening test is potentially a cost-effective option. However, it is worth noting that the model showed sensitivity to the parameters used and the incremental cost varied depending on i) incidence of major bleeding in the population, ii) relative risk (RR) reduction in patients genotyped, iii) cost of treating an episode of major bleeding and iv) cost of the test. Figure 7.3 shows the impact on the incremental cost per major bleeding avoided of varying key parameters when comparing the two options: genotyping versus not genotyping. By reducing the incidence of major bleeding in the Spanish population from 7% (base case scenario) to 4.43% the, incremental cost varies from €1,355 to €5,318, which almost reaches the cost of treating an episode of major bleeding (€5,451). On the contrary, when

*Table 7.2* Variables of the cost-effectiveness model and ranges for sensitivity analysis

| Variable | Value (base case scenario) | Sensitivity analysis (minimum/maximum) |
| --- | --- | --- |
| **Incidence (major bleeding)** | 7.00% | 4.43/13.30% |
| **Relative risk of major bleeding (RR):** | | |
| RR polymorphism in CYP2C9 | 1.649 | |
| RR polymorphism in CYP2C9 & VKORC1 | 3.85 | |
| **Reduction in RR in patients with CYP2C9** | 20% | 2/40% |
| **Reduction in RR in patients with CYP2C9 & VKORC1** | 37% | 5/50% |
| **Incidence of major bleeding (IMB):** | | |
| IMB polymorphism in CYP2C9 | 5.38% | 4.03/6.72% |
| IMB polymorphism in CYP2C9 & VKORC1 | 9.88% | 7.85/15.69% |
| **Cost of major bleeding (Spanish NHS)** | €5,451 | €2,204/8,698 |
| **Cost of test (Spanish NHS)** | €110 | €55/165 |

Source: Lindner et al. 2009

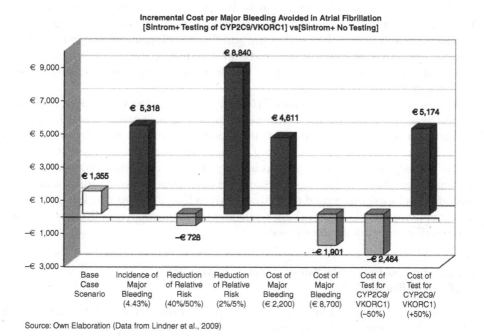

Source: Own Elaboration (Data from Lindner et al., 2009)

*Figure 7.3* Cost-effectiveness analysis of genotyping patients in treatment with acenocoumarol: results of varying key parameters

the incidence increases to 13.3%, the result shows an extra saving of €1,880. The relative risk reduction in patients genotyped, which accounts for the strength of the association between the genetic mutation and the health outcome, exhibits also a significant impact on results. When the relative risk reduction in patients with CYP2C9 moves from 20% to 40% and that from patients with both CYP2C9/VOKRC1 moves from 37% to 50%, an extra saving of €728 is obtained.

Conversely, if the RR reduction is set up at 2% and 5% for CYP2C9 and CYP2C9/VOKRC1, respectively, the incremental cost becomes €8,840. In its turn, by modifying the cost of an episode of major bleeding or the cost of the genetic screening, the results of the analysis change substantially. The higher the cost of the adverse event to be avoided (and the lower the price of the test), the better are the cost-effectiveness results.

## Economic Analysis of Targeting Chemotherapy for Early Breast Cancer: The Use of Gene Expression Profiling Along with Clinical Decision-Making Protocols

Gene expression profiling (GEP) is being used increasingly for risk stratification to identify women with lymph node negative, estrogen receptor-positive, early stage breast cancer who are most likely to benefit from adjuvant chemotherapy. A key challenge for patients with breast cancer and physicians while making treatment decisions relates to the decision to prescribe adjuvant chemotherapy. The argument for the use of adjuvant chemotherapy is the potential to reduce the risk of recurrence and mortality for patients with breast cancer. However, there is variation in the degree of benefit from adjuvant therapy, and the benefit is questionable for patients who have estrogen receptor-positive and lymph node-negative. Chemotherapy also is expensive for payers and may produce significant toxicities, which may have a substantial impact on quality of life.

To date, Oncotype DX (Genomic Health, Redwood City, California), a 21-gene profile assay that uses real-time (RT) polymerase chain reaction (PCR) for expression analysis of paraffin-embedded tissue, remains the most frequently used GEP in clinical practice in the United States. Oncotype DX uses a recurrence score (RS), which places patients in three categories: high risk, intermediate risk and low risk. MammaPrint (Agendia Inc., Irvine, California), a 70-gene profile microarray assay that was developed and is used more frequently in Europe, reports results in a binary mode: either high risk or low risk for recurrence. MammaPrint uses both fresh-frozen and paraffin-embedded tumor tissues.

### Prognostic and Predictive Values of Gene Expression Profiling in Breast Cancer

A key aspect with the use of genetic platforms in breast cancer is to demonstrate whether the genetic profile is superior to the conventional clinical criteria at the time of discriminating between subgroups of patients of high or low risk of recurrence. Figure 7.4 shows that the use of a gene expression profiling (e.g. MammaPrint) exhibits a more accurate and greater degree of discrimination than that from two different clinical decision-making protocols (e.g. the European St. Gallen Consensus and the US National Institute of Health (NIH) guideline). In the case of the NIH guideline, the results indicate that there are no differences statistically significative in the likelihood of recurrence among the pre-established risk groups; that is to say, those groups were set up with a significant margin of error. The St. Gallen consensus

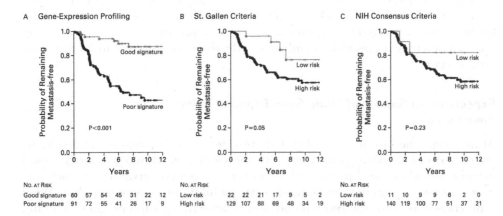

*Figure 7.4* Prognostic value of metastasis: genetic profile versus clinical consensus

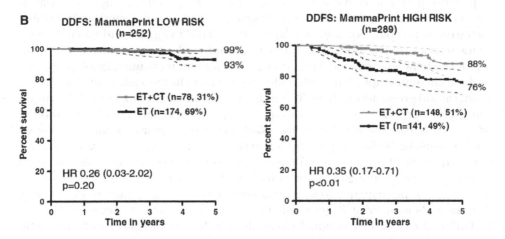

*Figure 7.5* Predictive value of chemotherapy in low- and high-risk patients based on GEP

informs that the likelihood of remaining metastasis free at year 8 is 70–80%, which appears to be very low on the basis of the expectations as for patients of low risk. This means that the use of the St. Gallen criteria gives rise to a significant number of patients mistakenly identified as low-risk patients (i.e. false low-risk patients).

Now, it remains to be seen whether a correct stratification between high-risk patients (poor signature) and low-risk ones (good signature) may be able to guide adjuvant chemotherapy decisions in patients with early breast cancer. Figure 7.5 shows results in terms of overall survival in a study of 541 patients (T1–T3, N0–N1, M0) where two alternative treatments are prescribed for each risk group of patients: i) only endocrine therapy (ET), ii) endocrine therapy plus chemotherapy (CT). For an average period of 7.1 years of follow-up, it can be observed that by treating the subgroup of low risk with a combination of therapies there is not a statistically significative difference in overall survival when compared with only endocrine therapy. As a result, prescription of chemotherapy in the subgroup of patients of low risk seems to be an ineffective option and probably harmful in terms of its negative impact on quality of life. As far as the subgroup of high risk is concerned, the option of adding up chemotherapy proves to be significantly effective in comparison with only endocrine therapy.

### Expected Cost Savings of Using Gene Expression Profiling in Breast Cancer

At this stage, the introduction of genetic platforms may be regarded as a complementary decision-making tool along with the clinic and histological criteria used in the real-world clinical practice in breast cancer. As a conservative approach, the gene expression profiling can be particularly useful in those situations where there is no consensus as for the recommendation of prescribing adjuvant chemotherapy. Table 7.3 shows a distribution of 862 early breast cancer patients among eight different subgroups on the basis of clinical decision-making protocols. For each subgroup of patients there is a recommended treatment based upon the European St. Gallen Consensus. As can be observed, in the subgroup of patients characterized by exhibiting estrogen receptor positive, overexpression of HER2 negative and specific tumor characteristics (tumor grade ii or number of lymph nodes between one and three or tumor size between 2 cm and 5 cm) there is no clear-cut recommendation as for prescribing chemotherapy along with endocrine therapy. In the Zanconati *et al.* (2011) study, this subgroup accounts for 37% of the total number of patients under scrutiny. The use of a genetic platform on this specific subgroup implies the identification of 58% of those patients as being at low risk of developing metastasis and, as a consequence, non-eligible for the prescription of adjuvant chemotherapy. In order to carry out a hypothetical exercise for estimating the potential cost savings with the use of gene expression profiling in breast cancer, two key parameters must be specified: i) screening cost per patient and ii) annual average cost of chemotherapy per patient. The cost of MammaPrint 70-gene signature is €2,675 per patient (Agendia, BV).

The total cost of conventional chemotherapy for breast cancer must take into account all its components. Table 7.4 shows the annual total average cost per patient based upon an estimation performed by Lacey *et al.* (2010) in the Irish NHS setting. In this sense, the total cost of prescribing chemotherapy to our target subgroup of patients (i.e. ER+, HER2−), which accounts for 323 patients, would be €2,249,695. In the case of excluding 58% of those patients, identified as being at low risk of metastasis via the genetic testing, from chemotherapy treatment the potential cost saving would account for €1,295,490. By discounting the total cost of the screening (€864,025) there will finally be a potential net cost saving of €431,465, which accounts for 19% of the total cost of chemotherapy for the entire subgroup of patients. As previously emphasized, this illustrative exercise was focused on guiding adjuvant treatment decisions with genetic testing on a specific subgroup of patients where there is no consensus of recommended treatment. Therefore, it represents a conservative approach. A less restrictive application of gene expression profiling in breast cancer may be able to yield larger potential cost savings provided that the cost of the avoided chemotherapy is sufficiently large in comparison with the cost of the genetic screening.

Table 7.3 Applying gene expression profiling to a subgroup of patients without clinical consensus regarding prescription of chemotherapy

| Clinical decision-making protocols | Recommended treatment based upon St Gallen Consensus | MammaPrint LOW RISK | MammaPrint HIGH RISK | Total number patients | LOW RISK (%) |
|---|---|---|---|---|---|
| < 1cm, LN0, PVI–, ER– | No treatment | 5 | 5 | 10 | 50% |
| < 1cm, LN0, PVI–, ER+ | Endocrine therapy | 23 | 10 | 33 | 70% |
| HER2+, ER– | Anti-HER2 + chemotherapy | 3 | 37 | 40 | 7% |
| HER2+, ER+ | Anti-HER2 + endocrine therapy + chemotherapy | 13 | 61 | 74 | 18% |
| ER– | Chemotherapy | 4 | 76 | 80 | 5% |
| ER+, HER2– (Gr III or 3LN or > 5cm or ER < 50%) | Endocrine therapy + chemotherapy | 103 | 171 | 274 | 38% |
| **ER+, HER2– (Gr II or LN 1–3 or 2–5cm)** | **Endocrine therapy + yes/no chemotherapy** | **186** | **137** | **323** | **58%** |
| ER+, HER2– (Gr I and LN0 and ≤ 2cm y ER > 50%) | Endocrine therapy | 23 | 5 | 28 | 82% |
| Total | | 360 | 502 | 862 | 42% |

Source: Own elaboration (data from Zanconati et al., 2011)

*Table 7.4* Average cost per patient of chemotherapy in the
          Irish health system

| Chemotherapy treatment components | Average cost |
|---|---|
| Cost of chemotherapy drugs | €1,002 |
| Cost of administration & monitoring | €1,646 |
| Cost of treatment of adverse events | €756 |
| Cost of preventing adverse events | €3,561 |
| **Total cost** | **€6,965** |

### Cost-Effectiveness of Gene Expression Profiling in Breast Cancer

In the field of economic evaluation, eight cost-effectiveness analyses have been published so far regarding gene expression profiles in breast cancer: i) four regarding the Oncotype-DX 21-gene assay versus clinical guidelines such as National Comprehensive Cancer Network (NCCN) and St. Gallen (Hornberger *et al.* 2005; Lyman *et al.* 2007; Kondo *et al.* 2008; Tsoi *et al.* 2010); ii) two regarding MammaPrint 70-gene signature versus clinical guidelines such as St. Gallen, National Institute of Health (NIH) and Adjuvant! Online (Oestreicher *et al.* 2005; Retel *et al.* 2010); and finally, (iii) two comparing the two commercialized available breast cancer genetic tests: Oncotype-DX and MammaPrint (Retel *et al.* 2011; Yang *et al.* 2012). In the reported CEAs regarding Oncotype-DX, all patients with an intermediate or high risk were assumed to receive hormonal (if endocrine responsive) and chemotherapy. In the two CEAs regarding MammaPrint, it was assumed that patients with a high risk test result would undergo hormonal (if endocrine responsive) and chemotherapy. In all CEAs the genomic profile in question was found to be cost-effective compared with the clinical guideline used. In one CEA comparing both genetic platforms, sensitivity and specificity were based on two datasets and the perspective of the analysis was the Dutch health system (Retel *et al.* 2011). The results indicated that MammaPrint seems to have the highest probability of being cost-effective when focusing on cost per QALY, while Oncotype-DX seems to have the highest probability of being cost-effective when focusing on cost per life year gained. In the second study comparing Oncotype-DX and MammaPrint (Yang *et al.* 2012), all patients started with a risk classification state based on an assessment by Adjuvant! Online. Subsequently, patients were reclassified into risk categories based on the two gene expression profiling tests using reclassification probabilities from the literature. The model suggested that MammaPrint is a more cost-effective test compared with Oncotype DX at a threshold willingness-to-pay of $50,000 per QALY. Because Oncotype DX is the most frequently used GEP in clinical practice in the United States, the authors concluded that the current findings have implications for health insurance reimbursement decisions. Figure 7.6 shows a summary of results of cost-effectiveness studies regarding the use of genetic platforms in early breast cancer. In all cases, the incremental cost-effectiveness ratios indicate that both the 21-gene assay and the 70-gene signature seem to be cost-saving and/or cost-effective strategies as compared with clinical–pathological guidelines. These favorable results can be explained by two main reasons: first, due to the cost savings of chemotherapy for those patients reclassified as low risk with the genetic testing

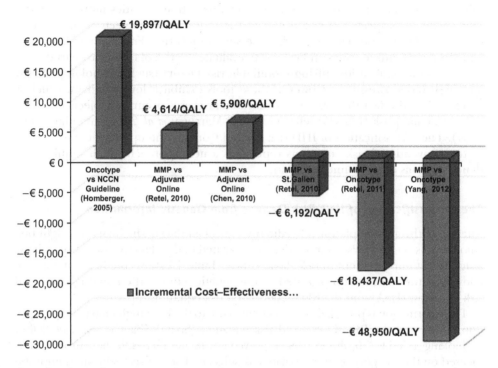

*Figure 7.6* Cost-effectiveness analysis results of comparing alternative genetic platforms in early breast cancer

and originally classified as high risk by the clinical-pathological guidelines; second, by the positive impact on quality of life in terms of avoiding minor, major, or fatal toxicity from chemotherapy for those patients who would not get any benefit from it. As for the comparison between the two genetic tests, it is not possible to get conclusions on the basis of just two studies. However, the fact that Oncotype-DX places patients in three categories (high, intermediate and low risk) rather than in two categories (high and low risk) deserves special attention in further analysis.

## The Use of Genetic Platforms to Reduce the Burden of Cardiovascular Disease: Adding Genetic Risk Information to the Standard Risk Equations

Cardiovascular disease is prevalent and expensive. The application of recommended activities could prevent a high proportion of the coronary artery disease events and strokes that are otherwise expected to occur in the adult population today. If every person could receive the prevention activities for which they are a candidate, myocardial infarcts could be reduced ≥60%, strokes could be reduced 30%, and everyone's life expectancy could be increased an average of 1.3 years and at a higher quality of life than currently experienced (Kahn *et al.* 2008). However, most of the prevention activities will substantially increase costs. If preventive activities are to achieve their full potential, ways must be found to deliver prevention activities more efficiently. One of the key aspects lies in the correct identification of subjects at high risk of cardiovascular disease. The use of risk-assessment tools (e.g. Framingham-based risk equation) accounts for the standard way to evaluate the risk of ischemic heart disease (IHD) on the basis of identifying modifiable risk factors (such as smoking, obesity and high blood pressure). However, these tools exhibit a low sensitivity, which is explained by the fact that 50% of cardiovascular events occur in subjects classified as intermediate risk (Lluis-Ganella *et al.* 2012; Marrugat *et al.* 2011; Greenland *et al.* 2004). The reclassification of IHD risk derived from adding up genetic information to the conventional risk equations represents a new approach which requires evidence in terms of economic evaluation.

### The Reclassification of IHD Risk Derived from Genetic Information

The use of the genetic platform Cardio-inCode® (Gendiag), which assesses eight polymorphisms (eight SNPs) independently associated to the classical risk factors, allows a significant improvement in risk classification. Table 7.5 shows the final outcome of adding up the information provided by the genetic score to the Framingham-based risk equation (USA) and the REGICOR-based risk equation (Spain).

The information is provided by the genetic score to the Framingham-based risk equation (USA) and the REGICOR-based risk equation (Spain) (Baena-Díez *et al.* 2009). By looking at Table 7.5, the greater improvement in the reclassification procedure is focused on the category of intermediate risk subjects. The net reclassification improvement (NRI), which offers a meaningful check of classification accuracy, indicates that the genetic score improves in 24.76% and 14.30% the original classification of intermediate risks derived from REGICOR and Framingham equations, respectively. In particular, as for the reclassification in the REGICOR cohort of patients, the standard risk equation identified 813 subjects in the intermediate risk category, while the genetic score places 690 subjects in that category. The former finding implies that 123 subjects were wrongly classified as intermediate risk by using classical risk factors information. This set of subjects actually has different probabilities of suffering IHD events than those correctly classified as intermediate risks, and consequently they require different schemes of preventive treatment on the basis of their actual genetic risk score (high or low risk).

### Cost-Effectiveness of the Risk Assessment of IHD Events with Genetic Platforms

A study performed by Ramírez de Arellano *et al.* (2013) conducted an economic analysis of the risk assessment of IHD with Cardio-inCode® (adding the genetic risk to the functions of REGICOR and Framingham) compared with the standard method (using only the functions). Figure 7.7 shows the Markov model developed with seven states of health (low, intermediate, high IHD risk, episode of IHD, recurrent episode of IHD, chronic IHD and death). The reclassification of IHD risk derived from genetic information and transition probabilities between states was obtained from a validation study conducted in cohorts of REGICOR (Spain) and Framingham (USA).

It was assumed that patients classified as intermediate risk by the standard method could be evaluated and reclassified with Cardio-inCode®. The utilities and

Table 7.5 Reclassification of risks of ischemic heart disease by including genetic information

**REGICOR**

Coronary events (cases)

| Classical risk factors | Classical risk factors + genetic score | | | |
|---|---|---|---|---|
| | Low risk | Intermediate-low risk | Intermediate-high risk | High risk |
| Low risk | 24 | 6 | 0 | 0 |
| Intermediate–low risk | 1 | 22 | 8 | 1 |
| Intermediate–high risk | 0 | 4 | 10 | 5 |
| High risk | 0 | 0 | 1 | 21 |

Coronary events (non-cases)

| | Low risk | Intermediate-low risk | Intermediate-high risk | High risk |
|---|---|---|---|---|
| Low risk | 1415 | 105 | 1 | 0 |
| Intermediate–low risk | 115 | 339 | 64 | 9 |
| Intermediate–high risk | 0 | 36 | 69 | 30 |
| High risk | 0 | 5 | 20 | 40 |

**FRAMINGHAM**

Coronary events (cases)

| Classical risk factors | Classical risk factors + genetic score | | | |
|---|---|---|---|---|
| | Low risk | Intermediate-low risk | Intermediate-high risk | High risk |
| Low risk | 60 | 11 | 0 | 0 |
| Intermediate–low risk | 7 | 36 | 5 | 0 |
| Intermediate–high risk | 0 | 4 | 30 | 9 |
| High risk | 0 | 0 | 8 | 84 |

Coronary events (non-cases)

| | Low risk | Intermediate-low risk | Intermediate-high risk | High risk |
|---|---|---|---|---|
| Low risk | 2014 | 50 | 0 | 0 |
| Intermediate–low risk | 57 | 444 | 49 | 1 |
| Intermediate–high risk | 0 | 47 | 207 | 30 |
| High risk | 0 | 0 | 34 | 350 |

**REGICOR**

| | All | Intermediate risk |
|---|---|---|
| NRI Coronary event | 12.17 [1.99;22.34] | 24.76 [7.62;41.91] |
| IDI Coronary event | 1.62 [0.72;2.51] | 0.54 [−0.38;1.46] |

**FRAMINGHAM**

| | All | Intermediate risk |
|---|---|---|
| NRI | 2.56 [−2.89;8.01] | 14.30 [3.08;25.51] |
| IDI | 0.22 [0.03;0.42] | 0.26 [−0.03;0.55] |

**META-ANALYSIS**

| | All | Intermediate risk |
|---|---|---|
| NRI | 6.37 [−2.85;15.58] | 17.44 [8.04;26.83] |
| IDI | 0.85 [−0.52;2.21] | 0.29 [0.01;0.56] |

Source: Lluis-Ganella et al. (2012)

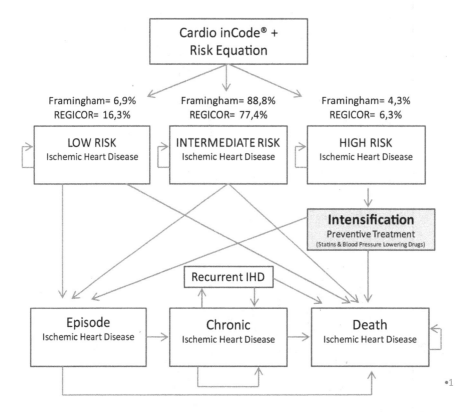

*Figure 7.7* Markov model used to perform cost-effectiveness analysis comparing [Genetic score + Risk equation] versus [Risk equation]

costs of Markov states were obtained from the literature and Spanish sources. The analysis was done from the perspective of the Spanish national health system, for a lifetime horizon. For a Cardio-inCode® price of €400, the cost per QALY gained compared with the standard method (ICER) would be €12,957 and €21,328 in REGICOR and Framingham cohorts, respectively (see Table 7.6). The threshold price of Cardio-inCode® to reach the ICER threshold generally accepted in Spain (€30,000/QALY) would range between €668 and €836. The greatest benefit occurred in the subgroup of patients with intermediate–high risk, with a high-risk reclassification of 23% of patients and an ICER of €1,650/QALY and €5,893/QALY (REGICOR and Framingham cohorts). Sensitivity analyses confirmed the stability of the study results.

## Conclusions

This chapter has intended to provide an overview of the current applications of economic evaluation on the field of pharmacogenomics. The relatively small number of cost-effectiveness evaluations of pharmacogenomics reflects the currently limited

*Table 7.6* Summary of cost-effectiveness analysis results based on three risk reclassification outcomes

**Reclassification from intermediate risk**
**REGICOR cohort**

| Comparator | Cost (€) | QALY | ICER (€) |
|---|---|---|---|
| Cardio-inCode® | 20,016.30 | 13.70 | 12,957.03 |
| Risk equation | 19,684.60 | 13.67 | |
| Difference | 331.70 | 0.03 | |

**FRAMINGHAM cohort**

| Comparator | Cost (€) | QALY | ICER (€) |
|---|---|---|---|
| Cardio-inCode® | 20,194.84 | 13.62 | **21,328.73** |
| Risk equation | 19,840.18 | 13.60 | |
| Difference | 354.66 | 0.02 | |

**Reclassification from intermediate (low/high) risk**
**REGICOR cohort**

| Comparator | Cost (€) | QALY | ICER (€) |
|---|---|---|---|
| Cardio-inCode® | 20,142.71/20,256.71 | 13.71/13.73 | **4,030.65/1,650.32** |
| Risk equation | 19,902.08/20,103.89 | 13.65/13.64 | |
| Difference | 240.63/152.82 | 0.06/0.09 | |

**FRAMINGHAM cohort**

| Comparator | Cost (€) | QALY | ICER (€) |
|---|---|---|---|
| Cardio-inCode® | 20,248.58/20,245.42 | 13.63/13.66 | **8,510.95/5,893.96** |
| Risk equation | 19,945.59/19,971.94 | 13.60/13.61 | |
| Difference | 302.99/273.48 | 0.03/0.05 | |

Source: Ramírez de Arellano et al. (2013)

use of these technologies as well as the complexity in combining a genetic test plus a drug as the relevant comparator in CEAs. The main hurdle for a drug/test combination being successful in terms of efficiency is the difficulty in calculating the likely cost savings in terms of reduced drug toxicity and/or improved efficacy. This is so because there is little evidence based on actual clinical practice. Additionally, adverse reactions and efficacy are invariably the outcome of both genetic and non-genetic factors. Nonetheless, the potential benefits, in both health and economic terms, are considerable. In this chapter, illustrative examples of successful cost-effectiveness analysis applications have been explained. In this sense, the key factors identified as influencing the cost-effectiveness of pharmacogenomic candidates are the following: i) establishment of a link between genotype and drug response, ii) strength of the association between the genetic mutation and clinical outcomes, iii) ease, rapidity and cost of genetic testing, iv) prevalence of genetic mutation as well as of the associated disease or health outcome, v) clinical and economic severity of the adverse reactions that might be avoided, vi) cost and effectiveness of alternative therapies, and vii) potential for improved monitoring of drug response. It is worth noting that therapeutic interventions based on individual genetic variation will not be applicable to all drugs and careful evaluation of cost-effectiveness will be needed on a case-by-case basis.

# References

Aspinall, M.G. and Hamermesh, R.G. (2007). Realising the promise of personalized medicine. *Harvard Business Review*, 85, 108–17.

Baena-Díez, J.M., Grau, M., Sánchez-Pérez, R., *et al.* (2009). La función calibrada de REGICOR mejora la clasificación de pacientes de alto riesgo tratados con estatinas respecto a Framingham y SCORE en la población española. *Revista Española de Cardiología*, 62, 1134–40.

Centers for Disease Control and Prevention (2010). *Genomic Testing: ACCE model process for evaluating genetic tests.* CDCP, Atlanta (available online at: www.cdc.gov/genomics/gtesting/ACCE).

Chiou, C.F., Hay, J.W., Wallace, J.F., *et al.* (2003). Development and validation of a grading system for the quality of cost-effectiveness studies. *Medical Care*, 41, 32–44.

Elkin, E.B., Weinstein, M.C., Winer, E.P., *et al.* (2004). HER-2 testing and trastuzumab therapy for metastatic breast cancer: a cost-effectiveness analysis. *Journal of Clinical Oncology*, 22, 854–63.

Greenland, P., LaBree, L., Azen, S.P., *et al.* (2004). Coronary artery calcium score combined with Framingham Score for risk prediction in asymptomatic individuals. *The Journal of the American Medical Association*, 2, 210–5.

Hopkins, M.M., Ibarreta, D., Gaisser, S., *et al.* (2006). Putting pharmacogenetics into practice. *Nature Biotechnology*, 24, 403–10.

Hornberger, J., Cosler, L.E. and Lyman, G.H. (2005). Economic analysis of targeting chemotherapy using a 21-gene RT-PCR assay in lymph-node-negative, estrogen-receptor-positive, early stage breast cancer. *American Journal of Managed Care*, 11, 313–24.

Kahn, R., Robertson, R.M., Smith, R. and Eddy, D. (2008). The impact of prevention on reducing the burden of cardiovascular disease. *Diabetes Care*, 31, 1686–96.

Knauer, M., Mook, S., Rutgers, E.J., *et al.* (2010). The predictive value of the 70-gene signature for adjuvant chemotherapy in early breast cancer. *Breast Cancer Research and Treatment*, 120, 655–61.

Kondo, M., Hoshi, S.L., Ishiguro, H., *et al.* (2008). Economic evaluation of 21-gene reverse transcriptase-polymerase chain reaction assay in lymph-node-negative, estrogen-receptor-positive, early stage breast cancer in Japan. *Breast Cancer Research and Treatment*, 112, 175–87.

Lacey, I., Chien, R. and Hornberger, J. (2010). Cost-utility of the 21-gene breast cancer assay (Oncotype-DX) in the Irish healthcare setting. *Cancer Research*, 15, 71.

Lindner, L., Lara, N., Tàssies, D., *et al.* (2009). Genotyping in patients in treatment with acenocoumarol cost-effectiveness. *Revista Española Economia de la Salud*, 8, 77–84.

Lluis-Ganella, C., Subirana, I., Lucas, G., *et al.* (2012). *Predictive capacity of the Framingham coronary risk function improved by including a genetic score.* Barcelona: Archive Ferrer inCode.

Lyman, G.H., Cosler, L.E., Kuderer, N.M. and Hornberger, J. (2007). Impact of a 21-gene RT-PCR assay on treatment decisions in early stage breast cancer: an economic analysis based on prognostic and predictive validation studies. *Cancer*, 109, 1011–8.

Marrugat, J., Vila, J., Baena-Diez, J.M., *et al.* (2011). Relative validity of the 10-year cardiovascular risk estimate in a population cohort of the REGICOR Study. *Revista Espanola de Cardiologia*, 5, 385–94.

Oestreicher, N., Ramsey, S.D., Linden, H.M., *et al.* (2005). Gene expression profiling and breast cancer: what are the potential benefits and policy implications? *Genetics in Medicine*, 7, 380–9.

Phillips, K.A., Veenstra, D., Van Bebber, S. and Sakowski, J. (2003). An introduction to cost-effectiveness analysis of pharmacogenomics. *Pharmacogenomics*, 4, 231–9.

Pirmohamed, M. and Lewis, G. (2004). The implications of pharmacogenetics and pharmacogenomics for drug development and health care. In: Mossialos, E., Mrazek, M. and Walley, T. (eds). *Regulating pharmaceuticals in Europe: striving for Efficiency, Equity and Quality.* Open University Press, Maidenhead.

Ramírez de Arellano, A., Coca, A., de la Figuera, M., *et al.* (2013). Economic evaluation of Cardio-inCode®: a clinical-genetic function for coronary heart disease risk assessment. *Applied Health Economics and Health Policy*, 11, 531–42.

Retel, V.P., Joore, M.A., Knauer, M., *et al.* (2010). Cost-effectiveness of the 70-gene signature versus St. Gallen guidelines and Adjuvant Online for early breast cancer. *European Journal of Cancer*, 46, 1382–91.

Retel, V.P., Joore, M.A. and Van Harten, W.H. (2011). Head-to-head comparison of the 70-gene signature versus the 21-gene assay: cost-effectiveness and the effect of compliance. *Breast Cancer Research Treatment*, 13, 627–36.

Secretary's Advisory Committee on Genetics, Health and Society (2007). Realizing the promise of pharmacogenomics: opportunities and challenges. *Biotechnology Law Report*, 26, 261–91.

Shah, J. (2003). Economic and regulatory considerations in pharmacogenomics for drug licensing and healthcare. *Nature Biotechnology*, 21, 747–53.

Shankaran, V., Bentrem, D.J., Mulcahy, M.F. *et al.* (2009). *Economic implications of Kras testing in metastatic colorectal cancer (mCRC)*. Abstract No. 298. Presented at the 2009 Gastrointestinal Cancers Symposium (ASCO).

Stallings, S.C., Huse, D., Crown, W.H., *et al.* (2006). A framework to evaluate the economic impact of pharmacogenomics. *Pharmacogenomics*, 7, 853–62.

Trusheim, M.R., Berndt, E.R. and Douglas, F.L. (2007). Stratified medicine: strategic and economic implications of combining drugs and clinical biomarkers. *Nature Reviews Drug Discovery*, 6, 287–93.

Tsoi, D.T., Inoue, M., Kelly, C.M., *et al.* (2010). Cost-effectiveness analysis of recurrence score-guided treatment using a 21-gene assay in early breast cancer. *The Oncologist*, 15, 457–65.

Van de Vijver, M.J., He, Y.D., Van't Veer, L.J. *et al.* (2002). A gene expression signature as a predictor of survival in breast cancer. *New England Journal of Medicine*, 347, 1999–2009.

Wong, W.B., Carlson, J.J., Thariani, R. and Veenstra, D.L. (2010). Cost-effectiveness of pharmacogenomics. *Pharmacoeconomics*, 28, 1001–13.

Yang, M.S., Rajan, S. and Issa, A.M. (2012). Cost effectiveness of gene expression profiling for early stage breast cancer. *Cancer*, 118, 5163–70.

Zanconati, F., Cusumano, P., Tinterri, C., *et al.* (2011). The 70-gene expression profile, MammaPrint, for breast cancer patients in mainly European hospitals. *The Breast*, 20, 45.

# Chapter 8

# *electronic* Health Economics (eHE)

*Olivier Ethgen, Justine Slomian and Mel Walker*

## Introduction

No need today to be an expert in information technologies (ITs) to realize that the internet is an integral part of our daily lives. Communicating through the web and connecting to electronic networks has become a daily reflex for both private and professional purposes. Lack of connection or poor quality connections are tolerated less and less. Instead, poor connectivity is often a major source of frustration, with hosting services expected to consistently provide high-speed, stable wireless connections.

Wikipedia[1] defines IT as the "branch of knowledge concerned with the development, management and use of computer-based information systems". Furthermore, information and communication technology (ICT) is presented as "a more specific term that stresses the role of unified communications and the integration of telecommunications (telephone lines and wireless signals), computers as well as necessary enterprise software, middleware, storage and audio-visual systems, which enable users to access, store, transmit and manipulate information". ICT is a full sector of the economy which hired about 14 million people in 2011. This sector now affects practically all others sector of the economy (OECD 2012, 2014). Despite the global economic crisis, the top ICT firms experienced a 6% annual growth in revenue between 2000 and 2011 (OECD 2012).

Admittedly, the ascendency of ICT in our daily lives was accelerated by the launch of the first smartphone in 2007. Since then, smartphones have been continuously developing and spreading. The arrival, only a few years later, of tablets with even higher storage capability has enhanced the predominance of ICT. This leap forward of mobile ICT, alongside ever-extending and accelerating high-speed wireless connections, allows for perfect user mobility, quasi-uninterruptable connectivity and virtual social interactions. In addition, progress in digitalization and micro-processing continues to enable faster transfers of even greater quantities of information. User applications also tend to multiply excessively while improving continuously to enrich user experience, handiness and shared conviviality.

Health and medicine are not unaffected by the upsurge in ICT use. On the contrary, medicine is one of the areas where ICTs hold one of their core promises (Topol 2012). The term "health information technologies" (HITs) is now broadly used to encompass ICT that has been designed or adapted to gather, record, store and communicate health information with the ultimate objective to improve clinical decisions and patient outcomes. In this chapter, we first introduce a series of HIT concepts. We then offer a discussion of the promises of HIT for health economics in the future.

## *electronic* Health (eHealth)

*e*Health is a rather broad term that encompasses the explicit use of ICT to record, store, access, exchange and analyze health-related information. Up to 51 definitions have been identified, spread over a large spectrum of themes but without a clear consensus about the exact meaning (Oh *et al.* 2005). There is, however, a tacit understanding of the meaning of *e*Health, covering two universal themes – health and technology – and six narrower themes – commerce, activities, stakeholders, outcomes, place and perspectives (Oh *et al.* 2005). *e*Health therefore has a broader meaning than telemedicine, which refers to the delivery of care when the clinician and the patient are separated by time and/or distance (Hersh 2009).

### Telemonitoring

Telemonitoring consists of using an electronic device that interfaces the patient and health care providers to provide remote real-time monitoring of medical conditions and to facilitate disease management and patient education (Vrijhoef *et al.* 2009; Polisena *et al.* 2010; Yang *et al.* 2012). The patient can be anywhere – at home, work, or any other places that their medical condition allows. Daily information is transmitted to a secure server over the phone (ordinary line or smartphone). Relevant time intervals can be used to segment information as clinically appropriate (hourly, bi-daily, weekly, etc.). Telemonitoring systems can be used very practically to feed data to patient registries, i.e. electronic data warehouse following up prospective cohorts of new patients from the onset of a new disease or the initiation of a new treatment. Patient registries can be used to make inferences over real-world effectiveness, toxicity and costs of treatments.

### Electronic Health Record (EHR)

Nowadays, in the developed world, virtually all places of health care delivery, such as physician offices, laboratories, pharmacies or hospitals, record and store medical information electronically. An electronic medical record (EMR) is the electronic record of real-world health-related information on an individual patient that is created, gathered, managed and can be consulted by the medical staff of a single health care organization involved in that patient's care. By extension, an electronic health record collects and provides patient information but from the multiple point of care. It corresponds to the longitudinal collection of patient-level data in real-world conditions as patients' seek and receive health care from multiple providers at different places of delivery (inpatient or outpatient).

An EHR thus has a broader scope as it allows the comprehensive collection of health information across multiple health care providers, via a unique patient identifier. An EHR embraces all medical aspects of a patient's health condition and clinical care pathway. However, an EHR generally must conform to nationally established interoperability standards so that the information can be gathered and consulted by multiple authorized health care providers across the entire national health system. An EHR can thus be considered as an EMR with interoperability features, i.e. with the possible integration of data across multiple health care providers' systems as enabled by technical, semantic and process standards.

An EHR can potentially result in better and more comprehensive communication of medical information across the health care continuum (OECD 2012). A data-capture system can be developed to gather data for specific study or modeling purposes. For instance, search parameters and algorithms can be designed to retrieve and compile relevant clinical practice information from EHRs, providing a comprehensive view of the treatment history and outcomes (Yamamoto *et al.* 2008).

The promises of EHR for improving quality, safety and effectiveness of health care while reducing operating costs are becoming increasingly established among policy makers (Hersh 2009; OECD 2012). The adoption of EHRs and the development of data-capture systems that would precisely integrate with EHRs to address particular research questions are increasingly considered as a priority health care investment by many governments of industrialized countries (OECD 2012; Takemura *et al.* 2012). The opportunities here for truly pragmatic trial designs that better reflect real-world outcomes are vast (van Staa *et al.* 2012).

### Personal Health Record (PHR)

A personal health record can be seen as the ultimate evolution of the EHR in the sense that it is a patient-controlled EHR. PHRs offer the possibility for patients to enter and manage their own health information and to have access to their health care providers' EHRs (Pearson *et al.* 2011). A PHR can thus be linked to multiple EHRs. Just imagine, a patient traveling with all their past and current health and treatment information at their fingertips on their smartphone or tablet. MicroSoft HealthVault[2] is a good example of a PHR. With a PHR, the integrity of the data and the control of access to the data are the responsibility of the individual patient. It is their responsibility to decide what information is stored and who has access to it. Interestingly, a PHR can include lifestyle, behavioral and environmental information in addition to past and current clinical information, making such a personal record clinically and epidemiologically meaningful (Figure 8.1). As increasingly user-friendly apps and monitoring devices are developed to support the storage of health information, PHRs are likely to become a significant source of real-world health outcomes data (Ved *et al.* 2011). However, the question remains as to whether these systems will be widely adopted, updated and properly managed by patients.

### Health Social Network

An increasing proportion of patients are turning to the internet to search for health and medical information. The internet has become an inexhaustible source of information, notably with highly effective and increasingly "intelligent" search engines. Patients not only seek health information on the internet, they also seem increasingly willing to share disease and treatment experience within virtual communities or forums. The social network phenomenon has taken hold of health and medicine as well. More specifically, health social networks (HSNs) are online social networks

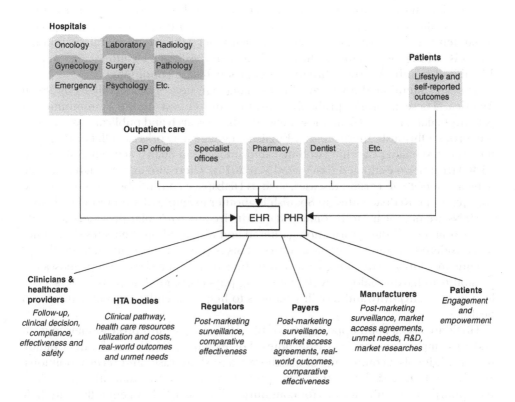

*Figure 8.1* Electronic health record (EHR) and personal health record (PHR)

where patients can interact, network, share experience and learn from each other about their medical conditions, treatments, outcomes and disease management. Nowadays, relatively large communities of patients are developing online. These HSNs are becoming a meaningful source of evidence as patient-reported data have been gaining increased relevance and credibility for clinical research (Frost 2011).

PatientsLikeMe[3] is probably one of the most visible HSNs and one of the most advanced in terms of research today. The site claims over 325,000 members reporting on more than 2,400 conditions. All this patient-level information represents approximately 27 million data points about disease and has contributed to more than 60 published research studies (last visited May 2015). CureTogether[4] is another HSN that more specifically focuses on the effectiveness of treatments. On its welcome page, the site proposes to "get access to millions of ratings comparing the real-world performance of treatments across 637 health conditions" (last visited May 2015). As with PatientsLikeMe, CureTogether is increasingly using its HSN community to compare and report on the effectiveness and use of popular treatments (Pearson *et al.* 2011).

Besides these generic HSNs, a host of disease-specific networks have popped up in the last few years. They usually have quite evocative names, such as TuDiabetes.org, MyBreastCancerTeam.com or AstmaAlliance.com. Some generic HSNs, probably confronted with the demand of their members for more tailored and disease-specific information, have compartmentalized their network by disease area. An example of this is Alliance Health, which operates a large "portfolio of condition-specific social networks", covering, for instance, diabetes, sleep disorders, migraine, multiple sclerosis, COPD, depression, arthritis or back pain.[5] Alliance Health claims to serve 1.5 million members across a broad set of chronic health conditions.

The sites mentioned above are English-language networks, notably from North America. These networks probably constitute the largest online communities of patients to date. It is also from these networks that research and publications are most numerous. Obviously, there are non-English-language networks as well. For example, the French-speaking Carenity[6] website claims more than 80,000 active members and 26,400 treatments evaluated (last visited May 2015). There also exist French-language networks specific to certain diseases, such as Diabspace.com (diabetes) or OncoCity. com (cancer). Redpacientes[7] in Spanish is another example of a non-English HSN.

HSNs are not meant to recommend or criticize any particular providers or medical treatments. All the information gathered and displayed on their sites should not be considered as suitable medical advice. This is precisely an issue that MedHelp[8] intends to address. This site goes a step further than other HSNs and proposes the possibility to have a dialogue with counseling physicians. MedHelp also offers a collection of connectivity and mobility services to help its members monitor their own health.

HSNs are also a good opportunity for physicians and health professionals to train and to compare anonymized case notes. For example, RadRounds[9] offers radiology professionals a community to collaborate and share cases and receive opinions. Sermo[10] and Ozmosis[11] are other examples of social networks that offer physicians the opportunity to submit cases for community discussion. They generally fund their sites with manufacturer sponsorships and advertisements.

### Quantified Self

Many HSNs now propose quantified self-tracking tools. The Quantified Self (QS) is a movement whose purpose is to further the quantitative measurement and analysis of self-owned personal data.[12] The QS is not a health-specific movement but health and wellness are among the core areas of QS applications. Health-related QS tools enable patients to catalogue, measure and report their personal health and well-being data over time in an analytical and standardized fashion (Pearson *et al.* 2012; Appelboom *et al.* 2014a). Symptoms, mood, feelings, medication effectiveness, toxicity, etc. can all be self-appraised, self-reported and analyzed online with QS tracking tools. The QS movement is the subject of a growing and global collaborative community of researchers, designers and users of self-tracking tools.

### mobile Health (mHealth)

ICT in medical applications has progressed to such an extent that today a multitude of medical parameters can be measured, monitored and recorded remotely by the patient themselves (Dobkin and Dorsch 2011; Appelboom *et al.* 2014b). This is all the more remarkable in that many of the technologies being developed are less and less invasive and increasingly user friendly (Slomian *et al.* 2014a). This trend is expected to strengthen in the future (Topol 2012). An increasing number of detectors (or sensors) are being made wearable and easy to use. They can be connected effortlessly to a mobile device, enabling real-time tracking and monitoring of the patient's progress under real-world conditions (Figure 8.2). Therefore, real-world data from the patients can be almost automatically and continuously transferred to servers. The information collected can then be processed and periodically redirected to clinicians as individual patient assessments or as aggregated statistics for a particular group of patients (Appelboom *et al.* 2014c).

Such novel ways of collecting real-world data through mobile phones is no longer science fiction. For instance, a company called SocialMoodLabs[13] launched a large-scale *m*Health application to measure and improve people's physical and psychological well-being. The app presents users with various tests and questionnaires through a notification system that guarantees the randomization of sampling throughout the day. The notifications can be presented even when the smartphone is offline, a feature that is of paramount importance since mental states are likely to be biased if they are measured exclusively when users are online (Kross *et al.* 2013). Tests involve various smartphone sensors, including the microphone, the touch screen and the camera. These sensors yield rich and comprehensive assessment of patients' health that is later sent to users through direct and personalized feedback available

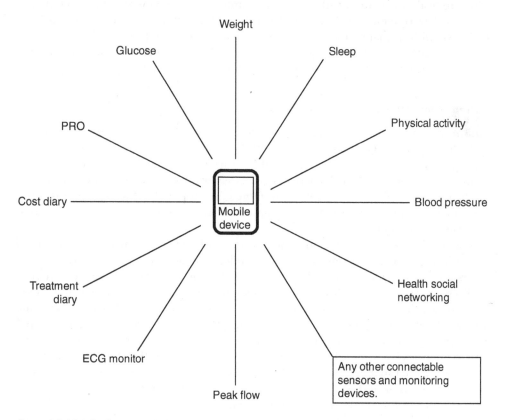

*Figure 8.2* Mobile devices to help patients and physicians for real-time health care monitoring
*Note:* PRO: Patient-reported outcomes; ECG: Electrocardiogram.

on their smartphones. Beyond helping individuals to measure and improve their well-being, this type of mobile app also represents a tremendous opportunity for researchers. As an example, Taquet *et al.* (2014) recently evidenced the importance of emotions in predicting people's behavior based on this app. The statistical models they developed can be used to predict what type of behavior patients are likely to engage in depending on their emotional states (e.g. risky, medication compliance).

Parameters assessed by SocialMoodLabs and other emerging companies are not limited to emotions. Such technology can be used to capture many real-time physical parameters or symptoms (e.g. heart rate, movement, cognitive ability, stress), health behaviors (e.g. sleeping, eating habits, time spent exercising), and medication impact (e.g. treatment efficacy, adverse events). See, for instance, Withings,[14] iHealth,[15] iBGStar,[16] PropellerHealth,[17] or Proteus.[18] Taken together, smartphone applications can be of great interest for patient and disease management by offering large datasets that will improve the diagnosis, the prognosis and ultimately the patient outcome.

Another recent innovation is noteworthy in terms of *m*health. A group of engineers has developed a thin and flexible microchip that can be literally stuck to the patient's skin. The chip is so thin that its developers do not hesitate to speak of "epidermal electronics" (Kim *et al.* 2011). The chip can be used to collect a variety of physiological information without any discomfort for the patient (Ma 2011). At this stage of development, cardiovascular, cerebral and muscular information has been collected with a quality and a reliability deemed equivalent to standard measures (Kim *et al.* 2011; Ma 2011). Again, it seems likely that such technologies will continue to develop and improve even further in the future (Topol 2012).

### Patient Engagement Platforms (PEPs)

Online patient engagement platforms are probably the most recently developed *m*Health initiative. The intention of a PEP is to facilitate patient monitoring and engagement in medical care using social networking, diaries, blogs, games, QS functions and connected medical devices. A great deal of effort is made to design tools and applications that are as user friendly and engaging as possible for the patients. They are meant to support clinical decisions based on real-life tracking of patient-reported experience and outcomes.

FolUp[19] is a good illustration of a PEP. This platform was specifically designed by clinicians (neurosurgeons) to support clinical management and research. FolUp offers a set of flexible and enabling services for clinicians, patients and researchers. It allows easy connection to a few medical technologies as well as connectable medical and health devices. The stated objective is to improve overall patient outcome and accelerate clinical discovery based on self-reported and quantified data collected online in a medically supervised environment. The medical supervision under which FolUp operates is a noticeable feature of PEPs that increases the clinical reliability of some of the data that are collected. It is a participatory clinician who invites eligible patients to register and to report online. The diagnosis is thus medically confirmed and patient responses are clinically superintended. This feature of PEPs sharply contrasts with HSNs where anyone can enroll online and self-declare specific health conditions online.

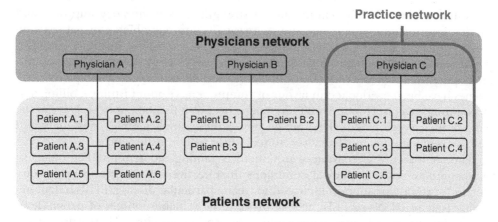

*Figure 8.3* The possible interweaving of multiple networks with PEP like FolUp (adapted from folup.com)

Figure 8.3 illustrates the different medically controlled sub-networks that can be generated with PEPs. These sub-networks can be useful to patients and physicians to help them to exchange their experiences and learn from each other. In addition, the information collected on these networks can be aggregated (statistically) and analyzed to inform the pattern of use and the performance of a specific health care technology or treatment in real-world conditions.

PowHealth[20] is another example of a PEP. It provides an online social environment for patients or carers to monitor, track and share changing lifestyle or health management needs with physicians or loved ones. A core focus of this platform is to leverage engagement tools and gamification mechanics to drive behavior change. Multiple connected devices can be added to conveniently capture evolutions. PowHealth also enables the patient to create and maintain their own secure PHR.

## Discussion

ICTs are increasingly available, useful and convenient. The services ICTs can render appear increasingly indispensable in our contemporary societies and nothing seems to limit their expansion. Medicine and health care are no exception to this general craze for ICTs. It is increasingly acknowledged that HIT can help to streamline health care and to improve patient outcomes. In the US, an authoritative physician announced "the creative destruction of medicine" (Topol 2012). The author described through detailed and concrete examples how the age of digitalized information is going to change the way medicine is practiced (Topol 2012). Convergence between ICTs and medical devices will further revolutionize our health care environment. Logically, if medicine capitalizes on the promises that HITs offer in terms of information gathering, storage and exchange, health economics will have to adapt in order to stay relevant.

The main advantage of HITs for health economists probably lies in the fact that they increasingly facilitate the quasi real-time follow-up of patients under real-world conditions. This valuable feature should strengthen as technology improves and health information systems become increasingly interoperable. The patient outcomes aspect of *e*Health and *m*Health is of particular interest for health economists. Until now, mostly payment and reimbursement issues have driven IT investments and operations in health care (Bates 2002). Clinical decision making and patient outcomes have been overlooked in favour of comprehensive administrative, billing and accounting systems. However, HITs are taking over with the patient experience at the core of their development. They are becoming increasingly mobile, convenient and reliable, enabling unequalled access to real-world patient experience.

The comparative effectiveness movement is gaining momentum. The objective is to compare under real-world conditions the effectiveness, safety and health outcomes for several treatments indicated to treat a particular disease. EHRs, telemonitoring systems, HSNs or PEPs may all prove to be valuable sources of patient-level data to inform comparative analyses under real-world conditions. These information systems or networks can provide clinicians, epidemiologists and health economists with relatively rapid access to a vast source of patient-based information that is not protocol-driven. Relatively large, anonymized and longitudinal patient databases can be generated in real-world conditions. Such sources of information can be used, for example, to identify specific sub-groups of patients with a greater likelihood of treatment response or greater risk of treatment failure or adverse events.

HITs can also serve as a lever for the implementation of large-scale comparative effectiveness studies. They can support real-world outcome studies and contribute to post-marketing surveillance systems. The range of services that HITs can render to streamline health care seems immense. The description of HIT potential sounds idyllic with the real-world patient experience at the core and indeed significant technological advances have already occurred. Health care providers are becoming progressively more reliant on mobile technologies and applications (Franko *et al.* 2012; Sclafani *et al.* 2013; Robinson *et al.* 2013). Medical information is now almost routinely digitalized and computerized. At a time when the demand for additional data by both regulators and payers is increasing to such an extent that many worry about the extra cost of drug development, HIT may actually offer a much-needed solution that will ensure that research remains feasible despite increasing evidentiary burden.

Medical information is still fragmented and warehoused across multiple databases. Many questions and obstacles remain to be overcome before HIT can be deployed and used to full capacity. The issue of interoperability between different systems is of particular concern (de la Torre *et al.* 2012 and 2013; PLOS Medicine Editors 2013). The issues of data access security, protection of privacy and data ownership may arise as well (Hsiao *et al.* 2012a, 2012b; Grams 2012). Regulators and payers have not yet really taken a position about the information collected on the basis of HIT in real-world conditions, for instance how data gathered from HSNs should be considered given the uncontrolled and unconfirmed nature of patient enrollment and reports. PEPs may help to resolve this drawback of HSNs by offering a medically controlled environment. However, this will function on a voluntary basis only and broad adoption by physicians is still to be proven as of today.

Massive amounts of medical and therapeutic information are now available at everyone's fingertips on the internet. The increasing inclination of patients to seek advice, share information and socialize online is a growing reality that can no longer be ignored (Thackeray *et al.* 2013; Zhang *et al.* 2013). The internet broadens the patient's knowledge about their illness, which makes patients even more empowered and engaged in their own care (Slomian *et al.* 2014b). The information found on the internet may also influence clinical decisions. Betsch *et al.* (2012a, 2012b) have specifically discussed this aspect for vaccination decisions. The authors called on public health officials to put additional effort into increasing the effectiveness of internet-based communication with easy-to-find and user-friendly websites, attractive presentation and readily available and reliable information about vaccination risks and benefits.

Internet and mobile devices are progressively transforming the clinical encounter. The patient–physician relationship is shifting from a paternalistic model to a much more balanced and collaborative model (Mascret 2012). As a matter of fact, medical and therapeutic information is becoming less and less asymmetrical between the physician and the patient. Even if this could be perceived as additional hassle for proper medical practice, the upsurge of mobile technologies in the patient–physician encounter relationship is also a major opportunity. Having good sources of information and exchange at the patient's disposal may actually contribute to more efficient health care as patients become better informed and more engaged in their care. "The doctor knows the disease but the patient experiences it in the flesh" (Lucas, cited by Mascret 2012). Patients and physicians can thus combine their complementary knowledge to adjust clinical decisions and foster compliance based upon mutually understood and agreed criteria. Mobile applications to improve adherence and patient follow-up between clinical encounters are seen as the most likely to develop and spread in the years to come (Topol 2012). Standardized patient-reported outcomes (PRO) questionnaires, including health utilities questionnaires, can be readily included, as well as health care resource utilization surveys or cost diaries.

The *raison d'être* of health economics models is to help health care decision makers and payers to make informed investment decisions by allocating the available resources as wisely as possible. Cost-effectiveness (CE) has clearly emerged as the preferred health economics modeling framework over the last two decades. The cost-effectiveness appraisal of an innovative technology needs a large amount of data. Generally, the necessary data are taken from pivotal phase III trials, systematic reviews, meta-analysis and claim databases. Experts' opinions and patients' charts reviews can also be used. It is thus mainly *ex-ante* and indirect evidence that document cost-effectiveness appraisals. Even in systems where CE is not the mainstay for decision making, clinical added value can be assessed through appropriate clinical modeling combined with new data sources.

It is becoming increasingly unpalatable for payers to fund health care technologies without some form of guarantee regarding the quality and value delivered under real-world conditions. Studies and models from the *ex-ante* (i.e. the investigational) world are necessary but not on their own sufficient to prove clinical benefit and economic value in the eyes of payers. As a result, the pricing and reimbursement processes for new health care technologies are changing. A greater emphasis is now given to real-world evidence. Moreover, payers tend to consider market access agreements such as coverage with evidence development or risk-sharing schemes that link the price of a technology to its real-world performance or volume of use.

It sounds premature to announce the end of the way health modeling is currently practiced. However, relying exclusively on *ex-ante* and indirect evidence to inform decision analytic models might well become obsolete. HITs are developing and spreading across the health care continuum and will be making it easier to implement comparative effectiveness analysis, adaptive study and modeling designs as well as market access agreements. Some practical applications have already emerged (Naversnik and Mrhar 2014). As described in this chapter, HITs hold great promise in terms of real-world and patient-centric data acquisition and processing. Therefore, health economists should consider the new route of evidence generation enabled by HITs, *e*Health and *m*Health initiatives in addition to the habitual clinical trials, systematic reviews and administrative databases.

## Conclusion

The path to digital medicine and mobile health is being paved from a technical standpoint. HITs are continually developing and improving. It is now rather a matter of broader adoption and diffusion throughout health care systems. The forthcoming generations of physicians and patients will be even more inclined to rely on HITs. Likewise, the future generation of health economists will need to consider HITs as a means of gathering and processing information. Economic and financial models could be populated and updated with patient-centric and real-world information in a timely fashion. This will enhance the value of health economics models and analyses for decision makers. One important avenue for future research would be the operationalization of *m*Health to design and implement adaptive coverage and reimbursement systems as information is collected and processed based on real-world patient experience.

## Disclosure

The authors of this chapter have no financial interest in any of the products, brands or companies cited in the chapter.

## Notes

1  http://en.wikipedia.org/wiki/Main_Page (last visited August 2014).
2  www.healthvault.com
3  www.patientslikeme.com
4  http://curetogether.com
5  www.alliancehealth.com
6  www.carenity.com
7  http://redpacientes.com/
8  www.medhelp.org/
9  www.radrounds.com/
10  www.sermo.com/
11  https://ozmosis.org/home
12  http://quantifiedself.com
13  http://socialmoodlabs.com/
14  www2.withings.com/uk/en/
15  www.ihealthlabs.com/

16  www.ibgstar.us/
17  http://propellerhealth.com/
18  www.proteus.com/
19  www.folup.com/
20  www.powhealth.com

## References

Appelboom, G., LoPresti, M., Reginster, J.-Y., *et al.* (2014a). The quantified patient: a patient participatory culture. *Current Medical Research & Opinion,* 30, 2585–7.

Appelboom, G., Camacho, E., Abraham, M.E., *et al.* (2014b). Smart wearable body sensors for patient self-assessment and monitoring. *Archives of Public Health,* 72, 28.

Appelboom, G., Yang, A.H., Christophe, B.R., *et al.* (2014c). The promise of wearable activity sensors to define patient recovery. *Journal of Clinical Neuroscience,* 21, 1089–93.

Bates, D. (2002). The quality case for information technology in healthcare. *BMC Medical Informatics & Decision Making,* 2, 7.

Betsch, C. and Sachse, K. (2012a). Dr. Jekyll or Mr. Hyde? (How) the Internet influences vaccination decisions: recent evidence and tentative guidelines for online vaccine communication. *Vaccine,* 30, 3723–6.

Betsch, C., Brewer, N.T. and Brocard, P., *et al.* (2012b). Opportunities and challenges of Web 2.0 for vaccination decisions. *Vaccine,* 30, 3727–33.

de la Torre-Diez, I., Gonzalez, S. and Lopez-Coronado, M. (2012). Analysis of the EHR systems in Spanish primary public health system: the lack of interoperability. *Journal of Medical Systems,* 36, 3273–81.

de la Torre-Diez, I., Gonzalez, S. and Lopez-Coronado, M. (2013). EHR systems in the Spanish Public health national system: the lack of interoperability between primary and specialty care. *Journal of Medical Systems,* 37, 9914.

Dobkin, B.H. and Dorsch, A. (2011). The promise of mHealth: daily activity monitoring and outcomes assessments by wearable sensors. *Neurorehabilitation and Neural Repair,* 25, 788–98.

Franko, O.I. and Tirrell, T.F. (2012). Smartphone app use among medical providers in ACGME training programs. *Journal of Medical Systems,* 36, 3135–9.

Frost, J.H. (2011). The case for using social media to aggregate patient experiences with off-label prescriptions. *Expert Review in Pharmacoeconomics and Outcomes Research,* 11, 371–3.

Ginsberg, J., Mohebbi, M.H., Patel, R.S., *et al.* (2009). Detecting influenza epidemics using search engine query data. *Nature,* 457, 1012–4.

Grams, R. (2012). In the world of medical alphabet soup – "Will a workable EMR or EHR please stand up?". *Journal of Medical Systems,* 36, 3079–81.

Hersh, W. (2009). A stimulus to define informatics and health information technology. *BMC Medical Informatics & Decision Making,* 9, 24.

Hsiao, T.-C., Wu, Z.-Y., Chung, Y.-F., *et al.* (2012a). A secure integrated medical information system. *Journal of Medical Systems,* 36, 3103–13.

Hsiao, T.-C., Liao, Y.-T., Huang, J.-Y., *et al.* (2012b). An authentication scheme to healthcare security under wireless sensor networks. *Journal of Medical Systems,* 36, 3649–64.

Kanas, G., Morimoto, L., Mowat, F., *et al.* (2010). Use of electronic medical records in oncology outcomes research. *ClinicoEconomics & Outcomes Research,* 2, 1–14.

Kim, D.-H., Lu, N., Ma, R., *et al.* (2011). Epidermal electronics. *Science,* 333, 838–43.

Kross, E., Verduyn, P., Demiralp, E., *et al.* (2013). Facebook use predicts declines in subjective well-being in young adults. *PLOS One,* 8, e69841.

Ma, Z. (2011). An electronic second skin. *Science,* 333, 830–1.

Mascret, D. (2012). La santé s'impose sur internet et les réseaux sociaux [French]. *Le Figaro,* 28 November.

Naversnik, K. and Mrhar, A. (2014). Routine real-time cost-effectiveness monitoring of a web-based depression intervention: a risk-sharing proposal. *Journal of Medical Internet Research*, 16, e67.

OECD (2012). Internet economy outlook 2012, OECD Publishing. DOI: 10.1787/9789264086463-en.

OECD (2014). Measuring the digital economy – a new perspective, OECD Publishing. DOI: 10.1787/9789264221796-en.

Oh, H., Rizo, C., Enkin, M. and Jadad, A. (2005). What is eHealth (3): a systematic review of published definitions. *Journal of Medical Internet Research*, 7, e1.

Pearson, J.F., Brownstein, C.A. and Brownstein, J.S. (2011). Potential for electronic health records and online social networking to redefine medical research. *Clinical Chemistry*, 57, 196–204.

PLOS One Editors (2013). A reality checkpoint for mobile health: three challenges to overcome. *PLOS Medicine*, 10, e1001395.

Polisena, J., Tran, K., Cimon, K., *et al.* (2010). Home telemonitoring for congestive heart failure: a systematic review and meta-analysis. *Journal of Telemedicine & Telecare*, 16, 68–76.

Robinson, T., Cronin, T., Ibrahim, H., *et al.* (2013). Smartphone use and acceptability among clinical medical students: a questionnaire-based survey. *Journal of Medical Systems*, 37, 9936.

Sclafani, J., Tirrell, T.F. and Franko, O.I. (2013). Mobile tablet use among academic physicians and trainees. *Journal of Medical Systems*, 37, 9903.

Slomian, J., Reginster, J.-Y., Ethgen, O., *et al.* (2014a). Opportunity and challenges of eHealth and mHealth for patients and caregivers. *Austin Journal of Public Health and Epidemiology*, 1, 3.

Slomian, J., Appelboom, G., Ethgen, O., *et al.* (2014b). Can new information and communication technologies help in the management of osteoporosis? *Women's Health*, 10, 229–32.

Takemura, T., Araki, K., Arita, K., *et al.* (2012). Development of fundamental infrastructure for nationwide EHR in Japan. *Journal of Medical Systems*, 36, 2213–8.

Taquet, M., Quoidbach, J., De Monjoye, Y.-A. and Desseilles, M. (2014). Mapping collective emotions to make sense of collective behavior. *Behavioral and Brain Sciences*, 37, 102–3.

Thackeray, R., Crookston, B.T. and West, J.H. (2013). Correlates of health-related social media use among adults. *Journal of Medical Internet Research*, 15, e21.

Topol, E. (2012). *The creative destruction of medicine*. Basic Books, New York.

van Staa, T.P., Goldacre, B., Gulliford, M., *et al.* (2012). Pragmatic randomised trials using electronic health record: putting them to the test. *British Medical Journal*, 344, e55, DOI: 10.1136/bmj.e55.

Ved, V., Tyagi, V., Agarwal, A. and Pandya, A.S. (2011). Personal health record system and integration techniques with various electronic medical record systems. *Proceedings of the Institute of Electrical and Electronics Engineers (IEEE), 13th International Symposium on High Assurance Systems Engineering (HASE)*, 10–12 November, pp. 91–4.

Vrijhoef, H.J.M., Janssen, J.J.M. and Greenbeg, M.E. (2009). Feasibility of telemonitoring for active surveillance of influenza vaccine safety in the primary care setting in the Netherlands. *Journal of Telemedicine and Telecare*, 9, 362–7.

Wicks, P., Keininger, D.L., Massagli, M.P., *et al.* (2012). Perceived benefits of sharing health data between people with epilepsy on an online platform. *Epilepsy & Behavior*, 23, 16–23.

Yamamoto, K., Matsumoto, S., Tada, H., *et al.* (2008). A data capture system for outcomes studies that integrates with Electronic Health Record: development and potential uses. *Journal of Medical Systems*, 32, 423–7.

Yang, C.-C. and Hsu, Y.-L. (2012). Remote monitoring and assessment of daily activities in the home environment. *Journal of Clinical Gerontology and Geriatrics*, 3, 97–104.

Zhang, Y. and Sang, Y. (2013). Facebook as a platform for health information and communication: a case study of a diabetes group. *Journal of Medical Systems*, 37, 9942.

# Chapter 9

# Population Needs, Opportunity Costs and Economic Methods for Financial Sustainability in Health Care Systems

*Stephen Birch and Amiram Gafni*

## Introduction

Equitable access to health care is an objective of many health care systems (Mooney *et al.* 1991). Policies aimed at extending coverage of health insurance or publicly funded health care provision to broader (or entire) populations are often a central part of health care reforms aimed at promoting equitable access to care. Removing price as the mechanism for allocating health care among competing demands increases the demand for care. Adopting need for care as the means of allocating health care resources instead of price combines concerns about equitable access to care (those with greater needs receive greater priority) with concerns about efficient resource use (maximizing expected health gain from available resources). Moreover, under universal public health care programmes governments are the sole (or major) purchaser of health care and hence in principle can use their monopsony power as a way of managing and controlling the costs of health care. However, in practice there is no evidence to suggest that publicly funded health care systems *per se* are any more successful at controlling health care costs than health care systems with a greater involvement of private financing. For example, based on OECD figures (OECD 2011), the rate of increase in the proportion of gross domestic product (GDP) spent on health care over the period 1989–2009 was greater in the UK (with a predominantly publicly funded system) than in the US (with a predominantly privately funded system). Yet other countries with predominantly publicly funded systems, such as Sweden and Canada, had lower rates of increase than either the UK or the US over the same period. In all these countries, health care continued to absorb an increasing proportion of what was, in the case of most countries, an increasing GDP. Hence, the type of health care system, although determining who has access to care, has little influence on cost control *per se*.

The failure to control health care costs as a result of market failure in a privately funded system is not solved by government intervention in the funding and provision of health care per se. Instead cost control (and hence sustainability of health care systems) will depend on the methods used for planning and evaluating health care resources use. If appropriate methods are not adopted, government intervention simply replaces market failure by government failure, leading to possible perceptions that health care systems aimed at maximizing population health gain from health care resources through policies of equitable access to health care are unsustainable. In this chapter we challenge this notion of equitable access to health care being unsustainable and show that the continuous increases in health care costs are the result of inappropriate assumptions underlying the methods for planning and evaluating health care resources.

We focus attention on two areas of planning and evaluation, economic evaluation of health care and health workforce planning, illustrating the failures of these approaches, as well as the lack of integration between the approaches to be responsible for the rapid increases in health care costs. We offer alternative approaches that relate directly to the needs of populations. These approaches provide effective means of cost control within a policy context of equitable access to care and the efficient use of health care resources.

## Illusions of Necessity: Needs Versus Demands

As noted above, allocating health care resources in accordance with relative needs for care combines considerations of equitable access to care with efficient use of resources. Much attention has been given to methods for accommodating relative needs for care in resource allocation mechanisms (e.g. Birch *et al.* 1993; Birch, *et al.* 1996; Eyles *et al.* 1991; Gravelle *et al.* 2003; Mays 1995). In contrast, little attention has focussed on population needs in planning health care systems, with financial, service and workforce planning each being performed separately and in isolation of explicit consideration of population needs for care (Birch and Maynard 1985a). Instead, planning has been based on incremental increases to existing resources to reflect ageing populations, advances in technology and changing public expectations on the implicit assumption that these factors are exogenous positive influences on health care resource requirements (Birch and Maynard 1985b). As a result, the costs of health care systems increase monotonically, usually at rates greater than the funding capacities of jurisdiction, leading to (1) questions being asked about the sustainability of publicly funded health care systems over time, and (2) policies proposed that generally detract from the objective of equitable access to care (e.g. reductions in the breadth or depth of public coverage and the introduction or increase in cost sharing). But none of these factors is directly linked to changes in needs for care.

Ageing populations relate to demographic as opposed to epidemiological trends and are driven primarily by reductions in age-specific mortality. The number of individuals at risk of illness or disability may change over time, but there is little attention paid to the levels of those risks. We would expect the average age-specific needs for health care per person to fall if average levels of health increase. Such reductions in need would therefore offset, at least partially, the increased health care needs arising from increased survival (i.e. more people at risk).

Advances in health technology involve developments that increase the productivity of health care providers (e.g. laprascopic surgery) and hence reduce the workforce (and other resources) required to support a particular level of service needs. Beyond productivity-improving technological change, developments that allow health care systems to "do more with more resources" represent increases in the scope of the health care system as opposed to increased efficiency, and need to be evaluated in the context of both the benefits produced within the health care system and the opportunity costs of the additional resource requirements.

Finally, patient expectations rarely represent exogenous shifts in patients' needs for care but are more likely to be influenced by providers exposing patients to possibilities for treatment often associated with new technologies. So, while each factor may be a source of increased demands for care, and hence increased costs to a health care system, none of these factors relates directly to changes in population needs for care (and hence the impact on the population health gain) or to the opportunity costs of satisfying those increased demands (what has to be forgone to meet these demands). Instead they are the result of the atypical nature of the demand for health care. In particular, individuals do not demand health care *per se*, because they have limited knowledge and information about the range, roles and effectiveness of different health care interventions. Instead individuals demand changes in the level of (or risk to) health.

In this way the demand for health care is derived from their demand for health status change in consultation with health care professionals who serve as agents to advise and prescribe what health care services should be demanded. Hence individuals' demand for health care is induced by suppliers. But suppliers also draw income from providing care and hence play a dual role as suppliers of care and agents of demanders of care. As a result, changes in demands are unlikely to reflect only changes in needs for care, particularly where changes in needs are likely to result in reduced demand for care, other things equal. Instead, demands for care will also be influenced by the number of providers and their expectations for workload and incomes. It is this divergence between the epidemiological concept of need for care and the economic concept of demand for care that lies behind what Evans (1985) described as the illusions of necessity in health care.

In the rest of this chapter we illustrate how this illusion of necessity occurs in two applications of health economics to the planning and evaluation of health care. We identify the underlying assumptions of the methods used, the inappropriateness of some of those assumptions and the consequences of employing these methods. We identify alternative approaches that relate directly to the needs of populations and show how financial sustainability can be maintained within a policy context of equitable access to care and the efficient use of health care resources.

## Economic Evaluation of Health Care as a Method for Sustainable Service Planning

Decision makers are continually faced with the new health care technologies offering the prospect of increased effectiveness for the treatment of particular conditions or patient groups. But increased effectiveness is not sufficient to warrant adoption given the constrained resources of a health care system. The challenge for decision makers is to determine whether choosing to adopt a new technology can be expected to increase health gains from the scarce resources available to the health care system. In other words, does adopting the new technology add more to health gains than whatever service or services are to be reduced or cancelled in order to fund the new technology? Even where a health care system receives greater funding, increased effectiveness is not sufficient to warrant the adoption of the new technology because other interventions not currently funded by the system, or the expansion of services already funded, may provide greater health gains than that offered by the new technology.

Cost-effectiveness analysis (CEA) has been presented in the health economics literature, and adopted in many jurisdictions, as the methodology to help decision makers allocate health care resources in ways that maximize the total health gain (Gafni and Birch 2006). Ministries of health in Australia, Ontario (Canada) and the UK all introduced mandatory requirements for economic evaluations as part of proposals for new drugs and interventions to be included in the publicly funded health care systems and explicit guidelines were developed for the conduct of such evaluations. Similar approaches have become fairly widespread, especially for the approval of new drugs (Drummond 2012).

However, evidence from the application of this approach shows that the total costs of the programmes has increased substantially. For example, expenditures increased by 14% per annum on the pharmaceutical benefits programme in Australia (Zinn 2002), while the adoption of economic evaluation guidelines by NICE in the UK was associated with an annual unplanned increase in NHS costs of £836 million (Gold and Bryan 2007). In Ontario, expenditure on the Ontario Drugs Benefits Plan increased by 10–15% per annum, resulting in questions being raised about the sustainability of the programme by provincial premiers, ministers of health and others (Laupacis 2002). This has led Drummond (2012) to conclude that after 20 years of formalized economic evaluation within health care systems, "the impact of economic evaluation on the allocation of healthcare resources is hard to ascertain".

Given that the fundamental concepts of economics – scarce resources require choices to be made that ensure the benefits generated from the way we choose to use resources exceed the benefits that would be generated by all alternative uses of the same resources – reflect the decision makers' concerns with efficiency, how has the use of economics resulted in this policy failure? As we show below, this can be explained by the attempts to simplify methods of economic evaluation by excluding considerations of opportunity cost (Gafni and Birch 2006). In particular the model that underlies the CEA method (Weinstein and Zeckhauser 1973) is based on several explicit theoretical assumptions that have no relevance to the practical challenges facing decision makers, namely perfect divisibility (a health care programme can be implemented for any quantity of available resources, e.g. one can implement one fifth of a CAT scanner) and constant returns to scale (increases in programme size produce the same proportionate increase in programme outcomes for all sizes of programme, e.g. doubling the size of a screening programme will double the number of positive tests) and perfect information on the incremental effects and incremental costs of all programmes (Birch and Gafni 1992 and 1993; Gafni and Birch 2006). Under these assumptions a threshold incremental cost-effectiveness ratio (ICER), $\lambda$, is calculated representing the opportunity cost of available resources at the margin. This is then used to determine whether investment of available resources in a new technology by diverting resources from other current uses represents a net health gain and hence an increase in efficiency of resource use.

In the absence of perfect information on all possible programmes, the threshold ICER cannot be determined. In practice, an arbitrarily determined threshold $\lambda$ is used instead, reflecting the subjective assessment of decision makers or researchers on what they consider to be a reasonable average price per unit health gain. For example, Laupacis et al. (1992) proposed a figure of $20,000 per QALY gain for use as the threshold for adopting new programmes in Ontario. Laupacis (2002) has since acknowledged that this figure was not derived from any consideration of opportunity costs but was simply made up. Because the threshold value is unrelated to and independent of the opportunity cost of the interventions under consideration, it provides no useful information for determining the efficiency of using available health care resources to support those interventions. This failure to incorporate opportunity cost in the decision-making process has led to unplanned rapid increased expenditures on health care programs noted above (Gafni and Birch 2006).

The choice facing a decision maker is not simply between a new intervention and the current way of treating the same patient group; a positive ICER means that the resources used by the current intervention are not sufficient to support the new intervention for the same number of patients. Additional resources must come from other uses in order to make up this shortfall, meaning that adopting new intervention requires replacing the current intervention and making cuts to other programs, in order to have sufficient resources to support the new intervention. To maximize health gains the decision maker needs to consider whether the population needs being met by the new intervention are greater than the population needs that could be met by using the resources the new intervention requires in other ways. By ignoring opportunity costs, the threshold approach to decision making continually adds to total costs without knowing whether total health gains increase, remain constant or decrease. So instead of producing the biggest bang for the buck, the use of CEA simply results in bigger bucks for the bang, without knowing the size of the bang (Birch and Gafni 2006).

How, then, can economics be applied in ways that avoid this threat to sustainability of health care systems aimed at maximizing health gains by providing equitable access to care? Drummond (1980) noted that the only way to ranking programmes in the context of a resource constraint is by mathematical programming, the traditional methodology for solving constrained maximization problems. However, decision makers are additionally constrained by indivisibilities in programmes representing either physical constraints (you cannot buy a part of an MRI machine) or policy constraints (screening 50% of children at risk may not be ethically acceptable). Integer programming (IP) is a special form of mathematical programming used to solve problems of constrained maximization in the presence of indivisibilities such as those faced by decision makers seeking to maximize health gain while subject to a health care constraint (Birch and Donaldson 1987; Gafni and Birch 1992). By incorporating the resource constraint explicitly into the analytical model, the approach encompasses opportunity cost considerations directly without the need for the unrealistic assumptions of the traditional CEA approach. In particular it is focussed on comparing different portfolios (or mixes) of health care interventions that can be supported from the available resources and identifying the portfolio that maximizes health gain. Hence it informs a decision maker as to whether introducing a new intervention into the portfolio of interventions can lead to an increase in health gain given the requirements of that intervention for additional resources from within the current resource constraint.

Consider the example of a health care organization allocated an additional $20 million to improve the health of its clients. The CEO approaches the therapeutic committee for recommendations for allocating the extra money. Table 9.1 describes four (hypothetical) new interventions that are potential candidates for implementation, aimed at treating four different conditions. Each intervention is described in terms of its additional effects and costs (for all patients with the disease) relative to the current way of treating these patients, as well as its ICER.

Suppose the committee decides that $50,000 per QALY is the maximum acceptable price to pay for health improvements. The only program acceptable is A, total additional health gains are 285 QALYs and $6 million is left unused. However, choosing B and C, neither of which meets the threshold, results in a larger total additional health gain (326 QALYs) with $2 million left unused. In other words, the organizations can achieve more health gain by deciding not to adopt the intervention with the lowest ICER.

In both cases it makes no sense to leave some of the allocated extra funds unused since there are enough resources left to purchase D, an intervention that produces additional health gains. However, if A, the intervention with the lowest ICER, is chosen, the additional health gain that can be generated with the residual budget is 51 QALYs (3 units of D, assuming constant returns to scale), producing a total additional health gain of 336 QALYs. If B and C are chosen, this leaves enough resources to purchase one unit of D and hence generate a total additional health gain of 343 QALYs. Hence purchasing A does not lead to an efficient use of resources. The use of ICER to decide which program to purchase fails to maximize the health gains from a given (additional) budget.

The key requirement of the IP approach is that the specification of the problem (i.e. objective function and constraints) must accurately reflect the decision maker's problem setting and variations on the approach have been presented to deal with different policy settings and constraints (Stinnett and Paltiel 1996). Moreover, the approach is not limited to operating under a single constraint and is easily adapted to deal with other multiple constraints. For example, separate constraints might be required to accommodate decision makers' equity goals. Only by incorporating these other requirements as additional constraints can we ensure that they are pursued efficiently (i.e. in ways that generate equitable outcomes at minimum opportunity cost).

The substantial data requirements of the IP approach, specifically the information on all costs and effects of all existing and new interventions, may be difficult to satisfy. However, these requirements reflect the complex nature of ensuring an efficient allocation of available resources. In practice, the IP approach has been used to inform decisions within individual programme areas. For example, IP approaches have been used to identify the efficient mix of HIV-treatment interventions in South Africa (Cleary et al. 2010) and the efficient mix of services for schoolchildren in a rural region of Southern Thailand (Tianviwat et al. 2011). Because these applications do not take into account all programs in the health care system, they are limited to identifying "local" solutions (i.e. restricted maximization of health gains within the programme area) where broader application that encompasses all health care intervention in the system might identify further health gains from reallocation of resources between programme areas. Nevertheless these applications reflect a decision maker's problem setting, i.e. within the context of a resource constraint, which is a prerequisite for the sustainability of the system.

An alternative approach is available which satisfies a modified objective of unambiguous increase in (as opposed to maximization of) health gain from available resources (Birch and Gafni 1992; Gafni and Birch 1993). This requires that the health gain of the proposed intervention be compared with the health improvements produced by that combination of interventions that is to be given up to generate sufficient resources to support the proposed intervention. Only where the health gain of the proposed intervention exceeds the health gains of the interventions to be given up (i.e. the health gain forgone or opportunity cost) does the new technology represent an improvement in the efficiency of use of available resources. Iterative application of the approach will of course lead to maximization of health gain when no further increases in health gain can be found from the reallocation of available resources. In this case resources are being allocated efficiently and any further health gain would require additional resources (which of course would need to be considered in the context of the opportunity cost of reallocating such resources from other sectors of society). The approach has been illustrated graphically in the form of a decision-making plane and extended to deal with the uncertain nature of costs and outcomes (Sendi *et al.* 2002).

## Incorporating Service Planning into a Model for Sustainable Workforce Planning

We argued above that in order to maximize health gains, decision makers must consider whether the population needs being met by the new intervention are greater than the population needs that could be met by using the resources the new intervention requires in other ways. In this way decisions about what services to provide are determined in relation to the needs of the population being served as opposed to the preferences of those providing services. As a result, decisions about the size and mix of the health care workforce must be linked directly to (or integrated with) decisions about the levels and mix of services required to maximize health gain. However, in practice there has been little if any integration of workforce planning with service planning. In this section the methods used for workforce planning are critically appraised and an approach for integrating workforce and service planning is presented.

### The "Inevitability" of Workforce Shortages

Although the number of practicing doctors per 1,000 population increased by 42% in the UK, 23% in Australia, 19% in New Zealand, 10% in the US and 9% in Canada over the first decade of the new millennium, each country reports serious shortages of doctors, as indicated by long wait times for treatments and poor access to primary care in some communities or population groups (OECD 2011). Given these substantial rates of increase appear to be insufficient to maintain reasonable levels of services, questions about financial sustainability of health care systems emerge. What explains this apparent never-ending need for more health care given the changes occurring in population health and the delivery of health care? For example, major improvements occurred in both oral health (particularly among children) and dentist productivity (associated with changes in the way care is delivered) over the last quarter century of the last millennium. However, dentist numbers continued to increase at rates faster than the increase in the size of the population (OECD 2009). Although one might have anticipated reductions in the average workload (and income) per dentist, this ignores the "rising expectations" in dentistry as reflected by, for example, the rapid expansion of orthodontics among children.

Where did this "expectation" come from? Mothers did not march on parliament demanding governments deal with the problem of children's "bent" teeth. Nor were governments identifying children's "bent" teeth as a threat to the economy, national security or general welfare. Instead, dentists, whose workloads were at risk as average needs per child fell and average productivity per dentist increased, took an interest in straightening children's teeth (for more on supplier-induced demand in UK dentistry see Birch 1988). This was not an unmet need that governments *planned* to address as part of oral health policy. Instead, services expanded to meet the provider workload expectations during periods when needs for care were falling.

Similarly, reductions in fertility rates and improvements in the average health of children currently observed in many countries seem inconsistent with trends in the numbers of paediatricians and expansion of children's hospitals. Shipman *et al.* (2004) identified this divergence in trends of supply and needs as a problem to the paediatric profession and offered three options for maintaining workloads: "provide significantly more medical services to the fewer children under their care, expand their patient populations to include more young adults, or attract a significantly greater proportion of children's visits currently going to non-paediatricians". Within four years the American Academy of Pediatrics introduced recommendations for screening children for high cholesterol from the age of two (Daniels and Greer 2008).

Because workforce planning methods do not respond to changes in the needs of the population or changes in productivity of providers serving those needs, the estimated required number of providers increases in line with the (age-adjusted) size of the population. As a result no attempt is made to integrate the needs of populations or the service requirements to meet those needs in determining the optimal supply of providers. Instead services respond to the workload preferences of providers. Using Evans' health care "income expenditure identity" (Evans 1984), developments that offer the prospect of reductions in health care expenditures, such as reduced needs and improved productivity, involve reductions in the aggregate income of providers, either through the use of fee-for-service remuneration systems or threats to the current levels of non-fee-for-service remunerated positions. Providers may therefore respond in order to maintain workloads and protect incomes and positions by identifying other "things to do" for patients –and creating illusions of necessity (Evans 1985).

## Health Workforce Planning or "Demography Gone Wild"?

Estimating the future supply of providers involves quantifying the current stock of potential providers, future additions to and losses from that stock, and the quantity of time for service production/delivery flowing from the stock (Birch *et al.* 2007). Aside from the careful identification and measurement of the determinants of these variables, estimating supply has provided few conceptual challenges.

Traditional methods for estimating future requirements for providers, $N_{t+1}$, where t+1 is the future time period, have also been relatively straightforward, being determined by applying a provider–population ratio to the estimated future size of the population, $P_{t+1}$. With the future population size being exogenous, future requirements are "controlled" through the provider–population ratio. In the simplest case the prevailing provider–population ratio $(N_t/P_t)$ is used and future requirements are driven entirely by the population size. Higher provider–population ratios may be used to respond to perceived shortages in providers (e.g. wait times), or ageing populations, or to coincide with some external provider–population ratio (in other jurisdictions or based on international recommendations). Nevertheless, the required number of providers is calculated as a fixed proportion of the population size. Levels of health or sickness (and by implication levels of need for health care) are absent. Two populations identical in size but with different health profiles would have the same provider requirements. Similarly, requirements would be independent of changes in population health over time. Only reductions in population size or decisions by planners that fewer providers per population are required would lead to reductions in the number of providers required. There is no evidence of either condition ever having occurred in health workforce planning. So, what gives rise to the requirement for providers under this approach is the amount of people to be served, not the amount of sickness or risks to health among those people.

In this way the traditional approach assumes that the required number of providers is a constant proportion of the size of the population (i.e. population numbers are used as a proxy for population needs for care) and that this relationship is constant over time and between different populations. Of course, if providers became more effective in treating needs, we would require fewer providers to serve the same population size. Similarly, if the role of providers changed by, for example, the adoption of new technology that required less provider time to deliver the same service (e.g. laser treatment for cataracts), we would also require fewer providers to serve the same population size. But the current approach, by adopting this simple analytical approach to determining requirements, implicitly assumes that what providers do, how they do it and what they achieve by doing it remain constant over time (and the same across populations).

So why do we observe persistent claims of provider shortages? Because health workforce planning has been performed in isolation of health service planning, providers and professional bodies can expand services in order to meet their workload preferences. As the new or expanded services become the norm, demand (as opposed to need) per capita grows and more providers are required to meet this expanded demand within a population increasing in size. So although we might expect provider–population ratios to fall over time as the average health of the population as well as productivity in health care increase, we observe the opposite.

### An Integrated Approach to Workforce Planning

To avoid these problems the conceptual basis of health workforce planning can be expanded to recognize that (1) need for health care is determined by the health of the population not simply its size, (2) the requirement for providers is derived from the requirement for services and (3) neither of these relationships is constant over time. The "simple" demographic model suggests

$$N_{t+1} = (N/P)^* \times P_{t+1}$$

Because there is no objective basis for the provider–population ratio, $(N/P)^*$, Birch *et al.* (2007) broke the ratio down into its constituent parts so that:

$$N_{t+1} = (N/Q)_{t+1} \times (Q/H)_{t+1} \times (H/P)_{t+1} \times P_{t+1}$$

where Q is the quantity of health care services to be delivered and H is the level of health in the population. Provider requirements are determined by four separate variables. *Demography* ($P_{t+1}$) remains a key determinant of requirements. However, this is now translated into health needs through explicit consideration of *epidemiology* (H/P), the average level and type of sickness in the population. No longer is the health profile of the population assumed fixed through time or across space. A third determinant, *level of service* (Q/H), represents the planned level and mix of services to respond to the health profile of the population, while *productivity*, the inverse of (N/Q), translates the quantity of service requirements into requirements for each type of provider involved in the production of those services.

Each element of the model is variable across different populations and over time. Hence planning must incorporate changes occurring in all four elements, e.g. the reduction in dental disease among children, the increased productivity in ophthalmology, etc. Moreover, each of these variables is potentially influenced by policies, although in the case of demography and epidemiology, potential policy levers are largely beyond the scope of health care planners. Levels of service and productivity, however, are influenced by planners through decisions about what health care to deliver and how it is to be delivered. Methods for the economic evaluation for sustainable service planning presented above provide an evidence base for these decisions. In practice, however, such policy levers have been largely left to professional interests, through adopting recommendations of professional groups for service expansions and controlling the deployment of alternative providers.

## Summary

Although governments continue to express concern about the rapidly rising costs of health care systems, and the increasing proportion of a country's resources absorbed by health care, they fail to recognize that this cost escalation is directly the result of the inappropriate methods used for planning services and allocating resources. The adoption of methods that align with the goals of health care policy (addressing the health care needs of the population) and reflect the problems faced by decision makers (health care resources are scarce, and use of those resources represents forgone opportunities for use in other ways) provides means by which expenditures can be controlled within the policy context of equitable access to care and efficient allocation of health care resources. It is not the economics of health care that threatens the sustainability of health care systems, only its misapplication in the way health care resources are planned and evaluated.

## References

Birch, S. (1988). The identification of supplier inducement in a fixed price system of health care provision: The case of dentistry in the United Kingdom. *Journal of Health Economics, 7,* 129–50.

Birch, S. and Donaldson, C. (1987). Application of cost–benefit analysis to health care: Departure from welfare economic theory. *Journal of Health Economics*, 6, 61–72.

Birch, S., Eyles, J., Hurley, J., *et al.* (1993). A needs-based approach to resource allocation in health care. *Canadian Public Policy*, 19, 68–85.

Birch, S., Eyles, J. and Newbold, B. (1996). Proxies for healthcare need among populations: Validation of alternatives – a study in Quebec. *Journal of Epidemiology and Community Health*, 50, 564–9.

Birch, S. and Gafni, A. (1992). Cost effectiveness/utility analysis: Do current decision rules lead us to where we want to be? *Journal of Health Economics*, 11, 279–96.

Birch, S. and Gafni, A. (1993). Changing the problem to fit the solution: Johannesson and Weinstein's (mis)application of economics to real world problems. *Journal of Health Economics*, 12, 469–76.

Birch, S. and Gafni, A. (2006). The biggest bang for the buck or bigger bucks for the bang: The fallacy of the cost-effectiveness threshold. *Journal of Health Services Research and Policy*, 11, 46–51.

Birch, S., Kephart, G., Tomblin-Murphy, G., *et al.* (2007). Human resources planning and the production of health: A needs-based analytical framework. *Canadian Public Policy*, 33, S1–S16.

Birch, S. and Maynard, A. (1985a). Dental manpower. *Social Policy and Administration*, 19, 199–217.

Birch, S. and Maynard, A. (1985b). Public expenditure planning for health and personal social services. In: Cockle, P. (ed.). *Public Expenditure Policy 1985–6*. London: Macmillan, pp. 223–42.

Cleary, S., Mooney, G. and McIntyre, D. (2010). Equity and efficiency in HIV-treatment in South Africa: The contribution of mathematical programming to priority setting. *Health Economics*, 19, 1166–80.

Daniels, S. and Greer, F. (2008). Lipid screening and cardiovascular health in children. *Pediatrics*, 122, 198–208.

Drummond, M. (1980). *Principles of Economic Appraisal in Health Care*. London: Oxford University Press.

Drummond, M. (2012). Twenty years of using economic evaluations for reimbursement decisions: what have we achieved? *Centre for Health Economics Research Paper 75*, University of York.

Evans, R. (1984). *Strained Mercy: The economics of Canadian health care*. Toronto: Butterworths.

Evans, R. (1985). Illusions of necessity: Evading responsibility for choice in health care. *Journal of Health Politics, Policy and Law*, 10, 439–67.

Eyles, J., Birch, S., Chambers, S., *et al.* (1991). A needs-based methodology for allocating health-care resources in Ontario: Development and application. *Social Science and Medicine*, 33, 489–500.

Gafni, A. and Birch, S. (1993). Guidelines for the adoption of new technologies: A prescription for uncontrolled growth in expenditures and how to avoid the problem. *Canadian Medical Association Journal*, 148, 913–7.

Gafni, A. and Birch, S. (2006). Incremental cost effectiveness ratio (ICERs): The silence of the lambda. *Social Science and Medicine*, 62, 2091–100.

Gold, M. and Bryan, S. (2007). A response to Birch and Gafni – some reasons to be cheerful about NICE. *Health Economics, Policy and Law*, 2, 209–16.

Gravelle, H., Sutton, M., Morris, S., *et al.* (2003). Modelling supply and demand influences on the use of health care: Implications for deriving a needs-based capitation formula. *Health Economics*, 12, 985–1004.

Laupacis, A. (2002). Inclusion of drugs in a provincial drug benefit program: Who is making these decisions and are they right ones? *Canadian Medical Association Journal*, 166, 44–7.

Laupacis, A., Feeny, D., Detsky, A. and Tugwell, P. (1992). How attractive does a technology have to be to warrant adoption and utilization? Tentative guidelines for using clinical and economic evaluations. *Canadian Medical Association Journal*, 146,,473–81.

Lorinc, J. (2006). How much are drugs worth? A fledgling medical science attempts an answer, *University of Toronto Magazine*, 37 (available online at: www.magazine.utoronto.ca/06Spring/drugs.asp).

Mays, N. (1995). Geographical resource allocation in the English National Health Service, 1971–1994: The tension between normative and empirical approaches. *International Journal of Epidemiology*, 24, S96–102.

Mooney, G., Hall, J., Donaldson, C. and Gerard, K. (1991). Utilisation as a measure of equity: Weighing heat? *Journal of Health Economics*, 10, 175–80.

NICE, National Institute for Clinical Excellence (2001). *Technical Guidance to Manufacturers and Sponsors on Making a Submission to a Technology Appraisal*. London: National Institute for Clinical Excellence.

OECD (2009). *Health at a Glance 2009*. Paris: OECD.

OECD (2011). *OECD Health Data 2011*. Paris: OECD (available online at: www.oecd.org/health/healthdata).

Sendi, P., Gafni, A. and Birch, S. (2002). Opportunity costs and uncertainty in the economic evaluation of health care interventions. *Health Economics*, 11, 23–31.

Shipman, S., Lurie, J. and Goodman, D. (2004). The general paediatrician: Projecting future workforce supply and requirements. *Pediatrics*, 11, 435–42.

Stinnett, A. and Paltiel, D. (1996). Mathematical programming for the efficient allocation of health care resources. *Journal of Health Economics*, 15, 641–53.

Tianviwat, S., Chongsuvivatwong, V. and Birch, S. (2011). Optimizing the mix of basic dental services for Southern Thai schoolchildren based on resource consumption, service needs and parental preferences. *Community Dentistry and Oral Epidemiology*, 37, 372–80.

Weinstein, M. and Zeckhauser, R. (1973). Critical ratios and efficient allocation. *Journal of Public Economics*, 2, 147–57.

Zinn, C. (2002). Plan to cut drug spending attacked by doctors. *British Medical Journal*, 324, 937.

# Chapter 10

# The Fiscal Impact of Investments in Health Care

*Mark Connolly*

## Intergenerational Consequences of Public Reimbursement

Policy decisions made by governments often have intergenerational fiscal consequences that are seldom considered in policy making. Publicly funded programs are often considered in relation to the intended target group directly influenced by a particular policy, for example changes to the minimum retirement age, taxation or provision of medical services to specific age groups, even reimbursement of new technologies. However, what is less often considered in relation to introducing new policies are the intergenerational fiscal consequences associated with these policies as the costs of introducing new policies will be passed onto other age cohorts expected to pay for new programs for generations to come.

The connectivity of policy making across generations was recently described by Lee and Mason in what was described as the generational economy (Lee and Mason 2011). The generational economy is defined by population age structures and the shares of people in education, working or retired, which fundamentally influences the economy and government fiscal accounts as individuals transition through life. The authors then suggest that in the coming decades, in nations with ageing populations, economies will increasingly be determined by choices made by the elderly, and the health of this age cohort. Specifically, whether older age cohorts will continue to work, spend down their wealth, and demands they are likely to make on health services.

The generational economy is not influenced only by the elderly – the health of current working-age adults and educational attainment of younger age cohorts can also have an impact. The health status of working-age adults and younger age groups, and behavioural choices made by these cohorts, are integral to economic gains that can be achieved by these age groups. These considerations are useful for helping us to recognize that the health and choices of one generation, both good and bad, will have consequences for other generations. For example, high rates of obesity and smoking in one age cohort will negatively impact health capital in these individuals and pose burdens on other generations expected pay for these excesses (Goldman *et al.* 2010). Conversely, high amounts of education capital accumulated by one generation will benefit not only those individuals but also other members of society due to higher rates of taxes paid on increased earnings. Because most public assistance programs and health spending are concentrated on older citizens, ageing populations have started to bring these issues to the fore as public debt has increased in relation to tax revenues and solutions to the debt crisis are being explored (Batini *et al.* 2011).

The intergenerational fiscal consequences of population health status are ever-present, although seldom evaluated and reported in the health economics literature. The typical economic framework for evaluating health conditions focuses on the direct costs of treatment and ignores the fiscal externalities of poor health or changes in health status achieved through publicly funded programs. By taking into consideration the macroeconomic effect of population health, it is possible to see that reduced health status of some individuals places demands on government resources not only for health services but also for disability payments and social services. In turn, the costs of these services will need to be paid for through tax contributions of the remaining workers.

When labour supply is plentiful and public finances are healthy, it is easy to overlook the effects of health on public finances and focus on the welfare gains for the recipient from publicly funded programs. However, ageing populations and shrinking numbers of working-age adults have heightened awareness about the necessity to pay for these programs with a dwindling number of workers. In 2005, a publication describing the contribution of health to economic growth in Europe highlighted that as the number of working-age adults starts to decline, it will be important not to lose workers due to avoidable disease and disability for maintaining economic growth (Suhrcke *et al.* 2005). Perhaps more concisely stated, Longman suggests that "with a shrinking labor supply, Europe's future economic growth will therefore depend entirely on getting more out of each remaining worker" (Longman 2004).

Such sentiment suggests that as the number of workers continues to decline, greater emphasis should be placed on disease prevention and maintaining healthy populations in order to sustain economic living standards. It is useful to highlight that ageing populations are not only about increasing numbers of elderly people but also the age cohorts of people working and supporting public programs.

Traditional approaches for evaluating the economics of health have ignored transfers and taxes, suggesting there is no welfare gain or loss associated with transfers and taxes (Drummond *et al.* 1997). While this may be true from a welfare economic perspective, from a fiscal accounting viewpoint this approach is flawed because taxes and transfers represent real costs for government. An illustration of these transfer costs was discussed in the report commissioned by the UK government describing the impact of ill health in working-age adults (Black 2008). The report suggested that in 2007 the impact of disability in working-age adults was £62–76 billion, of which £29 billion was workless benefits and £28–36 billion was lost tax revenue. As reported by Black, the health care costs of illness in working-age adults represented only 8–15% of total government costs, suggesting that health is a minor cost to government compared with workless benefits and lost taxes. The UK report highlights that applying a health service or societal perspective analytic framework to evaluate health in working-age adults would neglect approximately 90% of costs that fall on government. This highlights that in the current environment resources allocated within the health services are made without taking into consideration the broader consequences of health status changes on government fiscal accounts.

The examples described above reflect the difference between welfare economics and the reality of fiscal accounting, which defines the ability of governments to pay for public services. While welfare economics represents a theoretical framework for optimizing societal well-being, a noble goal worth achieving, it is divorced from the reality of fiscal constraint and the necessity to tax citizens in order to pay for government programs. Over the past several decades welfare economics has dominated thinking within many health services. However, in an era of shrinking numbers of workers and austerity there is reason to believe that understanding the fiscal impact of investments in health will gain in importance in coming years as ageing populations and sustainability of public finances will dominate public policy (European Commission 2009). The report prepared for the European Commission on the contribution of health on the European economy reminds us that "Policy-makers who are interested in improving economic outcomes (e.g. on the labour market or for the entire economy) would have good reasons to consider investment in health as one of their options by which to meet their economic objectives" (Suhrcke *et al.* 2005). In light of the fiscal challenges ahead this might suggest that an alternative compass for guiding health care and decision making might be required.

## Intergenerational Economic Framework

A government's financial situation is normally monitored by budget deficit and public debt. This approach to government finances provides a fiscal position only at a moment in time and is vulnerable to year-to-year expenditure and revenue changes. Furthermore, this approach fails to take into consideration future obligations in relation to projected revenue derived through taxation. In issues concerning the fiscal consequences of demographic change, a longer-term fiscal position might be more appropriate to anticipate future budget shortfalls.

One of the tools available to policy makers to evaluate the long-term intergenerational fiscal consequences of policy decisions is generational accounting. The methodology was developed by Auerbach *et al.* (1994) as an intergenerational framework to evaluate the fiscal consequences of government policy decisions. The generational accounting methodology rationalizes the intertemporal budgetary impact of policy decisions, taking into consideration age cohorts who will pay for policies now and into the future.

Connecting current and future policy obligations across generations using the generational accounting method enables policy makers to evaluate the intertemporal effects of policies, taking into consideration the consequences of policy making on current and future generations. The underlying premise of fiscal policy is zero sum over the long term, because government obligations must be met by current and future generations. Therefore, one of the questions that can be addressed using generational accounting is intergenerational fairness and whether one generation will be unfairly burdened with higher taxes, with the notion that different generations should face a similar lifetime tax burden. Unfortunately, because generational accounts are intimately linked with population age structures, current projections suggest that future generations will be likely to face higher tax burdens compared with current populations (European Commission 1999).

The fiscal policy discussion above should not be seen in isolation of health – in fact, the influence of population health is ubiquitous throughout generational accounts. Underlying the generational accounting framework are assumptions about the number of current and future working-age adults, productivity growth and demography – in essence, current and future population age structure and the ability of these age cohorts to produce things and contribute to economic growth – all of which are influenced by health.

Population health and in turn individual health play an important role in driving economic growth, as growth is driven by those supplying labour to the market. The health–growth relationship extends beyond simply increasing longevity and requires that those of working age are at optimal health to ensure human capital accumulation (i.e. education), labour force participation, being productive and creative, all of which drive economic growth (van Zon and Muysken 2005). Because social obligations for health, pensions and other social programs are paid from current workers and taxes, the ability of current and future generations to work and pay taxes provides a basis for sustainable public finances.

At the program and intervention level, funding decisions within health systems also have fiscal consequences. Because illness has the capacity to influence government fiscal accounts, the manner in which health services invest in health programs will have economic consequences. Considering that health is one of the main determinants on which retirement decisions are made, the health of older-age cohorts will influence fiscal accounts for government (van den Berg *et al.* 2010). The impact can be seen in terms of increased demand for social transfers, and these decisions in turn will need to be funded by those working; hence the intergenerational impact of health in one age cohort will influence costs in another (Manton *et al.* 2009).

## Health and the Fiscal Life Course

Public finance sustainability is influenced by two opposing population forces that influence government expenditure and tax revenues. As populations age, the opposing forces include economic growth influenced by labour market participation and age-related expenditure (European Commission 2009). By viewing opposing fiscal forces over the life course, it is possible to see how changes in population health status can influence the government balance sheet by increased transfers and reduced tax receipts. Consequently, applying a life course perspective to evaluate investments in health that change the life course, it is possible to estimate how investments in health will likely influence government fiscal accounts. From the government's perspective, health investment choices made by national and regional health services can positively and negatively influence government accounts dependent on the extent to which medical technology influence morbidity, mortality and labour force participation rates.

Over the course of life, individuals at different stages of life can be recipients of government transfers including healthcare, as well as transferring wealth to government in the form of various taxes and social insurances. By understanding the fiscal transfers between individuals and government, it is possible to derive a net fiscal position of an individual at any stage of life by deducting age-specific gross transfers from age-specific gross taxes (equation 1).

$$NPV_{fiscal} = \sum_{t=0}^{Te} \frac{Tax_t - Cost_t}{(1+r)^t} \tag{1}$$

where in year $t$

$$Tax_t = Direct\,tax_t + Indirect\,tax_t + National\,insurance_t \qquad (2)$$

$$Cost_t = Education_t + Health_t + Transfers_t + Pension_t \qquad (3)$$

Furthermore, and of relevance for fiscal accounts, health conditions that cause people to deviate from the normal life course will have fiscal consequences for government that can be evaluated using equation 1. For instance, events such as premature mortality, disability, early retirement or reduced labour force participation will reduce tax transfers to government (equation 2). Similarly, health conditions that increase demand for social transfer payments and disability payments will simultaneously increase costs for government (equation 3). The simultaneous consideration of fiscal costs and tax transfers provides insights to how some health conditions and resulting deviations will influence public finances. This could include avoiding early mortality, i.e. prevention, improving educational attainment and productivity, or delaying retirement decisions. In this respect, reduced labour force participation has the same effect as unemployment, as people are disengaged from the labour market while requiring increased publicly funded programs.

Assessing the fiscal impact of medical interventions requires some understanding of the degree in which a particular medical intervention and resulting health status changes will influence the labour market. From the government revenue-generating perspective, morbidity and mortality that influence productivity, retirement decisions and labour force participation will influence government revenues. For example, an intervention that maintains the health of a 62-year-old male and thus avoids early retirement due to ill health will generate increased tax for government and avoid disability costs and additional pension costs paid for early retirement. Additionally, the role that some medical conditions can have in human capital accumulation such as education and resulting wage effects can also be considered. Examples of this can include ADHD and hearing impairment in children, both of which can influence educational achievement and lifelong earnings and future employment opportunities (Sobanski *et al.* 2007; Access Economics 2006).

## Return on Investment from Health

By understanding how new medical interventions influence the fiscal life course of individuals, the analytic framework described above can be used to evaluate the return on investment in future net tax revenue associated with health status gains. Within publicly funded health services, if one considers that new medical interventions represent an increased cost for government, the increase expenditure ($K_t$) can be included in the expenditure equation (equation 4). In turn, if the new intervention prevents people from withdrawing from the workforce, delays health-related retirement or accelerates the return to work, this will have positive fiscal consequences for government that can be evaluated using this approach.

$$Cost_t = Education_t + Health_t + Transfers_t + Pension_t + K_t \qquad (4)$$

Figure 10.1 is an output that represents the average fiscal life course. While the degree of transfers and tax burden varies by country, the typical pattern is represented by government transfers during early life years in the form of education, health and allowances, and in later life state pensions, health care and other social assistance programs. Cumulative transfers are concentrated in both the early stages in life which have a relatively short time horizon, and then again once leaving the work environment.

When the consequences of disease and illness are considered over the life course, the figure helps to contemplate the fiscal consequences of premature mortality or early withdrawal from the workforce.

Generating quantitative output requires treating the medical intervention as an investment from the "government perspective" and can be evaluated using financial analysis methods such as net present value (NPV), internal rate of return (IRR) and return on investment (ROI). These analytic approaches differ from traditional health economics because they treat health care as an investment and not just a cost.

Initial pilot studies employed the fiscal health investment approach to investigate investments in publicly financed assisted reproduction (i.e. in-vitro fertilization). The externality of assisted reproduction is that its successful application leads to live births. The resulting children provide benefits not only for families but also for government as they mature and enter the workforce and start paying taxes. In some countries children conceived through assisted reproduction represent 4% of national births (de Mouzon *et al.* 2010). Consequently, when valued from a fiscal health investment perspective, the analysis suggested that a public investment of £13,000 to achieve a

*Figure 10.1* Cumulative fiscal life course for individual accounting for lifetime tax contributions and age-specific government transfers (Connolly, data on file)

live birth from assisted reproduction was worth £110,000 in discounted lifetime net tax revenue and £603,000 in undiscounted net taxes attributed to the resulting child (Connolly *et al.* 2009). In contrast, within a traditional health economics framework, for example cost-effectiveness analysis, the costs and consequences of increasing live births associated with a change in funding policy would not be captured because transfers and taxes are ignored (Drummond *et al.* 1997). The analysis has been useful for illustrating that what is often considered an expensive intervention for payers is actually an investment when a longer time horizon and a different perspective are used, i.e. ones that consider the fiscal consequences of an intervention's broader consequences.

The fiscal health investment framework described here has proven powerful in the appraisal of preventive health technologies. Immunizations represent a high-cost investment which pays off years or even decades after the actual immunization. Applications of the framework have evaluated investments in rotavirus vaccination in Egypt. In some countries the mortality and morbidity burden of rotavirus deaths are substantial, and the observation that indirect costs represent a significant proportion of costs suggests the fiscal effects will also be significant (Standaert *et al.* 2008; Parashar *et al.* 2003).

In the analysis performed, the costs associated with rotavirus ($K_i$) were treated as an investment cost with lifetime fiscal consequences. After deducting rotavirus vaccination costs, it was demonstrated that discounted net tax revenue from the vaccinated cohorts was greater than the unvaccinated cohorts, with incremental net tax revenues at year-25, year-50 and year-72 of $6.1 million, $58.1 million and $55.7 million, respectively. The fiscal benefits were achieved from reduced mortality associated with vaccination and increased labour supply in the future. To reflect the realities of life and the marketplace, the vaccinated cohort was adjusted for premature mortality due to non-rotavirus-related causes, unemployment and tax compliance.

The framework described here follows a generational accounting framework by considering age-specific per capita transfers. Constructing the accounts can be as detailed as the available data permit. When published sources are not available it will be necessary to derive such data for inclusion in the model as their omission may compromise the validity of the approach. However, unlike generational accounting, the analysis considers the cohort receiving an intervention and does not consider future generations, therefore the approach is a modified generational accounting one.

The methodological considerations in evaluating fiscal consequences attributed to health interventions vary from those considered in traditional cost-effectiveness analysis. Because many government transfers are adjusted for inflation, it is necessary to inflate government transfer payments over the life course of the treated cohort. Additionally, tax payments to government are influenced by wage growth, therefore it is necessary to adjust wages over time based on productivity growth projections. The choice of discount is an important consideration because many costs occur far in the future. In some instances, treasuries will publish recommended discount rates for cost–benefit analysis; if not, the interest rate on long-term treasury bonds can serve as an appropriate discount rate.

## Resource Allocation and Fiscal Accounts

The fiscal accounting framework described in this chapter highlights the relationship between population age structures and the role that health status can have for influencing life transitions with resulting fiscal consequences. Underlying the analytic framework described here is productivity and workforce participation. Because life transitions influence the fiscal relationship in terms of demand for government-funded programs and taxes paid, influencing health in a meaningful way will subsequently influence fiscal accounts. The framework and examples described here demonstrate that it is academically possible to analyze the relationship between health and fiscal accounts; however, what remains to be seen is the manner in which the methodology can influence decision making and resource allocation.

The current environment for evaluating health care favours achieving technical efficiency using cost-effectiveness analysis (CEA) rather than addressing allocative efficiency and which programs are worthy of funding. To do so would require more broad application of cost–benefit analysis, with all health and non-health benefits converted into monetary values. The fiscal health investment model described in this chapter shares many similarities with the cost–benefit approach, the difference being that all benefits are translated into future net tax revenues. In this regard the methodology can be thought to inform allocative efficiency at a fiscal level, although the approach described here does not account for the intangible benefits of being healthy, therefore it underestimates the benefits that people derive from improved health.

Evaluating the fiscal consequences of health programs using the methodology described in this chapter might appear to be a new approach for valuing health program costs. However, the approach is not entirely new considering that government tax revenue is a function of age-specific earnings which relate to productivity – a notion that is accepted within fiscal policy. In this respect the method should be seen as an extension of human capital economics. While productivity and human capital have gone out of fashion in the evaluation of health programs, methodologies that link public funding and future tax receipts are regularly considered in other areas of public policy. For example, education policy is regularly evaluated in relation to future tax revenue that will arise from changes in educational attainment (OECD 2009; Khatiwada et al. 2007).

The methodology discussed here suggests the possible need to align health policies and resource-allocation decisions with other macroeconomic policies, especially those that relate to labour policies. This is likely to prove challenging because productivity and labour activity are central to the fiscal health investment methodology described here, and at present productivity gains are not highly rated in the evaluation of health programs by many technology appraisal agencies (Knies et al. 2010). This illustrates the oddity of evaluating productivity gains linked to health care. While increased productivity is a major aim of most government macroeconomic policy initiatives (OECD 2011), productivity is seldom considered in relation to resource-allocation decisions in health. Surely productivity considered by labour economists and productivity evaluated by health services are not different? This might suggest that the macroeconomy can benefit from increased importance given to productivity gains from technology appraisal agencies. This approach is supported by the report to the European Commission noting the economic gains that can be achieved in Europe from investments in the health service (Suhrcke *et al.* 2005).

Applying a fiscal accounting approach to health care costs goes against the traditional welfare economics approach to evaluating health programs where the goal is to maximize societal welfare, however defined. However, in a society that is dependent on transfers between generations, it is possible to estimate the fiscal externality of changes in health status in one age cohort on another cohort. Taking a generational approach to health also helps to illustrate whether one generation consumes more than their lifetime tax revenues, highlighting the importance of intergenerational fairness on health spending. Furthermore, the approach brings to the fore the importance of sustainability of public finances and how health investments in one age cohort can produce fiscal benefits over many generations.

Considerations about the fiscal transfers between generations are often less salient in an era of population growth or sustainable population. However, population growth is declining and the number of working-age adults is starting to decline. Consequently the priorities and efficiency of the health service will influence the interaction between age cohorts and government accounts. The more effective the health service is at keeping retired people alive will influence other government costs such as pensions and retirement allowances. In contrast, the ability of public health services to prevent illness through vaccination or other preventative programs will avoid communicable diseases and most likely increase societal productive output. These two examples illustrate the challenges for government to prioritize health services in an era of ageing populations and shrinking numbers of working-age adults. Whether fiscal survival leads to joined-up policy making by governments is yet to be seen.

At the core of the fiscal health investment approach described here is productivity and its relationship to health and wealth, and the ability to pay taxes. Because of the dominant role of productivity in the analysis, many would object to its broad application in resource allocation as it may pose equity concerns since it would disfavour those not in the workforce. While this fact is unavoidable, sustainable public finances, economic growth and increasing living standards are all important goals for societies. At some point the ability to pay for all public services has to be rationalized against the ability to pay for these programs and the desire to achieve other macroeconomic goals.

As a minimum, the methodology described here helps to illustrate that some of the solutions to the ageing population conundrum should not be seen in isolation. Because of the special relationship between health and economic growth, if nations can employ their health services to improve economic sustainability in the face of ageing populations, then it might be in their interests to do so, particularly if the rewards from economic growth are shared among all members of society. As economies expand, this creates more opportunities for members in the society, and economic growth increases tax revenue for government. Increased revenue can then be re-deployed to support publicly funded programs.

In practice this might suggest that some resources should be re-deployed to health programmes aligned with other macroeconomic policies for stimulating growth, for example younger-aged and working-age cohorts. However, if all members of society can share the economic rewards, then it might be possible to maintain societal welfare by doing so. Conversely, ignoring opportunities for achieving economic growth by reallocating health services might seem perilous considering the mounting public debt faced by many governments.

## References

Access Economics (2006). *Listen hear! The economic impact and cost of hearing loss in Australia.* Access Economics Pty Ltd (available online at: www.audiology.asn.au/public/1/files/Publications/ListenHearFinal.pdf).

Auerbach, A.J., Gokhale, J. and Kotlikoff, L.J. (1994). Generational accounting: A meaningful way to evaluate fiscal policy. *The Journal of Economic Perspectives*, 8, 73–94.

Batini, N., Callegari, G. and Guerreiro, J. (2011). *An analysis of U.S. fiscal and generational imbalances: Who will pay and how?* International Monetary Fund, Washington (available online at: www.imf.org/external/pubs/ft/wp/2011/wp1172.pdf).

Black, C. (2008) Dame Carol Black's Review of the health of Britain's working age population. Working for a healthier tomorrow. London: Crown Copyright (accessed 28 February 2016: www.dwp.gov.uk/docs/hwwb-working-for-a-healthier-tomorrow.pdf).

Bonin, H. and Patxot, C. (2004). *Generational accounting as a tool to assess Fiscal Sustainability: An overview of the methodology.* Institute for the Study of Labor, Germany (available online at: http://papers.ssrn.com/sol3/papers.cfm?abstract_id=494223).

Commission on Macroeconomics and Health (2001). *Macroeconomics and health: Investing in health for economic development.* World Health Organization, Geneva (available online at: http://whqlibdoc.who.int/publications/2001/924154550x.pdf).

Connolly, M., Gallo, F., Hoorens, S. and Ledger, W. (2009). Assessing long-run economic benefits attributed to an IVF-conceived singleton based on projected lifetime net tax contributions in the UK. *Human Reproduction*, 24, 626–32.

Connolly, M.P., Topachevskyi, O., Standaert, B., *et al.* (2012). The impact of rotavirus vaccination on discounted net tax revenue in Egypt: A government perspective analysis. *Pharmacoeconomics*, 30, 681–95.

de Mouzon, J., Goossens, V., Bhattacharya, S., *et al.* (2010). Assisted reproductive technology in Europe, 2006: Results generated from European registers by ESHRE. *Human Reproduction*, 25, 1851–62.

Drummond, M.F., O'Brien, B., Stoddart, G.L. and Torrance, G.W. (1997). *Methods for the economic evaluation of Health Care programmes.* Oxford University Press, Oxford.

European Commission (1999). *Generational accounting in Europe: European Economy, 6.* Directorate-General for Economic and Financial Affairs, Luxembourg (available online at: http://ec.europa.eu/economy_finance/publications/publication8105_en.pdf).

European Commission (2009). *Sustainability Report 2009: European Economy, 9.* Directorate-General for Economic and Financial Affairs, Luxembourg (available online at: http://ec.europa.eu/economy_finance/publications/publication15998_en.pdf).

Goldman, D.P., Michaud, P.C., Lakdawalla, D., *et al.* (2010). The fiscal consequences of trends in population health. *National Tax Journal*, 63, 307–30.

Khatiwada, I., McLaughlin, J., Sum, A. and Palma, S. (2007). *The fiscal consequences of adult educational attainment.* National Commission on Adult Literacy, Boston (available online at: www.nationalcommissiononadultliteracy.org/content/fiscalimpact.pdf).

Knies, S., Severens, J.L., Ament, A.J. and Evers, S.M. (2010). The transferability of valuing lost productivity across jurisdictions: Differences between national pharmacoeconomic guidelines. *Value in Health*, 13, 519–27.

Lee, R. and Mason, A. (2011). *Population aging and the generational economy: a global perspective.* Edward Elgar Publishing, Cheltenham.

Longman, P. (2004). The global baby bust. *Foreign Affairs*, 83, 64–79.

Manton, K.G., Gu, Y.L., Ullian, A., *et al.* (2009). Long-term economic growth stimulus of human capital preservation in the elderly. *Proceedings of the National Academy of Sciences*, 106, 21080–5.

OECD (2009). *Education at a glance 2009: OECD indicators.* OECD, Paris (available online at: www.oecd.org/edu/skills-beyond-school/educationataglance2009oecdindicators.htm).

OECD (2011). *Economic policy reforms: Going for growth 2011.* OECD, Paris (available online at: www.oecd.org/eco/labour/economicpolicyreformsgoingforgrowth2011.htm).

Parashar, U.D., Hummelman, E.G., Bresee, J.S., *et al.* (2003). Global illness and deaths caused by rotavirus disease in children. *Emerging Infectious Diseases Journal*, 9, 565–72.

Sobanski, E., Brüggemann, D., Alm, B., *et al.* (2007). Psychiatric comorbidity and functional impairment in a clinically referred sample of adults with attention-deficit/hyperactivity disorder (ADHD). *European Archives of Psychiatry and Clinical Neurosciences*, 257, 371–7.

Standaert, B., Harlin, O. and Desselberger, U. (2008). The financial burden of rotavirus disease in four countries of the European Union. *The Pediatric Infectious Diseases Journal*, 27, 20–7.

Suhrcke, M., McKee, M., Arce, R.S., *et al.* (2005). The contribution of health to the economy in the European Union. *Public Health*, 120, 994–1001.

van den Berg, T.I., Elders, L.A. and Burdorf, A. (2010). Influence of health and work on early retirement. *Journal of Occupational and Environmental Medicine*, 52, 576–83.

van Zon, A. and Muysken, J. (2005). Health as a principal determinant of economic growth. In: Lopez-Casasnovas, G., Rivera, B. and Currais, L. (eds). *Health and economic growth: Findings and policy implications.* The MIT Press, Cambridge.

World Health Organization (2009). *WHO Guide to identifying the economic consequences of disease and injury.* World Health Organization, Geneva (available online at: www.who.int/choice/publications/d_economic_impact_guide.pdf).

# Chapter 11

# Does Health Economics Have a Future in Asia?

*Ning Lu and Eun-Young Bae*

## Introduction

After Weinstein and Stason published "Foundations of cost-effectiveness analysis for health and medical practices" (1977), many developed countries adopted health economics (also referred to as pharmacoeconomics (PE) hereafter)[1] in resource-allocation decision making. A majority of them have used health economics to evaluate pharmaceutical products. However, developing nations have not made similar advances (Singer 2008). Despite being the largest continent, with 60% of the world's population and a fast-growing economy, Asia's adoption of pharmacoeconomic evaluation has been slow over the past few years. So far only South Korea requires the use of pharmacoeconomic data in evaluation. Taiwan encourages the use of pharmacoeconomic data by offering premium pricing as an incentive, and Thailand is in the process of establishing such practice. The authorities in China and Japan have shown an interest in establishing a mechanism to formally incorporate pharmacoeconomic data into their decision making (Tarn *et al.* 2008; Yang 2009; EFPIA 2012; The Central People's Government of the People's Republic of China 2009).

Adoption of health economics as a decision-making tool is at an early stage and at different degrees of evolution in several developing countries, including some in Asia. Several researchers have raised the question as to whether there is a real role for health economics in these countries. The general conclusion seems to be that the benefit and likelihood of health economics adoption is uncertain in emerging markets (Singer 2008; Babar *et al.* 2010; Oortwijn *et al.* 2010). Due to the heterogeneity and complexity of emerging market social and economic development, it is unlikely that one conclusion fits all. A country's economic, political, social systems and value preferences all have an impact on the adoption of health economics as a decision-making tool. Therefore the authors have selected two representative Asian countries, China and South Korea, as case studies and will consider their needs as follows:

- First, is the need to manage rising health care cost reaching critical mass?
- Second, what is the level of resource infrastructure/capacity development for health economics adoption?
- Third, what are the country-specific challenges? Does the health care environment need the introduction of economic thinking and is the political will strong enough to implement health economics?

The need to effectively manage health care resource allocation has been a driving force of health economics adoption. Health economics was formally adopted by several developed countries only from the 1990s as the need to manage rising costs became more imminent. Given that individual demand for good health is infinite, income (gross domestic product, GDP) growth usually leads to rising health care costs, primarily through the actions of governments and employers who may pay on behalf of pools of consumers (Smith *et al.* 2009). Per capita health care expenditure usually goes up as GDP grows. The authors use two surrogate indicators, per capita health care spending and government spending on health as a percentage of total health expenditure, to identify whether the macro environment is ready for the adoption of health economics (Figure 11.1).

Developed countries that have introduced health economics to inform health care decision making, such as the UK, the Netherlands, Canada, Australia and Sweden, have similar economic characteristics: per capita health care expenditure above 3,000 PPP$[2] and government spending on health around 70–80% of total health expenditure in 2009 (Figure 11.1).

Among the emerging markets, South Korea, Poland and Slovakia have adopted the use of health economics in recent years. Per capita health care spending of these countries ranges from 1,476 PPP$ to 2,060 PPP$. Government spending on health as a percentage of total health expenditure was in the range of 59–73% (Figure 11.1).

- What is the level of infrastructure/capacity development required for successful health economics adoption to improve health care decision making?

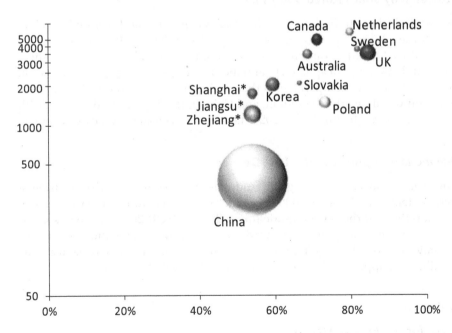

*Figure 11.1* Macroeconomic indicators for health economics adoption readiness: annual per capita health care spending, government spending on health as a percentage of total health expenditure

Health economics application requires a rigorous approach and consistent methodology and data analysis. The successful adoption of health economics in decision making requires significant human resource capacity: qualified professionals who can perform the analysis, policy makers who adopt and establish health economics as part of the decision-making process, and administrators who can implement and manage the use of health economics analysis.

Availability of local epidemiological, clinical, utility and cost data is critical to health economics evaluation.

The level of infrastructure development can facilitate or hinder health economics adoption.

• What are the country-specific challenges? Is the political will strong enough to overcome these challenges in order to implement health economics?

Last but not least, each country's health care system is unique, with its own challenges. The adoption of health economics is a paradigm shift of pricing and reimbursement decisions to a value-based approach. Health economics needs to be integrated into the overall health care system and society, which creates significant changes to organizations and processes on top of the already complex health system. Societal acceptance, and furthermore the political will to overcome all the challenges and to create new organizations/processes, is critical to health economics adoption.

### Case Studies: Why South Korea and China?

South Korea and China have similar health care system goals and planned development trajectories. Korea's per capita GDP was 2,7541 PPP$ in 2006 (OECD 2012) when it introduced health economics into decision making. Although there is still a significant gap between per capita GDP at national level, some regions in China will reach an economic level comparable to that of South Korea in the next few years. Korea has a universal health care system, and China is moving in this direction, with its health care reform "Healthy China 2020" targeting universal health care coverage.

### PE Guideline Development in the Last Decade

Korea and China started compiling PE guideline in 2003 and 2005 respectively – Korea has implemented PE since 2006 (Bae *et al.* 2009) and mandated its use in 2008, while China published the revised guideline in 2011 (IPSOR 2011). Korea's success and learning may inform China's future directions, while examination of China's specific challenges will also highlight how differences in country-specific factors may require a different approach from that followed so far in Korea

## South Korea

### Challenges for the Korean NHI

Korea has a universal health insurance system, the National Health Insurance (NHI) program, for which all residents in Korea are eligible except the beneficiaries of the medical aid program. The medical aid program targets the low-income groups specifically and is funded by tax. In 2010, 96.7% of the population of South Korea were covered by the NHI program and the remaining 3.3% were the beneficiaries of the medical aid program.

In 2000, NHI integrated hundreds of insurance funds into the National Health Insurance Corporation (NHIC) and established the Health Insurance Review and Assessment Service (HIRA) as an independent public agency, which reviews the medical claims and evaluates the appropriateness of the care provided by medical institutions. The Ministry of Health and Welfare (MOHW) is responsible for determining the benefit packages and setting up the regulations in guiding the health insurance policy (Figure 11.2).

Since Korean NHI started with a limited amount of resources, the scope of coverage was somewhat restricted, and even today some medically necessary services remain uncovered, although the MOHW continues to expand coverage of the benefit list. As a result, the share of the out-of-pocket payments in health care expenditure is relatively high in Korea (35.7% in 2006) (WHO 2012), compared with that of other developed countries. In addition, national health expenditure in Korea has grown rapidly at a rate higher than the income growth during the last decade (9.9%), which stirred up concern about the affordability of future medical demand (OECD 2012).

As for the Korean NHI, the future does not look promising in terms of financial sustainability, as Korea is one of the most rapidly ageing societies and has adopted the fee-for-service payment system which is known to be ineffective in controlling explosively increasing health care costs (Yang *et al.* 2008). Korean NHI should find a solution to cope with the two major conflicting issues: to control health expenditure at a sustainable level and to expand the NHI coverage without breaking the bank.

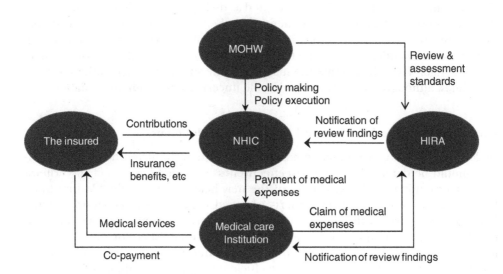

*Figure 11.2* National health insurance management system (South Korea)

### Reimbursement and Pricing Policies for Drugs

According to OECD health data 2012 (Yang *et al.* 2008), the share of drug spending in total health expenditure in South Korea was around 24.5% in 2006, the fourth highest among OECD countries. While per capita drug expenditure was slightly lower than the OECD average (359.6 PPP$ in 2006), it has increased more than the other medical expenditure, raising potential issues of allocative efficiency. The Korean government introduced several measures aimed at controlling drug expenditure after 2001, when the NHI budget was in a cumulative deficit. Most of them, however, were not terribly effective at slowing down the costs (IPSOR 2011). The pressure of skyrocketing drug expenditure resulted in the Korean government implementing "a drug expenditure rationalization plan" in 2006 and changing the listing from a negative list system to a positive one.

Under the positive list system (PLS), only clinically and economically valuable drugs can be listed, and pharmacoeconomic data are required for all submissions requesting higher prices than comparable drugs. HIRA is responsible for reviewing the submitted evidence and evaluating the value of the drug. Once HIRA has evaluated the submitted drug as effective and cost-effective, the price negotiation process between the company and the NHIC begins. If the negotiations fail, the drugs cannot be listed, unless they are essential drugs, for which the Benefit Coordination Committee establishes the prices, taking into consideration each party's requests and other conditions.

The Drug Reimbursement Evaluation Committee (DREC) is the advisory committee that gives recommendations to HIRA regarding the benefit status of all submitted drugs. DREC takes into account the effectiveness, cost-effectiveness and other benefits, including the availability of substitutes and the severity of the disease, in the process of its deliberation.

After the introduction of the PLS, 119 drugs were reviewed from 2007 to 2010 and among those, 84 were recommended for listing and 35 were rejected. For 84 of those recommended drugs, 67 were accepted as their prices were lower than those of the alternatives, and 11 were recommended as their ICER fell within an acceptable range, even though the price was higher than that of comparators. The remaining six were recommended considering their medical necessity (Bae 2011). For the quality of the data, HIRA found that the majority of the submissions had adhered to PE guidelines, although there were considerable uncertainties in submitted data.

### Pharmacoeconomic Adoption and Guideline Development

In 2001, the Korean government amended the rule that stipulates the way NHI benefits should be determined, and cost-effectiveness was added as one of the criteria when determining the benefit status of the new health technologies. At that time, however, there were only a few experts who had experience in economic evaluation, and it was rare for the companies to submit pharmacoeconomic data to get the reimbursement. Moreover, there were no guidelines established for the companies to adhere to. These circumstances drove HIRA to draft PE guidelines which allowed the company and HIRA to communicate efficiently with one another, and to ensure the quality of the submission. In the process of drafting the guidelines, the advisory committee convened to discuss the direction and the level of details the guidelines should provide to the reader. With the endorsement of DREC, the first version of these guidelines was officially published in 2006; it was revised in 2012 to reflect the experiences of the five years.

### Capacities for Pharmacoeconomics

Although Korea was the first Asian country to require pharmacoeconomic data in reimbursement decisions, capacities for pharmacoeconomics were not very different from those in other countries. Strong political will made it possible to adopt pharmacoeconomics despite the lack of infrastructure in this area.

- Human resources

As with other Asian countries, Korea did not have enough experts with experience in evaluating the cost-effectiveness of health technologies before implementing PE guidelines. The number of experienced experts can be inferred from the number of health economics studies published. Lee *et al.* (2005) reviewed 45 economic evaluation studies published from 1990 to June 2004, which were all carried out in a Korean context. Among these, 14 were CEA and 11 were cost–utility analysis (CUA). A similar number can be found in the paper written by Teerawattananon *et al.* (2007), which reviewed the 41 economic evaluation studies done in the Thai context – 27 were CEA and 2 were CUA.

The pharmaceutical industry also lacked experience in conducting and submitting pharmacoeconomic data. According to a survey carried out in Korea in 2002, only 9 among 19 companies that responded said they had experience in conducting pharmacoeconomic studies and only 3 had submitted them to HIRA (Bae *et al.* 2005).

- Data

There is a scarcity of local data needed for economic evaluations. This increases the uncertainty of the cost-effectiveness ratio in a local context (Lee *et al.* 2011). The lack of epidemiological data is known to be more problematic than the lack of efficacy data, given that it can influence the absolute size of effect and it is also less transferrable than efficacy data, especially for technologies which prevent adverse events. From 2005, the Korean government started to fund clinical studies and researcher-initiated clinical trials, which was expected to improve the availability of local clinical and epidemiological data. For costing, claims data are frequently used in measuring resource use, but only aggregated data are available in the *Health Insurance Statistical Yearbook.* Some submissions use hospital data, but representativeness of these data often comes into question. In 2011, HIRA offered sampled claim data for selected research projects, and from 2012 it was scheduled to be provided for more users, which will ultimately increase the availability of claims data, thus greatly contributing to the proliferation of quality costing studies in the future.

For utility data, there were no valuation studies based on the Korean population when the first PE guidelines were developed. At the time of writing, however, there were three studies published which surveyed the preferences of the general Korean population for different EQ-5D health states. The second version of the PE guidelines stressed the importance of local utility data since the preference for health states may differ from country to country, depending on social, cultural and economical context (Bae *et al.* 2012).

- Political will

The most influential driving force behind the adopting of pharmacoeconomics was the government's strong will to control drug expenditure. The MOHW wanted to expand the coverage rate and attain the efficient allocation of health care resources at the same time. Drug expenditure was considered a main contributor to the escalating health expenditure, therefore becoming the priority target for cost-containment efforts. Government officials thought there were too many drugs listed, and there was no room for the insurer to exert purchasing power in the listing process. They expected the PLS and pharmacoeconomics to contribute significantly to containing the costs and improving the efficiency in the system.

### Efforts Toward Evidence-Based Health Care

The PE adoption process was challenging for everyone concerned. Although the infrastructure for PE was limited, the relevant parties struggled to tackle the challenges in their own way.

- Industry

When the PLS was implemented, the industry experienced numerous difficulties in understanding the new system. Local companies especially found compiling dossiers complex. In order to adjust to the changes they established a market access department to deal with listing and pricing-related tasks (Lee *et al.* 2011). They also invested in staff training programs, and some companies recruited experts specializing in pharmacoeconomics.

- Academia

Professional groups in pharmacoeconomics decided to establish an academic society, the Korean Association of Health Technology Assessment (KAHTA), which aims to stimulate the communication among researchers, and educate the government and industry staff with theory and practice in health technology assessment. KAHTA provided training programs from 2006 on a biannual basis. University-based training programs have also been provided on an ongoing basis since 2007.

- HIRA

Since the implementation of PE, HIRA has tried to enhance the transparency of its decision making. Companies are granted the opportunity to comment on the reviews before the DREC meetings. After DREC's deliberation, the recommendation and opinion on the effectiveness and cost-effectiveness of the proposed drugs are published on the website. HIRA convenes a workshop where any changes in the process, decision rules, or the points frequently violated in the submission are discussed. In addition, HIRA provides a non-binding prior-consultation program to companies to prevent any unnecessary re-submissions. An economic sub-committee was formed in 2009 to offer advice on the technical aspects of economic evaluation to DREC.

### Prospects

When the MOHW first announced the introduction of pharmacoeconomics, the industry and academia were concerned about the lack of infrastructure for pharmacoeconomics in Korea. There are still a limited number of experts and data available in this area, but the capacity for evaluations has grown rapidly. Investment in infrastructure continues to increase where there is a need for it.

It is unclear whether or not pharmacoeconomics contributed to controlling drug expenditure in Korea. Several measures to contain the costs were implemented simultaneously in 2007, so it is difficult to distinguish each policy's contribution. More importantly, drug expenditure is determined not only by the price but also by the pattern of drug use. Since 2007, the prices of new-to-the-market drugs are known to be lower than in the past, but per capita drug expenditure is persistently increasing as a result of other cost-driving factors such as volume increases or shifts to higher-priced drugs.

The Korean government decided to introduce the mandatory diagnosis-related group (DRG) payment system for seven diseases starting on July 1, 2012, and planned to expand it across the board to incorporate all diseases. DRG is expected to contribute to attaining the efficiency of drug use to some extent, and will encourage the application of PE not only in reimbursement and pricing decisions but also in decision making for efficient drug use at hospitals throughout the country.

There has been a lot of progress made in terms of methodology in PE, but there are still many unresolved issues. How to judge the uncertainty of the evidence and how to incorporate social values into the reimbursement decisions remain critical issues. With regards to potential benefits that are not supported by concrete evidence, the industry suggested the adoption of risk-sharing schemes to circumvent the difficult decisions. However, some professionals have expressed skepticism over risk sharing, pointing out that it could be used to maintain high prices instead of lowering the prices to a cost-effective level. Despite the controversy, the newly elected government has adopted a risk-sharing scheme for drugs that is being used for severe diseases. Furthermore, compared with what was done in the past, a higher incremental cost-effectiveness ratio threshold for those drugs has been applied. To keep the balance between evidence-based decision making and rapid access to new medicine is a matter of great concern in Korea.

## China

### Health Care System Evolution, Reform and Complexities

China's health care system has transitioned several times during the past decades (Zhe *et al.* 2008). Despite that, GDP grew annually at an average of 9.6% from

1978 to 2004 (National Bureau of Statistics of China 2012) and the share of government spending on overall health care costs dropped from 32.2% in 1978 to the lowest at 15.5% in 2000 (China Healthcare Statistics Yearbook 2011). Health care became heavily privatized after that. Societal discontent after the outburst of SARS[3] in 2003 gradually triggered the political will to fundamentally reform the system (Teerawattananon et al. 2007). The government formerly initiated health care reform in 2007 with its "Healthy China 2020" program, with the ultimate goal to build a universal health care system. Mr. Chen, Minister of Health, pointed out that by 2020 national health care service and provision would be on the top level among all developing countries; east regions' and some mid-west regions' health care services and provisions would reach the mid level of developed countries' standard (Chen 2007).

After the reform, China's per capita health care expenditure grew to RMB 1,487 (around US$235) and government share of total health care spending increased to 28.6% in 2010 (SDPC 2012). Drug prices and spending have also increased significantly. The government introduced several measurements to contain drug prices, but none has been effective due to major complexities in the health care system, as we will discuss below. The adoption of pharmecoeconomics in decision making will also depend on how well the government tackles these complexities.

### Complexity 1: Universal Insurance Goal, However Different Schemes and Financing

By the end of 2010, 95% of the Chinese population had been covered by one of the three health care schemes: New Rural Cooperative Medical Scheme (NRCMS) (62%), Urban Residents' Basic Medical Insurance Scheme (URBMIS) (15%) and Urban Employee Basic Medical Insurance Scheme (UEBMIS) (18%) (Zhe et al. 2008).

NRCMS is managed by the Ministry of Health (MoH) and financed by government and individual contribution. The Ministry of Human Resources and Social Security (MoHRSS) manages the two urban schemes, URBMIS and UEBMIS. URBMIS is funded by government and individual contribution, while UEBMIS is funded by employer and employee insurance premium (Figure 11.3).

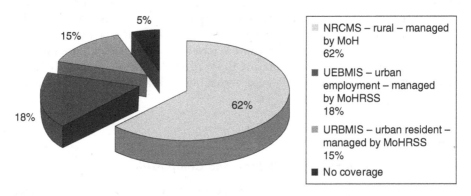

NRCMS – rural – managed by MoH 62%

UEBMIS – urban employment – managed by MoHRSS 18%

URBMIS – urban resident – managed by MoHRSS 15%

No coverage

*Figure 11.3* Health insurance overview: different schemes and fragmented management (China)

Regional MoHRSS determines the overall policy and coverage of the two urban schemes for the region. Regional MoH establishes the coverage and reimbursement level of rural NRCMS scheme. Provincial MoHRSS and MoH manage the funds and administration of the urban and rural schemes respectively. Reimbursement is typically capped at 4–8 times[4] of average annual provincial/municipal income level. Because of economic development disparity across provinces, as well as differences in urban and rural schemes, coverage varies to a great extent by the type of scheme and by region.

Differences in funding, insurance policy and coverage level of the three insurance schemes mean a fragmented approach in health care management.

### Complexity 2: Health Care Delivery – High Drug Prices to Subsidize Hospital Revenue

Health care delivery is organized through a three-tier structure (local/regional/national), with most hospitals being publicly owned. However, public hospitals are financed through multiple channels, mostly private: government subsidy, medicine markups, insurance payment and fee-for-service private payment from patients. Hospital charges are determined by national pricing authority. Prices are set below the cost of service in order to make it "affordable". Physicians' salaries are also kept at a low level due to low revenue budgets.

Because of historical health care privatization (Yip and Hsiao 2008), the Chinese government allowed hospital markup up to 15% of the medicine price to subsidize its revenue. This set the incentive for underpaid hospital services, as well as physicians, to over-prescribe and to prescribe more expensive drugs in order to make ends meet. Medicine markup on average consists of 40–50% of hospital income; in contrast, less than 10% of income is from government subsidy (National Bureau of Statistics of China 2012). The hospital financing model is the iceberg under water. It is a systematic overhaul involving society income distribution, hospital management and organizational issues. In order for any new pricing model to be successful, the first imperative is to fundamentally change the hospital financing model and establish the right incentives.

### Complexity 3: Drug Pricing and Reimbursement – Multiple Stakeholders, Fragmented Administration

Unlike other countries, the MoH in China does not oversee pricing and reimbursement decisions. Such responsibility is split among multiple organizations under a national–provincial two-tier system (Figure 11.4). MoHRSS at national level manages the two national reimbursement catalogs: the essential drug catalog (List A) and the innovative drug catalog (List B).

List A is enforced in principle in all provinces (Figure 11.5). At regional level, provincial and municipal MoHRSS determines up to 15% of variations of the reimbursement catalog of innovative drugs (List B). For example, Glivec has not been included on the national List B but is included on five provincial reimbursements List B. The majority of innovative, clinically proven effective and high-priced drugs are not yet reimbursed in China. MoHRSS suggests establishing a drug price negotiation

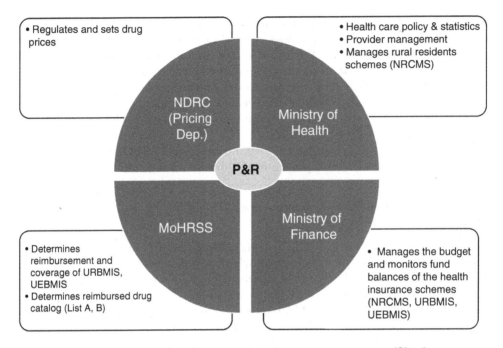

*Figure 11.4* Fragmented ownership of pricing and reimbursement management (China)

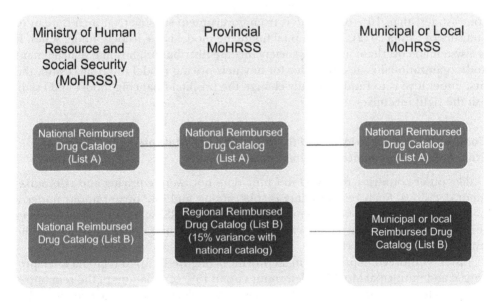

*Figure 11.5* National–provincial tiered reimbursement management (China)

mechanism with pharmaceutical companies, together with insurance companies, although details of such a negotiation mechanism are yet to be defined and published. This is likely the area where PE will be introduced.

The central government planning agency, NDRC, guides the overall pricing methodology and policy. NDRC determines pricing of prescription drugs on the national essential drugs catalog (List A) and the maximum price of List B drugs. Complementarily, the provincial pricing authority determines pricing of over-the-counter List A drugs, the price of provincial addition List B, and some drugs within provincial variation scope, etc. NDRC's price management focus is on the price of essential drugs, which is usually based on cost plus a certain margin. This innovative drug pricing method has transitioned from historically free pricing to government-guided pricing, with details yet to be revealed (SDPC 2012). Fragmented pricing and reimbursement ownership create challenges to developing and implementing health care policy systematically, due to lack of overarching organizational authority.

### Pharmacoeconomic Evaluation: Current Status and Guidelines in Development

Adoption of pharmacoeconomic analysis in decision making is still in its infancy in China. Government, academia and industry are at different stages with regards to the exposure and understanding of PE. So far most of the efforts toward PE adoption have been spearheaded by academia, although the government is starting to recognize the role of pharmaecoeconomic evaluation.

• Government

In March 2009 the government outlined, for the first time, the vision to apply pharmacoeconomic analysis in innovative and patented drugs pricing. However, there was a lot of work ahead to design the details, and to establish and implement the policy. The lack of PE expert resources in government was the main constraint in policy implementation.

At the time of writing this chapter (June 2012), use of PE was not required. Nevertheless, the government's vision has certainly ignited more interest among academia and industry, as evidenced by the multiple research centers and platforms initiated.

• Academia

Academic research in phamacoeconomics emerged in the mid 1990s and developed rapidly after 2002. The first research center, the Fudan Center for Pharmacoeconomic Research and Evaluation, was established in 2002 (Zhang *et al.* 2007) Multiple academic centers, including the Center of Pharmacoeconomic Evaluation (CPE) at the Chinese Medical Doctor Association (2005) and the Chinese Pharmaceutical Society Pharmacoeconomic Committee (CPSPC) (2008), were founded years after.

CPE's initiation of the China Guidelines for Pharmacoeconomic Evaluation project (thereafter The Guideline) at ISPOR 2005 marked a milestone step for China's pharmacoeconomic research. The Guideline was released in April 2011 as expert recommendations. Academic experts expressed high hopes that establishment of the CPSPC and publication of The Guideline would transform PE adoption from academic efforts to government mandate (Kang 2008).

- Industry

Pharmacoeconomic evaluation is not widely used by industry. According to a survey of 247 Chinese companies conducted from 2009 to 2010, only 35 companies (14.17%) had experience in using PE. Of those 35 companies, 16 (45.71%) used PE in the drug development stage prior to launch, 10 companies (28.57%) in the Phase IV post-marketing evaluation and 9 companies (25.71%) for pricing and reimbursement application (Zhang *et al.* 2010).

Pharmaceutical companies were initially the major pushback for implementation of The Guideline draft in 2007 due to lack of resources and operational practicality. After the government's March 2009 statement to introduce PE in decision making, industry-initiated activities increasingly began to emerge. Pfizer/Fudan launched a three-year joint training program for professionals in 2010, while a group of more than 20 Chinese pharmaceutical companies initiated the establishment of the Chinese Medicine Evidence-Based Pharmacoeconomic Evaluation Platform with academic institutions in May 2012.

- China Guidelines for Pharmacoeconomic Evaluation – 2011 version

The released guideline serves as a general framework for researchers and policy makers (China Guidelines for Pharmacoeconomic Evaluation 2011). The Guideline contains a comprehensive description of key pharmacoeconomic evaluation elements, with explanatory notes for key terminologies and concepts. Compared with established guidelines from agencies such as NICE in the UK, The Guideline serves more of an educational purpose than policy guidance, which is not surprising for a guideline yet to obtain political endorsement. The ICER threshold was mentioned and reference was made to the WHO recommendation that the threshold should be less than three times national GDP.

### Prospects of Pharmacoeconomic Evaluation in China

- Macro environment

China's per capita GDP reached 8,382 PPP$ in 2011 (IMF 2012). Although there is still a gap between its average economy and that of developed countries, several regions have per capita GDP of more than double the national average. Health care reform established the goal that by 2020 health care provision in all eastern regions and some mid-west provinces are expected to reach the middle level of that of developed countries, namely the US, Canada, Western European countries, Japan

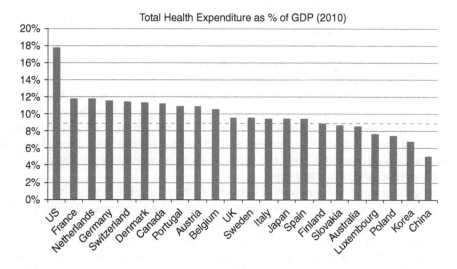

Figure 11.6 Total health expenditure as a percentage of GDP (multiple countries)

and Australia.[5] Total spending on health as a percentage of GDP was also expected to grow higher than the current 5% (2010 data) (Bae *et al.* 2012). If we use the lower range of total spending on health as a percentage of GDP (9%) from the developed countries, the top five municipalities/provinces in China would have per capita spending on health close to that of Korea and Poland, two countries that have adopted PE (Figure 11.6). The macro economic growth in China, and subsequently the rising health care costs, will reach the level that requires systematical cost management.

- Capacity for pharmacoeconomics

China experiences similar challenges in human resource and data availability as Korea during its implementation of PE. These challenges are recognized, and there have been multiple initiatives to bridge the gap.

On the human resources side, there are academia- and industry-initiated education programs. Some undergraduate curriculums also offer a pharmacoeconomic course, while several universities offer a pharmacoeconomics degree.

On the data and information system side, the establishment of a health care information system was listed as one of the development goals in the 12th (2011–2015) Five-Year-Plan (FYP). Most regions have adopted a smart card, Intelligent Card (IC), as the personal medical ID. The MoH goal was to increase the number of IC users to 800 million (about 60% of the total insured population) during the 12th FYP. Most of the IC cards can be used just within the issuing municipality, but some provinces are piloting integration of inter-region health IT information systems. Establishment of integrated health IT across regions will build up the data infrastructure on epidemiological and cost data. Similar to Korea, utility data seems to be the most challenging part. Several studies have been published on the preferences of the general Chinese population for different EQ-5D health states (Sun *et al.* 2011a, 2011b; Wang *et al.* 2012).

• Resolving the health care system complexities

The Chinese government embarked on an overhaul in its 12th Five-Year-Plan to tackle many of the health care system complexities. Hospital financing structure was ranked as the top priority (Xinhuanet 2012). The DRG payment system was considered one of the effective measurements and was being tested in six piloting hospitals in Beijing. Other provider payment models, such as capitation prepayment, were being tested in more than 40 cities.

The government also encourages provinces to pilot and explore the consolidation of the rural and urban insurance schemes. Many regions, such as Tianjin, Beijing, GuangDong and Nanjing, have consolidated or made plans to consolidate these two schemes. Equal coverage and reimbursement policy of rural or urban residents are also being discussed. As a natural development, establishing an overarching administrative organization will be unavoidable when the rural and urban schemes are consolidated. The NDRC started drug and medical service pricing reform in late 2009 with the goal of establishing a sound pricing system and mechanism that reflects the specific medical and health sector's needs by 2020. It also pointed out the use of health economics in determining the price of same category and innovative drugs and the need to scientifically evaluate pricing differences of drugs (Chen 2007).

Just like an old saying, Rome wasn't built in a day. The reform of China's health care system necessitates a gigantic overhaul, with many intricacies to be resolved over years. So far the government has shown great efforts toward building an efficient health care system. The complexities of the system will be tackled in the foreseeable future, and the adoption of health economics is just a matter of time.

## Concluding Remarks

In this chapter we have discussed several aspects of health economics adoption in two Asian countries and their development paths. The Korea and China case studies show that adoption of health economics in Asia depends not only on economic development and needs, and a favorable resource infrastructure, but most importantly on societal acceptance and political will. Health economics is one of the tools widely used to effectively manage health care resource allocation. With a global ageing population, individuals' growing demand for good health, and the financial austerity around the world, health care resource allocation will become increasingly important and health economics will certainly find its role in Asia as the economy grows.

## Acknowledgements

The authors would like to thank Professor William Hsiao, Professor Yuanli Liu, Ye (Yvonne) Xu and Chia-Wen Lee-Grossman for sharing their insights on the China market, Professor Tae-Jin Lee for his advice on the Korean market, and Eddie Hornby for general advice and proofreading.

## Notes

1 Application of health economics in the evaluation of pharmaceutical products is also called pharmacoeconomics (PE). PE does not include health economics evaluation of non-pharmaceutical courses of therapy or preventive strategies, such as surgical interventions or screening techniques. In this chapter, the authors use health economics and pharmacoeconomics interchangeably as all discussions refer to pharmaceutical products.
2 Purchasing power parity international dollar.
3 SARS: severe acute respiratory syndrome.
4 Reimbursement was capped at four times of average local income according to government policy in 2005. In the 12–5-Year-Plan, it has increased to six times of average income for urban employees and residents, and eight times of that number for rural residents.
5 United Nations composition of macro-geographical (continental) regions, geographical sub-regions, and selected economic and other groupings.

## References

Babar, Z.U. and Scahill, S. (2010). Is there a role for pharmacoeconomics in developing countries? *Pharmacoeconmics*, 28, 1069–74.

Bae, E.Y. (2011). Drug reimbursement decision in Korea, Australia, and Canada. *The Korean Journal of Health Economics and Policy*, 17, 1–21.

Bae, E.Y., Kim, J.H. and Choi, S.E. (2005). *Development of economic evaluation guideline and policy recommendation*. Seoul: Health Insurance Review and Assessment Service.

Bae, E.Y. and Lee, E.K. (2009). Pharmacoeconomic guidelines and their implementation in the positive list system in South Korea. *Value in Health*, 12, 36–41.

Bae, S.J., Lee, S.O., Jang, S.M. and Choi, S.E. (2012). *Development of 2nd version of Korean Pharmacoeconomic Guideline*. Seoul: Health Insurance Review and Assessment Service.

Chen, Z. (2007). Speech at China Association of Science & Technology Annual Meeting, (available online at: http://zt.cast.org.cn/n435777/n435799/n1204784/n1204788/44908.html).

China Healthcare Statistics Yearbook (2011) (available online at: www.stats.gov.cn/tjsj/ndsj/2011/indexeh.htm).

China Guidelines for Pharmacoeconomic Evaluations (2011). Instruction section. IMF World Economic Outlook Database (available online at: www.imf.org/external/ns/cs.aspx?id=28).

European Federation of Pharmaceutical Industries and Association (2012). *Japan position on the introduction of health technology assessment*. EFPIA, Brussels (available online at: http://efpia.jp/link/FINAL%20position%20on%20HTA20120420(E).pdf).

International Monetary Fund (2012). www.imf.org/.

International Society For Pharmacoeconomics and Outcomes Research (2011). *China Guidelines for Pharmacoeconomic Evaluations 2011*. IPSOR, U.S.A (available online at: www.ispor.org/peguidelines/source/China-Guidelines-for-Pharmacoeconomic-Evaluations_2011_Chinese.pdf).

Kang, Y.Y. (2008). China Guidelines for Pharmacoeconomic Evaluations – Government Push is Critical. Medicinal Economic Newspaper.

Lee, K.S., Brouwer, W.B., Lee, S.I. and Koo, H.W. (2005). Introducing economic evaluation as a policy tool in Korea: will decision makers get quality information? A critical review of published Korean economic evaluations. *Pharmacoeconomics*, 23, 709–21.

Lee, H.J., You, M.S. and Lee, T.J. (2011). Institutional change and organizational change: a multi case study on the organizational adaptation to the introduction of pharmacoeconomics. *Korean Journal of Health Policy & Administration*, 21, 425–56.

National Bureau of Statistics of China (2012). (Available online at: www.stats.gov.cn).

Oortwijn, W., Mathijssen, J. and Banta, D. (2010). The role of health technology assessment on phamarceutical reimbursement in selected middle-income countries. *Health Policy*, 95, 174–84.

Organization for Economic Co-Operation and Development (2012). *Health Status*. OECD, Paris (available online at: http://stats.oecd.org/index.aspx?DataSetCode=HEALTH_STAT).

SDPC (2012). *Opinion on reforming drug and medical service pricing policy and mechanism*. SDPC (available online at: www.sdpc.gov.cn/zcfb/zcfbtz/2009tz/W020091123362504424242.pdf).

Singer, M.E. (2008). Cost-effectiveness analysis developing nations left behind. *Pharmacoeconomics*, 26, 359–61.

Smith, S., Newhouse, J. and Freeland, M. (2009). Income, insurance and technology: why does health spending outpace economic growth? *Health Affairs*, 28, 1276–84.

Sun, S., Chen, J., Johannesson, M., *et al.* (2011a). Regional differences in health status in China. *Health Place*, 17, 671–80.

Sun, S., Chen, J., Johannesson, M., *et al.* (2011b). Population health status in China. *Quality of Life Research*, 20, 309–20.

Tarn, Y.H., Hu, S.L., Kamae, I. and Yang, B.M. (2008). Health-care systems and pharmacoeconomic research in Asia-Pacific region. *Value in Health*, 11, 137–55.

Teerawattananon, Y., Russel, S. and Mugford, M. (2007). Are the data good enough to be used by policy-makers? *Pharmacoeconomics*, 25, 467–79.

The Central People's Government of the People's Republic of China (2009). *Central government opinions on enhancing healthcare reform*. The Central People's Government of the People's Republic of China, China (available online at: www.gov.cn/test/2009-04/08/content_1280069.htm).

Wang, H.M., Patrick, D.L., Edwards, T.C., *et al.* (2012). Validation of the EQ-5D in a general population sample in urban China. *Quality of Life Research*, 21, 155–60.

Weinstein, M.C. and Stason, W.B. (1977). Foundations of cost-effectiveness analysis for health and medical practices. *New England Journal of Medicine*, 296, 716–21.

World Health Organization Global (2012). *Health Observatory Data Repository*. WHO, Geneva (available online at: http://apps.who.int/ghodata/?vid=1901).

Xinhuanet Beijing. Interview of Mr. Chen Zhu. 6 January 2012 (available online at: http://news.xinhuanet.com/politics/2012-01/05/c_111379068.htm).

Yang, B.M. (2009). The future of health technology assessment in healthcare decision making in Asia. *Pharmacoeconomics*, 27, 891–901.

Yang, B.M., Bae, E.Y. and Kim, J.H. (2008). Economic evaluation and pharmaceutical reimbursement reform in South Korea's National Health Insurance. *Health Affairs*, 27, 179–87.

Yip, W. and Hsiao, W. (2008). The Chinese health system at a crossroads. *Health Affairs*, 27, 460–8.

Zhang, Q.Y., Mo, S.X., Yang, D.W. and Xiong, G.L. (2007). Pharmacoeconomics development chronology. *China Journal of Pharmaceutical Economics*, 1, 34–43.

Zhang, X.Y., Feng, F.L., Li, M.H., *et al.* (2010). A survey of the use of pharmacoeconomics in Chinese pharmaceutical companies. *China Journal of Pharmaceutical Economics*, 3, 54–9.

Zhe, D. and Phillips, M. (2008). Evolution of China's health-care system. *The Lancet*, 372, 1715–16.

## Part III

# Decision Making and Assessment

# Chapter 12

# Patient Preferences in Health Technology Assessment

*Janine van Til and John F.P. Bridges*

## Introduction

Health technology assessment (HTA) is a comprehensive, systematic assessment of the conditions for and the consequences of using a health technology in the health care system (Banta 2003; Banta and Jonsson 2009). HTA was first conceptualized four decades ago as a response to the rise in health care costs and the increased need to regulate the introduction of new health technologies to the market (Wallner and Konski 2008; Banta and Jonsson 2009). The aim of HTA is to provide decision makers in health care with information that is relevant in making funding, planning, purchasing, investing and clinical decisions (Banta 2003). While this is a broad area of interest, HTA in practice is characterized by a focus on clinical impact and cost-effectiveness analysis of health technology (Banta 2003; Akkazieva *et al.* 2006). In recent years it was argued that social, legal and ethical aspects should be included in the assessment process of health care innovations to fulfill the aims of HTA and to realize its full potential (Banta 2003; Hailey and Nordwall 2006).

## Public and Patient Involvement in Medical Decision Making

Health care decision makers, patients and the public have expressed a strong desire for greater involvement in decision making in health care, to ensure that the patients' needs and wants are considered in decision making about their own care (Litva *et al.* 2002; Coulter 2012). In the last two decades the interest in shared decision making (SDM) between patients and clinicians during the clinical encounter has grown. In contrast to paternalistic decision models, in SDM the clinician and the patient share their values and preferences with regard to the process and outcome of care before coming to an agreed decision with regard to the optimal diagnostic or treatment plan. Research has shown that SDM enhances the effectiveness of the decision-making process, increases patient satisfaction and improves outcomes of care (Joosten *et al.* 2008), but SDM is not yet the norm in clinical practice (Elwyn *et al.* 2001; Coulter *et al.* 2011). The most important barriers for SDM are time constraints, information asymmetry and lack of applicability due to patient characteristics and/ or the clinical situation (Légaré *et al.* 2008).

More recently, including the patient perspective during the assessment stage of a technology was suggested to increase patient involvement (Coulter 2004; Bridges and Jones 2007). By including their perspective, patients' needs and wants in disease management could be contrasted with the benefits and harms of the technology, thereby allowing for a better fit between technologies that are offered to and those that are desired by patients (Parry *et al.* 1992; Pivik *et al.* 2004; Hansen and Lee 2011; Van Til and Ijzerman 2014). By taking into account patient preferences in access and reimbursement decisions, the legitimacy, accountability and effectiveness of the decision process itself are also thought to improve (Coulter 2004; Abelson *et al.* 2007; Danner *et al.* 2011). It is even suggested that if decision makers were more knowledgeable about patient preferences, health care as a whole could be cheaper and more effective (Brennan and Strombom 1998).

## Patient Involvement Models

Different conceptualizations of and mechanisms within public or patient involvement in health care decision making can be distinguished (Pivik *et al.* 2004; Gauvin *et al.* 2010). Gauvin *et al.* (2010) presented three decision-making domains (policy, organizational and research) and two main categories of the public (the general public and those that are directly affected by the decision making, i.e. the patient) (Gauvin *et al.* 2010). Within the patient involvement models in HTA, a clear distinction is made between direct and indirect approaches to include the patient or patient representative (Abelson *et al.* 2007). In the direct involvement in policy decision making, patients are a part of the decision-making panel itself, they take part in stakeholder consultation, give qualitative input to guidance development or assist in dissemination of the results to other patients (Kelson *et al.* 2009). One successful example of direct public involvement is the patient and public involvement program at the National Institute for Health and Clinical Excellence (NICE) in the UK. The program's main goal is to increase patients' access to the care to which they are entitled. The main strength of the NICE model of patient participation in decision making is its integration in the nationally supported framework for health policy decision making (Pivik *et al.* 2004). Similar initiatives have also been taken in other countries, but its full potential has not yet been reached (Nilsen Elin *et al.* 2006).

In this chapter, we will further concentrate on indirect approaches to include the patient as an assessor of health care technology by providing preferences on value-based aspects of the proposed health innovation that could maximize their welfare (Brouwer *et al.* 2008).

## Conceptualization of Patient-Based HTA

Patient preferences are the result of deliberation about the value of anticipated innovations that originate from cognitions, experiences and reflections of current health and the potential of innovation in the future. Traditionally, the value of a health technology was determined based on its ability to improve health and/or quality of life (Brazier *et al.* 1999). However, this does not evaluate organizational, social and ethical aspects of the health technology that are also important determinants of a technology's value. Moreover, it does not provide information on the choices patients make in satisfying their health care needs, which could be especially relevant to study of the actual impact of a technology (Casper and Brennan 1993; Bridges 2003; Johri and Norheim 2012).

The focus of this chapter will be on preference-based methods that enable valuation of health care innovation within the context of HTA (Litva *et al.* 2002; Bridges and Jones 2007). In this chapter we will assume the Welfarist perspective that the patient, i.e. the individual that faces the consequences of decision making, is the best judge of its value trade-offs (Brouwer *et al.* 2008). We refer to this subgroup of methods as patient-based HTA methods (Bridges and Jones 2007).

## Chapter Overview

In this chapter we aim to provide a broad overview of preference-based methods that are currently in use or could be useful in health technology assessment. As the methods originate from different backgrounds, for clarity purposes we will describe the methods based on their theories, strategies and methods of inquiry. The research theories are the basis for the type of knowledge that is gathered, while the research strategies refer to the process by which data are gathered. As the main strategies of inquiry we distinguish qualitative and quantitative approaches (Figure 12.1). In the following paragraphs, the particular aims, strengths and limitations of the methods and their usefulness in policy decision making within the context of patient-based HTA are discussed (Weernink *et al.* 2014).

## Qualitative Approaches to Patient-Based HTA

Qualitative research spans multiple theories, strategies and methods of inquiry (Ring *et al.* 2011). In this paragraph we focus on qualitative research methods that fall in the constructive theory of inquiry. In constructivism, researchers generate or inductively

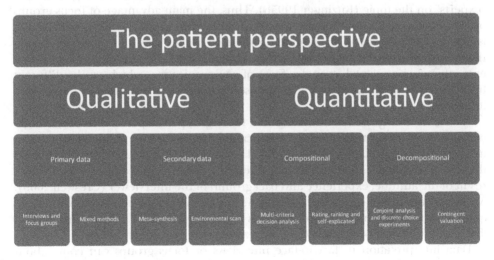

*Figure 12.1* Overview of qualitative and quantitative methods to study patients' preferences for health innovations

develop a theory about how respondents view the world. As methods for primary data collection we distinguish individual, group and mixed methods, and meta-synthesis and environmental scanning as methods for secondary data collection (Ryan *et al.* 2001) (Figure 12.1).

### Interviews and Focus Groups

Interviews and focus groups are qualitative methods for collecting primary data on patient preferences in patient-based HTA. Face-to-face interviews can be used to understand patient preferences for disease management in the context of their needs and wants (Eilertsen *et al.* 2010). There are three main types of interviews: in-depth, semi-structured and structured. In-depth interviews usually cover topics not defined prior to the encounter, but that come up during the interview itself. Their main strength is that preferences concerning a limited number of topics can be explored in great detail. Semi-structured interviews are conducted based on a loose structure of predefined topics related to the specific area of interest that needs to be explored. Questions in this type of interview are usually open-ended, and the researcher or the respondent may diverge from the primary structure to explore an item in further detail. In contrast, structured interviews make use of a predefined set of usually close-ended questions. For that reason, they do not fit the constructivist framework and are often perceived as questionnaires which are taken in person rather than interviews (Britten 1995; Coast 1999; Facey *et al.* 2010).

While interviews are interactions between a single respondent and inter-viewer, focus groups are controlled meetings of small numbers of patients (usually between 8 and 12) with one or more discussion facilitators. They rely on interaction between group members to stimulate discussion. Focus groups can be in-depth or semi-structured. Compared with (group) interviews, the interaction and group discussion in focus groups are thought to reveal additional information about the topic of inquiry that is valuable to the researcher, because it stems from the interaction of "experts" on the topic (Kitzinger 1995b). Thus, the main advantage of focus groups over interviews is that the researcher can stimulate the respondents to explore the issues important to them by generating their own questions and priorities, rather than those introduced by the researcher (Kitzinger 1995a). In addition, respondents interact in a relaxed, everyday form of communication, which can be different from the structured and reasoned responses that are usually elicited in face-to-face interviews.

A clear advantage of the interviews and focus groups compared with other methods of inquiry is that they allow for clarification and follow-up questions, which can improve the interpretation of the results. However, a major challenge to their use is the risk of so-called "interview effects", where the research outcomes are biased as a result of the attitude, experience and background of the interviewer (Creswell 2009). An important advantage of both interviews and focus groups compared with more quantitative, usually survey-based methods in patient-based HTA is that they do not discriminate against people who cannot read or write (Kitzinger 1995b).

Data interpretation in face-to-face interviews or focus groups can come about through inductive reasoning (Ring *et al.* 2011). It is used to define a structure for generating taxonomy, themes and theory with regard to the research subject and subsequently to generate hypotheses based on the results of the research (Bradley *et al.* 2007). Subsequent deductive analysis can be helpful in integrating well-known concepts in the existing literature (Bradley *et al.* 2007). In the context of patient-based HTA, the results of interviews and focus groups can offer in-depth understanding of the consequences of allowing or limiting access to health innovations for specific groups of patients (Coast *et al.* 2012).

### Mixed Methods

Mixed methods are qualitative methods for collecting primary data on patient preferences in patient-based HTA (O'Cathain *et al.* 2007). Their specific strength is to address one topic with quantitative and qualitative methods of inquiry to generate a deeper understanding of the subject than would ever be possible with either one alone (O'Cathain *et al.* 2007; O'Cathain 2009). In mixed methods the choice of the knowledge claims and strategies of inquiry is based on pragmatic grounds. In this chapter we opted to categorize mixed methods with the qualitative methods that use the constructivist theory of inquiry (to develop rather than to test hypothesis).

Mixed method designs use different methods of inquiry in a sequential, concurrent or transformative way (Creswell 2012). When used sequentially, qualitative research often precedes quantitative analysis, e.g. to identify important issues before they are further analyzed quantitatively. The aim of the (subsequent) quantitative phase is to add numbers to findings, to reduce information to a manageable volume or to identify those aspects that are most relevant to the research question. The quantitative phase of inquiry usually involves a combination of ranking (putting themes or aspects in order of importance) and rating (attaching a verbal or numerical judgment) to determine the relevance of each aspect to the patient (Kinter *et al.* 2009).

The main advantage of mixed methods within patient-based HTA is the ability to create an evidence base for generating and prioritizing issues to consider in further study or in the policy decision-making process. One major challenge is that the interpretation of results becomes difficult if data conflict. If so, value statements have to be made with regard to the strategies or methods of inquiry, to identify which are more important or more reliable in the interpretation of the study results (Moffatt *et al.* 2006). An extensive overview of the theory and practice of using mixed methods can be found in the literature (Creswell 2009).

### Meta-Synthesis

Meta-synthesis is a qualitative method for primary data synthesis of patient preferences in patient-based HTA (Coast 1999). Synthesis of qualitative studies is an important means to increase their generalizability and to ensure that decision makers have the best possible evidence base. Moreover, research synthesis helps to assess core patient aspects and to establish whether there is a need for more research (Ring *et al.* 2011).

In the interpretation of data from a range of secondary sources, there are multiple methods to synthesize qualitative studies. The most applicable ones are meta-ethnography, meta-study, meta-summary and thematic assessment.

Of these, meta-ethnography is the most commonly used (Ring *et al.* 2011). Meta-ethnography is a stepwise approach in which findings from multiple sources are brought together and reinterpreted. This method is mostly used to explore perceptions and experiences of disease and views on health services and innovations (Salter *et al.* 2008).

In meta-study, qualitative studies are first deconstructed based on the theory on which the study was built, methods used and their findings. After these analytical phases are completed, meta-synthesis is used to create a new interpretation of existing information.

Thematic synthesis is mainly (but not exclusively) used for separate analysis and then qualitative and quantitative information is integrated. Often, hypotheses are generated based on qualitative research and then subsequently tested using quantitative research synthesis. The meta-study method was developed to address mainly the questions of need, appropriateness, acceptability and effectiveness of interventions.

Lastly, meta-summary is a quantitatively oriented method for meta-synthesis of qualitative information. This makes it suitable for analysis of survey data, which is not possible with any of the other methods (Ring *et al.* 2011).

### Environmental Scan

A relatively novel method in patient-based HTA is the environmental scan. An environmental scan is a qualitative method for primary data synthesis of patient preferences in patient-based HTA. In contrast to meta synthesis, the environmental scan primarily focuses on content in the "soft" or "grey" literature (Porterfield *et al.* 2012). It can include examination of relevant websites, organizations, disease-specific social networks, videos, associations, workshops, presentations, governmental agencies, abstracts and other forms of unpublished resources ranging across topics beyond just health care (Garces *et al.* 2012). In examining data from this range of secondary sources, environmental scans aim to synthesize information around a particular focus in order to create a comprehensive view of a topic and incorporate a variety of perspectives that is often neglected by other sources (Maurer *et al.* 2012). The goal of the environmental scan is to find pertinent information from non-traditional sources outside of the medical community that can highlight certain trends, key players and stakeholders, relevant events and potential competitors to build an evidence-based perspective. Building specific constraints, such as a definition of the problem, a conceptual framework and outlining specific questions can aid in organizing an environmental scan providing a broad reach that is also targeted towards a topic.

With respect to patient preference, the environmental scan can be very helpful in identifying relevant groups and resources advocating for patient positions. Tracking patient preferences via an environmental scan may become more commonplace as patients are growing more connected to their care via wearable devices, social media websites and personal health records (Garces *et al.* 2012). As patients become more involved in their care and more information is available they can become more active in the decision-making process. Additionally, in assessment of the results of an environmental scan, attention can be drawn towards the gathering of information and developing metrics and identifying key gaps in subject matter or materials and tools (Maurer *et al.* 2012).

## Quantitative Methods in Patient-Based HTA

Quantitative research methods are based on the post-positivism theory of inquiry to relate causes to effects. It is reductionist in nature, as its basic principles are concrete hypotheses, which are tested through quantitative analysis. Interpretation of the findings is considered objective and the main aim is to develop numeric measures of outcome to test the behavior of a representative sample of the target population (Creswell 2009). The quantitative methods discussed in this chapter are ranking, rating and self-explicated methods and multi-criteria decision analysis as compositional approaches, and contingent valuation and conjoint analysis and discrete choice experiments as decompositional approaches to patient-based HTA (Green and Srinivasan 1978; Froberg and Kane 1989a). The compositional strategy of inquiry consists of methods that ask respondents to value individual characteristics of the outcome, which enables the researcher to build valuations for the whole (Froberg and Kane 1989a). In contrast, a decompositional strategy of inquiry requires the respondent to assign values to outcome as a whole (f.i. to express preferences for a health care scenario consisting of different aspects of the technology). Decomposed methods allow the attributes comprising the health outcome to be separated and their individual effects analyzed based on the judgment on relative preference or attractiveness of the whole.

A second distinction is based on the level of measurement that results from the different methods of inquiry, whether they result in ordinal, interval or ratio scaled outcomes (Froberg and Kane 1989b). Level of measurement is important because it influences the types of mathematical procedures that can be performed on the data, and thus the types of conclusions that can be drawn from them. Interval and ratio scaled data are preferred to ordinal data.

### Ranking, Rating and Self-Explicated

Ranking, rating and self-explicated methods are compositional techniques for quantitative assessment of patient preferences in patient-based HTA. In its most simple form, quantitative preferences can come about through ranking, rating or combinations of these methods of inquiry. Ranking and rating are direct scaling methods that enable the respondents to directly assign a relative importance value to outcomes (Froberg and Kane 1989b). In ranking, a prioritization of outcomes is given by putting outcomes in an order from most to least important (or vice versa), which results in an ordinal prioritization of outcomes. In rating, a prioritization of outcomes is given by rating them on some type of cardinal scale. Often used interval scales range from 0 to 10 or from 0 to 100. In the strategies of inquiry that combine these methods (compositional or self-explicated approaches), both ordinal rankings and cardinal ratings are assigned to determine the relative priorities with regard to different aspects of the technology.

In the second stage of the data analysis, rankings and ratings of the same aspects are multiplied and the result is a preference-based prioritization of outcomes of the health innovation (Bridges *et al.* 2011b). With respect to eliciting patient preferences, the self-explicated method is a stated preference-based method that enables people to state which outcomes of an innovation they prefer without asking for trade-offs with regard to importance (Pavlova *et al.* 2003; Bridges *et al.* 2011b). Although rating and ranking methods can be performed independently, combining the results of both in a self-explicated approach is superior with regard to the discriminating power of performing them alone (Read *et al.* 1984; Bridges *et al.* 2011b). In contrast to other compositional strategies of inquiry such as multi-criteria decision methods, rating and ranking require no, or only a few, explicit trade-offs on the relative importance of different aspects of a health innovation. This might explain the recent interest in ranking, rating and combined approaches, as it makes these methods more simple and easier to use compared with other stated preference-based methods (Pavlova *et al.* 2003).

### Multi-Criteria Decision Analysis

Multi-criteria decision analysis (MCDA) methods are compositional techniques for quantitative assessment of patient preferences in patient-based HTA. MCDA methods can be classified into three categories: value measurement models, outranking models and goal programming methods. In this chapter, we focus on value measurement methods, as they are used the most in patient-based HTA (Liberatore and Nydick 2008).

An MCDA is a multi-step process which combines different methods of inquiry. MCDA is an umbrella term for a wide range of techniques (Belton and Stewart 2002). Although most MCDA methods provide a systematic process for clarifying what is being taken into account (the "criteria"), how each of those criteria is to be measured ("the attributes") and how much importance ("weight") to put on each in making the final decision, they vary with regard to the complexity of the structuring process and the decision analysis (Devlin and Sussex 2011). Most methods require several steps before identifying the optimal decision, such as defining the problem, determining goals and requirements to the analysis, selecting criteria and determining their hierarchy, eliciting criteria importance and evaluating alternatives against criteria (Belton and Stewart 2002; Zhou and Ang 2009).

One critical step in which MCDA methods differ is the way in which preferences over criteria are established. One relatively simple method for preference estimation is the weighted sum method, or Simple Multi Attribute Rating Theory (SMART) (Thokola and Duenas 2012). In SMART, 100 points are divided over the criteria to reflect their relative importance (Van Til *et al.* 2008). Another method that was used successfully in the context of patient-based HTA is the analytical hierarchical process (AHP) (Danner *et al.* 2011). AHP makes use of indirect scaling of outcomes through the use of pairwise comparisons of criteria. Although the trade-offs made by the respondents have ordinal properties, a ratio scaled measure of outcome is obtained (Liberatore and Nydick 2008). Danner *et al.* (2011) used AHP to identify patient-relevant end-points in the treatment of major depression.

MCDA methods were previously used at the policy and management level of decision making (Liberatore and Nydick 2008), and more recently to capture the patient perspective in evaluation and selection of health care innovations (Dolan 2010; Ijzerman *et al.* 2012). The advantages of MCDA include (1) its ability to quantify both individual characteristics of health care innovations as the whole, (2) its ability to include and determine the relative importance of health, non-health and process attributes of care, and (3) its ability to prioritize future health care technologies in comparison with current advancements (Philips *et al.* 2002). In the context of patient-based HTA, quantitative prioritization of possible outcomes provides the policy maker with clear targets for decision making (Pavlova *et al.* 2003; Bridges *et al.* 2011b). MCDA methods vary with regard to their validity and complexity. The theoretical validity of MCDA methods is determined by their adherence to multi-attribute utility theory (Dyer *et al.* 1992), but the choice of the actual method to use also depends on pragmatic reasons (Dolan 2010). For support in deciding the most appropriate MCDA technique, see Guitouni and Martel (1998).

### Contingent Valuation

Contingent valuation (CV) methods are decompositional techniques for quantitative assessment of patient preferences in patient-based HTA. CV methods are direct methods used for eliciting a monetary valuation of health care technologies (Klose 1999). Their aim is to put a monetary value on health innovations to reflect their value to the individual or to the group (Cookson 2003). CV methods are often performed to broaden the perspective of cost–benefit analysis when it is difficult to value health care programs in direct clinical outcomes. In patient-based HTA, contingent valuation techniques are used to ask patients to state the amount of money they would be willing to spend to have access to the health innovation (willingness to pay), or alternatively, the amount of money the patient feels would compensate for being deprived of the health innovation (willingness to accept) (Froberg and Kane 1989b; Olsen and Smith 2001). CV methods are direct scaling methods (Froberg and Kane 1989b), where respondents are asked to judge the value of a health innovation as a whole in monetary terms. The number assigned to health innovations represents the absolute magnitude of desirability of the health innovation compared with others (Ryan *et al.* 2004).

CV methods have a strong foundation in welfare economics, which makes it theoretically strong. Also, CV offers a comprehensive valuation of outcomes that can include non-health outcomes and process outcomes of health care (Olsen and Smith 2001). CV methods have also shown high theoretical and convergent validity (Klose 1999). Yet CV methods have been criticized for being hypothetical, with low correspondence between expressed and actual values. The validity of CV methods depends on whether they can offer a realistic and believable representation of the decision context (Smith 2003). Major limitations of CV methods are that they are subject to both income and measurement bias (Cookson 2003). Willingness to pay (WTP) studies, for example, unadjusted for income will skew results towards the wealthy, because they are more able (not willing) to pay (Olsen and Smith 2001). Also, CV studies are sensitive to the magnitude of benefits and are skewed towards the particular interventions being valued, while budget constraint are not taken into account.

In the context of including patient preferences in policy decision making, the results of contingent valuation studies can aid policy decision makers by expressing intensities of preferences for health care programs competing for the same budget, or multiple interventions for the same disease/diagnosis (Olsen and Smith 2001). A discussion about the WTP method in the context of policy decision making in health is presented elsewhere (Cookson 2003).

## Conjoint Analysis and Discrete Choice Experiments

Conjoint analysis and discrete choice experiments are decompositional techniques for quantitative assessment of patient preferences in patient-based HTA. Conjoint analysis involves hypothetical scenarios, over which preferences are established by respondents through ranking, rating, or by choosing a particular scenario (Ryan 1999a; Bridges and Jones 2007). Among conjoint analysis methods the discrete choice experiment (DCE) is used the most often (Ryan and Farrar 2000). In a DCE, patients are asked to indicate their preferred scenario from a set of two or more scenarios.

A DCE has three specific advantages. First, it is methodologically sound as it is rooted in economic theory and based on multi-attribute utility theory (Louviere *et al.* 2010). Second, it can estimate the WTP for specific attributes of the health technology, by including cost as an attribute in conjoint analysis (CA) (Ryan and Watson 2009). Third, because a DCE uses holistic scenarios, it requires respondents to determine the relative importance and value of attributes of care within their context, in combination with all other attributes (Phillips *et al.* 2002). There are plenty of examples of DCEs in patient-based HTA (Ryan 1999b; Kinter *et al.* 2009; Bridges *et al.* 2012). For instance, Perreira *et al.* (2011) used DCEs to estimate the determinants of influenza vaccine purchase decisions in the US. DCEs were shown to be methodologically valid and acceptable to patients (Ryan *et al.* 1998; Van Til *et al.* 2008). In the past, efforts were undertaken to increase the quality of CA studies (Marshall *et al.* 2010). This recently resulted in the publication of good research practices for CA applications in health (Bridges *et al.* 2011a).

## Summary and Conclusions

As discussed in this chapter, there is increased interest in including the patient perspective in HTA, to get perspective on aspects of health technology that are not accounted for in traditional methods. We focused on preferences-based methods to establish the patient perspective in health technology assessment. Patient-based HTA can include a wide range of methods to capture the patient perspective. At present, quantitative methods are more frequently used in patient-based HTA. Quantitative methods allow for hypothesis testing and establishing quantitative assessments of preference towards technology innovations. Their value in determining the trade-offs of patients in the evaluation of health innovations has long been established. However, in recent years the use of qualitative methods in patient-based HTA has been increasing. Qualitative research methods' main strength is a more general assessment of the impact of technology, from the basis of more quantitative research or to offer increased understanding of the results of quantitative research outcomes. However, HTA researchers' lack of familiarity with the theories of inquiry and the specifics with regard to designing, executing and analyzing their results is one of the biggest challenges for the use of qualitative methods in HTA. Nevertheless, we feel that both qualitative and quantitative strategies of inquiry have their own specific role in patient-based HTA.

Patient-based HTA can help policy makers by providing an understanding of patient preferences, values and beliefs within their context, identifying relationships between these concepts and behaviors, and generating theoretical concepts to understand the feasibility of a technology within its wider context behaviors.

# References

Abelson, J., Giacomini, M., Lehoux, P. and Gauvin, F.P. (2007). Bringing 'the public' into health technology assessment and coverage policy decisions: from principles to practice. *Health Policy*, 82, 37–50.

Akkazieva, B., Gulacsi, L., Brandtmuller, A., *et al.* (2006). Patients' preferences for healthcare system reforms in Hungary: a conjoint analysis. *Applied Health Economics and Health Policy*, 5, 189–98.

Banta, D. (2003). The development of health technology assessment. *Health Policy*, 63, 121–32.

Banta, D. and Jonsson, E. (2009). History of HTA: introduction. *International Journal of Technology Assessment in Health Care*, 25, 1–6.

Belton, V. and Stewart, T.J. (2002). Multiple criteria decision analysis: an integrated approach. Springer Science + Business Media Dordrecht.

Bradley, E.H., Curry, L.A. and Devers, K.J. (2007). Qualitative data analysis for health services research: developing taxonomy, themes, and theory. *Health Services Research*, 42, 1758–72.

Brazier, J., Deverill, M. and Green, C. (1999). A review of the use of health status measures in economic evaluation. *Journal of Health Services Research & Policy*, 4, 174–84.

Brennan, P.F. and Strombom, I. (1998). Improving health care by understanding patient preferences: the role of computer technology. *Journal of the American Medical Informatics Association*, 5, 257–62.

Bridges, J.F. (2003). Stated preference methods in health care evaluation: an emerging methodological paradigm in health economics. *Applied Health Economics and Health Policy*, 2, 213–24.

Bridges, J.F. and Jones, C. (2007). Patient-based health technology assessment: a vision of the future. *International Journal of Technology Assessment in Health Care*, 23, 30–5.

Bridges, J.F., Hauber, A.B., Marshall, D., *et al.* (2011a). Conjoint analysis applications in health – a checklist: a report of the ISPOR Good Research Practices for Conjoint Analysis Task Force. *Value in Health*, 14, 403–13.

Bridges, J.F., Mohamed, A.F., Finnern, H.W., *et al.* (2012). Patients' preferences for treatment outcomes for advanced non-small cell lung cancer: a conjoint analysis. *Lung Cancer*, 77, 224–31.

Bridges, J.F., Slawik, L., Schmeding, A., *et al.* (2011b). A test of concordance between patient and psychiatrist valuations of multiple treatment goals for schizophrenia. *Health Expectations*, 16, 164–76.

Britten, N. (1995). Qualitative interviews in medical research. *British Medical Journal*, 311, 251–3.

Brouwer, W.B., Culyer, A.J., Van Exel, N.J. and Rutten, F.F. (2008). Welfarism vs. extra-welfarism. *Journal of Health Economics*, 27, 325–38.

Casper, G.R. and Brennan, P.F. (1993). Improving the quality of patient care: the role of patient preferences in the clinical record. *Proceedings the Annual Symposium on Computer Application in Medical Care*, 8–11.

Coast, J. (1999). The appropriate uses of qualitative methods in health economics. *Health Economics*, 8, 345–53.

Coast, J., Al-Janabi, H., Sutton, E.J., *et al.* (2012). Using qualitative methods for attribute development for discrete choice experiments: issues and recommendations. *Health Economics*, 21, 730–41.

Cookson, R. (2003). Willingness to pay methods in health care: a sceptical view. *Health Economics*, 12, 891–4.

Coulter, A. (2004). Perspectives on health technology assessment: response from the patient's perspective. *International Journal of Technology Assessment in Health Care*, 20, 92–6.

Coulter, A. (2012). Patient engagement – what works? *The Journal of Ambulatory Care Management*, 35, 80–9.

Coulter, A., Edwards, A., Elwyn, G. and Thomson, R. (2011). Implementing shared decision making in the UK. *Zeitschrift für Evidenz Fortbildung und Qualität Gesundheitswesen*, 105, 300–4.

Creswell, J.W. (2009). *Research design: qualitative, quantitative, and mixed methods approaches*. Sage Publications, Thousand Oaks, CA.

Creswell, J.W. (2012). *Educational research: planning, conducting, and evaluating quantitative and qualitative research*. Pearson, Boston, MA.

Danner, M., Hummel, J.M., Volz, F., *et al.* (2011). Integrating patients' views into health technology assessment: analytic hierarchy process (AHP) as a method to elicit patient preferences. *International Journal of Technology Assessment in Health Care*, 27, 369–75.

Devlin, N.J. and Sussex, J. (2011). *Incorporating multiple criteria in HTA. Methods and processes*. OHE, London.

Dolan, J.G. (2010). Multi-criteria clinical decision support: a primer on the use of multiple criteria decision making methods to promote evidence-based, patient-centered healthcare. *Patient*, 3, 229–48.

Dyer, J.S., Fishburn, P.C., Steuer, R.E., *et al.* (1992). Multiple criteria decision making, multiattribute utility theory: the next ten years. *Management Science*, 38, 645–54.

Eilertsen, G., Kirkevold, M. and Bjørk, I.T. (2010). Recovering from a stroke: a longitudinal, qualitative study of older Norwegian women. *Journal of Clinical Nursing*, 19, 2004–13.

Elwyn, G., Edwards, A., Mowle, S., *et al.* (2001). Measuring the involvement of patients in shared decision-making: a systematic review of instruments. *Patient Education and Counseling*, 43, 5–22.

Facey, K., Boivin, A., Gracia, J., *et al.* (2010). Patients' perspectives in health technology assessment: a route to robust evidence and fair deliberation. *International Journal of Technology Assessment in Health Care*, 26, 334–40.

Froberg, D.G. and Kane, R.L. (1989a). Methodology for measuring health-state preferences – I: measurement strategies. *Journal of Clinical Epidemiology*, 42, 345–54.

Froberg, D.G. and Kane, R.L. (1989b). Methodology for measuring health-state preferences – II: scaling methods. *Journal of Clinical Epidemiology*, 42, 459–71.

Garces, J.L.G., Wang, Z., Elraiyah, T., *et al.* 2012. *Eliciting patient perspective in patient-centered outcomes research: a meta narrative systematic review*. Mayo Clinic, Rochester, MN (available online at: www.pcori.org/assets/Eliciting-Patient-Perspective-in-Patient-Centered-Outcomes-Research-A-Meta-Narrative-Systematic-Review.pdf).

Gauvin, F.P., Abelson, J., Giacomini, M., *et al.* (2010). "It all depends": conceptualizing public involvement in the context of health technology assessment agencies. *Social Science and Medicine*, 70, 1518–26.

Green, P.E. and Srinivasan, V. (1978). Conjoint analysis in consumer research: issues and outlook. *Journal of Consumer Research*, 5, 103–23.

Guitouni, A. and Martel, J.-M. (1998). Tentative guidelines to help choosing an appropriate MCDA method. *European Journal of Operational Research*, 109, 501–21.

Hailey, D. and Nordwall, M. (2006). Survey on the involvement of consumers in health technology assessment programs. *International Journal of Technology Assessment in Health Care*, 22, 497–9.

Hansen, H.P. and Lee, A. (2011). Patient aspects and involvement in HTA: an academic perspective. *Pharmaceuticals Policy and Law*, 13, 123–8.

Ijzerman, M.J., Van Til, J.A. and Bridges, J.F. (2012). A comparison of analytic hierarchy process and conjoint analysis methods in assessing treatment alternatives for stroke rehabilitation. *Patient*, 5, 45–56.

Johri, M. and Norheim, O.F. (2012). Can cost-effectiveness analysis integrate concerns for equity? Systematic review. *International Journal of Technology Assessment in Health Care*, 28, 125–32.

Joosten, E.A.G., Defuentes-Merillas, L., De Weert, G.H., *et al.* (2008). Systematic review of the effects of shared-decision-making on patient satisfaction, treatment adherence and health status. *Psychotherapy and Psychosomatics*, 77, 219–26.

Kelson, M., Longson, C. and Littlejohns, P. (2009). NICE does consider patient views. *British Medical Journal*, 338, b652.

Kinter, E.T., Schmeding, A., Rudolph, I., *et al.* (2009). Identifying patient-relevant endpoints among individuals with schizophrenia: an application of patient-centered health technology assessment. *International Journal of Technology Assessment in Health Care*, 25, 35–41.

Kitzinger, J. (1995a). Introducing focus groups. *British Medical Journal*, 311, 299–302.

Kitzinger, J. (1995b). Qualitative research: introducing focus groups. *British Medical Journal*, 311, 299–302.

Klose, T. (1999). The contingent valuation method in health care. *Health Policy*, 47, 97–123.

Légaré, F., Ratté, S., Gravel, K. and Graham, I.D. (2008). Barriers and facilitators to implementing shared decision-making in clinical practice: update of a systematic review of health professionals' perceptions. *Patient Education and Counseling*, 73, 526–35.

Liberatore, M.J. and Nydick, R.L. (2008). The analytic hierarchy process in medical and health care decision making: a literature review. *European Journal of Operational Research*, 189, 194–207.

Litva, A., Coast, J., Donovan, J., *et al.* (2002). The public is too subjective: public involvement at different levels of health-care decision making. *Social Science & Medicine*, 54, 1825–37.

Louviere, J.J., Flynn, T.N. and Carson, R.T. (2010). Discrete choice experiments are not conjoint analysis. *Journal of Choice Modelling*, 3, 57–72.

Marshall, D., Bridges, J.F., Hauber, B., *et al.* (2010). Conjoint analysis applications in health – how are studies being designed and reported?: an update on current practice in the published literature between 2005 and 2008. *Patient*, 3, 249–56.

Maurer, M.D.P., Carman, K., Frazier, K. and Smeeding, L. (2012). *Guide to patient and family engagement: environmental scan report.* American Institutes for Research, Washington (available online at: www.ahrq.gov/research/findings/final-reports/ptfamilyscan/).

Moffatt, S., White, M., Mackintosh, J. and Howel, D. (2006). Using quantitative and qualitative data in health services research – what happens when mixed method findings conflict? *BMC Health Services Research*, 6, 28.

Nilsen Elin, S., Myrhaug Hilde, T., Johansen, M., *et al.* (2006). Methods of consumer involvement in developing healthcare policy and research, clinical practice guidelines and patient information material. *Cochrane Database of Systematic Reviews*, 19, CD004563.

O'Cathain, A., Murphy, E. and Nicholl, J. (2007). Why, and how, mixed methods research is undertaken in health services research in England: a mixed methods study. *BMC Health Services Research*, 7, 85.

O'Cathain, A. (2009). Mixed methods research in the health sciences: a quiet revolution. *Journal of Mixed Methods Research*, 3, 3–6.

Olsen, J.A. and Smith, R.D. (2001). Theory versus practice: a review of 'willingness-to-pay' in health and health care. *Health Economics*, 10, 39–52.

Parry, G., Moyser, G. and Day, N. (1992). *Political participation and democracy in Britain.* Cambridge University Press, Cambridge, England.

Pavlova, M., Groot, W. and Van Merode, G. (2003). The importance of quality, access and price to health care consumers in Bulgaria: a self-explicated approach. *International Journal of Health Planning and Management*, 18, 343–61.

Pereira, C.C., Mulligan, M., Bridges, J.F. and Bishai, D. (2011). Determinants of influenza vaccine purchasing decision in the U.S.: a conjoint analysis. *Vaccine*, 29, 1443–7.

Phillips, K.A., Maddala, T. and Johnson, F.R. (2002). Measuring preferences for health care interventions using conjoint analysis: an application to HIV testing. *Health Services Research Journal*, 37, 1681–705.

Pivik, J., Rode, E. and Ward, C. (2004). A consumer involvement model for health technology assessment in Canada. *Health Policy*, 69, 253–68.

Porterfield, D.S., Hinnant, L.W., Kane, H., *et al.* (2012). Linkages between clinical practices and community organizations for prevention: a literature review and environmental scan. *American Journal of Public Health*, 102, S375–82.

Read, J.L., Quinn, R.J., Berwick, D.M., *et al.* (1984). Preferences for health outcomes. *Medical Decision Making*, 4, 315–29.

Ring, N., Jepson, R. and Ritchie, K. (2011). Methods of synthesizing qualitative research studies for health technology assessment. *International Journal of Technology Assessment in Health Care*, 27, 384–90.

Ryan, M. (1999a). A role for conjoint analysis in technology assessment in health care? *International Journal of Technology Assessment in Health Care*, 15, 443–57.

Ryan, M. (1999b). Using conjoint analysis to take account of patient preferences and go beyond health outcomes: an application to in vitro fertilisation. *Social Science and Medicine*, 48, 535–46.

Ryan, M. and Farrar, S. (2000). Using conjoint analysis to elicit preferences for health care. *British Medical Journal*, 320, 1530–3.

Ryan, M. and Watson, V. (2009). Comparing welfare estimates from payment card contingent valuation and discrete choice experiments. *Health Economics*, 18, 389–401.

Ryan, M., Mcintosh, E. and Shackley, P. (1998). Methodological issues in the application of conjoint analysis in health care. *Health Economics*, 7, 373–8.

Ryan, M., Scott, D.A. and Donaldson, C. (2004). Valuing health care using willingness to pay: a comparison of the payment card and dichotomous choice methods. *Journal of Health Economics*, 23, 237–58.

Ryan, M., Scott, D.A., Reeves, C., *et al.* (2001). Eliciting public preferences for healthcare: a systematic review of techniques. *International Journal of Health Technology Assessment*, 5, 1–186.

Salter, K., Hellings, C., Foley, N. and Teasell, R. (2008). The experience of living with stroke: a qualitative meta-synthesis. *Journal of Rehabilitation Medicine*, 40, 595–602.

Smith, R.D. (2003). Construction of the contingent valuation market in health care: a critical assessment. *Health Economics*, 12, 609–28.

Thokala, P. and Duenas, A. (2012). Multiple criteria decision analysis for health technology assessment. *Value Health*, 15, 1172–81.

van Til, J.A. and Ijzerman, M.J. (2014). Why should regulators consider using patient preferences in benefit–risk assessment? *Pharmacoeconomics*, 32, 1–4.

van Til, J.A., Dolan, J.G., Stiggelbout, A.M., *et al.* (2008). The use of multi-criteria decision analysis weight elicitation techniques in patients with mild cognitive impairment: a pilot study. *Patient*, 1, 127–35.

Wallner, P.E. and Konski, A. (2008). The impact of technology on health care cost and policy development. *Seminars in Radiation Oncology*, 18, 194–200.

Weernink, M.G.M., Janus, S.L.M., van Til, J.A., *et al.* (2014). A systematic review to identify the use of preference elicitation methods in healthcare decision making. *Pharmaceutical Medicine*, 28, 175–85.

Zhou, P. and Ang, B.W. (2009). Comparing MCDA aggregation methods in constructing composite indicators using the Shannon–Spearman measure. *Social Indicators Research*, 94, 83–96.

# Chapter 13

# Multi-Criteria Decision Analysis

*Olivier Ethgen and Kevin Marsh*

## Introduction

Funding access to medical innovations, including pharmaceuticals and others medical technologies, is becoming increasingly challenging (Morgan *et al.* 2013). This is a situation that is not expected to ease in the near future. On the contrary, recent financial disturbances in the global economy are straining governments' budgets still more. Health care systems and their administrators, already under strict budget constraints, will very likely continue to face difficult decisions with regard to budget allocation. The prioritization of technologies for investment is one of the difficult choices confronting health care decision makers.

In response to this challenge of prioritizing investments in health technologies, health economists have given a prominent role to cost-effectiveness analysis (CEA). More precisely, CEA often aims to estimate the relative efficiency of technologies as the incremental cost per quality-adjusted life year (QALY) gained. This approach emphasizes the health impacts of technologies as defined and captured by the QALY metric. However, the introduction of a new health care technology may pose societal, political, financial, economic or ethical questions well beyond the sole consideration of clinical and cost-effectiveness.

Technologies generate a range of benefits that is not necessarily captured by a single metric such as the QALY. First, health gains that sit outside of the domains of the instrument used to measure QALYs are not taken into account. For instance, the EQ-5D is often used to estimate the QALY impact of technologies and includes five domains: mobility, capacity for self-care, conduct of usual activities, pain/discomfort and anxiety/depression. It is often argued that these domains exclude some health impacts of disease, such as vitality (Wailoo *et al.* 2010). Second, non-health outcomes, such as changes in health inequalities, innovation, or improvements in productivity, are excluded from the QALY. Further, the relative value of these outcomes will depend on the decision context, such as the target population, the level of unmet need, the budgetary constraints, and thus the public health priorities.

The relevance to health care decision making of this range of factors has led to calls for the development of methods to formally measure them and make this evidence available to decision makers. One of the most prominent of these calls was the UK government's Value-Based Pricing Initiative (Department of Health 2012), which aimed to value technologies based not only on their cost-effectiveness but also on the severity of disease and the social benefits generated by the technology. It is not that these factors are currently ignored by decision makers. Reviews have identified the wide range of factors considered as part of health technology assessment (HTA), including severity of disease, existence of alternative therapies, the size of the population that would benefit from an intervention, and budget impact (Golan *et al.* 2011; Tony *et al.* 2011). NICE, for instance, has acknowledged that while formal evidence requirements focus on clinical and cost-effectiveness, its committees consider a wide range of other factors when deliberating the evidence (Rawlins *et al.* 2010). Rather, concerns focus on the consistency, rigor and transparency with which these broader criteria are incorporated into decision making (Devlin and Sussex 2011).

The simultaneous consideration of multiple criteria is not straightforward, however, and can be cognitively demanding. Decision makers are faced with the complex task of assessing multiple interventions against multiple criteria, with multiple stakeholders and partial evidence. In addition, all criteria may carry different weight in the decision-making process and might not be considered as equally important in formulating a decision. In this context, it is not surprising to hear calls for the application of multi-criteria decision analysis (MCDA) to formally incorporate these factors into evidence generation.

The potential of MCDA extends beyond the support of reimbursement decisions (Marsh *et al.* 2014). For instance, MCDA has also received attention for its ability to support quantitative benefit–risk analysis and thus authorization decisions. Given prominent drug withdrawals over the past decade, regulatory agencies are searching for more rigorous, consistent and transparent approaches to benefit–risk assessment (BRA) (Guo *et al.* 2010; Garrison 2010). The European Medicines Agency's Benefit Risk Methodology project was precisely established to develop tools and processes for BRA to support informed, science-based, regulatory decision making about medicinal products (EMA 2012). It concluded that MCDA was an approach that could support BRA. In addition, the Pharmacoepidemiological Research on Outcomes of Therapeutics by a European Consortium (PROTECT) program has investigated and developed methodologies for BRA. It also concluded that MCDA could support quantitative benefit–risk assessment (PROTECT 2013).

MCDA methods are not new and interest in the approach is often traced to Keeney and Raiffa in the 1970s (Keeney and Raiffa 1993). MCDA is now often used to support decision making in a number of settings, including transport, environmental protection, construction, defence and finance (CLG 2009). The application of MCDA to health care has so far been limited in comparison with CEA. Interest in MCDA to support the allocation of health care resources is increasing, however, probably in response to the greater recognition of the complexity of such decisions and the relative narrow set of factors that is currently explicitly considered by the formal analysis undertaken to inform these decisions (Devlin and Sussex 2011). An increasing number of applications of MCDA in health care have been reported in the literature (Thokala and Duenas 2012; Marsh *et al.* 2012; Diaby *et al.* 2013; Adunlin *et al.* 2014).

This chapter introduces MCDA as an aid to decision making in health care. It is organized into three sections. The first section describes MCDA, the steps involved in its implementation, and how it can contribute to health decision making. The second section gives examples of MCDA applied to support health care decision making, and the lessons and challenges identified through these experiences. The final section summarizes the chapter and identifies future research required to support the application of MCDA in health.

## What is MCDA?

The term multi-criteria decision analysis encompasses a rather broad set of approaches and methods to guide decision making while accounting for multiple criteria (Baltussen and Niessen 2006; Devlin and Sussex 2011). These methods share the fact that they allow for the explicit trade-off between multiple criteria, establishing the relative importance of these criteria and thus generating a ranking of interventions (Baltussen and Niessen 2006; CLG 2009).

The term MCDA is used to mean different things. It is important to be clear about which definition of MCDA is being adopted. One definition is a method used to structure group decision making (Cross and Garrison 2008). This approach is concerned with eliciting and making transparent the judgments made in the decision-making process. An alternative and broader definition of MCDA is the set of methods that seeks to score, weight and ultimately aggregate the various criteria into an overall composite measure of benefit (NICE 2012). The second definition is inclusive of the first, but also includes a range of alternative and quantitative approaches, such as stated preference techniques for weighting criteria. In all instances, there are qualitative and quantitative approaches. Debate remains over whether qualitative approaches should be considered in the definition of MCDA.

While there is a range of MCDA methods, they share some common steps (CLG 2009; Devlin and Sussex 2011). A number of these steps are not specific to MCDA, but rather describe good research practice, such as defining the decision context and interventions of interest. These are summarized below in a seven-stage approach to conducting MCDA (this is based on the steps outlined in CLG (2009) and Devlin and Sussex (2011)).

1. Define the decision context
   The aim and scope of the MCDA exercise should be stated explicitly up front. The decision makers, such as the health care budget holder or the recommending committee, should be clearly identified. During this framing stage, it is important to define the specific MCDA approach that will be employed, including when and how the decision makers will input into the MCDA.
2. Shortlist the interventions
   The interventions to be appraised must be shortlisted. It is important to include all the appropriate alternatives and avoid the omission (addition) of relevant (irrelevant) options. This should consider standard of care in the setting of interest, and horizon scanning to identify any alternative interventions not yet on the market. Ideally, the decision makers involved in the MCDA exercise and identified at the previous stage should agree on the interventions selected for the analysis. It is also advisable, when the list of possible interventions is potentially controversial, to retain the opportunity to change the selected interventions as the MCDA progresses.

3. State the decision criteria

In selecting the value criteria, particular attention should be paid to the anticipated consequences of the interventions appraised. The criteria should be specific, relevant and measurable. They are meant to define the extent to which the different interventions being appraised will create value in the eyes of the decision makers identified at stage 1. Therefore, selected criteria should capture all the dimensions required by the decision makers to appraise the interventions.

A number of sources of information can be used to inform the identification of criteria, including reviews of previous decisions, such as decision makers' statements of the factors of relevance to their decisions, and reviews of the factors that are taken into account by decision makers (Guo *et al.* 2010). Interviews or a consultative process might also be undertaken with decision makers.

The number of criteria should be kept as low as is consistent with making a well-founded decision. There is no "rule" to guide this judgement. The number of criteria will vary from decision to decision, though criteria should be assessed against the following qualities (CLG 2009):

- Completeness: all relevant benefits and risks are covered by the criteria.
- Non-redundancy: no criteria should be included that are not relevant to the decision.
- Mutual independence of preferences: an assessment of the relative importance of a criterion should not be dependent on the score on another criterion.
- Double counting: it is important to avoid having criteria that measure the same thing or that can be considered as proxies for the same underlying concept.

Once all criteria have been listed, value trees can be used to organize criteria into groups, helping to assess whether the set of criteria selected is appropriate to the problem (CLG 2009). Figure 13.1 shows an example of a value tree.

4. Measure and score the performance of interventions against criteria

Once criteria have been defined, it is necessary to describe how the interventions perform for each of the criteria. A range of methods can be employed to generate this evidence. It is often necessary to undertake a review of the literature to identify the evidence required to measure performance. Where there are gaps in the existing evidence, these can be filled using modeling approaches or expert opinion. Performance estimates for each criterion and intervention are often organized in an effect table, making the data accessible to decision makers (Levitan *et al.* 2011). Depending on the specific MCDA approach adopted, it is sometimes necessary to convert estimates of performance into a common scale using performance scores (CLG 2009). It is conventional to score each criterion between 0 and 100 on an interval scale. This involves defining levels of performance corresponding to any two reference points on the scale. Two approaches are often distinguished for defining scales. First, global scaling assigns a score of 0 to represent the worst level of performance that is likely to be encountered, and 100 to represent the best level. Second, local scaling defines 0 as the performance level of the option in the currently considered set of treatments which performs least well and 100 as that which performs best. An advantage of global scaling is that it more easily accommodates new options at a later stage if these record performances that

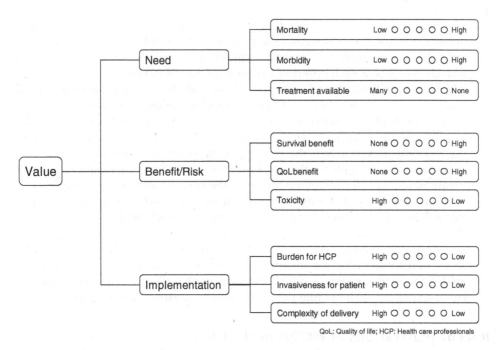

*Figure 13.1* Example of a simple value tree across nine criteria encompassing three value domains (need, benefit/risk and implementation)

lie outside those of the original set. This can help accommodate new data, for instance, or the addition of more treatment options to the analysis. However, it has the disadvantage of requiring extra, not necessarily helpful, judgements in defining the extremes of the scale.

5. Weight each decision criterion

In order to combine criteria measures and scores into an overall assessment of an intervention, it is necessary to determine the relative value of criteria. The elicitation of weights for criteria should be assigned independently of the measure or score of interventions against these criteria and should simply express the importance of the criterion relative to others.

A range of weighting methods can be employed in MCDA. The appropriate weighting methods will depend on the objectives of the MCDA. It is important to note that not all MCDA approaches employ a formal quantitative weighting of criteria. Of those that do, a number of key differences are often used to distinguish the weighting method employed in MCDA (CLG 2009). First, whose values are used to define the weights? A range of stakeholders' views has been drawn on to weight criteria as part of MCDA, including the public, patients, clinicians and decision makers. Second, which value elicitation method has been used? Again, a range of value elicitation techniques has been adopted, including the analytical hierarchy process (AHP) (Saaty 2008), swing weighting methods (CLG 2009) or survey-based techniques such as discrete choice experiment (DCE) (Lanscar *et al.* 2008; Ryan *et al.* 2008).

6.  Derive overall value
    The relative value of interventions is derived through the combination of their performance on the criteria and the judgment of the relative value of these criteria (i.e. the performance matrix, combining the scores of each intervention with the weights of each criterion to derive an overall value). This can be undertaken both qualitatively and quantitatively to rank the interventions considered (Baltussen *et al.* 2006). In a qualitative approach, decision makers simply interpret the performance matrix and make implicit judgments on the weights of the various criteria (stage 5 is carried out only implicitly). In a quantitative approach, the decision makers weigh the different criteria on the basis of their relative importance by multiplying the scores by the corresponding weights to obtain weighted averages for all interventions or the overall value score (stage 5 is carried out explicitly). The interventions can then be rank-ordered according to this weighed average (see, for instance, Youngkong *et al.* 2012).

7.  Run sensitivity analysis
    As for any modelling exercise, it is imperative to run sensitivity analysis. The aim is to document the sensitivity of the recommendations emanating from the MCDA to any uncertainty in the MCDA framework or the evidence used to populate the framework, including the performance measures and weights.

## Recent Illustrations of MCDA in Health Care

This section provides examples of MCDA as applied in health care and summarizes some of the challenges and lessons identified through this experience. The examples have been selected to illustrate the range of MCDA approaches available, in terms of both the health care-related decisions they are designed to support and the approaches employed.

### Example 1: Coverage Decisions in Thailand

Youngkong *et al.* (2012) described an MCDA to help in the selection of health interventions to be included in the universal health coverage benefit package of Thailand. They describe the project as a first attempt to achieve rational, transparent and fair health care rationing through the application of MCDA in a real-world context. The project began with a review of the international experience on developing health benefits packages. Seven health technology assessment (HTA) agencies were studied (the CADTH in Canada, the CAHTH in the Catalonian region of Spain, the DAHTH in Germany, the NICE in England and Wales, the Health Council of the Netherlands, the SBU in Sweden and the VATAP in the US). The review concluded that all the organizations considered multiple criteria and involved multiple stakeholders in their priority setting process. Four key steps in priority setting were also identified across the seven agencies: (1) nomination of interventions for assessment, (2) selection of intervention for assessment, (3) technology assessment of interventions, and (4) appraisal of interventions.

Consensus on the following decision criteria was reached by a consultation panel representing stakeholders: (1) the size of the population affected by the disease, (2) the severity of disease, (3) the effectiveness of interventions, (4) the potential variation in practice, (5) the economic impact of household expenditure, and (6) equity, ethical and social implications. The performances of each intervention considered were scored against each criterion on an ordinal scale from 1 to 5. No weights were elicited for the criteria considered; rather, the evidence was presented to the Subcommittee for Development of Benefit Package and Service Delivery (SCBP) for consideration. Thus, this particular approach corresponds with the qualitative approach to weighting criteria.

The authors note that the merits of this approach are especially clear when compared with the situation before, "where priority setting was said to be ad hoc and driven by the interests of stakeholder groups" (Youngkong *et al.* 2012). They draw a number of lessons from their experience. First, the process of deliberation is an important part of MCDA, allowing criteria other than those that have been quantified as part of the MCDA framework to be incorporated into the decision-making process. Second, the scoring scales for criteria, such as targeting the poor, can be difficult to define, requiring the input from experts. Third, there was a lack of comparable evidence on criteria such as severity of disease, calling into the question the value of including this criterion in MCDA. Fourth, there were challenges communicating the meaning of some criteria to participants, such as effectiveness. Fifth, the approach adopted by the authors did not include formal weighting of criteria.

### Example 2: Formulary Decision Making in Canada

Probably one of the most studied MCDA frameworks in health care is the EVIDEM framework – Evidence and Value: Impact on DEcision Making (Goetghebeur *et al.* 2008). The EVIDEM collaboration was launched to respond to the increasing demand for MCDA in HTA. Having reviewed decision-making processes in 20 jurisdictions, EVIDEM identified 15 criteria relevant to HTA and that fulfilled MCDA requirements (Geotghebeur *et al.* 2012). These criteria were used as the basis for an MCDA framework to inform HTA. The framework specifies that each criterion needs to be weighed by experts using a five-point scale. The scores for each alternative are then quantified using best-practice synthesis methods. Once the criteria have been quantified, experts use these data to score the criteria on a four-point scale. These quantitative criteria are supplemented with qualitative contextual criteria intended to focus decision makers' attention on "colloquial" forms of evidence.

The EVIDEM framework has been field-tested on several occasions. In Canada, for instance, Tony *et al.* (2011) looked at the usefulness of this framework for a drug advisory committee and tested the stability of estimates over time. The EVIDEM framework was also field-tested in South Africa for a screening test for cervical cancer as appraised by a private health plan committee (Miot *et al.* 2012). The experience of these pilots was that participants found the framework useful in supporting the systematic consideration of a broad range of criteria to promote a consistent, transparent, explicit and clear approach in appraising health care technologies, and that the framework was useful as a communication tool to convey the structure and transparency of the decision-making process. In turn, these benefits would enhance the acceptability of the health plan committee's decision. The pilots also revealed good consistency of scores, weights and MCDA values at an individual level, lending some support to the reliability of the approach.

The authors also noted a number of challenges posed by the framework. First, there was a higher variation in weights across individuals than there was across scores. This could be explained by the latter being based on evidence, while the former are based on individual perspective, though it may also be possible that variations are due to different understanding of the criteria, despite detailed definitions being provided. The authors noted that further exploration of weight elicitation methods was required to adapt the tool to the preferences and needs of users.

Second, some participants found it challenging to interpret the MCDA value estimates, causing them to question the utility of the outputs of the framework. The authors noted that this was likely the result of the fact that the scores were not used in a comparative context for ranking interventions, and that where this was the case the MCDA values were able to discriminate between interventions. Participants' concern is understandable, however, given the combination of multiple score and weights summarized in the MCDA value. It is exactly this complexity that the MCDA is designed to overcome, but as a consequence it is easy to see how the resulting single-number outcome can be difficult to understand.

### Example 3: Public Health in England

Marsh *et al.* (2013) used an MCDA to inform the prioritization of investments in public health interventions in England. Seventeen public health interventions were identified through reviews of NICE recommendations and interviews with UK public health decision makers. A review of previous MCDAs, workshops and surveys with decision makers, was used to identify three criteria: cost-effectiveness, the proportion of the population eligible for the intervention, and the distribution of the benefit of the intervention between disadvantaged and non-disadvantaged groups. Interventions' performance against the criteria was measured through a combination of reviews of the evidence and decision modeling. A DCE was employed to elicit weights for the criteria from public health decision makers and thus combine the criteria into an overall priority score.

The result of the MCDA was that taxation was ranked as the highest priority. Mass-media campaigns and brief interventions ranked in the top half of interventions. School-based educational interventions, statins and interventions to address mental health problems ranked in the bottom half of interventions.

According to the authors, the study demonstrated that it was possible to use an MCDA framework to systematically capture evidence on the dimensions relevant to public health coverage decisions. Furthermore, it does so in a manner that combines decision-maker requirements and preferences, and rigorous quantitative research methods to generate comparable evidence on interventions. They note, however, that the study raises a number of methodological questions that need to be addressed if MCDA is going to be applied to support decision making in the future. First, work is required to determine the appropriate balance between stakeholder opinion and quantitative research. It is likely that the answer to this question will vary between types of decisions and settings. Second, further discussion is required to determine whose values should be used to define weights and how these values should be elicited. Should payers', patients', or the publics' values be used to weight criteria? Should workshops, surveys of importance or surveys of preference be used to generate weights?

## Example 4: The Involvement of Patients by HTA Agencies

It is claimed that the QALY can be considered a form of MCDA in that it involves the combination of multiple dimensions (criteria) measuring different health outcomes using weights generated through surveys of patients or the public (NICE, 2012). However, a number of HTA agencies have rejected the QALY as tool to inform decisions. One such agency is IQWiG, which uses the efficiency frontier approach (Caro *et al.* 2010). This rejection of the QALY still leaves IQWiG with the challenge that the QALY was designed to overcome – converting multiple health effects in a standard scale. Multiple efficiency frontiers use different effectiveness measures and the question remains as to how to determine the value of a technology and thus an overall efficiency frontier.

Danner *et al.* (2011) tested the AHP as an alternative means of quantifying patient preferences to weigh the effects and thus inform IQWiG's assessment of interventions. The AHP was tested through two workshops, one with patients and another with health care professionals. Participants rated their preferences with respect to the importance of different criteria through pairwise comparison. The AHP involves participants answering a series of questions of the general form, "How important is criterion A relative to criterion B?" on a scale of equally important (1) to overwhelmingly more important (9).

The authors concluded that AHP is a well-structured technique whose cognitive demands are well handled by patients and professionals, delivering consistent results regarding the generation of preference-based weights. They argue that by breaking down problems into comparisons of pairs of criteria, AHP reduces the cognitive burden compared with other quantitative methods for eliciting patients' preferences, which require patients to state their preferences for health status in aggregate.

The authors also identified a number of methods challenges that emerged from the pilot. First, the AHP workshops were most effectively organized into small groups of individuals, raising questions about the resources required to conduct AHP surveys in this manner. Second, a major challenge was the selection of endpoints from the benefits measures in a manner that avoided overlap. This proved impossible, but the authors note that providing precise definitions of each endpoint helped reduce the potentially negative effects of overlap.

## Example 5: Vaccines

The US Institute of Medicine (IOM) has proposed an MCDA-based prioritization framework for vaccines (IOM 2012). Decision makers in vaccines are constantly challenged by rapidly changing demographics, epidemiology, economics, sciences, technologies and health systems. On this basis, the IOM designed a Strategic Multi-Attribute Ranking Tool for Vaccines, called SMART-Vaccines. The tool revisits the assumptions and limitations of the two previously proposed prioritization frameworks. For instance, the 1985–1986 approach was based on infant mortality equivalent as a proxy measure of health burden to prioritize vaccines. The 2000 approach was based on the incremental cost-per-QALY saved for ranking vaccines. The SMART-Vaccines initiative uses a multi-attribute utility framework to go beyond these earlier single-criterion frameworks and to embrace a broader range of multidimensional criteria that is likely to influence decision making in vaccines (IOM 2012).

SMART-Vaccines is an independent, adaptable and collaborative decision-making tool, with the potential of facilitating focused and informed discussion among the various stakeholders of a national vaccination strategy. Previous prioritization frameworks were deemed too limited in the sense that they were focused only on single and aggregated measures of health benefits such as infant mortality or QALY (IOM 2012). These single criteria have simply become two criteria among many others in this newly designed prioritization model, now including health, economic, demographic, public, scientific, business, programmatic, intangible values and policy considerations (Table 13.1). The framework proposed by the IOM requires that these criteria be measured. They acknowledge that this may mean a substantial data input from users, and recommend using expert opinion where it is not possible to collect data on all attributes. These measures should then be weighted based on the importance of attributes.

### Example 6: Benefit–Risk Assessment

The Benefit Risk Assessment Team (BRAT) framework is a set of processes and tools that provides a structured approach to pharmaceutical benefit–risk decision making (Coplan *et al.* 2011). Such decision making tends to rely on the subjective judgments of experts. The BRAT framework was developed to structure these pharmaceutical benefit–risk assessments, drawing on well-developed methodologies such as systematic evidence reviews and MCDA. The framework comprises six steps: defining the decision context; identifying outcomes; identifying and extracting source data; customizing the framework in light of the evidence; assessment of outcome importance; and display and interpret key benefit–risk metrics.

Levitan *et al.* (2011) applied the framework to a range of therapeutic areas and populations, selected to represent a diversity of the methodological challenges associated with BRA. All steps of the BRAT framework were implemented, with the exception of the assessing the importance of outcomes. Stakeholders involved in the project thought that the Framework could help facilitate a common understanding between sponsors and regulators, and it would be valuable as a discussion tool for understanding differences in viewpoints and alignment of opinions. Enthusiasm for the tool was compounded by the fact that it employed data already generated in the decision-making process.

The authors draw a number of lessons for MCDA to support health decisions. First, unambiguous definition of outcomes is essential and can be achieved with the help of a value-tree. Documenting the process of defining of outcomes encourages clear consideration of the relevant criteria and serves as a vehicle for communicating assumptions. Second, it is important to capture information on the strengths and limitations of data, something that can be lost in using a single score of study quality. Third, the BRA is a "living" tool that is revised and altered as new information is acquired over the life cycle of the product. Fourth, presenting the findings of the BRA in an accessible manner is a challenge. Tools employed by the BRAT framework, such as the "key benefit–risk summary" table and the risk/rate difference forest plot, can help.

Table 13.1 The multi-criteria framework of the SMART-Vaccines initiative (adapted from IOM, 2012)

| Criteria | Level 1 | Level 2 | Level 3 | Level 4 | Level 5 |
|---|---|---|---|---|---|
| **Health considerations** | | | | | |
| Premature deaths averted per year | >20,000 | 5,000–19,999 | 1,000–4,999 | <1,000 | — |
| Incident cases prevented per year | >75,000 | 50,000–74,999 | 10,000–49,999 | <10,000 | — |
| QALYs gained or DALYs averted | >50,000 | 20,000–49,999 | 5,000–19,999 | <5,000 | — |
| **Economic considerations** | | | | | |
| One-time costs | <$100 million | $100–$500 million | $500 million–$1 billion | >$1 billion | — |
| Annual net direct costs (savings) of vaccine use | <$0 (cost saving) | $0–$50 million | $50–$150 million | >$150 million | — |
| Annual net workforce productivity gained | >$10 billion | $5–$10 billion | $1–$5 billion | <$1 billion | — |
| Cost-effectiveness | <$0 (cost saving) | <$50,000 | $50,000–$150,000 | >$150,000 | — |
| **Demographic considerations** | | | | | |
| Benefits infants and children | Yes | No | — | — | — |
| Benefits women | Yes | No | — | — | — |
| Benefits socioeconomically disadvantaged | Yes | No | — | — | — |
| Benefits military personnel | Yes | No | — | — | — |
| Benefits other priority population (e.g. immunocompromised) | Yes | No | — | — | — |
| **Public concerns** | | | | | |
| Availability of alternative public health measures | No | Yes | — | — | — |
| Potential complications due to vaccines | No | Yes | — | — | — |
| Disease raises fear and stigma in the public | Yes | No | — | — | — |
| Serious pandemic potential | Yes | No | — | — | — |
| **Scientific and business considerations** | | | | | |

Table 13.1 (cont.)

| Criteria | Level 1 | Level 2 | Level 3 | Level 4 | Level 5 |
|---|---|---|---|---|---|
| Likelihood of financial profitability for the manufacturer | Almost certainly | | | | Almost certainly not |
| Likelihood of successful licensure in 10 years | Almost certainly | | | | Almost certainly not |
| Demonstrates new production platforms | Yes | No | — | — | — |
| Existing or adaptable manufacturing techniques | Yes | No | — | — | — |
| Potential litigation barriers beyond usual | No | Yes | — | — | — |
| Interest from NGOs, philanthropic organizations | Yes | No | — | — | — |
| **Programmatic considerations** | | | | | |
| Potential to improve delivery methods | Yes | No | — | — | — |
| Fits into existing immunization schedule | Yes | No | — | — | — |
| Reduces challenges relating to cold-chain requirements | Yes | No | — | — | — |
| **Intangible values** | | | | | |
| Eradication or elimination of the disease | Potential eradication | Potential elimination | No | | |
| Vaccine raises public health awareness | Yes | No | — | — | — |
| **Policy considerations** | | | | | |
| Special interest for national security, preparedness and response | Yes | No | — | — | — |
| Advances nation's foreign policy goals | Yes | No | — | — | — |

## Discussion

There is increasing support for using MCDA to support health care decisions. MCDA can support these decisions in a number of ways (Guo *et al.* 2012; NICE 2012; Thokala *et al.* 2012; Tony *et al.* 2011), including:

- improving the transparency, predictability and consistency of decisions;
- facilitating the incorporation of patients' values in decision making;
- supporting the communication of the benefits, risks and costs of treatments;
- ensuring decision makers are explicit about values;
- informing the design of data collection;
- understanding differences in viewpoints between stakeholders;
- sharpening signals to industry about what matters to decision makers.

MCDA can inform a range of health care decisions, such as manufacturers' judgments to invest in compounds, regulatory approvals, reimbursement decisions, health authority resource allocation decisions, and clinicians' prescription decisions. It should be noted, however, that MCDA is an aid to the decision-making process and is not meant to replace it. It is an analytical tool that renders explicit the impact the multiple criteria considered and the relative importance attached to them have on the decision (Devlin and Sussex 2011).

The use of MCDA to support health care decision making poses a number of methodological and practical challenges. First, how should stakeholders be involved in the MCDA? Different MCDA approaches involve stakeholders in different ways. Some examples use stakeholders to define the criteria of interest; others use stakeholders to also score and weigh criteria. The appropriate role of stakeholders will depend on the decision that the MCDA is intended to support. For instance, stakeholders should be involved in the different steps of an MCDA if it is being used to inform a specific decision, where the number of stakeholders is relatively small and where stakeholders' buy-in to the decision is important.

Second, and a related challenge, what weighting techniques should be used as part of the MCDA? The examples summarized in the previous section illustrate a range of weighting methods, including not explicitly weighting criteria (Youngkong *et al.* 2012), generation of weights through direct rating by experts in workshops (Tony *et al.* 2011), use of discrete choice experiments (Marsh *et al.* 2013) and use of the analytical hierarchy process (Danner *et al.* 2011). A range of factors should be considered when selecting the weighting method: time and resources available, whether trade-off or importance data are elicited, cognitive burden, consistency with the requirements of value measurement methods, correspondence between stakeholder preferences and the assumptions about the nature of preferences underlying the elicitation method, accessibility of the results to decision makers, the need to quantify uncertainty, whether population or patients' preferences are important to decision makers, and the theoretical basis of the weighting approach.

A key consideration when designing the weighting method is the accessibility of the final result of the MCDA. Many weighting methods, such as swing weights, produce results that are not meaningful outside of the specific MCDA within which they were generated. They are useful in comparing the value of interventions, but express this value only relative to these other interventions and within the content of the MCDA. Other methods, such as discrete choice experiments, claim to generate a result that has more meaning outside of the MCDA framework – the utility generated by the intervention to those who participated in the intervention, or the probability that these participants would prefer the intervention. This is important if the intention is to communicate the results of the MCDA beyond those who participated within it. More research is required to develop guidelines to help researchers select the appropriate weighting method.

Third, the assessment of the performance of interventions faces a number of challenges, including selecting endpoints that are clearly defined and avoid overlap, identifying data to measure performance, resolving differences across studies in the precise endpoint and/or population, and explaining endpoints to stakeholders. It is often necessary to get the input of therapy area experts to overcome these challenges.

Fourth, the inclusion of quantitative measures of uncertainty in MCDA is recommended. The above challenges imply that there will be uncertainty in the structure of the MCDA framework and the data used to populate it. The latter will include gaps in the evidence, different qualities of evidence, and heterogeneity in, for instance, participants' weights. It is important to test the implications of this uncertainty for results of the MCDA. A number of approaches have been used to understand the impact of uncertainty, including fuzzy logic, stochastic multi-criteria acceptability analysis and probabilistic sensitivity analysis. The importance of quantifying uncertainty should be considered when selecting the appropriate MCDA approach. These techniques are easier to apply with some approaches to MCDA (e.g. value measurement) than others (e.g. goal programming or outranking methods) (Thokala and Duenas 2012). Furthermore, work is required to develop approaches to present the implication of uncertainty to decision makers but also guide the selection of appropriate methods for assessing the impact of uncertainty. Of interest, Wen *et al.* (2014) have recently proposed two probabilistic approaches to incorporate clinical data uncertainty into MDCA for the benefit–risk assessment of medical products.

Fifth, it can be difficult to communicate the results of MCDA to decision makers. The authors of the examples of MCDA summarized in the previous section note the challenges communicating the meaning of criteria and overall MCDA value estimates to stakeholders. This is hardly surprising. MCDA is designed to structure complex problems that involve combining multiple criteria. It is easy to see how summarizing all this information in a single value can be difficult to understand. Work is required to understand which approaches and visualization techniques can help overcome this challenge.

## Conclusion

MCDA can help health economists and other researchers to explicitly capture the multiple factors and stakeholder preferences that impact a decision. This will ensure that their recommendations better align with the factors that are important to stakeholders. In view of the challenges facing health care decision makers, it is not surprising to observe the greater use of MCDA. However, a range of MCDA approaches is available, and the relevance of each approach will depend on the decision being informed. Further, as for any tools in decision sciences, MCDA has some specific features that researchers and decision makers should understand to ensure that the recommendations it generates are well informed and interpreted. Further guidance is required to ensure that MCDA is used in a way that best supports health care decision making.

## References

Adunlin, G., Diaby, V., Xiao, H. (2014). Application of multicriteria decision analysis in health care: a systematic review and bibliometric analysis. *Health Expectations*, 18, 1894–905. DOI: 10.1111/hex.12287.

Adunlin, G., Diaby, V., Montero, A.J., Xiao, H. (2014). Multicriteria decision analysis in oncology. *Health Expectations*, 18, 1812–26. DOI: 10.1111/hex.12178.

Baltussen, R., Niessen, L.W. (2006). Priority setting of health interventions: The need for multi-criteria decision analysis. *Cost Effectiveness and Resources Allocation*, 4, 14.

Caro, J.J., Nord, E., Siebert, U., *et al.* (2010). The efficiency frontier approach to economic evaluation of health-care interventions. *Health Economics*, 10, 1117–27.

CLG, Communities and Local Government. (2009). Multi-criteria analysis: A manual.

Coplan, P.M., Noel, R.A., Levitan, B.S., *et al.* (2011). Development of a framework for enhancing the transparency, reproducibility and communication of the benefit–risk balance of medicines. *Clinical Pharmacology & Therapeutics*, 89, 312–15.

Cross, J.T., Garrison, L.P. (2008). *Challenges and Opportunities for Improving Benefit–Risk Assessment of Pharmaceuticals from an Economic Perspective*. OHE, London (available online at: www.ohe.org/publications/article/challenges-and-opportunities-for-improving-benefit-risk-assessment-38.cfm).

Danner, M., Hummel, J.M., van Manen, J.G., *et al.* (2011). Integrating patients' views into health technology assessment: Analytical hierarchy process (AHP) as a method to elicit patient preferences. *International Journal of Technology Assessment in Health Care*, 4, 1–7.

Department of Health (2012). A new value-based approach to the pricing of branded medicines. A consultation (available online at: www.dh.gov.uk/en/Consultations/Liveconsultations/DH_122760).

Devlin, N.J., Sussex, J. (2011). *Incorporating Multiple Criteria in HTA. Methods and processes*. OHE, London.

Diaby, V., Campbell, K., Goeree, R. (2013). Multi-criteria decision analysis (MCDA) in health care: a bibliometric analysis. *Operations Research for Health Care*, 2, 20–4.

EMA, European Medicines Agency (2012). Benefit–risk methodology project. Work package 4 report: benefit–risk tools and processes.

Garrison, L.P. (2010). Regulatory benefit–risk assessment and comparative effectiveness research: strangers, bedfellows or strange bedfellows? *Pharmacoeconomics*, 28, 855–65.

Goetghebeur, M.M., Wagner, M., Khoury, H., *et al.* (2008). Evidence and value: impact on decision making – the EVIDEM framework and potential applications. *BMC Health Services Research*, 8, 270.

Goetghebeur, M.M., Wagner, M., Khoury, H., *et al.* (2012). Bridging health technology assessment (HTA) and efficient health care decision making with multicriteria decision analysis (MCDA): applying the EVIDEM framework to medicines appraisal. *Medical Decision Making*, 32, 376.

Golan, O., Hansen, P., Kaplan, G., Tal, O. (2011). Health technology prioritization: which criteria for prioritizing new technologies and what are their relative weights? *Health Policy*, 102, 126–35.

Guo, J.J., Pandey, S., Doyle, J., *et al.* (2010). A review of quantitative risk–benefit methodologies for assessing drug safety and efficacy – report of the ISPOR Risk–Benefit Management Working Group. *Value in Health*, 13, 657–66.

IOM, Institute of Medicine (2012). Ranking vaccines: a prioritization framework – Phase I: demonstration of concept and a software blueprint.

Keeney, R.L., Raiffa, H. (1993). *Decisions with Multiple Objectives: Preferences and Value Tradeoffs.* First published, John Wiley & Sons, 1976. Reprinted, Cambridge University Press.

Lanscar, E., Louviere, J. (2008). Conducting discrete choice experiment to inform healthcare decision making. *Pharmacoeconomics*, 26, 661–77.

Levitan, B.S., Andrews, B.E., Gilsenan, A., *et al.* (2011). Application of the BRAT framework to case studies: observations and insights. *Clinical Pharmacology & Therapeutics*, 89, 217–24.

Marsh, K., Dolan, P., Kempster, J., Lugon, M. (2013). Prioritising investments in public health: a multi-criteria decision analysis. *Journal of Public Health*, 35, 460–6.

Marsh, K., Lanitis, T., Neasham, D., *et al.* (2014). Assessing the value of healthcare interventions using multi-criteria decision analysis: a review of the literature. *Pharmacoeconomics*, 32, 345–65.

Marsh, K., Phillips, C.L., Fordham, R., *et al.* (2012). Estimating cost-effectiveness in public health: a summary of modelling and valuation methods. *Health Economics Review*, 2, 17.

Miot, J., Wagner, M., Khoury, H., *et al.* (2012). Field testing of a multicriteria decision analysis (MCDA) framework for coverage of a screening test for cervical cancer in South Africa. *Cost Effectiveness and Resource Allocation*, 10, 2.

Morgan, D., Astolfi, R. (2013). Health spending growth at zero: which countries, which sectors are most affected? OECD Health Working Papers, No. 60, OECD Publishing (available online at: http://dx.doi.org/10.1787/5k4dd1st95xv-en).

NICE, National Institute for Health and Care Excellence (2012). *Briefing Paper for Methods Review Workshop on Structured Decision Making.* NICE, London (available online at: www.nice.org.uk/media/C67/40/TAMethodsGuideReviewSupportingDocuments.pdf).

PROTECT, Pharmacoepidemiological Research on Outcomes of Therapeutics by a European Consortium (2013). IMI-PROTECT (available online at: www.imi-protect.eu/documents/HughesetalRecommendationsforthemethodologyandvisualisationtechniquestobeusedintheassessmento.pdf).

Rawlins, M., Barnett, D., Stevens, A. (2010). Pharmacoeconomics: NICE's approach to decision making. *British Journal of Clinical Pharmacology*, 70, 346–9.

Ryan, M., Watson, V., Gerard, K. (2008). Practical issues in conducting a discrete choice experiment. In: Ryan, M., Gerard, K. and Amaya-Amaya, M. (eds). *Using Discrete Choice Experiments to Value Health and Healthcare.* Springer, The Netherlands.

Saaty, T.L. (2008). Decision making with the analytic hierarchy process. *International Journal of Services Sciences*, 1, 83–98.

Thokala, P. and Duenas, A. (2012). Multiple criteria decision analysis for health technology assessment. *Value in Health*, 15, 1172–81.

Tony, M., Wagner, M., Khoury, H., *et al.* (2011). Bridging health technology assessment (HTA) with multicriteria decision analyses (MCDA): field testing of the EVIDEM framework for coverage decisions by public payer in Canada. *BMC Health Services Research*, 11, 329.

Wailoo, A., Davis, S., Tosh, J. (2010). *The Incorporation of Health Benefits in Cost Utility Analysis Using the EQ-5D.* Sheffield: Report by the Decision Support Unit.

Wen, S., Zhang, L., Yang, B. (2014). Two approaches to incorporate clinical data uncertainty into multiple criteria decision analysis for benefit–risk assessment of medicinal products. *Value in Health*, 17, 619–28.

Youngkong, S., Baltussen, R., Tantivess, S., *et al.* (2012). Multicriteria decision analysis for including health interventions in the universal health coverage benefit package in Thailand. *Value in Health*, 15, 961–70.

# Chapter 14

# Comparative Effectiveness from Real-World Evidence

*Billy Amzal, Roman Casciano, Lamiae Grimaldi-Bensouda and Lucien Abenhaim*

## Introduction

Over the last decade, both worlds of drug development and health care evaluations have undergone major changes impacting dramatically the way pharmaceutical companies envision their business models. One factor driving the drug development's paradigm shift is the emergence of real-world evidence as a new but critical market access hurdle.

The traditional well-structured drug development process was essentially focused and optimized around the market approval point and notably built on the Cochrane's hierarchy in which evidence from randomized control trials (RCTs) is the gold standard required to support public health decision making. A number of revelations concerning the unacceptable benefit/risk of widely used medicines stimulated a re-evaluation of the nature of evidence required for safe decision making around regulation and evaluation of drugs. Historically, observational data have been perceived as low-quality information, as many real-world conditions such as patient risk factors, concomitant prescriptions or patient compliance may be unbalanced across comparator arms, potentially biasing the true theoretical effect of a given drug. Although clinical trials continue to be regarded as a highly objective source of information able to isolate the pharmacological effects of a drug and provide proof of efficacy, they do not necessarily represent the best evidence to show how effective a drug may be in its likely actual setting of use in a given health system.

As a consequence, regulators worldwide have identified the need for, and begun to characterize the requirements of, more pragmatic evidence related to the real-world usage of drugs, specifically including the need for evidence of drugs' effectiveness. In parallel, payers and health technology assessment (HTA) bodies (notably within European countries where public health expenses are heavily scrutinized) have begun to base decisions and recommendations on such data in the absence of, or even in the face of, adequate data from RCTs. This is illustrated by the rising number of patients' access schemes or risk-sharing agreements deemed to align the public payers' decisions to the actual effect of a drug in a specific market rather than to a theoretical proof of efficacy for a drug "optimally used by an ideal patient".

This paradigm shift is being observed in most parts of the world. In Europe, the European Medicines Agency (EMA) issued a new Pharmacovigilance Directive 2010/84/EU (European Medicines Agency 2010) (in force in 2012) promoting the role of real-life evidence at all stages of benefit/risk assessments and created

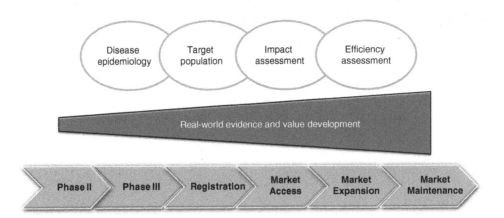

*Figure 14.1*  Real-world evidence on both disease and drugs is now required throughout drug life cycle

dedicated committees to appraise post-approval efficacy studies, the so-called PAES. Despite its name, PAES refers to effectiveness studies, described as "efficacy in the current medical practice". Country-specific HTA bodies are developing policies, structures and scientific guidance to generate and evaluate effectiveness arguments within the pricing and reimbursement process. In the US, the Patient-Centered Outcomes Research Institute (PCORI) refers similarly to the so-called "comparative effectiveness research" to reflect a comparable need to show how drugs' effects compare in the actual care practice, with a focus on evaluating the right drug for the right patient at the right time (PCORI 2010).

In order to align drug development to the actual needs and requirements set by regulators and payers, there is a growing mandate for industry to incorporate real-world evidence throughout the drug life cycle, as illustrated by Figure 14.1. Clearly, real-world evidence is required to defend reimbursement or market maintenance once the drug considered has been on the market. It is also becoming a critical piece of evidence to optimize strategic decisions during the development phase, for example to anticipate real-world effectiveness drivers, predict the public health impact and disease epidemiology, and optimize a target population accordingly.

In this chapter, we propose to describe the concepts and the practice of relative effectiveness studies, and how they can be technically conceived and analyzed to be relevant and impactful in addressing the current market access hurdles.

## The Practical Concepts of Relative Effectiveness

### Key Concepts of Relative Effectiveness

In this section, the key elements defining effectiveness are summarized, especially those differentiating relative effectiveness studies from efficacy trials.

Relative effectiveness studies are by nature based on real-world data reflecting the real-life conditions of prescribing and use of a compound in a given population. Such studies primarily aim at comparing a therapeutic option with the other options as used in a given routine practice. Conversely, clinical trials isolate the pharmacological effect of a chemical compound versus placebo or versus an active comparator via random treatment assignment in a homogenous setting of use. Such an effect, referred to as efficacy, is defined assuming optimal drug use.

Efficacy and effectiveness should not be treated as competitive concepts as they do not serve the same purposes. Instead they address complementary information needs. Efficacy assessment of a drug will always be required for drug development through explanatory trials aimed at demonstrating that a drug has some intrinsic effect on a disease. Once efficacy is established, effectiveness assessment of efficacious drugs takes the pragmatic viewpoint of a public health decision maker to establish whether the drug has a relative benefit superior to the existing therapeutic options in a given practice setting. Depending on how the real-world patterns of drug prescriptions and use interact with the drug effect, a compound may show higher efficacy than another but lower effectiveness than the same comparator, and vice versa. In fact, drugs well established in a given practice may typically show a larger effect in the actual clinical setting than in clinical trials, at least for good compliers, because physicians typically adjust their prescribing and dosing to the patients more likely to respond (Haynes 1999).

Both regulators and payers have shown an increasing interest in real-world evidence and consequently, relative effectiveness data have become a key piece of evidence for decision making. This is, not surprisingly, even truer still for HTA bodies whose focus of inquiry is usually on the pragmatic consequences of adopting new treatments given the current standards of care. Ideally, HTA evaluations would thus focus on real-world data, and all cost-effectiveness analyses or added therapeutic value assessments should theoretically be based on real-world data. In practice, such data of adequate reliability and accuracy are rarely available and efficacy data are often used instead. Especially at the time of launch of a new compound, HTA bodies typically face the dilemma of either using the large amounts of good-quality data from the development program that may not reflect the real-world effect of a drug or using more naturalistic data that may be strongly biased, incomplete or of a very small quantity. This trade-off between the robustness of the evidence and the real-world relevance of the evidence used by HTA bodies is typically made on a case-by-case basis and largely depends on the therapeutic area and the perceived public health needs in the therapeutic area. For example, a new HIV drug may not require further evidence of effectiveness beyond the clinical trial data given the high perceived unmet needs in the setting. In such cases, delaying the use of a proven efficacious drug may be unethical and inefficient, and perhaps more importantly, unpopular. The expected effectiveness in the real-world setting despite the use on a broader population or in a differing point in the treatment pathway may thus be assumed adequately comparable to the demonstrated efficacy given the unmet needs. Conversely, a new inhaled corticosteroid for asthma patients may face greater scrutiny concerning the potential difference between efficacy and effectiveness due to a lower perceived public health need. As a consequence, while the HIV treatment may receive a favourable assessment based solely on clinical data, there may be a requirement for strong and specific relative effectiveness data for the asthma treatment.

In theory, the effectiveness of a new compound versus the standard of care could be assessed by comparing, without any intervention, two very same practices: one with the new drug as a therapeutic option and one without. In reality, this way of assessing drugs is not practicable and thus relative effectiveness analysis requires customized study designs and/or epidemiologic models. Hereinafter, we will review the nature of real-world studies, the tools to analyze them for relative effectiveness analyses, and two key real-world factors that are central considerations in the quantification of relative effects: those affecting the actual exposure to the drug and those changing the drug effect.

### Exposure Modifiers in the Real-World Setting

In the real-world setting, drug exposure depends on how prescribers and patients behave. Prescribers may follow guidelines or not, they may adapt treatment and dose based, for example, on the treatment and effectiveness history, on patients' responsiveness and also on the local reimbursement policies. Patients may similarly change how they use a drug, how compliant they are or for how long they stay on treatment based on factors such as their perception of effectiveness, the drug regimen they are on or the local reimbursement policy. The factors influencing exposure to treatments, their changes over time and the dynamic exposure this creates are key focal points of effectiveness research which are commonly (and necessarily) explored within real-world cohorts. A variety of tools and methodological approaches has been developed to address the challenges of this complex environment. Propensity scores are one such tool that has been developed and adopted widely in recent years to characterize the comparability of populations vis-à-vis their likelihood of exposure (Rothman 2002) given a set of characteristics and other factors. Via propensity scoring, researchers attempt to harness the available information about factors which are influencing exposures in order to emulate an experimental design. Additionally, beyond the consideration of factors influencing exposures at any given point in time, advanced statistical models are required for robust analysis of cohort data given the typically complex dynamics created by the constantly shifting exposures in groups of patients and within individual patients over time.

Addressing these aforementioned issues is critical to ensuring the validity of the findings of any real-world study of effectiveness. Analyses that fail to account for the way prescribers adapt their prescriptions to the patients' conditions over time may have severe flaws and result in misleading conclusions. A common phenomenon that must always be considered when evaluating a new treatment in the real-world setting is the channelling effect which is often observed when a drug is introduced to a setting with already existing effective alternatives. In such a context, the first patients to be prescribed the new drugs may be those who are not responding to the current alternatives or those with the highest severity among the target population. Cohort data collected during this period of time which does not contain detailed data about each patient's circumstances, or analyses which do not take into consideration such available data, may erroneously attribute worse outcomes to the new treatment, rather than more appropriately concluding that the patients were simply more severe or treatment resistant.

This effect is all the more important in that the channelling effect is often most pronounced immediately after the product launch at the time when post-marketing studies are typically required, and when decision makers' interest in and scrutiny of results is likely to be the strongest. Figure 14.2 illustrates how the failure to account for the channelling effect can lead to severely flawed results. In this study (for which

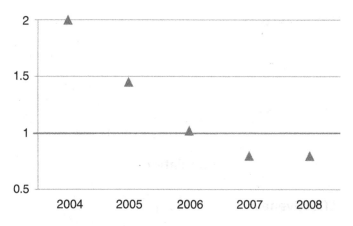

*Figure 14.2* Relative risk of hospitalization according to time from launch (2003) of a new drug, based on a cohort study with dynamic exposure

few details are given, to preserve confidentiality), the primary effectiveness outcome was the risk of hospitalization. The new drug was introduced in the market in 2003. The analysis showed that up to two years after launch, the drug showed to be less effective than other alternatives with significantly higher risks of hospitalization. However, four years after launch, the channelling vanished to the extent that the new drug showed to be significantly more effective than alternatives.

### Effect Modifiers in the Real World

Given equivalent exposure to an intervention, there is often also a wide variation in the observed effects of a given intervention which cannot be sufficiently explained by random chance. In other words, there are other factors (besides exposure) influencing the effects of an intervention (see Figure 14.3). Such factors include, for example, patient demographics, genetics and health characteristics, lifestyle, treatment history, co-prescriptions and co-morbidities.

Appropriately designed real-world effectiveness research must ultimately aim to:

- identify the factors that modify treatment effects;
- characterize all such factors by assessing whether they are intrinsic to a drug or a disease or if they apply for a specific and local situation (for example, the impact of age on effects is likely to be intrinsic, whereas the impact of employment status on effects may be a local phenomenon);
- quantify in a given country the distribution of all effect modifiers.

As for exposure modifiers, factors affecting the effect of an intervention may be universal (as described in RCTs) or related to real-world practice, and they can be country specific or not (see Table 14.1). These distinctions are key when planning for evidence generation, leveraging or not the existing information from clinical trials or different countries.

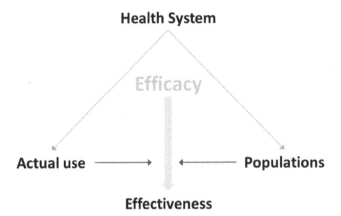

Figure 14.3 In the real-life context, efficacy of interventions interacts with the actual population and drug use

Table 14.1 Effect and exposure modifiers can be country-specific or not, and can be real-world-specific or not

|  | Country-specific | Non-country-specific |
|---|---|---|
| Real-world-specific | Treatment pathways, exposure modifiers, drug utilization | Adherence effect, co-prescription and off-label use |
| Intrinsic | Population characteristics, drugs prescribed | Pharmacological effects, effect modifiers |

## Implementation of Relative Effectiveness Studies in the Real World

### Generating Real-World Data for Relative Effectiveness Analysis

When there is no registry or electronic health care database ready-made to serve a relative effectiveness study, prospective field data collection is required. Effectiveness studies should in essence be as naturalistic and non-interventional as possible, employing a variety of observational study design approaches (e.g. cohort registry, case-control, or survey) as well as the so-called pragmatic trial approach.

The pragmatic trials, while still attempting to reflect a real-world research setting, nonetheless generally employ a randomization step to reduce the problems of exposure and effect modification. While explanatory trials tend to recruit a selected and homogeneous population, pragmatic trials are supposed to reflect the heterogeneity of patient types, circumstances and treatment pathways encountered in everyday clinical practice and aims to inform choices between treatments given this more representative real-world environment. More specifically, pragmatic trials typically differ from explanatory trials in that:

- the study population will be defined as the actual population typically being prescribed the drug under evaluation;

- the comparator will be defined among the other treatment options, which may include the "no-treatment" option or can be anything else besides the drug under evaluation;
- the actual use, adherence and drug switches would be observed as they are, rather than imposed according to a strict protocol as in an explanatory trial;
- the study outcome will preferably reflect a tangible clinical and/or public health outcome (e.g. hospitalization);
- protocol-dictated interactions with patients and other interventions are minimized (e.g. less frequent mandatory follow-up visits, fewer diagnostic tests unless part of routine care).

By construction, there is no prospective randomized trial that can exactly reflect the real-world practice of medicine. For example, the fact that patients formally consent to take part in a study, the fact they received information on the study and the fact that visits may be planned according to a predefined schedule will always influence study results to some degree relative to what might have been expected in the absence of these factors. The randomized pragmatic trial is often seen as a compromise between the randomized clinical explanatory trials and a purely observational study. In fact, there is a continuum in the pragmatism of a trial design rather than a dichotomy, depending on a number of practical aspects of the study conduct.

Table 14.2 summarizes the main components typically differentiating efficacy trials from effectiveness studies.

Aside from pragmatic randomized trials, other observational study designs can be implemented to assess the relative effectiveness of a given compound. For effectiveness studies with rare outcomes or for risk studies, case-control designs can be utilized, provided the collection of cases is conducted with minimal intervention (Shapiro 2004). For other non-randomized effectiveness studies, a disease cohort design accounting for dynamic exposure is often a relevant approach provided data collection is possible and the data analysis is adequately specified and performed. Such studies should include a broad and representative group of the target

*Table 14.2* Comparison of the main study characteristics between efficacy trials and effectiveness studies

|  | *Efficacy trials* | *Effectiveness studies* |
|---|---|---|
| Setting | Experimental setting | Routine practice |
| Comparator | Placebo controlled | Standard of care |
| Blinding | Yes to minimize bias | No to reflect treatment adaptation |
| Protocol | Standardized | Minimize study interventions to reflect routine practice |
| Population | Selected, homogeneous | Heterogeneous, representative of the actual population |
| Sample size | Usually smaller | Usually larger |
| Endpoint | Usually clinical short-term endpoint | Usually public health-relevant benefit/risk outcomes |
| Follow-up | Usually short term | Usually long term |
| Validity | High internal, low external | High external, low internal |
| Analysis | Standard test | Model-based and ad hoc |

population of patients and follow them over time with minimal intervention and no scheduled visits other than those that would routinely occur through the usual care process. All prescriptions, switches and treatment interruptions are ideally recorded, with the dynamics of exposure reflecting how prescribers and patients behave in the real-world setting. Specific statistical methods are required to capture this dynamic and derive robust relative effectiveness measures out of it.

In general, real-world studies may be prospective or retrospective if relevant data exist. However, explanatory studies by design must be prospective due to the need for the randomization of the intervention which cannot be implemented retrospectively. In the case of risk studies, or if the effectiveness primary outcomes is a rare adverse event, a retrospective case-control study may be conducted in dedicated registries containing sufficient information on drug exposure and patients' characteristics for matching (Grimaldi-Bensouda *et al.* 2011). Such a retrospective study has the advantage of minimizing study-specific interventions biasing outcomes.

More so than for RCTs, the analysis plan for effectiveness studies should be developed at the same time as they are designed to ensure that all potential sources of bias can be handled and confounding adequately adjusted for. All important factors interacting with both exposure and effect should ideally be collected. In the study conduct, many practical choices will have to be made based on clinical expertise and logistical constraints, including aspects such as defining metrics for adherence, treatment groupings and severity measures. The success of real-world data collection is largely dependent on such choices along with the quality of study operations (e.g. patient/physician recruitment, case report form (CRF) design, drug delivery system, patient tracking).

### Relative Effectiveness Studies to Assess Public Health Value

There are numerous potential pitfalls associated with the conduct of relative effectiveness studies in the real world which can often lead to erroneous or ambiguous conclusions. However, when well conducted, a relative effectiveness study can provide key information on public health value of an intervention that no explanatory clinical trial can provide.

A case in point can be observed with the market entry of the long-acting risperidone formulation (R-LAI) in France. R-LAI was the first long-acting atypical antipsychotic to be launched in the schizophrenia indication. Intuitively, in a setting such as schizophrenia where patient compliance with medication regimens is so critical to treatment effectiveness, a long-acting formulation may provide an advantage. In 2005, reimbursement was refused in several European countries due to the lack of hard evidence of a relative effectiveness advantage compared with other available treatments. However, reimbursement was secured in France at the time through a risk-sharing agreement in which reimbursement was contingent upon proof of relative effectiveness, with hospitalization rate as primary outcome of interest. In contrast to the typical clinical trial outcomes in schizophrenia (e.g. positive/negative symptoms), hospitalization rates reflect a critical public health goal of interventions in schizophrenia. Such effectiveness outcomes can be measured in the real-life context only, based on the compliance of the actual patient population. Compliance, being a behavioural factor, is often difficult to assess within the artificial construct of a

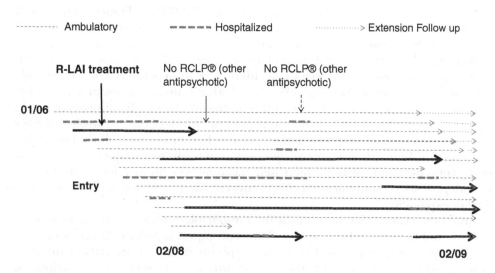

*Figure 14.4* Schematic view of the disease cohort with dynamic exposure in the CGS study (each line represents a patient experience)

clinical trial where frequent interactions with investigators are imposed by the trial. Similarly, hospitalization rates may be highly influenced by the participation within a trial where the monitoring of patients is more stringent.

To study the effectiveness of R-LAI in reducing the hospitalization rate, a prospective observational relative effectiveness study design (disease cohort of 2,500 schizophrenia patients with dynamic exposure) was agreed upon with the French Transparency Committee and the ensuing Cohorte Générale de Schizophrénie (CGS) study was implemented over the three following years. The dynamic exposure (see Figure 14.4) was described and accounted for in the statistical analysis using a Poisson model for repeated data. Ultimately, R-LAI was shown to be associated with a hospitalization risk reduction of 34% compared with all other treatments (Grimaldi-Bensouda *et al.* 2012). This favourable result for the manufacturer could never have been proven in a clinical trial, and importantly it fulfilled the contingency criterion for continued reimbursement of R-LAI in France.

### Electronic Health Care Database Studies for Relative Effectiveness

With the rise of information technology (IT) systems and electronic management of care, health care databases have been built and used for pharmacoeconomic evaluations and, more recently, for risk and effectiveness research. Electronic health care databases (eHCD) include:

- insurance claims databases;
- electronic medical records (eMR);
- health surveys;
- national or local registries;
- pharmacy prescriptions/dispensing data.

Data owners include public health insurers (e.g. CNAMTS in France), private sick funds (as in Germany), health maintenance organizations (as in the US), or regions, local practices or hospitals, as is often the case with European registries.

By nature, eHCD are naturalistic and reflect actual health care practice, especially those reporting prescriptions, claims, health records from patients' visits or expenditures in a given practice. Although eHCD are obviously useful for resource utilization or drug use studies, some of them can also be considered for effectiveness research, e.g. when medical insurance claims and prescription data can be linked together via a common patient identifier, and especially when these can be linked with electronic medical records, including laboratory results. As a consequence, the use of both claims data and eMRs has increased massively over the last decade in the area of both pharmaco-economics and effectiveness research, and thus the topic warrants further exploration.

Insurance claims data are records for the billable interaction between insured patients and the care delivery system. They encompass inpatient claims, outpatient claims and pharmacy claims. Claims data typically include basic patient information (e.g. gender, age, etc.), intervention records, dates of service or prescriptions, diagnosis/ICD codes (except in the case of pharmacy claims), and costs incurred by intervention or hospitalization.

As mentioned, claims data have a broad range of potentially useful applications; however, such data are subject to a number of limitations which must be considered thoroughly depending upon the research questions being asked:

- Claims data are dependent on professional ICD coding, which may be used inaccurately or inconsistently across clinical settings or companies.
- Claims data apply only to the insured population, which may cause severe biases in the analysis. For example, a so-called "healthy worker" bias may be problematic as severe patients too sick to work may not appear in professional health care database as such. Similarly, the elderly population is not well represented.
- Claims data do not include over-the-counter or non-reimbursed items.
- Clinical outcomes data are typically missing, as are data on severity and patient history prior to the diagnosed event. In the case of data linkage with registries or EMR repository, the long-term and exhaustive tracking of patients who change practices or hospitals can also be a challenge for robust effectiveness studies.

Electronic medical records are computerized patients' charts collected from local practices in a standard format via some dedicated software. eMRs typically document patient demographics, their medical history, diagnosis and treatment prescribed, laboratory results and treatment response. Major limitations of eMRs are the data inconsistency across practices and missing data for key information such as prescriptions or care received from other practices not participating in the particular eMR. Furthermore, the length of follow-up is often limited as patients may switch health care providers frequently and the new practitioner often will not have a linked eMR with the previous provider.

Given that many of the limitations of both claims data and eMR are related to the missing information that is typical in each type of data source, data linkage is a key step towards integrated effectiveness research in databases. Enhancing the ability to track and measure broader sets of information and patient outcomes data across settings and practices can even enable the conduct of randomized studies within eHCD.

In the US, given the large variety of private health insurance companies, managed care organizations and provider networks, all of which hold vast quantities of data, there are numerous available sources of eHCD, in particular insurance claims data and eMRs, which are increasingly being linked.

Kaiser Permanente, one of the largest managed care organizations in the US, and one of the few captive group model HMOs in operation in the US, is tracking millions of health records (including both claims and eMR data) from health plan members, hospitals and local health care practices. Given the captive group model, this ensures nearly complete data capture as patients are easily followed through both their claims and eMRs as they seek care across the group practices of the Kaiser Permanente network. This provides a large longitudinal database which can be considered for effectiveness research as one patient can be tracked through different care practices hospitals, with most of their prescriptions and health outcomes.

When the US FDA wanted to investigate the link between the use of Vioxx (rofecoxib) and increased risk of coronary heart disease, Kaiser Permanente was used to provide 1.4 million Kaiser enrollees' medical records. Such a study of sufficient size and quality could establish that the use of Vioxx did indeed increase the risk and ultimately led to the drug's withdrawal (Graham *et al.* 2005).

Europe has fewer eHCD options for effectiveness research than the US. Still, some nationwide data linkages (e.g. Sweden, Denmark and the Netherlands) are being established associating claims data, registries and hospital eMRs. However, access to such data is not open and requires the implementation of a dedicated research project to be conducted through local academic structures.

Clinical Practice Research Datalink (CPRD) is the new NHS observational data and interventional research service in the UK, designed to maximize the way anonymized NHS clinical data from local practices and registries can be linked to enable many types of observational research. The upcoming widespread implementation of electronic records in clinical practice, such as the CPRD, will lead to a significant opportunity for effectiveness research, provided this information is compiled into well-designed databases and analyzed with appropriate statistical methods.

In principle, most epidemiological designs and analyses can be implemented in retrospective data analyses. Even randomized control trials are foreseen to be implemented in real time within databases such as the CPRD (Van Staa *et al.* 2012). In practice, however, data depth, availability and technical challenges drive the feasibility of such studies. For example, the CGS prospective effectiveness study described above would have been difficult to achieve in an eHCD given the specific data needs to adequately correct for potential bias due to exposure and effect modifiers which were critical to the analysis but not typically available in any existing electronic data platform in existence.

### Model-Based Evaluations: "Adjusting for the Real World"

Statistical adjustments and model-based analysis are generally needed more for the analysis of relative effectiveness studies than for the analysis of randomized clinical trials for which the design and the patient selection have already addressed most of the potential biases. Basic comparison tests or ANOVAs are usually sufficient for the primary analysis of RCTs. Instead, to address a relative effectiveness question using real-world data, two options may be considered:

- Population matching to correct for imbalances in effect/exposure modifiers between patients. Matching methods consist of the selection of subpopulations from the study data in order to ensure that the key effect and exposure modifiers are evenly distributed between treatments to be compared. Data size and quality must be sufficient to allow for this matching approach. By definition, such an approach can be *ad hoc* only for a given outcome with a small number of parameters to account for (Rothman 2002).
- Statistical modeling to adjust and account for all parameters interacting with both exposure and effects. Regression models or more complex dynamic models can be used to reflect exposure and effect dynamics and their interaction with a number of real-world parameters.

There is a wide variety of statistical models and analytic approaches that could be used to handle such observational data and limit misinterpretation of results. As mentioned previously, the use of propensity scores (Rothman 2002) is one such technique. Propensity score analysis consists of modeling the chance to be prescribed a drug versus any other alternative given some population characteristics, usually via logistic regression. The distribution of the patients' characteristics in a given sub-group therefore translates into the distribution of their propensity scores reflecting the difference of exposure explained by the patients' characteristics. Comparing distributions of propensity scores from two groups can help identify potential bias due to differential exposure which can be addressed by the statistical analysis.

Regression analysis is the basis of the majority of models most often used to analyze observational data and to adjust for a number of effect and exposure modifiers. In practice, data on important factors may not be available, or the variability, the size or the quality of the data may not be sufficient. As a result, as with any model, validation of their robustness requires careful evaluation.

While regression techniques and adjustment for effect and exposure modifiers are well understood and commonly employed by researchers today, other equally important factors are surprisingly often neglected and can lead to erroneous conclusions if they are not adequately considered. For example, relative effectiveness studies involving longitudinal data in patients with constantly changing prescription patterns (i.e. dynamic exposure) and health outcomes over time for each patient require dynamic models, often more complex to handle statistically. The possible approaches include Poisson models or time-to-event processes with repeated data structure which accounts for intra-individual correlation of outcomes and prescriptions.

Statistical models can address some of the biases and data complexity in the analysis of effectiveness studies, provided they are utilized within their scope of validity. In practice, this implies a careful and close interaction between clinicians, epidemiologists and statisticians at the time of analysis.

Finally, it is important to note that models are used not only to analyze observational data (inference models). The dual use of the same models can be the simulation of future patients or of future outcomes of existing patients (predictive models). Simulation models can be useful decision-support tools, too. In the context of relative effectiveness studies, they can be used to test and optimize the design of future studies.

## Towards More Integrated Efficacy and Effectiveness Assessments

The use of real-world evidence has gained considerable importance in the drug evaluation paradigm, directly impacting drug development strategies and the pharmaceutical business model (Eichler *et al.* 2011). Nevertheless, there is a long way to go to align such evidence needs with the actual data sources and methodologies to handle them. The generation of robust evidence is not a rapid process, but drug development, authorization and pricing and reimbursement decisions must be made in a timely fashion. To this end, patient access schemes and risk-sharing arrangements can be developed. These arrangements usually assume some levels of relative effectiveness based on efficacy data from trials or from evidence-synthesis exercises (e.g. from mixed-treatment comparisons using published clinical trials). For the reasons highlighted in this chapter, such approximation can be flawed and uncertain, even over the limited period of time post-product launch as the evidence base is developed. As a consequence, more robust or efficient methodologies for extrapolating relative effectiveness from efficacy in a given population are being developed.

For this purpose, one emerging concept is the design of a so-called bridging study. Generally speaking, such a study aims to bridge efficacy to effectiveness by using all available and relevant data and by integrating those data via *ad hoc* statistical models. Typically, a bridging study will be composed of:

- a dedicated source of real-world data, e.g. on adherence, effectiveness, drug use, prescriptions;
- other sources of data, e.g. clinical data, patient demographics in a given country;
- a bridging model able to simulate relative effectiveness from this data in a specific population.

Such an approach has the advantage of integrating all available information, hence providing the best estimate possible for relative effectiveness projections. Indeed, as illustrated by Table 14.3, real-world data are required only to inform specific effect or exposure modifiers while other sources of data can be used to inform the non-country-specific and/or non-real-world-specific effects.

*Table 14.3* Data sources used for bridging studies

|  | Country-specific | Non-country-specific |
| --- | --- | --- |
| **Real-world-specific** | Local real-world data | Real-world data from other countries |
| **Intrinsic** | Local trials, national surveys or registries | Clinical trials |

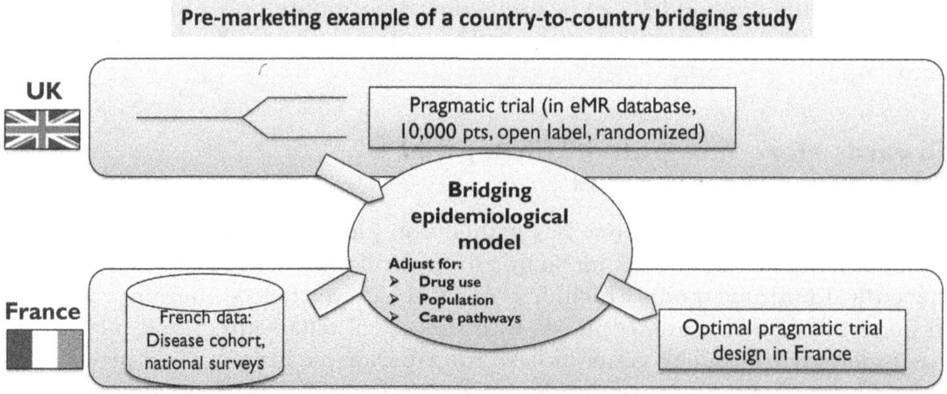

*Figure 14.5* Example of a UK-to-France bridging study combining an eMR database analysis and a predictive model, used for optimal design

When conducted properly, the model projections are associated with the quantification of uncertainty, allowing for quantitative gap analysis. As a simulation platform, bridging models also can be used for decision analysis and optimal planning of real-world evidence generation.

Although such bridging studies are not yet considered as standard tools for evidence generation, precedents have been successfully accepted (e.g. by HAS in France, e.g. with ongoing study – https://clinicaltrials.gov/ NCT01414192) and interest from both HTA and industry is growing fast. Bridging studies can be implemented in both pre-marketing and post-marketing stages. Figure 14.5 illustrates an example for a country-to-county bridging in which UK real-world evidence could be bridged to the French context using a bridging simulation model which adapts the population characteristics and drug use to the French population.

## Conclusion

While effectiveness research is a relatively old concept in pharmaco-epidemiology, the practice of effectiveness evaluations and related tools are far from being established. Interestingly, regulators and payers or HTA bodies are showing increasing pragmatism in the way they consider drug value has to be evaluated. This creates a dynamic environment for the development of new practices and tools to create standards yet to be defined. Until then, large databases allowing the conduct of effectiveness research remain rare and specific to certain disease areas or outcomes. Indeed, many nationwide registries or claims databases are available but were not constructed to fit the purpose of effectiveness studies, which require a relatively high standard of quality and consistency. Furthermore, unlike randomized clinical trials, tools and databases will never be fully applicable in a similar way in all local settings, as by nature real-world drug evaluations are specific to the local context, practice and data available in the health care practice. Aside from the improvement of information systems and databases, which will take time, methodological developments such as bridging modeling and innovative multi-country study designs will create precedents and shape the future of drug value development and assessment.

## References

Eichler, H.-G., Abadie, E., Breckenridge, A., *et al.* (2011). Bridging the efficacy–effectiveness gap: a regulator's perspective on addressing variability of drug response. *Nature Reviews – Drug Discovery*, 495–507.

Graham, D., Campen, D., Hui, R., *et al.* (2005). Risk of acute myocardial infarction and sudden cardiac death in patients treated with cyclo-oxygenase 2 selective and non-selective non-steroidal anti-inflammatory drugs: nested case-control study. *The Lancet, 365, 475–81.*

Grimaldi-Bensouda, L. (2011). Guillain-Barre syndrome, influenzalike illnesses, and influenza vaccination during seasons with and without circulating A/H1N1 viruses. *American Journal of Epidemiology*, 326–35.

Grimaldi-Bensouda, L. (2012). Does long-acting injectable risperidone make a difference to the real-life treatment of schizophrenia? Results of the Cohort for the General study of Schizophrenia (CGS). *Schizophrenia Research*, 187–94.

Grimaldi-Bensouda, L., Rouillon, F., Astruc, B., *et al.* (2012). Does long-acting injectable risperidone make a difference to the real-life treatment of schizophrenia? Results of the Cohort for the General study of Schizophrenia (CGS). *Schizophrenia Research*, 187–194.

Haynes, B. (1999). Can it work? Does it work? Is it worth it? *British Medical Journal*, 319, 653–54.

PCORI (2010). www.pcori.org/.

Rothman, K. (2002). *Epidemiology: An Introduction.* New York: Oxford University Press.

Shapiro, E. (2004). Case-control studies of the effectiveness of vaccines: Validity and assessment of bias. *The Pediatric Infectious Disease Journal*, 127–31.

Van Staa, T.-P., Goldacre, B., Gulliford, M., *et al.* (2012). Pragmatic randomised trials using routine electronic health records: putting them to the test. *BMJ*, 344–55.

# Chapter 15

# Mathematical Programming Modeling: An Alternative to Incremental Cost-Effectiveness Analyses and Budget Impact Analysis to Optimize Allocations of Health Care Interventions

*Nadia Demarteau, Baudouin Standaert and Stephanie Earnshaw*

## Introduction

Health economics analysis normally provides a rationale for an efficient allocation of scare resources in health care. The incremental cost-effectiveness ratio (added marginal cost divided by added marginal effect of a new intervention) has been the standard for measuring the economic benefit of a health care technology and has been used for several decades. This analysis has been adopted by many national guidelines providing results that help local decision makers in their economic appraisal of new interventions (ISPOR 2008). The cost-effectiveness of a given product is assessed against this incremental cost-effectiveness ratio and accepted when the ratio is below a pre-defined threshold value (€20,000 in the Netherlands, £20,000–30,000 in the UK, three times the gross domestic product (GDP)/capita as set by the WHO, etc.) (McCabe *et al.* 2008; WHO 2008; Rogoza *et al.* 2009).

Although cost-effectiveness analyses have been implemented to assess the relative value of new health care interventions, these analyses do have their limitations. One noted limitation is that the cost-effectiveness threshold per country has remained unchanged for many years now. Specifically, there have been no adjustments due to inflation, arrival of new expensive therapies or other factors. Another limitation is that cost-effectiveness analyses do not consider affordability/budget availability. Budget impact analysis provides a measure of affordability that is also considered by decision makers before adopting a new technology. However, this type of analysis typically presents cost over time and is not linked to achievement of a specific outcome measure to be reached. To consider the cost-effectiveness of health care interventions in an efficient manner such that affordability is taken into account, one should consider listing and ordering interventions by their incremental cost-effectiveness ratios (i.e. order interventions by most cost-effective to least cost-effective). In this approach, interventions that are most cost-effective should be financed first. Interventions in the cost-effective list should be financed until the whole budget is exhausted. This way of acting is rarely applied in practice. In 1990, however, the US state of Oregon attempted to allocate health care resources on the basis of QALY-based CE ratios (Klevit *et al.* 1991; Nelson and Drought 1992;

Kaplan 1994; Hardorn 1996; Tengs *et al.* 1996; Blumstein 1997). The commission was created to rank a list of health services by CE.

As a consequence, the implementation of cost-effectiveness analysis has resulted not in a more efficient allocation of budgets but rather budget increases (Donaldson *et al.* 2009).

Another limitation of cost-effectiveness analysis for allocating resources efficiently is that it has difficulties evaluating combinations of different interventions under various constraints (Claxton 1999; Hutubessy *et al.* 2001; WHO 2003; Adang *et al.* 2005). The selection of cost-effective health care interventions rarely considers the relationship of the new therapy to the other treatment options financed. Considering combinations of different interventions rather than considering individual interventions could actually yield more efficient allocations. Finding an optimal mix of several complementary interventions to provide the most efficient use of health care resources is, however, a challenge using the economic tools typically applied today.

Finally, the way in which cost-effectiveness is calculated, using an incremental cost-effectiveness ratio, entails a risk over the exact interpretation of the results, especially when the numerator and/or denominator are very small. Specifically, the incremental cost-effectiveness ratio has meaning only if it operates in a mature health care market where there is still room for improvement in health gain and the cost offset can be substantial. At the extremes of the analysis – for instance, a high health gain impact but with no cost offset for a new intervention, as would be the case in a developing country – we may come to the paradox that the result is very cost-effective at a price higher in low-income countries compared with middle-income countries (Postma and Standart 2013).

## Optimization

It is these specific and questionable issues about the use of the incremental cost-effectiveness ratios of new health care interventions that make it attractive to consider alternative economic evaluation methods for allocating funds for health care interventions such as resource-allocation models. These evaluations allow optimal allocation of resources under specific constraints to be determined. Resource allocation models in the form of mathematical programs provide an alternative to incremental cost-effectiveness evaluation for allocating health care resources in an efficient manner. Mathematical programming is a system of equations that is set up to optimize specific objective criteria by allocating a combination of health care interventions while satisfying a fixed set of constraints (Drummond 1980; Stinnett and Paltiel 1996; Weniger *et al.* 1998; Earnshaw *et al.* 2002; Earnshaw *et al.* 2007; Epstein *et al.* 2007; Richter *et al.* 2008). Any number of constraints upon which the allocation may be enacted can be added to the objective criteria. An example of a mathematical program may be to maximize health outcome (objective) among a combination of health care interventions (decision variables) subject to the funding of the interventions being under a certain budget (constraints). While a fixed budget constraint may be thought of as a constraint to always work under, constraints of access and equity may also be added which are often omitted in cost-effectiveness modeling.

Mathematical programming is typically used to allocate resources efficiently. The most widely used mathematical programming models are linear. In these models, the equations that are derived to represent the objective along with the set of constraints are linear (Earnshaw and Dennett 2003). The decision variables may be continuous (i.e. linear program) or integer (i.e. integer linear program).

This technique is not new – it was applied in many different settings, such as transport, agriculture, industry and banking (Luenberger and Yinyu 2008), before it reached the medical community. Since then, it has been applied to several health care situations (Stinnett and Paltiel 1996; Weniger *et al.* 1998; Earnshaw *et al.* 2002; Epstein *et al.* 2007; Richter *et al.* 2008; Demarteau *et al.* 2012). Health care technologies upon which budget optimization using this approach were first used include the vaccine domain (Weniger *et al.* 1998), the allocation of funds for HIV prevention (Zaric and Brandeau 2001a; Zaric and Brandeau 2001b; Earnshaw *et al.* 2007; Richter *et al.* 2008) and the treatment of type 2 diabetes (Earnshaw *et al.* 2002). The first to suggest the use of this evaluation method for health care budget allocation were Gafni and Birch in the early 1990s (Birch and Gafni 1992; Gafni and Birch 1993), followed by Sendi in the early 2000s (Sendi 2002).

Budget optimization exercises are normally performed in two steps. The first step uses an evaluation model to estimate the cost and outcomes associated with each intervention assessed. The second step is to apply the resource allocation model to optimally allocate the health care interventions. Specifically, the output of the first step is used as input to the resource allocation model (i.e. the linear program) to determine the optimal combination of interventions to achieve a specific health goal while being subjected to various constraints (budget, screening/vaccination coverage).

We present here two applications of linear programming to optimize a health care budget allocation. One uses the method to optimally allocate a cervical cancer prevention budget (Demarteau *et al.* 2012). The other uses the approach to optimally allocate interventions in type 2 diabetes treatment (Earnshaw *et al.* 2002).

## Optimization of Cervical Cancer Prevention Strategies

Human papilloma virus (HPV) infection is causally linked to the development of cervical cancer (CC) (Bosch *et al.* 1995; zur Hausen 1996; Walboomers *et al.* 1999). Two major prevention strategies are currently available: primary prevention with HPV vaccination and secondary prevention with screening or early detection of pre-cancerous lesions followed by treatment.

The evaluation model in the optimization exercise here is a Markov cohort model constructed in Microsoft® Excel, which assesses the clinical and economic effect of cytology-based screening combined with or without vaccination. Details for the UK adaptation of the model have been published elsewhere (Debicki *et al.* 2008; Colantonio *et al.* 2009).

The different prevention strategies available for cervical cancer prevention in the UK are screening from the age of 25 to 68 years, vaccination, screening plus vaccination, and no screening or vaccination. The screening intervals are varied from annual to every 25 years (i.e. women are then screened only twice over their lifetime), with a one-year increment between each subsequent scenario. It is assumed that vaccination induces life-long protection and targets 12-year-old girls. For each scenario, the model is run over a lifetime of the age cohort and the number of cervical cancer cases and total cost expected are estimated. To estimate the projected number of cases at vaccine steady state per year, the total projected lifetime number of cases is divided by the total number of life-years lived by the cohort. The estimated cervical cancer cases and the cost of each prevention scenario obtained by the evaluation cohort model are then used as input variables in the resource allocation model.

The resource allocation model is also developed in Microsoft Excel® using the solver tool that is applying linear programming. It distributes the population between the 52 different prevention strategies to achieve the health goal of minimizing the number of cervical cancer cases. The resource allocation model resolves issues such as the optimal mix of cervical cancer prevention strategies to minimize the expected cervical cancer incidence rate within a fixed budget, with additional constraints on screening and vaccination coverage. Formulation of the resource allocation problem in terms of linear programming is convenient because only minor adjustments are needed to reformulate different optimization problems with different constraints. There is only one criterion that needs to be fulfilled when using linear programming and that is that a linear change in an independent variable results in a linear change in the dependent output measure (i.e. doubling the input variable results in doubling the output measure). This is the case in the current analysis.

The mathematical problem is defined as follows:

$$\text{Minimize} \sum_{i=1}^{52} CC_i \cdot x_i \tag{1}$$

$$\text{Subject to}: \sum_{i=1}^{52} b_i \cdot x_i \le B \tag{2}$$

$$\sum_{i=1}^{52} x_i = 1 \tag{3}$$

$$\sum_{s=1}^{50} x_s \le Cov_1 \tag{4}$$

$$\sum_{v=1}^{26} x_v \le Cov_2 \tag{5}$$

$$x_{nprev} \ge Minimum\,value\,between\,1 - Cov_1\,and\,1 - Cov_2 \tag{6}$$

$$0 \le x_i \le 1 \text{ for } i = 1,...,52 \tag{7}$$

where

Indices

$i = 1, ..., 52$, index for strategies based on screening and vaccination: screening alone defined as strategies $1, ..., 25$ in which the screening interval varies from 1 to 25 years, vaccination alone defined as strategy 26, vaccination combined with screening defined as strategies $27, ..., 51$ in which the screening interval varies from 1 to 25 years, and no prevention measure defined as strategy 52

$s = 1, ..., 25, 27, ..., 51$, index for screening strategies: screening alone defined as 25 strategies in which the screening interval varies from 1 to 25 years and vaccination combined with screening defined as strategies $27, ..., 51$ in which the screening interval varies from 1 to 25 years

$v = 26, ..., 51$, index for vaccination strategies: vaccination alone defined as strategy 26 and vaccination combined with screening defined as strategies $27, ..., 51$

$x_{nprev} = 52$, index for the no prevention measure defined as strategy 52

*Decision variables*

$x_i$ = Proportion of the population treated via strategy $i$

*Parameters*

$CC_i$ = Number of cervical cancer cases at steady state for 100,000 women as estimated by the evaluation model if strategy i was implemented

$b_i$ = Budget required for 100,000 women at steady state under the strategy i as estimated by the evaluation model

$B$ = Overall budget held by the budget holder (corresponding to the pre-vaccination budget in the base case)

$Cov_1$ = Upper bound for coverage in terms of screening

$Cov_2$ = Upper bound for coverage in terms of vaccination

The objective function minimizes the number of cervical cancer cases out of 100,000 women. The constraints in the linear program include a budget constraint [2]; the proportion of women in the population assigned to all strategies is 100% [3]; the proportion of women in the population assigned to screening strategies is less than or equal to the screening coverage upper bound [4]; the proportion of women in the population assigned to vaccination strategies is less than or equal to the vaccination coverage upper bound; [5] the proportion of women in the population assigned to no preventive measure cannot be smaller than the minimum value between the proportion not covered by vaccination or screening when taken alone; it reflects that screened individuals are likely to also be the one vaccinated; [6] the value of the decision variables need to be between 0 and 1.0.

The base case analysis assumes that:

- the maximum screening coverage is the current coverage (65% of women are screened in the UK, with a screening interval of every three years) (Debicki *et al.* 2008; Colantanio *et al.* 2009; Department of Health 2004);
- the maximum vaccination coverage is set to 80%;
- the budget is not higher than the current budget allocated to screening and treatment of cervical lesions.

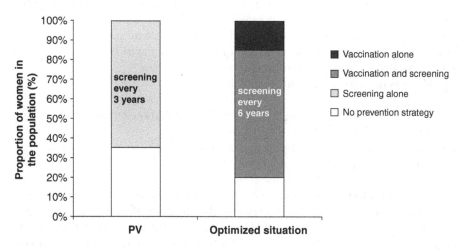

*Figure 15.1* Pre-vaccination strategy (PV) and base case optimal budget allocation
*Source:* PharmacoEconomics/2012. With kind permission from Springer Science and Business Media.

In addition, if any difference exists between vaccine coverage rate and screening, it is assumed that the women who are not vaccinated are also not screened and vice versa. As a result of this assumption, the percentage of the population receiving no preventive intervention is equal to the percentage of the population remaining when the maximum permitted vaccination coverage of 80% is achieved.

The results of this optimal resource allocation exercise are presented in Figure 15.1, with the pre-vaccination situation shown for comparison. The stacked columns represent the proportion of women in the population receiving each intervention. The screening interval is reported on the screened portion of the graph. Compared with the pre-vaccination situation in which 65% of the women are screened every three years, the optimal scenario would be that 65% of the women are vaccinated and also screened every six years, and that 15% would be vaccinated but not screened, taking the total vaccination coverage rate to the maximum level of 80%. The remaining 20% would receive no prevention. This mix of interventions would lead to a reduction of 41% in the number of cervical cancer cases from the pre-vaccination level with no change in budget.

## Optimization of Diabetes Treatments Strategies

The evaluation model in this example is also a Markov model that estimates the cost and the QALYs associated with 16 interventions which are made up of a combination of 4 possible type 2 diabetes treatments. These treatments are intensive glycemic control, intensified hypertension control, cholesterol reduction, and smoking cessation. These different interventions were evaluated among 56 population subgroups based on age (25–34, 35–44, 45–54, 55–64, 65–74, 75–84 and 85–94 years), hypertension level (normal or above normal), cholesterol level (normal or above normal) and smoking status (non-smoker or smoker). The model was developed for the US setting. Total diabetes costs, intervention costs, QALYs and number of individuals in each subgroup were extracted from the evaluation model for input into the resource allocation model.

The "base case" resource allocation model was structured as a linear program. The objective function selected was to maximize QALYs over a lifetime across the population. The constraints were constructed to ensure that all patients received at least standard of care while the other treatments were allocated by means of linear programing to solve the optimization problem.

The model was used to answer three questions:

1. What is the benefit of increasing funding for type 2 diabetes treatment?
2. What is the effect of including equity constraints?
3. What is the impact of increasing the budget for any diabetes care versus increasing the budget for specific interventions?

Each question was addressed by adding constraints to the base linear program.

For understanding the impact of increasing the funding of diabetes treatments, a constraint on diabetes costs was added using four different values: the current cost budget, a 10% increase in current cost budget, a 20% increase in current cost budget, and no funding at all. For understanding the impact of considering equity, two constraints were tested. The first constraint required that all subgroups receive one and only one "non-standard" intervention (intensive glycemic control, intensified hypertension control, cholesterol reduction, or smoking cessation). A second constraint required that population subgroups receive intervention funding that was proportionate to each population subgroup's size. For understanding the last question, constraints were added to restrict the funding for diabetes care versus restricting the funding of interventions where budget increases of zero, $5 billion, $10 billion or $15 billion were considered.

For the first question, the resource allocation model showed that management could be optimized within the current budget by implementing intensified hypertension control that led to cost savings. It allowed for free budgeting for other treatment options. When further increasing the budget, more interventions were shown to be sponsored and hence more QALYs gained. The largest increase in QALYs occurred between a 0% and 10% increase in budget versus between a 10% and 20% increase in budget because smaller incremental gains in QALYs occurred. Eliminating the budget constraint demonstrated that a budget increase of 43% was required to maximize QALYs gained. The evaluation of the equity question showed that equity has a substantial cost in that more budget is needed to fulfil that criterion. Of course, removing the equity constraint while keeping the budget fixed allowed for more QALYs to be gained. When assessing the impact of restricting funding for diabetes care versus for specific interventions, it was shown that more QALYs were gained when diabetes care costs were constrained rather than when interventions costs were constrained.

## Discussion and Conclusion

The two linear programming applications presented here address similar but different questions. Both applications show that the budget could be better allocated than it is currently the case. Other scenarios could be investigated, however. For the cancer prevention exercise, questions could be investigated such as what would be the impact of an increase in the budget, a change in the vaccine or screening profile, a decrease in the maximum proportion of the population that could be covered by either prevention program on the optimal resource allocation. Overall, each scenario would lead to a different result, but the model allows the user to address specific questions within a specific environment by incorporating its own constraints adapted to the question addressed. This optimization exercise demonstrates an approach to identifying the most efficient or optimal program for health authorities. It is therefore more informative than performing the classical cost-effectiveness evaluation, which assesses the efficiency of only one technology compared with another.

It should be noted that the application of mathematical programming models is especially valuable when the selection of health care interventions is to be performed among a large number of combinations. However, when the selection of health care interventions is to occur among a small number of interventions, mathematical programming may not be needed, because the problem is much simpler to solve. Hence, the classical approach of performing cost-effectiveness evaluation combined with a budget impact analysis to answer the question of affordability may suffice.

## References

Adang, E., Voordijk, L., Jan van der, W.G. and Ament, A. (2005). Cost-effectiveness analysis in relation to budgetary constraints and reallocative restrictions. *Health Policy*, 74, 146–56.

Birch, S. and Gafni, A. (1992). Cost effectiveness/utility analyses. Do current decision rules lead us to where we want to be? *Journal of Health Economics*, 11, 279–96.

Blumstein, J.F. (1997). The Oregon experiment: the role of cost-benefit analysis in the allocation of Medicaid funds. *Social Science & Medicine*, 45, 545–54.

Bosch, F.X., Manos, M.M., Munoz, N., *et al.* (1995). Prevalence of human papillomavirus in cervical cancer: a worldwide perspective. International biological study on cervical cancer (IBSCC) Study Group. *Journal of the National Cancer Institute*, 87, 796–802.

Claxton, K. (1999). The irrelevance of inference: a decision-making approach to the stochastic evaluation of health care technologies. *Journal of Health Economics*, 18, 341–64.

Colantonio, L., Gómez, J.A., Demarteau, N., *et al.* (2009). Cost-effectiveness analysis of a cervical cancer vaccine in five Latin American countries. *Vaccine*, 27, 5519–29.

Debicki, D., Ferko, N., Demarteau, N., *et al.* (2008). Comparison of detailed and succinct cohort modelling approaches in a multi-regional evaluation of cervical cancer vaccination. *Vaccine*, 26, F16–F28.

Demarteau, N., Breuer, T. and Standaert, B. (2012). Selecting a mix of prevention strategies against cervical cancer for maximum efficiency with an optimization program. *Pharmacoeconomics*, 30, 337–53.

Department of Health (2004). Department of Health Bulletin – Cervical Screening Program, England, 2003–2004. www.dh.gov.UK/assetRoot/04/09/63/75/04096375.pdf 2004 October 1 [cited 2010 July 1].

Donaldson, L.J., Rutter, P.D., Ellis, B.M., *et al.* (2009). Mortality from pandemic A/H1N1 2009 influenza in England: public health surveillance study. *British Medical Journal*, 339, b5213.

Drummond, M.F. (1980). *Principles of economic appraisal in health care.* Oxford University Press, Oxford.

Earnshaw, S.R. and Dennett, S.L. (2003). Integer/linear mathematical programming models: a tool for allocating healthcare resources. *Pharmacoeconomics*, 21, 839–51.

Earnshaw, S.R., Hicks, K., Richter, A. and Honeycutt, A. (2007). A linear programming model for allocating HIV prevention funds with state agencies: a pilot study. *The Health Care Manager*, 10, 239–52.

Earnshaw, S.R., Richter, A., Sorensen, S.W., *et al.* (2002). Optimal allocation of resources across four interventions for type 2 diabetes. *Medical Decision Making*, 22, S80–S91.

Epstein, D.M., Chalabi, Z., Claxton, K. and Sculpher, M. (2007). Efficiency, equity, and budgetary policies: informing decisions using mathematical programming. *Medical Decision Making*, 27, 128–37.

Gafni, A. and Birch, S. (1993). Guidelines for the adoption of new technologies: a prescription for uncontrolled growth in expenditures and how to avoid the problem. *Canadian Medical Association Journal*, 48, 913–7.

Gafni, A. and Birch, S. (2006). Incremental cost-effectiveness ratios (ICERs): the silence of the lambda. *Social Science and Medicine*, 62, 2091–100.

Hadorn, D. (1996). The Oregon priority-setting exercise: cost-effectiveness and the rule of rescue, revisited. *Medical Decision Making*, 16, 117–9.

Hutubessy, R.C., Bendib, L.M. and Evans, D.B. (2001). Critical issues in the economic evaluation of interventions against communicable diseases. *Acta Tropica*, 78, 191–206.

International Society For Pharmacoeconomics and Outcomes Research (2008). *Pharmacoeconomic guidelines around the world*. IPSOR, U.S.A (available online at: www.ispor.org/PEguidelines/index.asp).

Kaplan, R.M. (1994). Value judgment in the Oregon Medicaid experiment. *Medical Care*, 32, 975–88.

Klevit, H.D., Bates, A.C., Castanares, T., *et al.* (1991). Prioritization of health care services. A progress report by the Oregon Health Services Commission. *Archives of Internal Medicine*, 151, 912–6.

Luenberger, D.G. and Yinyu, Y. (2008). *Linear and nonlinear programming*. New York: Springer.

McCabe, C., Claxton, K. and Culyer, A.J. (2008). The NICE cost-effectiveness threshold: what it is and what that means. *Pharmacoeconomics*, 26, 733–44.

Nelson, R.M. and Drought, T. (1992). Justice and the moral acceptability of rationing medical care: the Oregon experiment. *Journal of Medicine and Philosophy*, 17, 97–117.

Postma, M.J. and Standaert, B.A. (2013). Economics of vaccines revisited. *Human Vaccines and Immunotherapeutics*, 9, 1139–41.

Richter, A., Hicks, K.A., Earnshaw, S.R. and Honeycutt, A.A. (2008). Allocating HIV prevention resources: a tool for state and local decision making. *Health Policy*, 87, 342–9.

Rogoza, R.M., Westra, T.A., Ferko, N., *et al.* (2009). Cost-effectiveness of prophylactic vaccination against human papillomavirus 16/18 for the prevention of cervical cancer: Adaptation of an existing cohort model to the situation in the Netherlands. *Vaccine*, 27, 4776–83.

Sendi, P. (2002). Some reflections on cost-effectiveness analysis and budget allocation in medicine. *Expert Review Pharmacoeconomics & Outcomes Research*, 2, 191–3.

Stinnett, A.A. and Paltiel, A.D. (1996). Mathematical programming for the efficient allocation of health care resources. *Journal of Health Economics*, 15, 641–53.

Tengs, T.O., Meyer, G., Siegel, J.E., *et al.* (1996). Oregon's Medicaid ranking and cost-effectiveness: is there any relationship? *Medical Decision Making*, 16, 99–107.

Walboomers, J.M., Jacobs, M.V., Manos, M.M., *et al.* (1999). Human papillomavirus is a necessary cause of invasive cervical cancer worldwide. *The Journal of Pathology*, 189, 12–9.

Weniger, B.G., Chen, R.T., Jacobson, S.H., *et al.* (1998). Addressing the challenges to immunization practice with an economic algorithm for vaccine selection. *Vaccine*, 16, 1885–97.

World Health Organization (2003). *Making choices in health: WHO guide to cost-effectiveness analysis*. World Health Organization, Geneva (available online at: www.who.int/choice/publications/p_2003_generalised_cea.pdf).

World Health Organization (2008). *WHO guide for standardization of economic evaluations of immunization programmes.* World Health Organization, Geneva (available online at: http://whqlibdoc.who.int/hq/2008/WHO_IVB_08.14_eng.pdf).

Zaric, G.S. and Brandeau, M.L. (2001a). Optimal investment in a portfolio of HIV prevention programs. *Medical Decision Making,* 21, 391–408.

Zaric, G.S. and Brandeau, M.L. (2001b). Resource allocation for epidemic control over short time horizons. *Mathematical Biosciences,* 171, 33–58.

zur Hausen, H. (1996). Papillomavirus infections – a major cause of human cancers. *Biochimica Biophysica Acta,* 1288, F55–F78.

# Chapter 16

# Bridging Health Economics and Capital Investment Modeling Methods to Improve Portfolio Management

*Essè Ifèbi Hervé Akpo, Cédric Popa, Dogan Fidan and Ömer Saka*

## Background

Research and development (R&D) of innovative bio-pharmaceutical products requires considerable investment from the industry firms. The process of introducing such innovative products to the market is a long one, with additional challenges due to uncertainties in attaining value perception, meeting market demand and achieving a successful take-up (Rogers *et al.* 2002).

Technological uncertainties concern researchers' inability to guarantee that a drug would demonstrate non-toxicity and adequate benefit through clinical trials which may take as long as 10–12 years and then gain regulatory authorities' approval. For every approved drug, roughly 10,000 molecules are tested and discarded (Carr 1998). Moreover, even if the primary endpoint is met in pivotal clinical trials, the chances of failure are still significant when submitted for approval to regulatory authorities, given the ever-changing and tightening regulatory requirements. On the other hand, market uncertainties capture the gap in translating the technical success of a drug into market value. In fact, only 30% of drugs achieve cost recovery and increasingly fewer drugs are in the blockbuster category (Grabowski and Vernon 1994; Banerjee 2003). As a consequence, any attempt to improve the precision of overall product success estimates for earlier stage assets is vital to sponsors of drug research. Here, product success should be defined as achieving regulatory approval, positive reimbursement review supporting optimal pricing, as well as patient and physician acceptance.

There is therefore a need for robust decision-making tools to value, determine and prioritize the molecules to invest in or to abandon/disinvest the non-promising ones. The selection, design and application of such tools is made more complicated by the fact that pharmaceutical products must demonstrate value on two very different but interrelated scales: that of financial value to commercial stakeholders, and that of clinical and cost-effectiveness assessed by payers and regulatory authorities. The acceptance by physicians and patients is another crucial element of overall success; however, this is beyond the scope of this chapter.

Although R&D and commercial functions are increasingly under pressure to demonstrate the value proposition of drugs from early development to later market access stages, they often use independently different quantitative methods to appraise project uncertainties (both risks and benefits) during the basic, the translational, the clinical and the pricing and reimbursement research phases. For instance, commercial stakeholders may rely on strategic business case models and on financial analyses such as return on investment (ROI), economic value added, return on equity, discounted cash flow (DCF) or real options valuation (ROV) methods. Meanwhile, researchers and health economists make use of health impact assessment, multi-criteria decision methods and conjoint analysis in the basic research and translational research phases, frequently referred to as health technology assessment (HTA) (Ijzerman and Steuten 2011). In the clinical and market access stages, cost-effectiveness models, mixed-treatment comparison, horizon-scanning systems, clinical-trial simulation and value-of-information (VOI) modeling are deemed very useful. However, it is difficult to find a systematic framework to merge components of health economics with portfolio evaluation.

In the framework of product portfolio management under budgetary limitations, the connection between commercial, R&D and health economics models is becoming of increasing interest. In this chapter, we argue, in five sections, that the use of capital investment appraisal techniques alongside health economics methods would enhance the efficiency of an investment portfolio decision-making process.

- Sections 1 and 2 are a non-exhaustive description of the conventional tools used in capital investment decision making and health economics evaluation, respectively.
- Section 3 is devoted to an in-depth discussion of how health economics could be combined with capital investment methods for the early value proposition of an internal drug.
- Section 4 discusses the application of these methods in the context of optimal portfolio selection and management.
- Section 5 illustrates this approach in the context of value-based pricing.

## Methods for Capital Investment Decisions

Investors and business managers in various sectors use a range of investment decision and capital allocation approaches with the aim of optimizing the risk–return parameters of investments, while taking into account information availability, complexity of analysis, overall value contribution, etc. Such approaches range from the simplest ones (e.g. the payback period (PB) and ROI) to more complex approaches such as internal rate of return (IRR), the DCF and even ROV methods. Within life sciences, the complexity and long time horizon of drug development portfolios usually require a sophisticated investment decision approach. Two main approaches are described below.

**The DCF methods:** These are considered as the standard valuation approach. They consist of calculating the present value of all future cash flows generated by a project, using a relevant discount rate. In addition to projected benefits, DCF methods take into account the time value of money as well as the risk of getting the expected returns. The outcome of a DCF analysis is the net present value (NPV), which is the difference between the present value (i.e. discounted value) of a future cash inflow and the investment sum required to purchase that stream (Mills 1988).

$$NPV = -C_0 + \sum_{1}^{y} \frac{C_y}{(1+r)^y}$$

where $C_0$ = investment outlay at commencement
$C_y$ = cash inflow at end of year $y$
$r$ = required rate of return.

A positive NPV indicates that the investment will achieve at least the minimum rate of return and that the project should be undertaken. A negative NPV means a worse return than the discount rate (minimum accepted rate of return) and the project should be rejected. With a null NPV, the project would generate neither loss nor benefit if pursued. Consider, for example, a project with an outlay of €100,000, which is expected to generate net revenue of €15,000 after the first year, €35,000 after the second year and €60,000 after the third year. If we suppose that the return rate is 10% and the product life is three years, the NPV will be –€12,359 and the project should be rejected.

An inherent weakness of the NPV approach is the difficulty of reflecting flexibility in a project in response to changes in product expectations as more information becomes available during the R&D process, and in response to market and technology uncertainties. Furthermore, it is difficult to calculate the probability of technical as well as market access success rates. Therefore, especially for the early assets (before the proof of concept studies), the NPV valuations may vary significantly, leaving senior management with large confidence intervals, which are often not useful. This has led to consideration of real options techniques to value R&D investment, as discussed below.

**Real options valuation analysis:** In corporate finance an option commonly refers to a financial instrument that gives the owner the right, but not the obligation, to buy (call option) or to sell (put option) assets at a predetermined price (exercise price), on or before an agreed expiry date.

The drug development pipeline is characterized by staged investments – the clinical phases – that can be viewed as a series of call options on an underlying asset (the R&D project and the related products) with uncertain returns. The clinical R&D pipeline starts with the decision to invest or not in the pre-clinical phase. Each phase can then be considered as an opportunity (call option) to continue development, with its associated investment cost, without the obligation to take further that opportunity, depending on whether or not the phase requirements have been met. Various financial option pricing models, such as the Black–Scholes formula, the binomial option pricing model, risk-adjusted decision trees and Monte-Carlo simulations, could be used to price these options according to the level of complexity of the valuation analysis. Given a portfolio of drugs in different clinical R&D phases, different equation parameters would then be required to determine the optimal drug development portfolio that maximizes profitability. Such parameters may include the probability of technical success, the period to "maturity" (i.e. market access or the next stage of investment), the investment required for the remaining stages and the forecasts for future market revenues. The application of financial option pricing models to real options valuation can be complex, since financial market concepts such as volatility of an underlying asset and risk-neutrality (as well as other input parameters such as investment return, maturity, etc.) need to be "translated" into real-world equivalents or proxies which can be estimated. Accordingly, while this approach can be useful for investment analysis, it also has risks related to, among others, its complexity and limited transparency, and hence to the risk of incorrect or incomplete modeling of real-world parameters, leading to incorrect decision making. The health economics approaches analyzed below could therefore play an important role in defining the assumptions and parameters of such models.

An example of the application of ROV is its use by Merck & Co. Inc to value the potential profitability of the in-licensing of Davanrik, a drug that could potentially treat both hypertension and obesity (Nichols 1994; Zhang 2006). A close collaboration between senior researchers, marketers and manufacturing managers enabled the identification of the Black–Scholes equation parameters, including the potential return based on characteristics of the drug, the market size and the potential competition, the probability of success of each clinical phase, and the completion time required for each phase. Additional parameters in Merck's analysis included the capital required to produce the drug and an estimate of the volatility of the related biotechnology stocks index traded at the NASDAQ.

Another interesting area which is not covered in this chapter is the implication of the firms' risk behavior. There are many clinical areas in which there are huge unmet needs with limited drug therapies (such as Alzheimer's). In these areas, the likely commercial returns (and hence the overall NPV) could be significant, despite the very low probability of success. In this case, some sponsors may select drugs with low risk and low return to de-risk their portfolio. The differences in firms' risk behavior may also partly explain the wide variations of the product valuations in the business development field.

### Methods for Health Economics Evaluation

Health economics has been shown to be of interest in early value proposition assessment (Cosh *et al.* 2007; Vallejo-Torres *et al.* 2011). A series of methods could be used to identify the value of a drug at the basic research stage or when the product may just be an idea or a concept.

**Headroom analysis:** Early (Bayesian) health economics modeling can be used to answer the question as to whether or not the product under consideration would be cost-effective if it works as well as the best available alternative. It estimates the maximum additional cost for which a new treatment could be brought to market and still be cost-effective. As no clinical data are yet available in the early R&D process, the analysis is based on the strengths and weaknesses of the current technology the new product aims to substitute or to compete with. Data related to clinical parameters and resources used can be further gathered from the literature, expert opinions, patient questionnaires and/or assumptions regarding the impact on cost and effectiveness of the new technology (Vallejo-Torres *et al.* 2011). The headroom is calculated as:

$$max\Delta Cost = WTP.max\Delta QALY$$

where $max\Delta Cost$ is the maximum additional cost of the new treatment over the comparator for the new treatment to be deemed cost-effective

$WTP$, the willingness to pay
and $max\Delta QALY$, the effectiveness gap.

If there is little or no likelihood that the technology could be marketed at a price that would keep the maxΔQALY below the cost-effectiveness threshold, then either the parameters related to the technology could be revisited or it should not attract further investment (Cosh *et al.* 2007). The difference between the QALY values multiplied by the maximum potential duration of the clinical benefit expected from the new treatment will represent the effectiveness gap. The headroom analysis method also allows the exploration of which attributes of the new treatment will enhance its value, so research can be focused on those attributes. This method is useful in defining the minimum requirements for a commercially viable target product profile; however, it is of limited value for later-stage investments, as it does not incorporate other decision factors considered by payers, such as budget impact.

**Multi-criteria decision analysis (MCDA):** This is a transparent and explicit technique for decision-making processes that uses criteria to quantify the value of a product and a weight that reflects the relative importance of each criterion (Johal and Williams 2007). Methods to perform an MCDA include sum methods and analytical hierarchy processes (AHP) to elicit preferences and value of a product (Thokala and Duenas 2012). The result is a prioritized list of possible decisions, backed by an explicit and transparent methodology that organizes all relevant information. Because the process is explicit and transparent, results can be explained or adjusted to accommodate new information or changes in relative preferences toward decision-making criteria. Furthermore, the application can be extended to countries where QALY assessments are not universally accepted. A limitation of MCDA is the burden of implementing it, which involves data capturing from many stakeholders, consensus building, and data aggregation through specialist tools and software.

AHP is a decision-making framework whereby both "subjective and objective measurements" are taken into consideration to solve complex, multi-party criteria problems through the assessment of alternatives against a variety of criteria (Danner *et al.* 2011). First the problem and the preferred solution are defined. Then a hierarchy tree of the problem from a top-down viewpoint is provided. Next a pairwise comparison of each of the nodes in the hierarchical tree is developed, ensuring they equate to 100%, and based on that weights are calculated. Finally, priorities are derived from each alternative node, allowing consideration for a variety of actions.

The use of AHP in the early decision-making process has been explicitly illustrated in the medical devices field. For example, out of a number of other concepts, one may set clinical value, barriers to entry and market size as criteria for selecting a device to invest in. An expert panel could elicit the relative weight (most likely pairwise) for these criteria. The percent weight for each criterion would then be computed and the performance compared across devices. Hummel *et al.* (2000) used the AHP method to compare a new blood pump with its potential competitors, focusing on their performance, safety, ease of use and their applicability. They further described the use of AHP-derived estimations to model the cost-effectiveness of photo acoustic mammography (PAM) compared with magnet resonance imaging (MRI) to support early internal investment decisions (Hummel *et al.* 2011). Their study demonstrated the use of AHP as an adjustment tool for health utility measures based on criteria such as patient comfort and the safety of the devices. Dolan further demonstrated the use of AHP to change prescription behavior and improve the process of patient care (Dolan 1989; Dolan 1995).

**Value of information:** This analysis quantifies decision uncertainty in monetary units and can be applied in probabilistic health economics models, at even the earliest stages of their development (Sculpher and Claxton 2005). VOI analysis can inform clinical decisions on investing in a treatment, given resource constraints, by quantifying the collective view on the societal value of additional research that would be needed to reduce the uncertainty of the decision. The term VOI covers different decision analytics, including the expected value of information (EVI), expected value of perfect information (EVPI), the expected value of sample information (EVSI) and the expected value of perfect information for parameters (EVPPI) (Briggs *et al.* 2006; Griffin *et al.* 2010; Hall *et al.* 2012). EVI quantifies the expected gain in net benefit from obtaining specific further information to inform the decision. The EVPI is a concept used by decision makers in reimbursement decisions based on the existing level of evidence. The EVPI is simply the difference between the expected value of the decision made with perfect information about the uncertain parameters, and the decision made on the basis of the existing level of evidence. The larger the EVPI, the greater the value of the existing uncertainty associated with a project (Sculpher and Claxton 2005). This concept could be used in a staged-investment decision-making model, in which EVPI effectively represents the value of eliminating these uncertainties during the next investment stage. Consequently, a project for which the investment cost is larger than the EVPI would not be developed further unless it has a positive impact beyond current forecasts (e.g. for obtaining a new indication), as the added value of reducing risk in the current forecasts is not worth the investment costs. Conversely, a project with an investment cost equal to or lower than the EVPI could be pursued. If the investment costs are lower than the EVI or EVPI, then the EVSI or EVPPI can be used to identify parameters where additional research would bring more value than the required investment.

Vallejo-Torres *et al.* (2008) proposed an adaptation of VOI to inform the company rather than the reimbursement decision maker to prioritize at an early stage those projects that are worth investing in and to identify parameters that would drive the value of a new medical device. Willan and other scholars had successfully used EVI to optimize trial sample size in order to maximize the difference between the cost incurred by a trial phase and the value of information gained from the trial results (Willan 2007; Lee and Liu 2008; Willan 2008). They did this by calculating the EVI provided by trial data, in relation to the increase in expected profit due to an increased probability of getting regulatory approval with these data. Conversely, Bayesian value of information can be used to prioritize the trials that maximize the trade-off between the expected value and the research costs. As an illustration,

Girling *et al.* (2007) assessed at an early developmental stage the cost-effectiveness of left-ventricular assist device (LVAD) implantation as a therapy in end-stage heart failure. They concluded that the technology was unlikely to be cost-effective compared with the best standard of care at a cost of £60,000, even with additional information. Investing in such a trial would then be worthwhile only if the price of the device would be lower than £60,000.

In the next section, we will discuss how health economics could support the commercial roadmap of a company's business through the appraisal of those products that would likely be cost-effective prior to attracting any investment.

### Combining Health Economics and Capital Investment Methods in Early Value Proposition Assessment

A business model describes the rationale of how an organization creates, delivers and captures value. It is based on the nature of the market (in life sciences this corresponds to the burden of disease, existing treatments and their related cost, as well as payers' willingness to pay), the proposed product value (the patient outcome benefits as well as the value to physicians and payers) and the value chain of the business (R&D, manufacture, marketing and sales, commercial agreements, distribution, etc.), all leading to an estimate of the expected revenue and net income forecasts.

A robust approach to creating a comprehensive product portfolio management system aimed at developing the right (combination of) products to be presented to the market is to make use of analytical tools to support decisions. Decision process has to focus on selecting the "right" internal and/or in-licensed molecules that would be of high value for the company and also for the health of the public at large. For such an exercise, economic models are powerful tools to predict and forecast the impact of potential performance of a particular drug.

Commercial stakeholders ground their decisions on economic models that capture estimated cash inflows and outflows, as well as market and technology uncertainties (Figure 16.1). These input values serve for calculating individual criteria, including the payback period, the ROI/IRR and the NPV, to further support investment-related decisions under conditions of uncertainty. Health economics modelers, meanwhile, use predictive distribution of treatment effects to assist decision makers to reach appropriate conclusions on the cost-effectiveness of alternative treatments based on collected evidences and population characteristics. As they are often deemed to serve different purposes, commercial and health economics models are currently used independently from each other and without coherence in the timing and modality of their implementation, especially in the early value proposition framework. Strengthening the bridge between clinical and commercial objectives would enable the successful implementation of business models that capture both the cost-effectiveness and the profitability of drug portfolios.

Figure 16.2 shows how health economics assessment could be of value to support investment decisions. At the early stages of the R&D effort, headroom analysis could potentially inform on the likelihood of an investment being cost-effective. Such an analysis could be supported by the EVPI or MCDA to aggregate the qualitative value of the treatment options and consolidate the effectiveness measures.

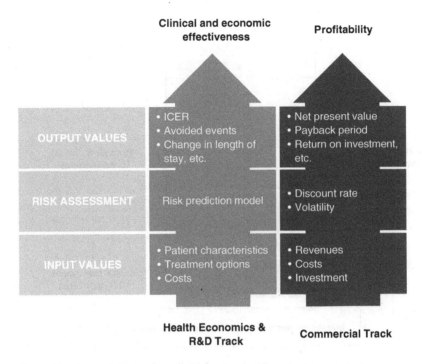

*Figure 16.1* Comparison of health economics and commercial models structure
*Note:* ICER, incremental cost-effectiveness ratio.

However, early health economics evaluation may attract criticism given the lack of data in the early drug development process. Although this may be true, at phase I and II clinical evidence of the tolerability and efficacy of the drug under development as well as the initial cost estimates may become available. Under these conditions, the early modeling of cost-effectiveness may be refined and updated and uncertainty in the decision explored. Grabowski (1997) reported the testimony of Paul Freiman, former chief executive of Syntex Corporation, Palo Alto, California. Freiman explained how the integration of pharmacoeconomic models in early decisions had led to the abandonment of the development of an antiemetic drug in the serotonin3 receptor antagonist. Indeed, phase II did not achieve the projected gain in efficacy for this drug to demonstrate cost-effectiveness at the price level that would generate profits to make the investment worthwhile. As a result, costly phase III trials were not further undertaken. Finally, it makes sense to use Bayesian models as they are quantitative tools recommended by HTA agencies to synthesize cost-effectiveness evidences (Cosh *et al.* 2007).

Capital investment decisions answer the question as to whether it is worth, in terms of revenue and profits, spending a substantial amount of capital in an R&D project portfolio. They involve analyzing the drugs independently by studying the trade-off between success rates and NPVs. Products with low success rates and low NPVs should not be prioritized, and in a real-life situation involving limited capital and resources they should not attract further investment. The risk associated with products with low success rates and high NPVs

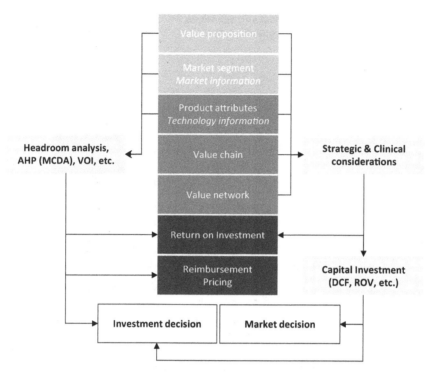

*Figure 16.2* Mapping health economics analytics onto the company's commercial roadmap

can be reduced by carrying out more extensive testing in early development phases, thereby reducing the risk of late-stage failure. For products with high success rates and low NPVs, additional value can be created through indication-extension. Finally, investment should be prioritized in products with high success rates and high NPVs.

Figure 16.3 shows how health economics modeling can be integrated in real options models as a preferred capital investment valuation tool. The analogy with financial options is also depicted. The potential gain, or NPV, of a particular product could be determined with the backwards induction method. The main parameters for the model to be populated are the probability of success at each stage, which depends on the drug's pharmacological profile and the therapeutic area of application, the related investment costs (cash flows) and the discount rates.

The decision-tree approach presents the advantage of clearly communicating the investment opportunities in the staged R&D process. As the uncertainties are resolved, the cost-effectiveness assessment and the investment opportunities are redefined and updated in an iterative fashion in order to subsequently balance the composition of the drug portfolios that would maximize the expected NPV. The ROV approach further improves the strategic thinking and captures the management's flexibility. Indeed, while with DCF methods, products with negative NPVs would be discarded, they could be evaluated, for example, as out-licensable products

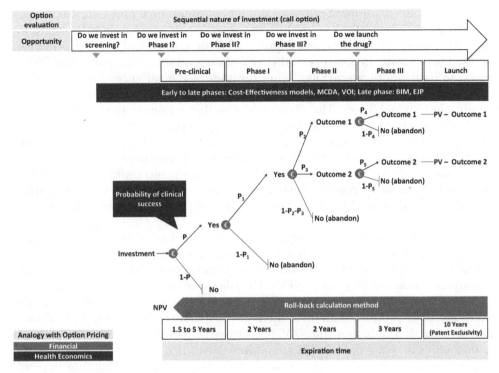

BIM, budget impact model; EJP, economically justifiable price; MCDA, multi-criteria decision analysis; NPV, (probability-adjusted) net present value; PV, present value; ROV, real option valuation; VOI; value of information. The quantitative metrics described here are not exhaustive.

*Figure 16.3* Early value proposition of a drug through the sequential appraisal with health economics and capital investment methods

with additional revenue streams in the ROV framework. A survey by Hartmann and Hassan showed that only 20% of the pharmaceutical firms use ROV to value their projects (Hartmann and Hassan 2006). The mathematical rigor required to use ROV, which then can be perceived as technical complexity, may be one of the reasons hampering its adoption by managers. Another point that needs to be mentioned is that such a modeling approach assumes that there is no replacement for projects as they fail. This shortcoming can be accommodated by carrying out a number of assessments and comparing the outcomes from the company's perspective.

The probability of success (P) of a clinical study can be obtained from historical data from the pharmaceutical industry (Gallaher *et al.* 2007; DiMasi *et al.* 2010; Kaitin and DiMasi 2011). For the sake of simplicity, only two outcomes are displayed. The investment in a subsequent clinical phase is conditional to the success of the preceding one.

### Optimal R&D Portfolio Composition

As illustrated by several scholars, early decision making should be grounded on a portfolio selection rather than on evaluating investment decisions on a project-by-project basis (Rogers *et al.* 2002; Evans *et al.* 2009). This view raises the question of what an optimal portfolio should be. An optimal portfolio should contain drugs candidates that (1) would meet payers' requirements and (2) maximize NPV for a given risk level. In this approach, Monte Carlo simulations of NPVs can be used to calculate the variance of the NPV of each product (Rajapakse *et al.* 2006), with the total risk of a portfolio being the sum of the variance of the (positive) NPV of the products that compose the portfolio. Simulations should also capture product interdependency. The drug portfolios that minimize the risk for a given level of return form an efficient frontier that is the most efficient trade-off between risk (budgetary level) and return. The modeling of the efficiency frontier should be dynamic, as the optimal portfolio structure may change depending on the total amount available for investment (e.g. where a larger project with a higher return may displace smaller projects previously considered optimal under lower capital availability conditions). Figure 16.4 summarizes the processes of portfolio composition and selection.

Figure 16.4a describes how health economics and capital investment perspective can be used to select products that should attract further investment. Drugs are plotted in a bubble chart with X-values as the difference (delta) between EVPI and investment costs and Y-values as NPVs. The diameter can be either the investment cost or the probability of making it to market. NPVs could be calculated with ROV methods. Drug products with investment costs equal to or lower than EVPI should be considered. The higher the NPV, the higher the profitability. Figure 16.4b is a scatter plot where portfolio NPVs are plotted versus risk. Portfolios located on the efficient frontier are deemed optimal. Budget constraints and drug interdependency are additional parameters to consider for portfolio composition.

In addition to financial modeling defining the efficiency frontier and optimal portfolio, companies will use non-financial considerations in their portfolio selection:

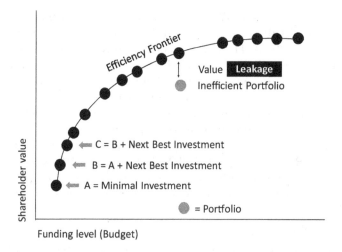

*Figure 16.4* Trade-off of risk and return

- the company strategy and culture (e.g. target therapeutic areas, areas of scientific excellence, internal communication);
- economies of scope and scale (e.g. having an existing franchise for one disease area would significantly reduce the operating expenditure (OPEX) of products);
- extended value (some products or projects may not add much commercial value *per se* but may significantly augment the value of another drug, such as companion diagnostics, additional health care services around the blockbuster product);
- the timing of product cash flows (i.e. ensuring smooth cash flows through the combination of products at different maturity/development stages).

### An Illustration of Portfolio Management in the Context of Value-Based Pricing

A recent development in HTA, in particular in the UK, is value-based pricing, which has been proposed as an approach to link the price of a drug to its clinical value. Under this scheme, the price calculation should be grounded on (1) the drug's ability to tackle the burden of illness and (2) to improve health, (3) on its innovativeness, and (4) on the proof of wider social benefits (Sussex *et al.* 2013). Within this context, the use of more detailed quantitative and qualitative assessment methods will be required in order to derive sufficient and appropriate value propositions for those technologies. The methods we have discussed in this chapter could be applicable from the point of decision making on investing into such technologies all the way to pricing and market access:

- Cost-effectiveness and budget-impact analyses are quantitative instruments that measure the price level that a given product can achieve, benchmarked against that of competitors. This allows the value for money to be perceived by payers and enables companies to evaluate the extent to which their innovative drug can be rewarded and revenue generated.
- Less tangible issues would also have to make their way into a formal decision-making process. Such qualitative criteria may include the patient's perception of the way the new drug is administered, the daily dosing frequency, whether or not regular monitoring is required, and the impact of the treatment on family, carers or the society as a whole. MCDA presents an opportunity to incorporate such parameters into the decision-making process and has been growing in importance in the past few years.

### Conclusion

Prior to investing their capital in the lengthy and risky R&D process, it is crucial for pharmaceutical companies to identify at an early stage those products that would meet regulatory bodies' and payers' requirements for their drugs to be rewarded. We argue that on top of the conventional capital investment tools and strategies, market access analysis and health economics assessments should be employed at all stages:

- The health technology assessment process should be started at the earliest development stage for companies to decide up front on those drugs that would be deemed to be cost-effective according to the willingness-to-pay thresholds employed in HTAs.
- The measure of effectiveness should be extended to cover qualitative evidence, including the patients' view, and MCDA could cater for this need. The management of a product portfolio would then be considerably improved through the interaction between the commercial, the R&D and the health economics activities.
- For pharmaceuticals to get the most from the health care marketplace, market access analysis should be conducted in order to ensure pricing strategy copes with the assessment of the value for money dictated by third-party payers.

Among the variety of quantitative analytics that could be used to monitor the decision process, real options analysis, supported by the approaches set out above, appears to be well suited to capture both the potential return and the possibility to abandon an R&D phase if it does not meet the expected requirements. Therefore, applying health economics methods, not only at the late R&D stage but alongside capital investment tools from the earliest R&D stage onwards, could increase the likelihood of selecting the right products that would compose an effective investment portfolio.

## References

Banerjee, A. (2003). Real option valuation of a pharmaceutical company. *Vikalpa*, 28, 61–74.

Briggs, A., Claxton, K. and Sculpher, M. (2006). *Decision modelling for health economic evaluation.* Oxford University Press, New York.

Carr, G. (1998). The alchemists: a survey of the pharmaceutical industry. *The Economist*, 21, 1–18.

Cosh, E., Girling, A., Lilford, R., *et al.* (2007). Investing in new medical technologies: a decision framework. *Journal of Commercial Biotechnology*, 13, 263–71.

Danner, M., Hummel, J.M., Volz, F., *et al.* (2011). Integrating patients' views into health technology assessment: analytic hierarchy process (AHP) as a method to elicit patient preferences. *International Journal of Technology Assessment in Health Care*, 27, 369–75.

DiMasi, J.A., Feldman, L., Seckler, A. and Wilson, A. (2010). Trends in risks associated with new drug development: success rates for investigational drugs. *Clinical Pharmacology & Therapeutics*, 87, 272–7.

Dolan, J.G. (1989). *Choosing initial antibiotic therapy for acute pyleonephritis in the analytic hierarchy process: applications and studies.* Springer-Verlag, London.

Dolan, J.G. (1995). Are patients capable of using the analytic hierarchy process and willing to use it to help make clinical decisions? *Medical Decision Making*, 15, 76–80.

Evans, R., Hinds, S. and Hammock, D. (2009). Portfolio analysis and R&D decision making. *Nature Review Drug Discovery*, 8, 189–90.

Gallaher, M., Petrusa, J., O'Connor, A. and Houghton, S. (2007). *Economic analysis of the technology infrastructure needs of the U.S. biopharmaceutical industry.* National Institute of Standards and Technology (N.I.S.T.), Gaithersburg, U.S.A (available online at: www.nist.gov/director/planning/upload/report07-1.pdf).

Girling, A.J., Freeman, G., Gordon, J.P., *et al.* (2007). Modeling payback from research into the efficacy of left-ventricular assist devices as destination therapy. *International Journal of Technology Assessment in Health Care*, 23, 269–77.

Grabowski, H. (1997). The effect of pharmacoeconomics on company research and development decisions. *Pharmacoeconomics*, 11, 389–97.

Grabowski, H.G. and Vernon, J.M. (1994). Returns to R&D on new drug introductions in the 1980s. *Journal of Health Economics*, 13, 383–406.

Griffin, S., Welton, N.J. and Claxton, K. (2010). Exploring the research decision space: the expected value of information for sequential research designs. *Medical Decision Making*, 30, 155–62.

Hall, P.S., Edlin, R., Kharroubi, S., *et al.* (2012). Expected net present value of sample information: from burden to investment. *Medical Decision Making*, 32, E11–E21.

Hartmann, M. and Hassan, A. (2006). Application of real options analysis for pharmaceutical R&D project valuation – empirical results from a survey. *Research Policy*, 35, 343–54.

Hummel, M.J., van Rossum, W., Verkerke, G.J., and Rakhorst, G. (2000). Assessing medical technologies in development. A new paradigm of medical technology assessment. *International Journal of Technology Assessment in Health Care*, 16, 1214–9.

Hummel, M.J.M., Steuten, L.M.G., Groothuis-Oudshoorn, K.G.M. and Ijzerman, M.J. (2011). How the analytic hierarchy process may fill missing gaps in early decision modeling. *Ispor Connections*, 17, 9–10.

Ijzerman, M.J. and Steuten, L.M. (2011). Early assessment of medical technologies to inform product development and market access: a review of methods and applications. *Applied Health Economics and Health Policy*, 9, 331–47.

Johal, S. and Williams, H. (2007). Decision-making tools for medical device development. *Journal of the ABHI*, 20, 2.

Kaitin, K.I. and DiMasi, J.A. (2011). Pharmaceutical innovation in the 21st century: new drug approvals in the first decade, 2000–2009. *Clinical Pharmacology & Therapeutics*, 89, 183–88.

Lee, J.J. and Liu, D.D. (2008). A predictive probability design for phase II cancer clinical trials. *Clinical Trials*, 5, 93–106.

Mills, R.W. (1988). Capital budgeting – the state of the art. *Long Range Planning*, 21, 76–81.

Nichols, N.A. (1994). Scientific management at Merck: an interview with CFO Judy Lewent. *Harvard Business Review*, 72, 88–99.

Rajapakse, A., Titchener-Hooker, N.J. and Farid, S.S. (2006). Integrated approach to improving the value potential of biopharmaceutical R&D portfolios while mitigating risk. *Journal of Chemical Technology and Biotechnology*, 81, 1705–14.

Rogers, M.J., Gupta, A. and Maranas, C.D. (2002). Real options based analysis of optimal pharmaceutical research and development portfolios. *Industrial & Engineering Chemistry Research*, 41, 6607–20.

Sculpher, M. and Claxton, K. (2005). Establishing the cost-effectiveness of new pharmaceuticals under conditions of uncertainty – when is there sufficient evidence? *Value in Health*, 8, 433–46.

Sussex, J., Towse, A. and Devlin, N. (2013). Operationalizing value-based pricing of medicines: a taxonomy of approaches. *Pharmacoeconomics*, 31, 1–10.

Thokala, P. and Duenas, A. (2012). Multiple criteria decision analysis for health technology assessment. *Value in Health*, 15, 1172–81.

Vallejo-Torres, L., Steuten, L.M., Buxton, M.J., *et al.* (2008). Integrating health economics modeling in the product development cycle of medical devices: a Bayesian approach. *International Journal of Technology Assessment in Health Care*, 24, 459–64.

Vallejo-Torres, L., Steuten, L., Parkinson, B., *et al.* (2011). Integrating health economics into the product development cycle: a case study of absorbable pins for treating hallux valgus. *Medical Decision Making*, 31, 596–610.

Willan, A.R. (2007). Clinical decision making and the expected value of information. *Clinical Trials*, 4, 279–85.

Willan, A.R. (2008). Optimal sample size determinations from an industry perspective based on the expected value of information. *Clinical Trials*, 5, 587–94.

Zhang, H.R. (2006). *Application of real options valuation to R&D investments in pharmaceutical companies.* Nottingham Business School, United Kingdom.

# Index